LITIGATION AND ADMINISTRATIVE PRACTICE SERIES
Litigation
Course Handbook Series
Number H-562

Avoiding Workplace Litigation

Strategies for Lawyers and Human Resource Professionals

Chair
Martin F. Payson

To order this book, call (800) 260-4PLI or fax us at (800) 321-0093. Ask our Customer Service Department for PLI order number H4-5261, Dept. BAV5.

Practising Law Institute
810 Seventh Avenue
New York, New York 10019

"This publication is designed to provide information in regard to the subject matter covered. It is sold with the understanding that the publisher is not engaged in rendering legal, accounting or other professional service. If legal advice or other expert assistance is required, the services of a competent professional person should be sought."

—from Declaration of Principles jointly adopted by Committee of American Bar Association and Committee of Publishers and Associations

ISBN 0-87224-321-4

Foreword

This course handbook is one of about 150 published each year by the Practising Law Institute.

Its primary function is to serve as an educational supplement to each program. It may also be used as a reference manual by attorneys and related professionals unable to attend the sessions.

The method of reproduction utilized has been chosen to insure that registrants receive these materials as quickly as possible and in the most usable form practicable.

The Practising Law Institute wishes to acknowledge its debt and extend its sincere appreciation to the authors who have rendered this valuable service. They exemplify the finest tradition of our profession by sharing their expertise with their colleagues.

We also wish to thank Executive Enterprises for their cosponsorship of this program.

Prepared for distribution at the
AVOIDING WORKPLACE LITIGATION:
STRATEGIES FOR LAWYERS AND HUMAN RESOURCE PROFESSIONAL
Program
April 1997

CONTENTS:

1

WHAT A PLAINTIFF'S LAWYER LOOKS FOR WHEN EVALUATING A POTENTIAL LAWSUIT

Kyle M. Francis

Reprinted with permission of the New Jersey Institute for Continuing Legal Education and was published in its "1997 Labor Law Forum."

WHAT A PLAINTIFF'S LAWYER LOOKS FOR WHEN EVALUATING A POTENTIAL LAWSUIT

(These materials were previously submitted to the Institute for Continuing Legal Education and are reprinted with permission.)

by Kyle M. Francis, Esq.
Smith Mullin, P.C.
West Orange, New Jersey

Every case begins with the initial consultation between a potential client and the attorney. The initial consultation typically lasts an hour. During that time, the attorney should gain the information which will help decide whether to accept a case, either for negotiation or litigation. Following are some questions often used to evaluate a case from the plaintiff's perspective.

I. WHO ARE THE PROPER DEFENDANTS?

Who is the employer?

Determine the name of the employer, its location, and the location of other facilities. Ask the client the name of the entity on his paychecks.

Where did the plaintiff work?

In most cases it will be the place of employment, not the plaintiff's residence, that will determine what laws will apply. For example, a plaintiff living in New Jersey and commuting to work in New York will likely be governed by New York, not New Jersey, law. Buccilli v. Timby, Brown & Timby, 283 N.J. Super. 6 (App. Div. 1995).

Is there a parent corporation that may be liable?

Parent corporations may be responsible for the unlawful employment action where the parent exercises control over the subsidiary, or played a role in the unlawful action. See generally Berkowitz v. Allied Stores of Penn-Ohio, Inc., 541 F. Supp. 1209 (E.D.Pa. 1982)(test for determining parent corporation liability for ADEA violation are (1) "integrated enterprise" test; (2) the "alter ego" test; and (3) "mere instrumentality" test.) In truth, there is little substantive difference between the three tests. Id. at 1215.

Should individual defendants be named?

The reasons in favor of naming individual defendants are that (1) wrongdoers may be held personally liable for injuries that they have caused; and (2) the presence of non-diverse individual defendants will defeat federal diversity jurisdiction.

Clients often feel strongly in favor of naming individual defendants. However, the decision to name an individual defendant should be a legal, and not an emotional, decision. The primary disadvantage to naming individual defendants is that each individual defendant may retain counsel, thus giving the plaintiff numerous adversaries instead of one.

Will an individual be held liable under the applicable law?

A. New Jersey Law Against Discrimination

The scope of individual liability is currently under debate. Numerous decisions have allowed, and impliedly affirmed, personal liability of individual defendants. See Andersen v. Exxon Co., 89 N.J. 483 (1982); Peper v. Princeton Univ. Bd. of Trustees, 151 N.J. Super. 15, 26 (App. Div. 1977), rev'd on other grounds, 77 N.J. 55 (1978). But see Tyson v. Cigna Corporation, 918 F. Supp. 836 (D.N.J. 1996)(holding that individual liability under LAD is limited to supervisory employees who affirmatively engage in discriminatory conduct while acting within the scope of employment).

Statutory authority: Under LAD, it is an unlawful practice for an "employer" to discriminate. N.J.S.A. 10:5-12 (a). The definition of "employer" includes "all persons" defined by the statute. N.J.S.A. 10:5-5(e). "Persons" is defined as (among other things), "one or more individuals." N.J.S.A. 10:5-5(a).

Are there accomplices to the acts of discrimination?

N.J.S.A. 10:5-12(e) provides that it is unlawful discrimination for "any person, whether an employer or employee or not, to aid, abet, incite, compel or coerce the doing of any of the acts forbidden under this act, or attempt to do so." See also Baliko v. Stecker, 275 N.J. Super. 182 (App. Div. 1994)(holding that individuals can be personally liable as aiders and abettors to discrimination).

2

B. Common Law

Individuals may be found liable for other wrongful discharge torts. See Borecki v. Eastern International Management Corporation, 694 F. Supp. 47 (D.N.J. 1988)(holding that individual may be held liable for Pierce wrongful discharge under New Jersey law).

C. Title VII

Individual employees are not liable under Title VII. Sheridan v. E.I. Dupont de Nemours and Company, 100 F.3d 1061 (3d Cir. 1996).

Is the defendant a philanthropic, charitable or religious organization?

Juries may be reluctant to award significant damages where the defendant is a philanthropic, charitable or religious organization. Such organizations may not have sufficient assets to pay judgments. Moreover, with religious organizations, one runs the risk of falling within the exceptions to the LAD's provisions. N.J.S.A. 10:5-12a.

Is the defendant a public entity?

Tort claims against public entities are governed by the Tort Claims notice provisions of the Tort Claims Act. Discrimination claims do not fall within the Act's scope. Therefore, notice of discrimination claims does not have to be filed. Fuchilla v. Layman, 109 N.J. 319, cert. den. 488 U.S. 826 (1988).

II. WHAT ARE THE CAUSES OF ACTION?

Counsel should carefully question the client to determine all the relevant facts. Clients may omit important details, not realizing that those details may have tremendous legal significance. Every lawyer can recall an experience where a client, while preparing to leave the office, says, "By the way, I have this document...."

In assessing a client's case, plaintiff's counsel should make sure that the facts fit the legal claim, and not struggle to make the claim fit the facts. Creative lawyering is essential to success in any area, and is the means by which new law gets created. However, counsel should take care to ensure that any claims raised are meritorious. Not only must we comply with the

Rules of Professional Conduct, we must also protect our clients, preserve our professional reputations, and safeguard the integrity of the discrimination laws.

Does the client have a statutory, contract or common law claim?

A. New Jersey Law Against Discrimination, N.J.S.A. 10:5-1 et seq.

The New Jersey Law Against Discrimination ("LAD") prohibits discrimination on the basis of race, creed, color, national origin, ancestry, age, marital status, affectional or sexual orientation, sex, atypical hereditary cellular or blood trait or handicap.

Sexual harassment is a violation of the LAD. Hostile environment sexual harassment occurs where the conduct (1) occurred because of the employee's gender; (2) is severe or pervasive; (3) makes a reasonable woman believe that (4) the working environment is hostile. Lehmann v. Toys 'R' Us, Inc., 132 N.J. 587 (1993). The conduct does not have to be overtly sexual to form the basis for a sexual harassment claim. Muench v. Township of Haddon, 255 N.J. Super. 288 (App. Div. 1992).

B. The New Jersey Conscientious Employee Protection Act, N.J.S.A. 34:19-1 et seq.

The New Jersey Conscientious Employee Protection Act ("CEPA") prohibits an employer from retaliating against an employee because the employee (1) discloses or threatens to disclose an activity, policy or practice that the employee reasonably believes is in violation of the law; (2) provides information to a public body, or objects to or refuses to participate in activity which the employee reasonably believes is in violation of law, regulation or public policy.

C. New Jersey Family Leave Act, N.J.S.A. 34:11B-1 et seq.

The New Jersey Family Leave Act ("FLA") requires employers to provide employees with a maximum of 12 weeks leave of absence for (1) the birth of a child; (2) the adoption of a child; or (3) the serious health condition of a child, parent or spouse.

Is there a public policy violation?

New Jersey also recognizes claims for discharges in violation of public policy. Pierce v. Ortho Pharmaceutical, 84 N.J. 58 (1980).

Is there a written or oral contract?

New Jersey recognizes the rights of employees to enforce implied written and oral contracts relating to employment. Woolley v. Hoffmann-LaRoche, Inc., 99 N.J. 284, modified 101 N.J. 10 (1995)(implied written contract existed); Shebar v. Sanyo Business Systems Corp., 218 N.J. Super. 111 (App. Div. 1987), aff'd 111 N.J. 276 (1988)(oral contract of employment). There are no decisions regarding the statute of limitations for Woolley or Shebar claims. Both Woolley and Shebar claims are treated as contract claims and analyzed under basic contract principles.

Are there tort claims?

Counsel should consider whether the facts will support a tort claim. Such claims might include defamation, invasion of privacy, intentional infliction of emotional distress claim, assault or negligent supervision.

III. WHEN IS THE STATUTE OF LIMITATIONS EXPIRED?

Counsel should, of course, routinely calculate the Statute of Limitations on claims while evaluating a case. If there is a lengthy time period before the statute runs, counsel may be able to engage in negotiations concerning the claims. Negotiations may help assess the strength of the claim, as well as the client.

A. New Jersey Law Against Discrimination

1. Division on Civil Rights ("DCR")

A verified complaint must be filed with the Division on Civil Rights within 180 days of the unlawful discrimination. N.J.S.A. 10:5-18, 10:5-13. Filing a non-verified complaint with the 180 day period may satisfy this requirement under certain circumstances. Decker v. Elizabeth Board of Education, 153 N.J. Super. 470, 473-474 (App. Div. 1977), certif. denied 75 N.J. 612 (1978).

When was the individual notified of the adverse job action?

The statute of limitations begins to run on the date that the individual is notified of the discriminatory action. Delaware State College v. Ricks, 449 U.S. 250 (1980). But see Keelan v. Bell Communications Research, 289 N.J. Super. 531 (App. Div. 1996)(holding that the statute of limitations for Conscientious Employee Protection Act ("CEPA") claims begins to run on the date of employee's termination, and not on notification date).

The "discovery rule" is rarely applicable to cases under the New Jersey Law Against Discrimination. See e.g., Walden v. Hiram Walker, Inc., 92 NJAR2d (CRT) 95 (holding that complaint was time barred after 180 days and rejecting plaintiff's discovery rule argument).

Is there a "continuing violation"?

A "continuing violation" occurs where charges involve a particular company policy, practice or procedure used by the employer which has a discriminatory impact. Decker v. Elizabeth Bd. of Ed. , 153 N. J. Super. 470, 473-74 (App. Div. 1977), certif. den. 75 N.J. 612 (1978)(holding that wage discrimination is a continuing violation). See also Erdmann v. Union Cty Regional High School Board of Education, 541 F. Supp. 388, 392-94 (D.N.J. 1982)(discussing continuing violations); Pilot v. New Jersey Dept of Health, 7 NJAR 150 (DCR 1982)(holding that where a timely complaint is filed as to current violations, prior(otherwise time barred) acts may be litigated. Terry v. Mercer Cty Freeholders Board, 173 N.J.Super. 249, 253 (App. Div. 1980), aff'd on other grounds, 86 N.J. 141 (1981)(discussing recoverable damages for continuing violations).

A continuing violation exists where there is a present and ongoing violation of Title VII (as opposed to simply the present effect of past discrimination.) United Air Lines Inc. v. Evans, 431 U.S. 553 (1977).

2. Filing in Superior Court under the LAD

There is a two year statute of limitations. Montells v. Haynes, 133 N.J. 282 (1993)(holding that the statute of limitations for civil actions under LAD is two years; six year statute for acts occurring prior to July 27, 1993).

B. Title VII[1]

Charge of discrimination must be filed with the Equal Employment Opportunity Commission within 180 days of the act of discrimination, in states in which there is no state agency (42 U.S.C. 20000e-5(e)) and within 300 days in states where there is a state agency. 29 CFR 1601.13.

Has the client received a right to Sue letter?

A Right to Sue letter is required for bringing suit. 42 USC 2000e-5(f). A party has 90 days from the receipt of the formal right to sue letter to file suit. 42 USC 2000e-5(f)(1).

C. Age Discrimination in Employment Act, 29 USC 623(a)

Just as with Title VII, no civil action under the ADEA may be taken until an individual has filed a charge with the EEOC. No civil action may occur until 60 days after the individual has filed the charge with the EEOC. 29 USC 626(d).

In a deferral state, a charge must be filed within the earlier of 300 days after the discriminatory act or 30 days after receipt of notice of the termination of state law proceedings. 29 USC 626(d)(2). In a non-deferral state, the charge must be filed within 180 days of the alleged discriminatory practice. 29 USC 626(d)(1). A civil suit must be filed within 90 days of the notice of dismissal or termination of the EEOC proceedings. 29 USC 626(e).

D. Americans with Disabilities Act, 42 USC 12101 <u>et seq.</u>

The ADA utilizes the same procedural requirements as those applicable to Title VII. 42 USC 12117(a).

E. Public Policy violation

Public policy claims have a two year statute of limitations. <u>N.J.S.A.</u> 2A:14-2 (two year statute of limitations on personal

---

[1]These procedures apply to non-federal employees. Federal employees are governed by separate rules which shall not be explored here.

injury claims).

F. Conscientious Employee Protection Act (CEPA), N.J.S.A. 34:19-1 et seq.

CEPA claims have a one year statute of limitations. N.J.S.A. 34:19-5. See also Young v. Schering Corp., 275 N.J. Super. 221, 229 (App. Div. 1994), aff'd 141 N.J. 16 (1995).

The statute of limitations for CEPA claims begins to run on the actual date of the employee's termination, not notification date. Keelan v. Bell Communications Research, 289 N.J. Super. 531 (App. Div. 1996).

G. Defamation

Defamation claims are governed by a one year statute of limitations. N.J.S.A. 2A:14-3.

H. Other tort claims

Other tort claims are generally governed by a two year statute of limitations. N.J.S.A. 2A:14-2 (two year statute of limitations on personal injury claims).

IV WHAT ARE THE DAMAGES AVAILABLE?

Under the LAD and FLA, a plaintiff is entitled to all remedies available in common law tort actions, including compensatory damages for lost wages and benefits. Under Title VII and ADEA, a plaintiff can receive reimbursement for back pay and benefits.

Computing a client's wage and benefit loss is the best way to evaluate the value of a case. Wage and benefit loss can be proven with precise financial evidence, and the help of an economic expert. Unlike emotional distress or punitive damages, wage and benefits loss is not speculative.

Has or can the client mitigate?

The failure of a client to mitigate damages by making a reasonable and diligent job search can limit the client's recovery of compensatory damages. Goodman v. London Metals Exchange, Inc., 86 N.J. 19 (1981).

What are potential punitive damages?

Most causes of action in employment litigation, with the exception of contract claims, allow for the recovery of punitive damages.

Punitive damages may be awarded against public entities in CEPA actions. Abbamonte v. Piscataway Township, 138 N.J. 405 (1994). Most likely, the Abbamonte reasoning will allow for punitive damages against public entities in LAD claims.

Under the Punitive Damages Act, N.J.S.A. 2A:15-5.9, a defendant shall not be liable for more than five times the amount of compensatory damages or $350,000, whichever is greater. Discrimination actions are excluded from this limitation. The Act is applied prospectively from its effective date (October 27, 1995).

As a practical matter, cases should rarely be evaluated on a potential award of punitive damages. Awards of punitive damages are speculative at best.

Is there insurance coverage?

The possible existence of insurance coverage will generally not affect the decision as to whether to accept a case. However, plaintiff's counsel will want to determine during discovery whether there is insurance to cover either defendant's litigations costs or the judgment. Insurance coverage will often affect the valuation of a case. Plaintiff may also make an offer to settle within the policy limits, which may place additional pressure on the insurers to settle. Rova Farms Resort v. Investors Ins. Co., 65 N.J. 474 (1974).

Are attorneys' fees recoverable?

Attorneys' fees may be awarded pursuant to statutory causes of action. A contingency enhancement may be awarded under the NJLAD. Rendine v. Pantzer, 141 N.J. 292 (1995).

V. WHAT IS THE EVIDENCE?

It is almost too obvious to point out that an attorney should assess the evidence when evaluating a potential case. If a case appears speculative, do not accept a case on the hope of developing evidence during discovery. Not only may such actions violate the Rules of Professional Conduct, it is unfair to the client and dangerous to a practice.

However, do not expect a discrimination case to be easy to prove. There will rarely be direct evidence of discrimination claims. Most cases will be proven through circumstantial evidence. Always ask the client for the reasons she believes that adverse action was taken against her. Ask the client why she believes a decision was discriminatory. Be sure to ask about the existence of direct evidence.

Determine if there are witnesses to the discrimination. Ask the client who would make good witnesses, and determine whether you may speak to those individuals ex parte. Find out if there are other victims of discrimination or harassment. Such incidents will likely be admissible.

In sexual harassment cases, employer liability varies according to the facts of the case. An employer is strictly liable for equitable relief. Agency principles, which include negligence, should be applied to determine if an employer is liable for compensatory damages. Punitive damages may be assessed against the employer in the event of actual participation by upper management or willful indifference. Lehmann v. Toys 'R' Us, Inc., 132 N.J. 587 (1993). Therefore, inquire of the client whether there have been other complaints against the harasser, or whether the client has any information to suggest that the employer knew of the harasser's propensities.

Evidence will also include the employer's response to a sexual harassment complaint. To determine whether an employer has taken effective remedial action under the LAD for sexual harassment, plaintiff should seek discovery of documents relating to any internal investigation. Such documents are discoverable. Payton v. New Jersey Turnpike Authority, 292 N.J. Super. 36 (App. Div. 1996), certif. granted 146 N.J. 495 (1996).

VI WHO IS MY CLIENT?

In litigating any action, consider that you are going to be working closely with the plaintiff until the case goes to trial. Ultimately, the plaintiff's case is going to rest upon the impression the plaintiff makes with the jury. Therefore, it is important for an attorney to feel comfortable with a client, and to trust that a jury will be favorably impressed with the plaintiff.

Assess the client to determine whether he or she can withstand litigation, and the abusive discovery tactics that too often get used by defendants. It will be important that the client is committed to helping in the litigation of his case, which means responding to information requests, making time to prepare for depositions, and remaining calm in the face of delays or difficult motions. Determine that the client is willing to honor the financial arrangement made regarding litigation.

Determine that the plaintiff is credible and likable. Inquire as to plaintiff's work history and past performance evaluations. If there will be a claim for emotional distress, inquire about past psychological treatment. Ask the client if the employer will contend that he is guilty of misconduct or dishonesty.

Never lose sight of the fact that an attorney's responsibility is to help the client obtain the justice he seeks. Always ask a client what he wants or what he thinks would be a fair outcome. Occasionally, a client will desire an outcome which is, in your mind, unreasonable or unreachable. In those cases, the attorney should discuss the matter clearly and explain what results might realistically be obtained. Do not accept a case where the client wants what you cannot possibly achieve.

Finally, consider the fact that "law" and "justice" might sometimes actually be synonymous. Some cases, while not presenting enormous financial rewards, are of such import that they should be litigated. Most clients are nice people in need of help. Although plaintiff's attorneys sometimes worry that "no good deed goes unpunished," do not live by that rule. Sometimes, take a case because it is simply the right thing to do.

NOTES

2

WHAT A PLAINTIFF'S LAWYER LOOKS FOR WHEN EVALUATING A POTENTIAL LAWSUIT

Wayne N. Outten

TABLE OF CONTENTS

PART A: EVALUATING PLAINTIFF'S CASE.

I. Introduction

A. Often, an employee's decision to seek counsel is prompted by the employee's perception of having been treated unfairly. This perception may be based not only on the fact of termination, but also on the manner of termination, such as a sudden pronouncement, a demeaning encounter, or defamatory remarks. Due to unfavorable common law standards on termination in many states (e.g., New York), sometimes the most promising claims are those arising from the manner of termination or surrounding circumstances.

B. The initial task of employee's counsel is to evaluate the case. This usually involves several in-depth interviews with the client, both to gather the facts (to see whether the client's expectations and objectives may reasonably be met) and to get a sense of the client's relevant personal strengths and weaknesses. Next, employee's counsel must carefully evaluate each potential cause of action and its recoverable damages; especially in New York State where employees have so few common law remedies available to them, plaintiff's counsel must analyze the facts closely and think about them creatively. Before initiating litigation, plaintiff's counsel often should try to resolve the dispute without resorting to litigation. Sometimes, the employer is unaware of the nature of the employee's feelings or of the extent of the wrong the employee has incurred; occasionally, this will enable the parties to reach a settlement in lieu of litigation. At this juncture, the parties should seriously consider alternative dispute resolution (ADR) procedures, such as mediation and arbitration. If these strategies fail, and the decision to litigate is made, certain strategic considerations, such as choice of forum, must be resolved immediately. Thereafter, the principal objectives of employee's counsel in litigation generally are to sustain all meritorious causes of action, to get through discovery in an efficient and productive manner, and to get to a jury whenever possible.

C. Part A this outline addresses the pre-trial phases of litigating an employee's claim, including evaluating the case and the client, weighing procedural and strategic concerns, drafting of pleadings, and ADR. Part B addresses the negotiation and drafting of severance agreements, which frequently results in the "settlement" of employee claims.

II. Case and Client Evaluation

A. Introduction

1. Obviously, plaintiff's counsel must do a thorough investigation before commencing a lawsuit based on employment matters. Indeed, counsel should do a thorough investigation before undertaking to represent a potential plaintiff in such a matter or before advising a client about the merits of a potential claim.

2. Moreover, under Rule 11 of the Federal Rules of Civil Procedure, plaintiff's counsel, by signing, filing, or submitting the complaint and other court papers, thereby

certifies that

> "to the best of the person's knowledge, information, and belief, formed after an inquiry reasonable under the circumstances,-
>
> (1) it is not being presented for any improper purpose, such as to harass or to cause unnecessary delay or needless increase in the cost of litigation;
>
> (2) the claims, defenses, and other legal contentions therein are warranted by existing law or by a nonfrivolous argument for the extension, modification, or reversal of existing law or the establishment of new law;
>
> (3) the allegations and other factual contentions have evidentiary support or, if specifically so identified, are likely to have evidentiary support after a reasonable opportunity for further investigation or discovery; and
>
> (4) the denials of factual contentions are warranted on the evidence or, if specifically so identified, are reasonably based on a lack of information or belief."

B. <u>Evaluating the Client</u>

1. Initial Interview

a. The first and most important step in the investigation is the initial interview with the employee. Plaintiff's counsel should ask the client to bring to the initial interview all potentially useful documents, including copies of correspondence and memoranda, job evaluations, personnel manuals, summary plan descriptions, diary notes and, where possible, the personnel records. Additionally, it is often helpful for the client to prepare and bring to the initial interview:
(1) a chart describing key players and their relationships to

each other and the employee; and (2) a concise statement of the sequence of events.

b. At the initial interview, plaintiff's counsel must filter out the relevant facts, analyze those facts critically and objectively, and ascertain whether the facts support a claim. Moreover, counsel must critically and objectively evaluate the interviewee as a prospective client, litigant, and witness.

c. While the interview questions and techniques are too numerous and variable to enumerate here, some of the questions and subjects useful in evaluating the facts and the client include the following:

- What adverse personnel action has been taken? When (earliest notice)?
- What reason(s), if any, did the employer give for taking the adverse personnel action? What does the employee believe are the real reasons? If asked by a neutral third-party, what reasons would the employer probably give?
- Does the client believe he or she was discriminated against for illegal reasons, i.e., on the basis of sex, race, religion, national origin, age? Why?
- What are the worst things the employer may say about the employee or his/her work?
- What is the employee's work record with the employer? (All past positions, promotions, evaluations, problems, etc.) Were there performance appraisals; and, if

so, what did they say?

- Who are the key managers/decision-makers involved in the adverse personnel action?

- What are the relevant personality, political, and power factors affecting the situation?

- Who are potential witnesses? Former employees? Others? Are they "friendly"? Can they be contacted?

- What records does the employer have? Where? Who controls them? Are they likely to help or hurt the claim?

- Were there any warnings regarding the relevant adverse personnel action? Any witnesses?

- Who is left on the job? What happened to the client's work? Were younger employees kept or hired?

- What damages does the employee believe he or she has sustained? (Back pay, benefits, pension, front pay, emotional distress, etc.) Has the employee mitigated damages (e.g., sought re-employment). Kept records of efforts?

- What steps, if any, has the employee already taken to seek redress? Discussions with line managers or personnel managers? Administrative filings? Unemployment insurance sought? What happened?

- What does the employee want? Are the objectives reasonable? Realistic? (If not, the potential exists for serious attorney-client problems.)

5

- What steps might be taken, short of litigation, to try to obtain the objectives?
- What kind of retainer arrangements are appropriate and workable?

2. Result of Initial Interview: The foregoing represents only a sample of the types of inquiries to make at the outset. Plaintiff's counsel should then discuss with the potential client the strengths and weaknesses of the potential claims. (This evaluation process is discussed in greater detail in Section II C below.) That discussion often leads to a mutual recognition that some or all potential claims lack sufficient actual or potential merit to warrant asserting a claim. Sometimes, the decision may be to investigate further, which may entail gathering further documentation, interviewing potential witnesses, having additional interviews with the client, and researching legal issues. In any event, as described in greater detail in Section II D below, plaintiff's counsel and the client should explore non-litigation avenues for the client to achieve his or her objectives. Finally, assuming that such measures do not result in a satisfactory result and that the investigation supports the viability of a claim, plaintiff's counsel and the client must determine the litigation strategy most suitable to the situation. See Section II E below.

C. Evaluating the Causes of Action and the <u>Recoverable Damages</u>

1. <u>Introduction</u>

a. As wrongful discharge litigation has expanded during the last several years, large damage awards have become common in some states. Although wrongful discharge claims rarely survive motions to dismiss or for summary judgment in New York, the plaintiff's attorney should know what damages are available for each possible cause of action. To do so, it is helpful to consider how other jurisdictions have handled damages in employment cases.

b. Plaintiff's attorney should research potential causes of action and the availability of damages for those in each jurisdiction in which the lawsuit might be maintained.

2. <u>Contract Actions</u>

a. Since <u>Hadley v. Baxendale</u>, 156 Eng. Rep. 145 (1854), a plaintiff in a breach of contract action generally can recover those damages that are reasonable and foreseeable at the time the contract is made. Usually computed at the time of the breach, these damages are awarded to place the injured party in as good a position as the party would have been in had the contract not been breached. <u>See</u>, <u>e.g.</u>, <u>R&I Electronics, Inc. v. Newman</u>, 66 A.D.2d 836, 411 N.Y.S.2d 401 (2d Dep't 1978).

b. Because contract damages are not designed to place the injured party in a better position than he would otherwise have been, punitive damages and damages for pain and suffering or for emotional distress generally are not recoverable. See Wehringer v. Standard Security Life Insurance Co. of New York, 57 N.Y.2d 757, 440 N.E.2d 1331, 454 N.Y.S.2d 984 (1982); Purdy v. Consumers Distributing Co., Ltd., 648 F. Supp. 980 (S.D.N.Y. 1987). See also Restatement (2d) of Contracts §355 ("punitive damages are not recoverable for a breach of contract unless the conduct constituting the breach is also a tort for which punitive damages are recoverable"). But see Mulder v. Donaldson, Lufkin & Jenrette, 623 N.Y.S.2d 560 (1st Dep't 1995) (punitive damages recoverable for a bad faith or dishonest failure to carry out a contract).

c. The clearest situation for damages arises when the suit is based on an express employment contract for a definite term. See, e.g., Frank B. Hall & Co., Inc. v. Buck, 678 S.W.2d 612 (Tex. App. 1984), cert. denied, 105 S. Ct. 2704 (1985) (plaintiff received jury award that included $414,000 for lost wages).

d. Some courts have imposed what they consider a reasonable time limit based on their determination of the parties' expectations at the time of making the contract. See, e.g., Rogozinski v. Airstream by Angell, 152 N.J. Super. 133, 377 A.2d 807 (N.J. Super Ct. 1977), modified on other grounds, 164 N.J. Super. 465, 397 A.2d 334 (App. Div. 1979) (two years considered limit of contract "in perpetuity").

e. Where the employment is at-will, the damage awards based on contract have varied greatly from state to state; however, damages generally do include back pay. See, e.g., Pine

River State Bank v. Mettille, 333 N.W.2d 622 (Minn. 1983) (damage award based on employee's lost wages from time of discharge to time of trial because measure of damages for breach of employment contract is the compensation the employee would have received had the contract been carried out according to its terms; on these facts, employee probably would not have been discharged before date of trial).

f. In considering what relief to demand, plaintiff's attorney should consider recoverability of commissions, bonuses and fringe benefits, including medical insurance, life insurance, and severance pay. See, e.g., Gorrill v. Icelandair/Flugeleidir, 761 F.2d 847 (2d Cir. 1985) (fringe benefits).

g. Where breach of an implied covenant of good faith and fair dealing is treated as a contract cause of action, recovery may be more limited than in cases in which it is treated as a tort. See Monge v. Beebe Rubber Co., 114 N.H. 130, 316 A.2d 549 (1974).

h. A terminated employee has a duty to mitigate damages. The employee's recovery for lost wages is reduced not only by income actually earned (and to be earned) by the employee, but also by income that could be earned with "reasonable diligence." McClelland v. Climax Hosiery Mills, 252 N.Y. 347, 169 N.E. 605 (1930) (Justice Cardozo). Nonetheless, the wrongdoer (i.e., the employer) has the burden of proving any potential items of mitigation. See, e.g., Air Et Chaleur, S.A.

v. Janeway, 757 F.2d 489, 494 (2d Cir. 1985); Katz Communications, Inc. v. The Evening News Association and KTVY, Inc., 705 F.2d 20, 26 (2d Cir. 1983). Employee's counsel should be sure to advise the employee to make diligent efforts to find a suitable new job, and to keep careful records of such efforts.

i. In some situations, plaintiff's recoverable damages may be reduced by payments received from collateral sources, such as insurance proceeds or unemployment insurance benefits. Generally, under the "collateral source" rule, damages recoverable for a tortious wrong are not reduced by insurance proceeds received by the injured party. See, e.g., Healy v. Rennert, 9 N.Y.2d 202, 206, 173 N.E.2d 777, 213 N.Y.S.2d 44 (1961); Restatement of Torts 2d, §920A. Although originating in tort, the collateral source rule has been applied to contract cases. See, e.g., Gusikoff v. Republic Storage Co., Inc., 241 App. Div. 889, 272 N.Y.S. 77 (2d Dep't 1934); Rutzen v. Monroe County Long Term Care Program, Inc., 104 Misc.2d 1000, 429 N.Y.S.2d 863 (Sup. Ct. Monroe Co. 1980) (unemployment benefits do not reduce damages under employment contract); Cornell v. T.V. Development Corp., 17 N.Y.2d 69, 268 N.Y.S.2d 29, 33, 34 (1966). See also Schwarze v. Solo Cup Co., 112 Ill. App.3d 632, 68 Ill. Dec. 228, 445 N.E.2d 872, 877 (Ill. App. Ct. 1983); Rabago-Alvarez v. Dart Industries, 55 Cal. App.3d 91, 127 Cal. Rptr. 222, 227 (Cal. Ct. App. 1976); Brown v. A.J. Gerrard Mfg. Co., 715 F.2d 1549 (11th Cir. 1983) (Title VII); Kauffman v. Sidereal Corp., 695 F.2d 614 (9th Cir. 1983) (Title VII). But see Syvock v. Milwaukee Boiler Mfg. Co., 665 F.2d 149 (7th Cir. 1981); Naton v. Bank of California, 649 F.2d 691 (9th Cir. 1981). See generally National Labor Relations Board v. Gullett Gin, 340 U.S. 361 (1951).

j. Plaintiff's counsel should, of course, be alert for grounds to seek attorneys' fees. See, e.g., Section 706(k) of Title VII of the Civil Rights Act of 1964, 42 U.S.C. §2000e-5(k); Age Discrimination in Employment Act of 1967, 29 U.S.C. §626. But see Evans v. Jeff D., 106 S. Ct. 2909 (1986) (upholding settlement conditioned on waiver of attorneys' fees).

3. Tort Actions

a. Where breach of an implied covenant of good faith and fair dealing is treated as a tort, punitive damages may be recoverable. See Cancellier v. Federated Department Stores, 672 F.2d 1312 (9th Cir. 1982); Gates v. Montana Insurance Co., 668 P.2d 213 (1983); Kelsay v. Motorola, Inc., 74 Ill.2d 172, 384 N.E.2d 353 (1978).

b. Tort damages include those based on lost wages, benefits and pension rights as well as damages for emotional distress and mental anguish. See Harless v. First National Bank, 289 S.E.2d 692 (W. Va. 1982); Moniodis v. Cook, 494 A.2d 212 (Md. App. 1985).

c. The standard for determining the availability of punitive damages is based on a showing of fraudulent, criminal or dishonest acts - or morally culpable conduct directed at the general public. See Purdy v. Consumers Distributing Co., Ltd.,

648 F. Supp. 980 (S.D.N.Y. 1986), and cases cited therein.

4. Statutory Actions

a. Because statutory claims often provide greater and more varied remedies, plaintiff's counsel should endeavor to include such claims when possible. Although this list is far from exhaustive, note the following:

b. Federal Statutes

- Title VII of the Civil Rights Act of 1964 allows relief in the form of back pay, reinstatement, injunctive relief, retroactive promotion, attorney's fees, and other relief. As of November 1991, compensatory and punitive damages are recoverable, subject to caps based on the employer's size.
- ADEA allows relief in the form of back pay, front pay, reinstatement, promotion, liquidated damages (where the violation is willful), attorney's fees, and other relief.
- Section 510 of ERISA prohibits retaliation against participants and beneficiaries for exercising their rights to ERISA benefits and prohibits interference with the attainment of ERISA benefits. It allows awards of back pay, front pay, and continuation of long-term disability and health insurance coverage. In ERISA §502 actions, attorney's fees may be awarded.
- The Americans with Disabilities Act prohibits discrimination against qualified individuals with disabilities and requires reasonable accommodations in some

circumstances. Basically, the remedies are comparable to Title VII remedies.

c. State and Local Laws

° Although ADEA does not allow awards for pain and suffering, state statutes often do. Thus, in New York, for example, a prudent plaintiff's attorney in an age case will include pendent state claims under the Human Rights Law to enable the employee to seek compensatory damages.

° Plaintiff's counsel must also be aware of other damages available under other state laws. See, e.g., New York Business Corporation Law §630 (providing enforcement mechanism for employees to recover in certain instances directly from ten largest shareholders of closely-held corporation). See Sasso v. Vachris, 66 N.Y.2d 28, 484 N.E.2d 1359, 494 N.Y.S.2d 856 (1985).

° Local statutes may provide additional rights and remedies. See, e.g., New York City Human Rights Law, Admin. Code Sections 8-101 et seq. (unlimited punitive damages and emotional distress damages).

D. Steps That Can Be Taken In An Effort To Avoid Litigation

1. In view of the expense of litigation, it usually makes sense for plaintiff's counsel to try to achieve the employee's objectives without litigation by contacting the employer directly and attempting some sort of negotiation; to achieve the employee's objectives through negotiation, the

employee should be able to articulate and espouse some legally cognizable claim(s), though that is not always essential. Sometimes a telephone call will lead to a meeting of the parties and their counsel.

2. Often, a carefully-crafted, direct letter giving notice of the claims in sufficient detail to indicate that counsel has done a thorough investigation of the facts will lead to negotiations.

3. If the claims are particularly strong, a letter accompanied by a well-drafted proposed complaint asserting meritorious claims may be an effective tool in negotiations.

4. Consider alternative dispute resolution mechanisms, which are discussed below.

5. For more on negotiating severance packages, see Part B of this outline.

E. Other Issues to Consider Before Initiating Litigation

1. If negotiation fails, and plaintiff has decided to litigate, several strategy decisions must be addressed before actually initiating the litigation. These concern choice of forum and applicable statutes of limitations.

2. Choice of Forum: Which State. When an employee resides in a different state than the employer, or when the employer has relevant offices in more than one state, the employee may have a choice of more than one state in which to commence the action. Obviously, the employee's attorney should

analyze state causes of action and choice-of-law rules to ascertain which state is best for the client.

3. Choice of Forum: State v. Federal Court. Whether to bring the action in state or federal court depends on, among other things, which forum is most likely to be receptive to the causes of action, which forum offers the broader range of remedies, and which forum is better on procedural and discovery matters. For example, in California, plaintiff's attorneys generally favor state court, given the favorable compensatory and punitive damages awards employees have been awarded. On the other hand, in New York, where the lower courts have applied Weiner narrowly to common law claims, the plaintiff may be better off in federal court where, based upon Gorrill v. Icelandair/Flugeleidir, 761 F.2d 847, 852-53 (1985), a Weiner-type claim may have a better chance of surviving a motion to dismiss. But see Sabetay, supra; Lapidus v. New York City Chapter of the New York State Association for Retarded Children, Inc., 118 A.D.2d 122, 504 N.Y.S.2d 629 (1st Dep't 1986). Moreover, plaintiffs in New York generally favor federal court due to procedural advantages (e.g., better calendar practices, better discovery rules and controls. A multi-state employer may seek to change the forum based upon more favorable treatment of certain claims or certain choice-of-law rules. See, e.g., Smith v. Teledyne Industries, Inc., 578 F. Supp. 353 (E.D. Mich. 1984) (employee residing in Michigan filed suit against Ohio employer in federal court based upon diversity. Held: Ohio law governs

claims for wrongful discharge of employee-at-will; Michigan law governs defamation and negligent and intentional infliction of emotional distress claims).

4. Choice of Forum: Administrative v. Court Proceeding. As is well-known, some statutes require compliance with or exhaustion of administrative procedures as a prerequisite for filing a court action. E.g., Title VII and ADEA. In some states, filing a complaint with a state agency bars the plaintiff from commencing an action in court; plaintiffs must therefore elect their remedy. See, e.g., N.Y. Exec. Law §§297(a), 300 (generally bars employee who files complaint with New York State Division of Human Rights from filing state law action in court, except when the agency grants an administrative convenience dismissal).

5. Effect of Administrative Determinations on Subsequent Litigation in Court. In some state courts, a finding in an administrative agency is res judicata on issues in court. See, e.g., Ryan v. New York Telephone Co., 62 N.Y.2d 494, 467 N.E.2d 487, 478 N.Y.S.2d 823 (1984) (unemployment insurance decision; overruled by statutory amendment).

6. Removal. If federal jurisdiction exists, a defendant may remove the case from state to federal court pursuant to 28 U.S.C. §1441. In a diversity case, an employee can commence and keep a case in state court by joining a non-diverse defendant, thereby defeating the complete diversity requirement. See, e.g., Green v. Amerada Hess Corp., 707 F.2d

201 (5th Cir. 1983), cert. denied, 464 U.S. 1039 (1984). If a case is removed to federal court, a jury demand must be made within 10 days of removal, unless it has been already expressly made in state court. Fed. R. Civ. P. 81(c).

7. Preemption. Certain federal statutes may preempt state law claims. National Labor Relations Act, 29 U.S.C. §§151 et seq. (employee discharge for union organizing activities). Others do not. E.g., Title VII of the Civil Rights Act of 1964, 42 U.S.C. §2000e-7 (discrimination claims). Others, such as ERISA, may preempt in certain circumstances, but not others. See, e.g., Gilbert v. Burlington Industries Inc., 765 F.2d 320 (2d Cir. 1985) (severance pay preempted), aff'd, 477 U.S. 901 (1986); California Hospital Association v. Henning, 770 F.2d 856 (9th Cir. 1985) (vacation benefit not preempted).

8. Statutes of Limitations. Plaintiff's counsel must also be aware of the different statutes of limitations applicable to different claims, e.g., those of state discrimination laws may be different from those of federal discrimination laws. Notably, if the EEOC finds that discrimination has occurred and enters into conciliation, that tolls the statute of limitations for the EEOC but not for the private plaintiff.

9. Insurance Coverage. The way you draft the complaint may determine whether your claims are covered by the defendant's insurance. For example, general commercial liability insurance generally will cover negligent, but not intentional, acts; and director's and officer's liability insurance coverage

may be triggered if you name individual directors or officers as defendants. Moreover, during the past several years, some companies have obtained a new type of coverage - employment practices liability insurance - which covers a wide range of employment claims including discrimination claims. Generally, the plaintiff will be better off where insurance coverage exists, for several reasons: a more objective, dispassionate decision-maker (e.g., the insurance carrier) is involved, which may lead to earlier and better settlements; another "pocket" is available to contribute to a settlement fund; the defendant's solvency is not a concern; and an insurance carrier may not select an experienced employment lawyer for the defense.

IV. Pleadings

A. Drafting a Complaint With Multiple Causes of Action. The complaint should include those claims -- both state and federal -- that are viable or colorable and should exclude those claims that are without sound basis in law and fact. Because the law in some states (e.g., New York) is so unfavorable, plaintiff's counsel may often be litigating based on relatively little legal support. This should not prevent plaintiff from litigating certain claims (e.g., fraudulent inducement to contract) where the facts and damages support such a claim. The degree of specificity in the complaint depends in part on the amount of factual and documentary support available to plaintiff's counsel. Often, the complaint is the first document (except perhaps a demand letter) that defendant's attorneys see; it begins the process of educating the defendant, its counsel, and eventually the court, about the strengths (and weaknesses) of plaintiff's case. A well-drafted complaint can be an important tool for both litigating and settling the case. Therefore, plaintiff's counsel must put sufficient thought and effort into its preparation. Be sure to demand a jury trial whenever possible; if defendant removes to state court, be sure to comply with applicable state rules for demanding a jury.

B. Choice of parties.

1. Individual v. Corporate Defendants. The plaintiff's attorney must decide whether to include individual defendants as well as corporate defendants. The federal courts are currently divided over whether individuals can be held liable under federal discrimination statutes. Compare Hamilton v. Rodgers, 791 F.2d 439 (5th Cir. 1986) (individuals can be liable under Title VII), with Tomka v. The Seiler Corp., 66 F.3d 1295 (2d Cir. 1995)(no individual liability under Title VII, but such liability under New York's Human Rights Law). In certain cases, e.g., sexual harassment, it may be appropriate to include individual defendants. In other cases, e.g., wrongful discharge, it may be better to sue the corporate defendants only, alleging that the company is liable for the acts of its employees because they acted within the scope of their employment. When the employer is a small company, it is sometimes appropriate to assert claims against the principal officer(s) personally,

especially if the company is of questionable solvency. One advantage of naming individuals is assuring access for discovery.

2. Parent v. Subsidiary. It may be advisable to join a parent corporation as a defendant, especially if the solvency of the subsidiary defendant is unknown or suspect or if the subsidiary has too few employees to be covered by a particular statute (e.g., Title VII, 15 employees). In such cases, the pleading should reflect the parent's control over the personnel practices and policies of the subsidiary.

C. Rule 11 duties.

As noted earlier, Rule 11 requires the attorney signing, filing, or submitting a pleading to certify that, to the best of his or her knowledge and after reasonable inquiry, the allegations and contentions in the pleading have evidentiary support or are likely to have such support after further investigation or discovery. The threat of Rule 11 sanctions and proceedings has been used by some defense attorneys to try to intimidate or pressure plaintiff's counsel; this should be recognized as the intimidation tactic it is. The extent of plaintiff's counsel's investigation of the facts and law while drafting the complaint should offer some measure of reassurance. Indeed, because of Rule 11, plaintiff's counsel should feel free - in investigating while drafting the complaint - to interview former employees and current employees (to the extent permitted by ethical standards) and, when appropriate, to insist on a written response to any demand letter.

D. Answering the defendant's counterclaims.

Counterclaims against employees for various alleged breaches of duty or violations of employment contracts are not uncommon. See, e.g., Mandelblatt v. Devon Stores, Inc., 132 A.D.2d 162, 521 N.Y.S.2d 672 (1st Dep't 1987). Sometimes, a defendant counterclaims for damages in an amount equal to or more than those sought by plaintiff. If, upon investigation, plaintiff's counsel believes such counterclaims are without merit, plaintiff's counsel may advise defendant's counsel, that unless they are withdrawn, plaintiff will move to strike or to seek Rule 11 sanctions. If there are discrimination claims in the complaint, plaintiff might assert an additional claim for retaliation based on the counterclaims.

V. Alternative Dispute Resolution Mechanisms

A. Generally, employees and their counsel should seriously consider using so-called alternative dispute resolution (ADR) mechanisms. Broadly speaking, ADR encompasses a wide spectrum of ways to try to resolve disputes other than through judicial proceedings. ADR might be more accurately described as "primary" problem solving or dispute resolution, inasmuch as it should be considered before litigation, not merely as an alternative to litigation.

B. The vast majority of employment-related disputes do not need or warrant litigation, which is simply too expensive, slow, inefficient, and inflexible for many such disputes. Nonetheless, litigation is a necessary alternative (perhaps, a "last resort") when other mechanisms to avoid or resolve a dispute have failed. The availability of litigation, of course, is sometimes essential to spur parties to engage seriously in ADR procedures.

C. An escalation-of-confrontation approach can be especially useful in employment disputes. That is, the employee should begin to try to resolve a problem through the approach that is least confrontational but that has a reasonable prospect of success (e.g., direct negotiations between parties), and then progress as and when needed to more confrontational or adversarial approaches (e.g., internal corporate procedures, then external or formal mediation, then non-binding arbitration). The benefits to this approach are that disputes often can be resolved faster and better, with less aggravation for all concerned, than may occur when parties rush into more adversarial forums.

D. Over the past twenty years, more and more companies have instituted internal review procedures. Given that these are internal, employees and their counsel may legitimately view such procedures with some skepticism. Companies that are serious about such programs must be aware of such skepticism and should take care to design and run the programs in a way that enhances their credibility; assuring fair procedures and neutral evaluators, for example, are important factors. For companies, these procedures can be excellent for personnel relations, if they are done properly -- not merely as litigation avoidance schemes. In any event, unless the employee perceives that the internal process is unfair or futile or that use of the process would be prejudicial, the employee should seriously consider using such procedures. They may work; and even if they don't, the employee probably will learn in the process about the strengths and weaknesses of each party's positions.

E. Once an employer decides to take a dispute "outside" the company, various alternatives are available. In employment discrimination cases, of course, the employee can go to the EEOC or to a state or local human rights agency. Such agencies are using ADR techniques, especially mediation, more and more to try to reduce their backlog of charges.

F. Mediation is an increasing popular ADR procedure for employment disputes. The key benefit of mediation is that it is voluntary and non-binding. The parties can design the process to suit the dispute, can choose the mediator, and can retain control over whether and how to settle. Done right, mediation can resolve disputes relatively quickly and amicably that could not be settled through direct negotiations An effective mediator is essential. Not everyone can be a good mediator; retired judges do not necessarily make good mediators, though some are. The most important characteristics for a mediator are good interpersonal and listening skills, creative problem-solving skills, and credibility with the parties. Substantive knowledge of the law is helpful, but not essential. While any employment dispute is a good candidate for mediation, prime candidates are cases involving on-going relationships (e.g., an employee still working for the company), emotional or sensitive issues (e.g., potentially bad publicity), and problems with non-financial aspects that may lend themselves to creative problem-solving. Examples include sexual harassment cases and cases involving reasonable accommodation of a disability. A lawyer representing employees -- or employers -- should consciously consider mediation in virtually every significant employment dispute that cannot be resolved through direct negotiations.

G. Binding arbitration raises a set of considerations that are altogether different from those arising from mediation. Of course, a dispute may be submitted to non-binding arbitration, which could be considered a hybrid of mediation and arbitration -- the object being to facilitate a consensual agreement on settlement terms. Binding arbitration, however, entails surrendering the authority to resolve the dispute to a third-party neutral. Arbitration may be suitable for employment discrimination claims, if and only if the parties enter into the agreement to arbitrate knowingly and voluntarily and as a product of comparable bargaining positions. Thus, an employee, with aid of counsel, could agree with the company to submit such a dispute to arbitration if the employee decided that the procedures were fair in the circumstances. (In fact, this rarely happens in employment discrimination cases, for a variety of reasons.) So-called "pre-dispute" mandatory arbitration procedures -- those imposed by an employer on employees, as a condition of initial or continued employment, before a dispute has arisen -- inevitably are not the product of a knowing and voluntary choice by an employee with a comparable bargaining position (except perhaps in the cases of senior executives, professionals, etc.) Moreover, such procedures often do not provide the kind of full and fair procedures (e.g., discovery) needed for discrimination cases, and sometimes purport to limit the remedies available to the plaintiff. Such coercive or unfair procedures should be resisted by employee's counsel.

PART B: NEGOTIATING AND DRAFTING SEVERANCE AGREEMENTS ON BEHALF OF EMPLOYEES

I. Common Scenarios

A. Employee fired and given employer's severance letter or agreement.

B. Employee fired but not given a severance letter or agreement.

C. Negotiated departure.

II. Negotiation

A. Should the employee negotiate for a better package or agreement? Generally, yes. If you don't ask, you don't get. It doesn't hurt to ask.

B. Can the employer rescind or withdraw the package if the employee asks for more? Generally, yes, but it virtually never happens. A standard package provided under company policy or an ongoing exit or reduction program will not be withdrawn. Under the Older Workers Benefit Protection Act (see below), the employer probably cannot withdraw during the 21/45 day consideration period.

C. Who to negotiate? It depends. Generally, the employee should try, with counsel in the background. It's cheaper and less confrontational. If that fails, the attorney can step forward.

D. With whom do you negotiate? Sometimes, you have no choice; the contact person may be named in the agreement, through you might ignore that. Other times, it is obvious in the circumstances. Try to find someone with decision-making authority, a willingness to negotiate, and an inclination to help the employee. Often, the employee is better off negotiating with his or her management rather than human resources or counsel types. Generally, prefer HR types to counsel.

E. What negotiating leverage does the employee have/use? Obviously, that depends on the situation. If the employer has a legal claim (strong? viable? colorable?), that is the best leverage, through occasionally it pays to hold that in reserve. Even absent such a legal claim -- or before asserting one -- the employee can try to "push the buttons" of the employer (especially people in the company who know and like the employee). The "buttons" include fairness, guilt (can be a great motivator), fear (e.g., bad publicity, government, higher management), friendship, etc. In some companies with some employees, it works. This is especially true where proposed changes will cost the employer little or no money while helping the employee.

F. Typically, it is harder to negotiate potential changes in the context of a RIF or large-company standard severance policy. The employer's representatives (HR, counsel, etc.) will say they can't or won't make changes that could undermine the standard or create a bad precedent. Even in the face of such a mindset, changes can be obtained -- even substantial ones -- through creative approaches (discussed below).

III. The Older Workers Benefit Protection Act ("OWBPA")

A. Effective October 16, 1990, OWBPA amended ADEA by creating strict requirements for waiver of ADEA rights or claims. The provision was codified at 29 U.S.C. 626(f).

B. Under OWBPA, an individual may not waive any ADEA right or claim "unless the waiver is knowing and voluntary";[1] and "a waiver may not be considered knowing and voluntary unless" it meets certain minimum requirements. In other words, any purported waiver of ADEA rights or claims will be totally ineffective unless it meets the minimum requirements. Note: A waiver that fails to comply with OWBPA can still waive non-ADEA rights and claims.

C. In short, the minimum requirements are:

(1) an agreement written "in a manner calculated to be understood by such individual or by the average individual eligible to participate";

(2) specific referral to "rights or claims arising under" ADEA;

(3) no waiver of rights or claims "that may arise after the date the waiver is executed";

---

[1] This codifies the well-established principle that waiver of any statutory rights must be knowing and voluntary to be effective.

(4) waiver "only in exchange for consideration in addition to anything of value to which the individual already is entitled";[2]

(5) advised in writing to consult with an attorney prior to executing the agreement;

(6) given at least 21 days within which to consider the agreement; and

(7) given at least 7 days to revoke the agreement after signing.

D. Where the waiver is requested "in connection with an exit incentive or other employment termination program offered to a group or class of employees":

(1) the consideration period is 45 days, not 21;

(2) the employer must inform the individual in writing as to

(a) any class, unit, or group of individuals covered by such program, any eligibility factors for such program, and any time limits applicable to such program; and

(b) the job titles and ages of all individuals eligible or selected for the program, and the

---

[2] Thus, an ADEA waiver would be ineffective if signed to get a standard severance package. But if there is enhanced severance for a release, the consideration requirement is met. Many companies now have a standard package available without a release, plus an enhanced package with a release. A few companies have stated that they provide no severance pay . . . but will give severance in exchange for a release.

ages of all individuals in the same job classification or organization unit who are not eligible or selected for the program.

Query: If 2 or 3 persons are fired at the same time and are provided a standard employment package, is this information requirement triggered? And does the failure to comply invalidate the waiver? (I think the answer is yes to both questions.)

E. Under a literal interpretation of the language of OWBPA, a waiver that fails to meet even one of these requirements is ineffective. Thus, an employee could take the benefits and still assert ADEA rights.

Query: In that event, can the employer require the employee to restore the consideration? (The courts are divided.)

F. Presumably, the employer cannot withdraw the proposed agreement during the 21/45 day consideration period.

IV. Economic Terms of Severance Agreements

A. COBRA

As is well-known, a discharged employee has the right under COBRA to continue group health/medical insurance coverage, with the existing coverage and rates, for up to 18 months after the off-payroll date (up to 29 months if the employee is disabled under Social Security standards). The employer may require the employee to pay up to 102% of the applicable premium.

B. Pay

1. Choices: The basic choices are lump sum and salary continuation. Typically, benefits end when a lump sum is paid and most benefits continue during a continuation period, though exceptions occur both ways. Employers will sometimes negotiate a switch from one to the other at the employee's request.

2. Effect of Choices: During a severance continuation period, employers often will continue to pay for health/medical benefits on the same terms as during active employment, though the employer may require the employee to pay up to 102% of the cost. Employers sometimes will continue other benefits, such as life insurance coverage, pension/401(k) contributions and accruals, stock plans, etc. Employers generally do not continue disability benefits or vacation/sick day accruals during a salary continuation period, though sometimes vacation accruals can be negotiated.

3. Termination of Severance Pay:

(a) An important negotiating point is whether severance continuation pay will end when the employee gets a new job. Some severance arrangements so provide, with a forfeiture of pay and benefits thereafter; such a provision may or may not impose a duty to mitigate on the employee. Other arrangements provide that the employee may choose to cease severance pay and obtain a lump sum payment for the balance, upon starting a new job or merely upon request. Of course, if the proposed agreement contains a defeasance or mitigation provision or lacks an option to choose a lump sum payment, you may try to negotiate for a change.

(b) An employee who is concerned about the prospect of running out of severance pay before finding a new job may try to negotiate a trade-off: trading a fixed amount or duration of severance pay for a potentially larger variable amount of duration, depending on when the employee gets a job. In such a situation, the employer will always insist on an outside deadline or ceiling and a duty to mitigate. For example, in lieu of 26 weeks fixed severance pay, an employee may prefer to receive severance until (and only until) reemployment, which could happen after only 10 weeks or after 40 weeks. Sometimes a combination of fixed and variable pay is negotiated, providing a floor and a ceiling.

(c) A modified arrangement sometimes is negotiated to meet the employee's security objectives (i.e., limiting the risk of missing paydays), while meeting the employer's concern that the employee won't try hard enough to find a job. Thus, for example, under a variable payment arrangement with an outside date, the employee may receive pay until reemployment and then split (50:50?) with the employer the amount of severance covered by the remainder of the severance period. This shares risks and benefits.

4. Base salary: Severance pay is typically based on base salary and does not include bonuses, incentive pay, commissions, etc. Nonetheless, employees should be alert to opportunities to lay claim to such compensation. Such claims have special merit toward the end of the business year when the compensation would normally accrue or be paid, especially if the employee has met most or all of standards for the extra compensation. Discussion of such claims is beyond the scope of this outline, but they can be quite substantial.

5. Creative Approaches: When an employer refuses to alter a standard severance pay amount or period, look for creative ways to improve the package "around the edges" while leaving the core intact.

Examples:

(a) Defer the effective date of the termination. This could be in the form of a "notice period" or simply continued employment. If the off-payroll date is postponed, the employee gets paid longer before getting the standard package. It may be understood (or better, stated) that the employee will not be expected to perform any or much service during all or part of the extended period, presumably while looking for a new job.

(b) Add a consulting agreement (discussed later).

(c) Convert some unimportant benefit to cash. For example, if the employee does not need proffered outplacement services, occasionally an employer will allow the cost of that service to be "traded in" for severance pay; this can be as much a 15% of the employee's salary. Similarly, if the employee does not need medical coverage (e.g., when covered under a spouse's plan), the cost of such coverage might be traded in.

(d) Get increased leave pay (see below).

(e) Agree to a restrictive covenant, such as a covenant not to compete or to solicit customers or employees (see below).

6. Leave pay: Always ascertain the employee's entitlement or potential claim to accrued but unused vacation or other leave pay. Sometimes, you can get the whole year's allotment; other times, all you can get is the pro rata portion. Check the employer's manuals and policies and ascertain what other employees have gotten. Increasing the amount of vacation pay is a way to enhance the package without "breaking the mold" of the standard package.

7. Offsets: Employers are not allowed to offset

unilaterally against "wages" any amount that the employer contends the employee owes the employer (*e.g.*, cash advances, loans, alleged thefts). *See* New York Labor Law § 193.

8. Income Taxes:

(a) Obviously, to the extent an employee can receive money upon severance that is tax-free, the employee is better off. Severance pay *per se* is taxable; so is accrued vacation or other leave pay.

(b) Before August 20, 1996, it was sometimes possible to structure and allocate settlements so that some or all of the proceeds would be non-taxable, specifically amounts received as compensation for emotional distress under tort or statutory claims. *See* *Schleier v. Commissioner*, ___ U.S. ____, 115 S.Ct. 2159, 132 L. Ed. 2d 294, 63 U.S.L.W. 4557 (1995). On August 20, 1996, President Clinton signed the Small Business Job Protection Act, which included a provision that amended Internal Revenue Code Section 104(a)(2) to eliminate that exclusion from taxable income. The new law permits exclusion from income only for damages received "on account of personal *physical* injuries or *physical* illnesses." (emphasis added). For these purposes, "emotional distress shall not be treated as a physical injury or physical illness," except to the extent of damages paid for medical care. This change became effective immediately, except for payments received after August 20, 1996 "under a binding agreement, court decree, or mediation award in effect on (or issued on or before) September 13, 1995."

(c) Under the new law, the opportunities for tax-free settlement amounts appear to be all but eliminated. The open possibilities for tax-free amounts include (a) damages paid for the costs of medical care, (b) amounts paid into tax-deferred accounts (e.g., 401(k)s and pension plans), and (c) direct payment by an employer of attorneys' fees for the employee's attorney (where the claim asserted permits recover of attorneys' fees). Also, keep in mind that amounts received as compensation for emotional distress, though subject to <u>income</u> taxes, may not be considered <u>wages</u> for purposes of FICA and other taxes and contributions.

C. Benefits

1. As discussed earlier, COBRA provides rights

regarding medical coverage, and some benefits are commonly extended during a salary continuation period. In any event, as to all benefits, employees should gather all pertinent information as soon as possible, including benefit and account statements, plan documents, summary plan descriptions, etc. This is especially applicable to any severance plan documents. With these documents, the employee and counsel can assess the effects of the severance on those benefits -- what is being preserved and what may be lost (e.g., due to inadequate accrual or vesting). This process can lead to identification of problems, clarification of ambiguities, and improvements that can benefit the employee, often without substantial cost to the employer.

2. Be alert to the possibility that the employer might be terminating the employee for the purpose of preventing the employee from obtaining a benefit[3] (e.g., vesting in a pension). While obviously hard to prove, such a purpose would violate ERISA § 510.

3. Where the employee is close to but short of a date for vesting or accruing some benefit, try to negotiate a way to bridge to that date. This is especially applicable to pensions, 401(k)s, and stock plans. Ways to do that include: getting a longer severance period; spreading the same severance pay over a

---

[3] Similarly, if an employer terminates an employee for the purpose of preventing the employee from obtaining compensation (e.g., a large commission or bonus), there may be a breach of the implied covenant of good faith and fair dealing. See Wakefield v. Northern Telecom, 769 F.2d 109 (2d Cir. 1985) and 813 F.2d 535 (1987).

longer period; getting an authorized leave of absence (i.e., continuing employment status without pay); or getting credit for some prior service. Sometimes an employer can be persuaded to provide some cash in lieu of the forfeited benefit.

D. Consulting

1. Sometimes, it is advantageous for both the employer and employee to enter into a consulting agreement after the end of employment. The employer may have use for the employee's expertise, contacts, etc. and the employee can obtain additional income that may not interfere with other employment. Sometimes, a consulting agreement is a way for the employer to assure the employee's good will/non-disparagement in the trade. A consulting agreement is thus a way for the employee to obtain more money in exchange for something of real value to the employee, which makes it easier for the employer to agree to.

2. Sometimes, a "no-show" consultancy can be arranged. For example, the employee may be paid to "be available" or to be "on call". Obviously, the employee should be careful to assure that the agreement is not drafted in a way that imposes real, significant obligations as a condition for payment, if that is not the intent; otherwise, the employer could stop payments for alleged non-performance.

3. Consulting agreements are especially useful when the employer does not want to alter a standard package but is otherwise willing to improve the deal.

V. Other Severance Issues

A. Outplacement Services

1. Some employers offer professional outplacement services. If this option is not offered and the employee could benefit from it, ask.

2. If the employee doesn't need or want such professional help, the employer may be willing to trade-in the cost for cash. Some employers refuse to do so, however, taking the position that outplacement service is offered to help the employee find a new job/career and the employee can take it or leave it.

3. In the absence of professional outplacement assistance, the employee may ask for and obtain help from the employer in looking for a job, such as use of a company office, secretarial and reception services, a telephone, photocopying, etc. This can be of substantial benefit, especially when it helps preserve the appearance that the employee is "looking for a job from a job."

B. Personal Property and Perquisites

1. Be alert to issues over personal property, such as the employee's rolodex, personal papers and files, copies of some "business" documents, office furnishings, etc. As to documents, ascertain whether a confidentiality agreement is already in place.

2. Employers sometimes allow employees to keep (or purchase at a reduced price) such company property as the

employee's personal office computer, home fax machine, cellular telephone, or even company car. (It doesn't hurt to ask.)

C. Confidentiality

1. Employers almost always want the terms of a severance package to be kept confidential whenever the employee gets a non-standard package. Generally, employees have no real problem with this, as long as they accept the financial terms. Such confidentiality provisions obviously make it harder for other employees (and their attorneys) to learn about enhanced severance terms -- that is the whole point from the employer's perspective.

2. The typical confidentiality clause contains some exceptions but they usually are incomplete. The employee should ask for the following exceptions: (a) the employee's professional advisors (attorney, accountant, financial planner, etc.); (b) the employee's immediate family (and perhaps other specified family, friends, etc.); (c) use in any proceeding arising under or pertaining to the severance agreement; (d) disclosure in response to any subpoena or other compulsory legal process (though employers sometimes ask/insist that the employee give notice of any such process received, so the employer can move to quash, etc.). Be careful about <u>retroactive</u> application of a confidentiality clause, i.e., proscribing disclosures that the client may have made before the deal was made. Also, it is sometimes useful to have a "safe harbor" clause, specifying what your client can say safely, if asked what happened (e.g., "We

entered into an amicable resolution.")

3. A review of case law reveals that confidentiality clauses are very, very seldom the subject of litigation.

D. Releases/Waivers

1. When an employer provides an enhanced severance package, it invariably insists on a release of any and all claims and rights by the employee against the employer (and its agents, representatives, successors, assigns, etc., etc.). For adequate consideration, that is fair and appropriate.

2. Note that a waiver that does not conform to the requirements of the OWBPA is ineffective as to ADEA rights. It would still be effective as to all other rights and claims, assuming it is otherwise knowing and voluntary and does not violate some other statutory limitation (e.g., minimum wage and overtime pay claims under the Fair Labor Standards Act and workers' compensation claims).

3. Releases in typical severance agreements are often unduly broad, perhaps unknowingly. For example, read literally, such releases often would encompass an employee's rights under benefit plans, vested or otherwise. Such a release would undoubtedly be unenforceable as to vested rights, but the release language should be clarified anyway. In any event, be sure to exclude specifically from the scope of the release all benefits that should be excluded.

4. A release by the employer of any rights and claims against the employee may be desirable or even essential.

Employers generally resist such releases, especially in a typical severance situation. When they are agreed to, employers sometimes want an exception for after-discovered claims, such as any claim for defalcation or theft against the employee. Such exceptions must be narrowly tailored.

5. In the release, be careful not to forfeit reimbursement for business expenses. The employee should submit the expenses and get reimbursed before signing the agreement, or at least reserve the ability to submit the expenses for reimbursement.

E. References/Non-Disparagement

1. A good job reference can be very valuable to an employee. Forestalling a bad job reference can be even more valuable.

2. An agreed upon form of reference letter is a good idea. I usually suggest that the employee draft a reasonable proposed letter that the employer should accept, and then negotiate from that draft. I prefer to have the agreed upon letter annexed to the severance agreement. The letter can be used in two forms: as a "To Whom It May Concern" letter that the employee can use any time, and as the standard letter to be sent out by the employer in response to any requests.

3. The content of the letter can also be the script for any oral references given. It is advisable to name specific individuals who are deemed acceptable/trustworthy to respond to any call for a reference; obtain assurances that no one else will

handle such a call.

4. In the absence of the foregoing, try to obtain agreement that, in response to any reference request, the employer will state that, pursuant to standard company policy, it can only confirm limited employment information (such as last position held and dates of employment).

F. Restrictive Covenants

1. In some contexts, employers try to include in severance agreements restrictive covenants, such as a covenant not to solicit employees or customers ("non-solicitation"), a covenant not to compete for a period of time within certain geographic and/or business parameters ("non-competition"), or a covenant not to disclose confidential or proprietary information ("non-disclosure"). Sometimes, an employee may already be subject to such restrictions, in which event the employer may ask to confirm their continued validity or to extend their scope, or the employee may seek to narrow or eliminate them.

2. Such covenants present obvious limitations on an employee's ability to earn a living after leaving the employer. A logical argument can be made that such restrictions should not extend beyond the end of the severance pay period; or put another way, that severance pay should be paid for the entire duration of any such restrictions.

3. Generally, non-competition and non-solicitation covenants are enforceable in New York to the extent that they are reasonable in time, place, and scope. In New York, unreasonable

provisions can be "blue-pencilled" to make them reasonable. Such covenants are treated differently in other states. Some places (like Florida) consider such covenants as promoting public policy and encourage them by statute or common law; others, like California, consider such covenants to be against public policy and therefore totally or largely unenforceable; some states declare any unreasonable provision to be unenforceable, without "blue-pencilling" to preserve reasonable aspects.

4. One way of handling an employer's legitimate non-competition or non-solicitation concern is to be very specific about what is prohibited. For example, the employee may covenant not to solicit named employees or customers for a period of time or not to compete as to named clients; a list can be attached as an exhibit to the agreement.

5. It is important to keep in mind the difference between non-solicitation and non-hire or non-competition. A clause that prohibits an employee from soliciting co-workers to leave the employer would not prohibit the employee from actually hiring a co-worker who approaches the employee. The same thing applies to customers and clients.

G. Cooperation

1. Employers sometimes want to assure that former employees will cooperate in the future if necessary for a lawsuit or claim as to which the employee has knowledge. For example, the employer's counsel may want to interview the employee or to have the employee available for an affidavit, deposition, or

trial.

2. While the employee is receiving severance benefits, the employer may have some self-help remedies. Otherwise, the employer may wish to obtain a written assurance of cooperation.

3. If the employee is willing to assure future cooperation, some ground rules are appropriate. For example, it may be agreed that the employee will be available only outside business hours (so as not to interfere with a subsequent job) or only up to a certain amount of time. Moreover, it is often advisable to negotiate a per diem or per hour compensation arrangement for such services, sometimes with a small amount of time (say, one day) provided free, plus assurance of reimbursement for all expenses. In addition, sometimes you can obtain a commitment that the employer will pay reasonable legal fees incurred by the employee in connection with such cooperation.

H. "Gag" Clauses

Employers sometimes seek to prohibit former employees from providing information to regulatory agencies and from voluntarily cooperating with such agencies or with other persons who might have claims against the employer. For example, such a clause might provide that the former employee may not file a charge with the EEOC, may not voluntarily assist the EEOC or any other administrative agency, may not voluntarily appear as a witness or party in any judicial or administrative proceeding in which the employer is a party, and must notify the employer of any subpoena and cooperate with any efforts by the employer to resist such a subpoena.

These clauses present a tension between public policy considerations (e.g., encouraging and facilitating disclosure and investigation of potentially unlawful conduct by employers) and private considerations of the parties (e.g., the desire by an employer to try to assure complete peace, which an employee may be willing to provide in exchange for appropriate consideration). Because of the public policy considerations, such gag clauses may not be enforceable. See, e.g., Connecticut Light & Power Co. v. Secretary of Labor, 85 F.3d 89 (2d Cir. 1996) (employer's proposed settlement provision, which would have prohibited employee's voluntary appearance as a witness or party against the employer, found to violate the Energy Reorganization Act's anti-discrimination provision); EEOC v. Astra, U.S.A., Inc., ___ F.3d ___ (1st Cir. 9/6/96) (settlement agreement clause that prohibited former employees from assisting the EEOC held to violate public policy).

I. Attorneys' Fees

Try to get the employer to pay the employee's attorneys' fees. Sometimes it works. Sometimes, this may be traded off against other amounts that would be subject to income taxes and/or FICA, thereby saving some taxes.

J. Unemployment Insurance ("UI")

1. You should always remind the terminated employee of the right to collect UI benefits. Those benefits are not payable

until the employee applies.

2. UI benefits are not payable to employees who quit without sufficient reason or are fired for misconduct.

3. If there is a doubt about what the employer will tell the UI office about the termination, try to get that straightened out beforehand and acknowledged in the agreement.

4. Strictly speaking, UI benefits generally are not payable while an employee remains on the payroll receiving severance pay, but are payable despite a lump sum severance payment or a fixed period of salary continuation. It appears that the ban on UI benefits while receiving severance benefits is not uniformly enforced.

5. If an employee is denied UI benefits improperly, an appeal should be filed; initial determinations are routinely reversed on appeal in New York.

6. New York UI law prohibits an attorney from charging a fee for handling an UI proceeding, except as ordered by the ALJ. Presumably, however, an attorney who is helping an employee preserve and enforce rights under discrimination laws or under the common law (e.g., contract claims) can help the employee with the UI proceeding in aid of the other claims.

7. For help in New York, an employee can be referred to the Unemployment Action Center, (212) 998-6568, (516) 463-6048.

#32675

NOTES

NOTES

3

PROACTIVE STEPS FOR HUMAN RESOURCE EXECUTIVES TO TAKE IN WORKING WITH DEFENSE COUNSEL TO AVOID WORKPLACE LITIGATION

Jackie Gordon, S.P.H.R.

Proactive Steps for Human Resource Executives to take in Working with Defense Counsel to Avoid workplace Litigation.

By Jackie Gordon, S.P.H.R.

Once upon a time, when an Human Resource executive received a discrimination charge or an employment lawsuit, she would call the Company's defense Counsel and arrange to send over the charge, the relevant records and then wait until further notice for the next step. It was easy but often resulted in litigation that was costly both in time and dollars.

Then came the lean and mean years of lowering costs in areas managed by Human Resource executives. We were suddenly expected to better manage our resources in every area including legal costs. But no one sent out a plan on how to accomplish this. We were not attorneys. How could we possibly tell then what to do or suggest an alternative. For many of us, the transition was difficult.

Human Resource executives who have successfully made the transition, came to terms with the necessity to establish a business relationship with their legal partners. This business relationship means you can ask questions, expect responses and talk about costs. There are some key elements to effectively managing that relationship.

*** Human Resource executives should know their organization's culture and how employment practices and litigation fit into the business plans.**

1. Communicate those plans to your counsel from the beginning of the business relationship.

2. State your standard code of operation as it relates to your expectations of updates and involvement from counsel.

3. Talk about your organization's view on expenses and any specific limits you have established for case management.

4. Let counsel know if your organization prefers to avoid litigation and why, even if the rationale is unusual.

5. And outline, the general practice and feelings about mediation, arbitration and settlements.

You've established a good business relationship with your defense counsel. Together you are able plan strategies, look at alternatives and determine a course of action. That's great! You've made progress. But are you still waiting for the answer from counsel. You wouldn't be so dependent on counsel if you had proactive steps to take to prevent the cases.

***Human Resource executives should encourage their organization to develop a peer review process to provide employees who disagree with disciplinary decisions, a vehicle in which to channel those concerns.**

1. Review process should be in writing and distributed to every employee at the time of hire.

2. This process should be included in the employee handbook.

3. The review process must be user friendly, clear, simple and understood by all levels of employees.

4. Custom design the process to fit your organization's needs, don't settle for a one size fits all program.

5. The process should be designed to be implemented in stages, not all at once.

6. Before implementation of the process, counsel should review and approve to ascertain no conflicts exist.

7. And most important. you must have periodic review of all decisions by counsel to ensure the review process is working as planned and the decisions made have not placed your organization in a vulnerable position.

You have a peer review process in place and most employees choose to use it and get a expedient response to their concerns. That's great. But you have a few more areas you want to monitor to make sure other programs and practices are in place, to minimize potential claims.

*** Human Resource executive's need to look at many things we have taken for granted because there have not been any complaints, yet. And maybe some programs you haven't tried that could be beneficial in keeping the communication doors open.**

1. Is the appraisal process realistic and measurable? Does it result in fair pay practices?

2. Read that handbook and see if what you've printed is what you do.

3. Are those policies up to date? Have you amended those that are affected by regulatory changes, i.e. **COBRA FMLA and Minimum Wage.**

4. Do you have any rotating employee suggestion groups to measure the pulse of your organization?

5. And when location make it improbable that there will be visits by other management members or Human Resource executives, a third party administered telephone concern call center with specific follow-up procedures may provide the means for employees to ask questions.

And after getting your proactive plans in place you've got a better chance of minimizing claims and litigation. However, we have to be prepared to handle those that do emerge. As Human Resource executives we should be confident in our business relationship with our defense counsel to make them immediately aware of any asserted claim. What you do and how you manage that claim will depend on how well you have built that business relationship. If you have taken most of those proactive steps, both you and counsel will be able define a plan that meets your needs and does not create a barrier for counsel to effectively represent your concerns.

NOTES

NOTES

NOTES

NOTES

NOTES

4

HOW DEFENSE COUNSEL AND HUMAN RESOURCES EXECUTIVES CAN WORK TOGETHER TO AVOID WORKPLACE LITIGATION

Lynne E. DiStasio

How Defense Counsel and Human Resources Executives Can Work More Effectively Together To Avoid Workplace Litigation

Lynne E. DiStasio[1]
Associate General Counsel
Metropolitan Life Insurance Company

An active partnership forged between counsel and executives in the Human Resources function of an organization can contribute greatly to the workplace environment as well as decrease the risk of litigation. Individuals from these two functions each bring something unique and valuable to the partnership, facilitating the sharp focusing of counsel's legal knowledge on the issues of greatest concern to, or which have greatest impact on, the organization.

For maximum impact, strategies for litigation avoidance should be a constant subject under discussion between counsel and Human Resources executives. Both must keep in mind that their perspectives are different but equally valid, and that "litigation avoidance" can mean different things to each because of those perspectives. Counsel might be able to offer a number of approaches to avoid the assertion of certain claims, but some or all of those approaches may simply not be right for the organization. Counsel and Human

[1]Ms. DiStasio acknowledges with appreciation the editorial assistance of Associate Counsel Suzanne C. Auclair of the MetLife Law Department in the preparation of this material. She also wishes to acknowledge, with sincere thanks, the many outstanding Human Resources professionals at MetLife, who have enabled her to experience first-hand the partnership that this paper describes.

Resources executives must be continually mindful (and respectful) of their differing perspectives, and looking for the strategies that are optimal from both perspectives.

One key element around which some consensus should begin to form in the developing relationship between counsel and a Human Resources executive is an understanding of the point at which litigation avoidance is no longer a particular organization's main objective. There might be issues that are not to be compromised, or that represent important principles. There might also be situations where the avoidance strategy is seen as too costly in terms of organizational impact or important organizational imperatives. These establish one of the parameters within which potential and actual claims can be evaluated, and having that parameter established in general, in advance, can help counsel and Human Resources executives focus their activities and discussions in the most productive directions. In working with counsel to define these general parameters for his or her organization, a Human Resources executive will identify and communicate the organization's philosophy and imperatives, which can prompt a useful discussion within the organization itself. Counsel who offers a litigation avoidance strategy that is at odds with the organization's philosophy can anticipate that it will be met with resistance at least, if not outright rejection. If it is a strategy that merits consideration nonetheless, of course counsel should advance it, but anticipate that it will not be readily embraced and be prepared to address the organization's concerns. Better still, counsel should anticipate the reaction and formulate alternative strategies that address counsel's concerns in ways that will be acceptable to organizational sensibilities.

For the partnership to work efficiently and effectively, the roles of counsel and the Human Resources executives cannot be too precisely or rigidly defined. Each needs to know at least some aspects of the other's role. Obviously, a Human Resource executive must have at least a general familiarity with key employment-related laws and, ideally, counsel should have some familiarity with the organization and its philosophy, policies and procedures. The goal of the partnership, in my opinion, is to identify the best approaches for the organization to take to minimize the risk of the assertion of claims as it pursues its business goals. This is facilitated by counsel and Human Resources executives joining forces as a team, not with each overly focused on a precise role.

The best time to contemplate litigation avoidance is before there is any threatened litigation on the horizon. I would suggest that there are five questions that should be part of the on-going dialog between counsel and Human Resources executives to enable an organization to reach and maintain its desired maximum level of litigation avoidance:

What are we doing now, and should we continue to do it?

The Human Resources executive should be sure that all of the organization's printed material is periodically reviewed both by Human Resources professionals and by counsel, so that it may be updated and revised as necessary to reflect changing circumstances, of both the organization and the law. This should include the obvious candidates for such review (employee handbooks, policy and procedure manuals, benefit plans and summary plan descriptions) and some less immediately obvious documents (applications, forms of agreements, brochures distributed to employees). Human Resources professionals and counsel should be sure to also periodically review the practices and procedures followed by the organization, to be sure that they continue to satisfy the objective that led the organization to implement them in the first place, and that they continue to meet evolving legal requirements, as well.

What should we consider doing now that we are not doing?

In this on-going dialog, Human Resources executives might identify changes or issues of concern to the organization, or matters that have arisen in the workplace, or counsel might observe developments in a particular area of the law that suggest a new approach that the organization should at least consider. For example, no one needed an Internet policy ten years ago, but most organizations should consider that today. Where arbitrations were once seen almost exclusively in the context of unionized workplaces, more and more organizations are giving serious consideration to implementing a variety of alternative dispute resolution programs, including the arbitration of workplace disputes in non-union settings. The implications of the changes, the new policies and procedures suggested, and the impact of all of these on the organization should be carefully discussed between counsel and the Human Resources executives to establish approaches that address organizational imperatives while minimizing liability and avoiding litigation where possible or desirable.

What might we need to do in the future?

At times, it seems that we are bombarded by new laws, rules, orders, requirements and regulations. Counsel should continually monitor the important developments in the law that apply to or impact the organizations that he or she advises, and evaluate the impact that these developments are likely to have on them. As counsel reports on these developments to the Human Resources executives, and shares observations about approaches that would appear to be most responsive to the changes and within the organization's philosophy, they can begin to work together to plan and implement appropriate and effective compliance strategies, the cornerstone of evolving litigation avoidance strategies.

Are we reaching the right audiences, in a timely and appropriate manner?

There is clearly need to review training programs, to be sure that they continue to address important topics and reflect current law and policy, and to be sure that the right people in the organization are attending them. Delivery methods of the programs should also be periodically assessed. Special attention should also be paid to the appropriate messages for managers and non-management employees on important topics. This review should not be strictly limited to training programs, but cover generally the communications or outreach programs used within the organization to convey significant information.

Are we doing this right?

This is the point at which specific actions, rather than programs or policies in general, are the focus of discussion between counsel and Human Resource executives. This particular aspect of the dialog between counsel and Human Resources executives in furtherance of their partnership will be the most individualized for each organization. The extent to which counsel might be asked this question can vary widely among organizations and within an organization, based on a variety of factors. For example, in some situations, all individual personnel actions will routinely be reviewed with counsel before implementation. In other situations, only particular personnel actions will be reviewed, or perhaps an organization might not feel that this is necessary in any situation. In these cases, counsel's review can help the organization assess the risk factors of the proposed action in light of applicable law. If there are concerns about the proposed actions, alternative steps can be suggested to achieve the same, or essentially the same, business objective. Counsel might become involved in evaluating planned actions such as layoffs or workforce consolidations, or the implementation of a new program, where the availability of the attorney-client privilege can shield certain discussions and evaluations from discovery in (unavoidable) future disputes. Counsel can also initiate some reviews by requesting them of the Human Resources executives, potentially invoking both the attorney-client privilege as well as the self-critical evaluation privilege.

Even in a workplace environment in which much time and thought has been given to avoiding the opportunity for claims to be asserted, it is inevitable that disputes will arise, and a lawsuit might result. At this point, "theories" and "potential claims" are replaced by facts. My assumption here is that the Human Resource executive becomes aware of the dispute first, by way of some communication from or on behalf of the employee. My premise is that the response of the organization to the dispute, not the timing of the initial consultation of the Human Resources executive with counsel, will be most determinative of whether the organization can avoid litigation on this particular dispute. Accordingly, the objective here should be to assemble the maximum resources available within or to the organization to evaluate and address the dispute appropriately and in a timely manner.

The Human Resources executive will first want to determine the facts of the dispute. The investigation that would be necessary to do this could be quite straightforward and simple, or very involved and complex. If counsel and the Human Resources executive have created a process for the organization to follow to accomplish investigations, even a complex investigation could be undertaken by the Human Resources organization without feeling the need to consult specifically with counsel on this particular matter during an investigation. At the other end of the spectrum, the Human Resources executive might choose to consult with counsel immediately, and even ask him or her to conduct the investigation. A certain element of personal and/or organizational preference is at work here. If the matter is particularly sensitive or problematic, or if the Human Resources executive feels that his or her staff should not be called upon to conduct this particular investigation, the earliest possible direct involvement of counsel might be seen to be appropriate.

Of course, the facts that the investigation uncovers are not themselves privileged, so the involvement of counsel in the investigation at this stage does not serve to shield the actual facts from discovery because of the privilege that attaches to attorney work product or to attorney-client communications. The privilege could avoid the creation of discoverable documents, or shield certain discussions and evaluations, however.

Litigation can usually be avoided by giving the person who asserts a claim what he or she wants, and there might be no need to consult with counsel to achieve that result. If an employee claims that there was a mistake in calculating his vacation time, and review of relevant records indicates that the employee is correct, the most appropriate response might be to correct the calculation on the spot, credit him with the right amount of vacation, and conclude the matter right there. Sometimes, however, apparently straightforward situations contain wrinkles or tangential issues and a Human Resources executive might want to consult with counsel, before determining that the matter is completely ended. This is a judgment call for the Human Resources executive, one that might be facilitated by having had the chance to develop a close working partnership with counsel in advance.

Few employment-related disputes are ever that simple, however, as we all well know. In most situations, the Human Resources executive will want to consult with counsel at least by the point that the investigation is concluded and the next steps are being evaluated. This will assure that the matter receives the most thorough evaluation possible, as potential approaches for resolution are considered, and that any resolutions proposed will truly end the matter. Consideration should be given to securing releases whenever that is appropriate. I recommend that counsel be consulted whenever releases of claims will be a part of the resolution of individual claims, and also when adverse action will be taken against another employee as the result of the resolution of the claim.

I have not distinguished between in-house counsel and outside counsel in the references to "counsel" above. For purposes of most of that discussion, there is no need for any such distinction. As noted above, no privilege attaches to the facts themselves, so there would be no difference from that perspective if an investigation is conducted by in-house or outside counsel. Further, in-house counsel are accorded the same attorney-client privilege as are outside attorneys. However, it is the unique position of in-house counsel that they might simultaneously be viewed as officers or members of the management of the organization, as well as counsel, and this duality can contribute to a perceived blurring of the line between legal and business consultation. Only advice rendered in the capacity of counsel will be protected by the attorney-client privilege. In-house counsel should always be mindful, especially when asked to conduct a particularly sensitive investigation into the facts of a particular situation, or when asked to render advice on a matter where the lines between the legal advice and business advice might be blurred, of the possibility that he or she might express an opinion or participate in an action that is seen to flow from the business, not counsel, role, and thereby be deprived of the traditional privileges that attach to an attorney in the performance of his or her professional duties. It should not be assumed that an organization always wants to shield its in-house counsel from becoming a fact witness, however. That will almost always be the case, but there can be exceptions. Ideally, exceptions will always be made knowingly and with the full intention of making an exception.

An organization that takes great care with its policies and procedures and shows great attention to its handling of individual employee concerns and complaints can eliminate the initiation of many lawsuits on those bases alone. A careful and thoughtful process of evaluating complaints and disputes quickly can allow the organization to take corrective action, or implement appropriate settlements of disputes before they become lawsuits. The end result of this will not be the total absence of lawsuits, because there undoubtedly will be situations in which the organization cannot appease an aggrieved employee on any basis that it deems reasonable. However, the end result of this process will tend to limit lawsuits to claims that the organization acknowledges cannot be resolved by any means satisfactory to it, and claims that it deems to have no merit and which it will not compromise. If this defines the types of lawsuits pending against an organization, it can declare itself a success at the task of litigation avoidance, and the counsel and Human Resources executives whose partnership has helped achieve this result share much of the credit for this success.

NOTES

5

HOW TO RESPOND EFFECTIVELY TO CHARGES OF SEXUAL HARASSMENT

Presented by Meryl R. Kanard

HOW TO RESPOND EFFECTIVELY TO
CHARGES OF SEXUAL HARASSMENT

Presented by Meryl R. Kaynard and Pamela S. Poff

Outline prepared by the law firm of
Jackson, Lewis, Schnitzler & Krupman

I. INTRODUCTION

Sexual harassment lawsuits have become one of the most frequently litigated employment-related claims. Some observers attribute this increase to national events, such as the Clarence Thomas confirmation hearings and the Paula Jones lawsuit against President Clinton, which have lessened the reluctance of employees to "go public" with complaints of sexual harassment. Unquestionably, part of the increase in litigation is directly attributable to the Civil Rights Act of 1991, which amended Title VII of the Civil Rights Act of 1964 to provide for jury trials and compensatory and punitive damages. Whatever the cause, the number of cases in which an employee accuses another of sexual harassment is increasing, and there is no indication that this trend will reverse.

Sexual harassment is a form of gender discrimination in violation of Title VII of the Civil Rights Act of 1964, as well as state fair employment practices laws.[1] Sexual harassment is created by unwelcome sexual advances, requests for sexual favors, or other conduct of a sexual nature when: (1) submission to that conduct is made a term or condition of employment, whether explicitly or implicitly; (2) submission to, or rejection of, sexual advances is a basis for employment-related decisions; or (3) such conduct has the purpose or effect of unreasonably

---

[1] Except where noted, this discussion is limited to federal law.

interfering with the victim's work performance or of creating an intimidating or offensive work environment. EEOC Guidelines on Sexual Harassment, 29 CFR §1604.1(a). The first and second of these general categories constitute quid pro quo harassment. The third is referred to as a hostile environment.

In recent years, there have been an alarming number of multi-million dollar jury verdicts and/or settlements against employers based on claims of hostile environment sexual harassment. This trend is particularly disturbing given the fact that the EEOC guidelines and earlier case law suggest that liability for hostile environment sexual harassment can be avoided if the employer (1) has a clear policy prohibiting sexual harassment, (2) has a well-established record of no prior knowledge of the offending conduct, (3) conducts a prompt investigation once allegations of inappropriate conduct are raised, and, (4) takes remedial action. The experience of Baker & McKenzie, a national law firm whose $3.5 million dollar jury verdict sent shockwaves through the business community, illustrates the importance of each of these factors.

There are three critical elements to avoiding liability after a complaint of sexual harassment has been filed: 1) conducting a prompt and thorough investigation; 2) taking appropriate remedial action; and 3) documenting the investigation and any resulting remedial action.

II. INVESTIGATING THE COMPLAINT

The ultimate goal of the investigation is to evaluate whether there has been inappropriate conduct, and if so, to take remedial and preventive action to insure the conduct will not be repeated. Evidence of prior instances of similar offending conduct is tantamount to establishing that the employer had prior knowledge and should be held strictly liable. In investigating a complaint, the employer should recognize that it may be impossible to establish absolutely the truth or falsity of allegations, and it may be necessary to make a credibility determination. Thus, the credentials of the investigator are important.

A sexual harassment policy that provides a definition of "sexual harassment" and gives examples of what actions would constitute sexual harassment should be helpful in determining whether or not the offending conduct is unlawful. However, the types of conduct which constitute sexual harassment have changed over time, and any policy should clearly define the categories of potentially offensive conduct. Lastly, the investigation should aid in making a determination whether remedial action is required and, if so, what action is appropriate.

A. Laying The Foundation -- The Sexual Harassment Policy

The first step in preventing sexual harassment or later avoiding liability should be the implementation of a strong policy against sexual harassment. The policy should include anti-retaliation provisions to encourage potential victims to come forward. It also should include a clear definition of the types of conduct which can constitute sexual harassment. In implementing such a policy, an employer is not seeking to regulate its employees' morality. Rather, it is taking a necessary step to reduce the likelihood that the law will be violated and the employer found liable. This policy may serve to discourage employees from sexually harassing other employees, and thereby reduce the possibility that claims will be made or lawsuits filed against the employer.

One of the most important features of the policy is the establishment of a formal complaint procedure by which an employee may bring a claim to a designated management official or any other management representative, if for some reason the employee does not wish to take the claim to the designated management official.

An official should be assigned to receive sexual harassment complaints and to investigate and remedy violations of the employer's policy. This individual should have training in conducting interviews and should be regarded as neutral or impartial by the employees. Note that Title VII does not require that the investigator be the same gender as the complainant. In Stafford v. Missouri, 835 F. Supp. 1136 (D.C. W.Mo. 1993), the district court held that the employer was not biased when it chose not to honor the employee's request to have a female investigator appointed to handle her complaint.

B. Conducting The Investigation

All allegations of inappropriate conduct be responded to immediately with an effective and impartial investigation. Failure to respond in a timely manner may not only subject the employer to sexual harassment suits but tort actions as well. See Prunty v. Arkansas Freightways, 16 F.3d 649 (5th Cir.), reh'g and reh'g en banc den'd, 21 F.3d 1110 (5th Cir. 1994) (where the employer was held liable for intentional infliction of emotional distress when it failed to investigate the employee's complaint, which it had actual knowledge of, until after a company official was contacted.)

The employer that immediately investigates complaints and responds quickly and effectively, preferably within 24 hours, taking disciplinary action proportionate to the severity of any improper conduct, is in the best possible position to avoid, and if necessary, defend, sexual harassment lawsuits. See Saxton v. AT&T, supra (where employer commenced investigation on same day it received complaint and transfer of alleged harasser occurred immediately after employer determined that complainant did not want to move); and Bouton v. BMW of North America, 29 F.3d 103 (3rd Cir. 1994) (where the employer was not found liable because it investigated and took remedial action even after finding no support for the sexual harassment allegations.) An investigation which is conducted properly may dissuade the complainant from even seeking administrative or court intervention. Additionally, the investigation may serve to deter future sexual harassment from occurring.

The harassee's immediate supervisor or department head and personnel officials should be notified about the complaint. If the harassee is an employee covered by a collective bargaining agreement, a union representative also should be contacted. For other employees, the harassee should contact the appropriate official who has been designated to handle such complaints. The investigation should be fully documented as it proceeds and should be comprehensive even if the harassee does not wish to cooperate fully.

Interviewing the complainant, the alleged harasser, and all purported witnesses who may have knowledge and information concerning the alleged harassment is essential to the investigation. These interviews should be conducted in private to prevent others not involved in the investigation process from overhearing any statements. Any overheard statements may form the basis of a suit brought by a party claiming the negligent publication of the incident or invasion of privacy. Additionally, negligent and intentional infliction of emotional distress claims also can be brought.

When interviewing the alleged harassee, it is critical not to create an atmosphere of fear or mistrust.[2] When obtaining information about the alleged harassment, ask for

---

[2] A California employer recently settled a case for $2.2 million because the investigation into four female employees' sexual harassment complaints, from its inception, was conducted in an atmosphere of mistrust and lack of cooperation among those doing the investigation. The (continued...)

"documenting facts" about the incident, including what was said and done and what the harassee regards as "inappropriate behavior." It is important to ask the alleged harassee if his or her job performance has been affected or if there was any psychological injury during the period of harassment. Should the employee deny the harassment has negatively impacted job performance or psychological well-being, then any corrective action that is taken to prevent the recurrence of sexual harassment should be sufficient to preclude a successful lawsuit if a claim is subsequently brought by the harassee. In the event the employee claims the harassment has negatively impacted job performance or mental state, specific examples should be obtained. These claims should be evaluated and, if substantiated, steps should be taken to alleviate the problems identified.

With respect to the confidentiality of the investigation, the individuals being interviewed should be advised that the investigation will proceed as professionally and discreetly as possible. However, a guarantee of confidentiality should not be given. Every effort should be made to keep information concerning the investigation limited to those "with a need to know." A conditional privilege may exist to shield the employer against defamation claims where communications are limited. In the following sexual harassment/defamation cases, the courts granted the employers' summary judgment motions: Manning v. Signa, 807 F. Supp. 889 (D.Conn. 1991); Scherer v. Rockwell Int'l Corp., 766 F. Supp. 593 (N.D. Ill. 1991), aff'd, 975 F.2d 356 (7th Cir. 1992); Moss v. Mutual of Omaha Ins. Co., WL 485666 (D.Vt. 1990); Roberts

---

[2](...continued)
employer had demonstrated a lack of concern about the allegations made and credited the alleged harasser's denials even though the plaintiff's allegations were corroborated by others. Because of the flaws in its investigation, the employer felt that settling was more advantageous than having these facts presented to a jury. Aquino, Jorge, "Chevron's Road To Settlement," The Recorder, March 15, 1995 referring to Vandell v. Chevron, No. SCV-945302 (Cal. S.Ct. 1992).

v. Louisiana Bank & Trust Co., 550 F. Supp. 809 (La. App. 1989); Stockley v. AT&T Info. Sys., Inc., 687 F. Supp. 764 (E.D. N.Y. 1988); and Hanly v. Riverside Methodist Hosp., 603 N.E. 2d 1126 (Ohio App. 1991).

After identifying the need for an investigation, the threshold issue for management is who will conduct the inquiry. Typically, attorneys are first considered. The skills required for an effective investigation -- interviewing employees and non-company personnel, identifying and reviewing relevant documentation while determining how these facts relate to relevant law -- are skills used every day by lawyers. Moreover, as discussed below, an attorney investigation may permit the results and supporting documentation of the investigation to be protected from disclosure as attorney work product and by the attorney-client privilege. If it is determined that an investigation should be conducted by an attorney, the selection of in-house or outside counsel to conduct the inquiry poses a separate issue for management.

With regard to investigations involving employee relations issues there is another choice -- experienced human resources professionals. Both company employees and outside consultants are excellent factfinders and deciders of credibility.

1. The benefits of using in-house counsel

When a company initiates an internal investigation, a person that likely would be consulted is its in-house attorney. He or she is an employee of the company, and, therefore, is readily available.

An in-house attorney is probably familiar with the company, its business and operations. He or she will know the people, the organizational structure, and the shortcuts to conducting an efficient and thorough investigation. This knowledge often is crucial in saving time and expense.

In-house counsel's unique knowledge also is helpful when an investigation leads to litigation. During litigation, outside counsel's major focus will be on winning the case at hand. However, in-house counsel's knowledge of a company's operations, customers and suppliers will be important. The manner in which litigation is conducted, as well as winning or losing, may have greater ramifications after its conclusion than outside counsel would recognize initially. Thus, having in-house counsel involved in an investigation at the point of an allegation may prove invaluable if a lawsuit ultimately is initiated.

Finally, the primary reason that companies elect to have their in-house counsel conduct internal investigations is cost. The use of outside counsel for an internal investigation typically is more costly in the short run than if in-house counsel conduct the same investigation. Moreover, if litigation does arise, the legal fees alone may be more disruptive to the company's business operations than would a quick settlement.

2. The downside to using in-house counsel

The use of in-house counsel in conducting an internal investigation should not be undertaken prior to evaluating the potential negative factors.

As discussed above, there is a presumption that an in-house attorney, as an employee of the company, has a better understanding of both the workings of the company and the nature of its business. This presumption is overcome, however, when an in-house attorney is asked to conduct an internal investigation of a subsidiary or separate division. Moreover, the attorney's expertise should be considered. A highly rated tax attorney, for example, may not have the necessary experience to conduct an investigation arising from a sexual harassment complaint. An in-house attorney also may have been the drafter of policies under review and, therefore, may lose his or her objectivity. Further, counsel's judgment may be affected by biases built up during his or her tenure, and previous confidences with witnesses may be threatened. In addition, there may be political considerations mitigating against the use of in-house counsel. For example, it may not be wise to ask an in-house attorney to investigate the conduct of his or her direct or indirect superiors. Finally, even if an investigation is protected by the attorney-client privilege, it may be best for the company if the investigation not remain privileged.

Accordingly, the size of a company, in-house counsel's role in that company, his or her professional and personal experiences while at the company, the political circumstances and the desire, if possible, to keep the investigation privileged must all be considered in choosing an appropriate investigator.

3. The benefits of using outside counsel

As an initial matter, hiring outside counsel to conduct an investigation may prove indicative of a high degree of commitment by a company. The importance of this is highlighted in the sexual harassment context and in satisfying the business judgment rule. An attorney experienced in conducting an investigation -- interviewing witnesses, identifying and collecting documents and integrating facts with relevant law -- is likely to be readily available. In addition, an outside attorney may be less influenced by political considerations.

4. <u>The downside of using outside counsel</u>

Outside counsel are not generally as familiar with company operations as in-house counsel. Further, they do not usually have the benefit of knowing the people involved in the investigation. Of course, use of outside counsel may prove to be more costly. Finally, if the company takes action based on the investigation, it may not be desirable to keep the investigation privileged. It may be necessary for the investigator to testify in a future action. If that investigator is your outside counsel, he or she may not be able to represent you in a subsequent litigation in which the company's actions and responsibilities are put in issue.

5. <u>Human resources professionals</u>

In employment situations, experienced human resources professionals are good alternatives to in-house or outside counsel as investigators. Human resource professionals often are knowledgeable in the law, are well-trained in talking to employees, and are careful fact gatherers. Further, juries may tend to give more credibility to a non-attorney investigation.

III. <u>SOLUTIONS TO REMEDY THE COMPLAINT</u>

The step after the investigation is to determine what, if any, corrective action should be taken. The investigator should prepare a confidential report of his or her findings and recommendation, which are to be reviewed by the appropriate company officer(s) as well as counsel.

Before taking any corrective action, counsel should make sure that the charge has been substantiated or corroborated by third parties and that the alleged harasser was given an opportunity to rebut the charges by responding to evidence against him or her. If it is determined that harassment did occur, the corrective action should be commensurate with the severity of the conduct.

The phrase "prompt remedial action" has been defined to mean that an employer must take prompt and appropriate remedial action "reasonably calculated to end the harassment." See, e.g., Waltman v. International Paper Co., 875 F.2d 468 (5th Cir. 1989) The courts all seem to agree that "what is appropriate remedial action will necessarily depend on the particular facts of the case - the severity and persistence of the harassment, and the effectiveness of any initial remedial steps ... not every response by an employer will be sufficient to discharge its legal duty. Rather, the employer may be liable despite having taken remedial steps if the plaintiff can establish that the employer's response was not 'reasonably calculated' to halt the harassment." Id. at 479. Kotcher, supra. (Transfer and demotion of alleged harasser followed by restoration of the alleged harasser to his original position after the complainant left the company held to be insufficient remedial action.) Additionally, if the harasser is a high-level employee, there is a noticeable trend among the courts to find the company responsible for acts of hostile environment regardless of prior knowledge that the offensive conduct was occurring.

In the Karibian v. Columbia University case cited earlier, the employee alleged that she had been sexually harassed by one of her supervisors. The district court granted summary judgment on the basis that the plaintiff sustained no economic loss, and further, that the University was not liable for the supervisor's conduct because it had no prior knowledge that the offensive conduct was occurring. In this regard, the district court held that the plaintiff had to prove that the employer either provided no reasonable avenue for employees to bring sexual harassment complaints or knew of the harassment but did nothing about it. Id. at 777.

The U.S. Court of Appeals for the Second Circuit reversed, holding that the district court applied the wrong standard in evaluating employer liability in hostile environment cases and holding "that an employer is liable for the discriminatory abusive work environment created by a supervisor, if the supervisor uses his actual or apparent authority to further the harassment, or if he was otherwise aided in accomplishing the harassment by the existence of the agency relationship . . . [a]t some point ... the actions of a supervisor at a sufficiently high level in the hierarchy would necessarily be imputed to the company." Id. at 779-80. Thus, the court held that Columbia University was liable for the acts of the alleged harasser, regardless of the absence of notice or the reasonableness of its complaint procedures, because the supervisor capitalized upon his authority over the plaintiff's employment to force her to endure offensive conduct.

These cases illustrate the importance not only of the investigation but also the action taken in response to the complaint. Put simply, appropriate remedial action is action that stops the conduct. Termination, however, is not the only alternative. Kotcher, supra. Indeed, the Second Circuit in Kotcher held that not every response to a complaint of sexual harassment must take the form of dismissal. Id. at 63. However, in the Weeks v. Baker & McKenzie case noted earlier, the jury concluded that the company had failed to take effective action based on testimony from several women that the alleged harasser had engaged in similar conduct toward them and that they had complained about the offensive conduct.

Whether or not remedial action is taken, the harassee should be encouraged to report any future perceived harassment or retaliation. The employer should still follow-up with the employee after the investigation to inquire if harassment still persists. If the employee states that the harassment has ceased, this would preclude a successful negligent retention or sexual harassment suit from being brought. See Harrison v. Edison Bros. Apparels Store, 924 F.2d 530 (4th Cir. 1991), where the court held that no negligent retention liability existed for acts which occurred after the plaintiff's complaint because she did not complain of any further harassment even though she was asked.

IV. EFFECTIVE RECORDKEEPING DURING AND AFTER INVESTIGATION

Documentation of the investigation process should be segregated from both employees' (alleged harasser and harassee) personnel files, unless it is concluded that harassment occurred and discipline is imposed. Contained in the segregated file should be the employee's complaint and other documents and notes recorded or memorialized during the investigation. Additionally, the file should contain copies of applicable federal and state laws, employer policy statements (including notices, handbooks and the applicable personnel manual provision) and a written plan of who is to be interviewed.

It is important to record what was said during the interviewing process and what was done because such evidence gathered can be used to support an employer's corrective action, or lack thereof, during and after the investigation. The contents in the file should be protected and preserved as they will more than likely be used as part of the employer's defense in a potential sexual harassment, retaliation, defamation, or similar suit filed by any of the parties involved.

Because the contents of the file later may be discoverable, care should be taken not to make any derogatory or editorial notations when recording what went on during the investigation process. Any personal opinion about what is being communicated to the investigator should be excluded as these statements may end up placing the employer at a disadvantage in subsequent litigation. To better safeguard against potential lawsuits and to maintain confidentiality, avoid using support staff to type, copy, file, or deliver documents contained in the file.

At the conclusion of the investigation, a report should be prepared to document the entire investigation. The report should include:

- a summary of the allegations and the alleged harasser's responses;
- a summary of those individuals interviewed;
- a summation of the findings of fact;
- a discussion of the conclusions drawn about the allegations; and
- a discussion of the recommendations for remedial or corrective action to be taken.

If a report is generated, special care should be taken that it accurately reflects the contents of the investigative notes. Additionally, all subsequent follow-up with the complainant and communications to the alleged harasser and other parties involved should continue to be documented.

V. PRIVILEGE ISSUES SURROUNDING AN INTERNAL INVESTIGATION

An internal investigation, which encompasses interviewing witnesses, examining documents, and drafting reports raises several issues relating to the attorney-client privilege, the work-product doctrine, and the self-evaluative privilege. Prior to commencing an investigation, the company must decide whether it desires to keep the investigation privileged. In a sexual harassment investigation, proof of an immediate and effective investigation and appropriate remedial action can relieve a company from liability. See generally Gary v. Long, 59 F.3d 139

(D.C. Cir. 1995). In such a situation, the company will want to disclose the investigation and have its investigator testify.

The remainder of this section presumes an investigation where the company desires to keep the investigation privileged. If privilege is desired, safeguards must be put in place to assure that a potential plaintiff will not gain access to investigative materials.

A. The Attorney-Client Privilege

The attorney-client privilege protects the information furnished to counsel to help him or her render an informal opinion, as well as the professional legal advice provided by the attorney to the client.

The elements of the privilege are well-settled in both state and federal courts. For example, in New York the attorney-client privilege is codified as protecting "confidential communications made between an attorney ... and the client in the course of professional employment..." N.Y. Civ. Prac. L. & R. §4503 (McKinney 1992). To sustain a claim of privilege, the party invoking it must demonstrate that the information at issue was a communication between client and counsel, that it was intended to be and was in fact kept confidential, and that it was made in order to assist in obtaining or providing legal advice to the client. Matter of Bekins Record Store Co., 465 N.E.2d 345 (N.Y. 1984).[3]

---

[3]A more thorough, but similar description of the privilege, is offered by Wigmore:

> (1) the asserted holder of the privilege is or sought to become a client; (2) the person to whom the communication was made (a) is a member of the bar of a court, or his subordinate and (b) in connection with this communication is acting as a lawyer; (3) the communication relates to a fact of which the attorney was informed (a) by client (b) without the presence of strangers (c) for the purpose of

(continued...)

A corporation may invoke the attorney-client privilege to protect a communication. Upjohn Co. v. United States, 449 U.S. 383 (1981). To assert the privilege, the following must be shown:

1. the communication was made for purposes of securing legal advice;

2. the employee making the communication did so at the direction of his corporate superior;

3. the superior made the request to secure legal advice;

4. the communication is within the subject matter of the employee's corporate duties; and

5. the communication has not been disseminated beyond those persons who, because of the corporate structure, need to know its contents.

The attorney-client privilege is not restricted to communications involving litigation; it includes any matters with respect to which the client seeks legal advice. However, the privilege protects only the "communications" between a lawyer and the client. It can not be used as a shield for the client's knowledge of the facts themselves. Accordingly, communications by a client to counsel will not be protected if the attorney's role is to serve solely as a fact finder.[4]

---

[3](...continued)
securing primarily either (i) an opinion on law or (ii) legal services or (iii) assistance in some legal proceeding, and not (d) for the purpose of committing a crime or tort; and (4) the privilege has been (a) claimed and (b) not waived by the client. See 8 J. Wigmore, Evidence §2292 (McNaughton rev. 1961).

[4]Documents that do not themselves contain confidential communications to a lawyer do not become privileged from the transmittal of them to an attorney. Darnell v. McMurray, 141 F.R.D. 433, 434 (W.D.Va. 1992) ("preexisting documents which could have been obtained by court process from the client when he was in possession may also be obtained from the attorney by similar process following transfer by the client in order to obtain more informed legal advice").

Attorney-client communications relating solely to non-legal business matters are not privileged. Rossi v. Blue Cross & Blue Shield of Greater N.Y., 540 N.E.2d 703, 705 (N.Y. 1989); Bowne of New York City, Inc. v. AmBase Corp., 150 F.R.D. 465 (S.D.N.Y. 1993). However, where a communication is mixed between legal and non-legal advice, the privilege may be invoked where the legal character of the communication is predominant.

Generally, an investigative report by counsel will be protected by the attorney-client privilege provided it primarily reflects legal advice. Spectrum Sys. Int'l Corp. v. Chemical Bank, 581 N.E.2d 1055 (N.Y. 1991) (upholding privilege with respect to report prepared by special counsel retained to investigate possible fraud by bank's employees and suppliers, where primary purpose of report was to "render legal advice to the client"); Kraus v. Brandseter, 586 N.Y.S.2d 280 (N.Y. App. Div. 1992) (reports containing both facts and legal analysis were privileged where it was "clear that they were made in order to render legal services or advice").

B. The Work-Product Doctrine

The work-product privilege provides an attorney with protection for materials prepared in anticipation of litigation. It encompasses the "mental impressions, conclusions, opinions or legal theories of any attorney." Fed R. Civ. P.26(b)(3). The doctrine generally extends to all material prepared or reviewed by the attorney in anticipation of litigation. Sporck v. Peil, 759 F.2d 312 (3d Cir.), cert. denied, 474 U.S. 903 (1985). It is, therefore, much broader than the attorney-client privilege.

The immunity from discovery provided by the work-product doctrine, however, is conditional. It may be set aside if a party demonstrates a sufficiently pressing need for the information. See, e.g., Golden Trade, S.R.L. v. Jordache, 143 F.R.D. 508, 510 (S.D.N.Y.

1992). Under the federal rules, proof must be shown that the inquiring party "has [a] substantial need of the materials in the preparation of [his] case and that [he] is unable without undue hardship to obtain the substantial equivalent of the materials by other means." Fed. R. Civ. P. 26(b)(3).

Whether the work-product doctrine is applicable in the absence of an actual threat of litigation is dependent on two factors. The first is the temporal proximity of the potential litigation. Some courts have adopted a liberal standard and have held that for the work-product doctrine to apply, the materials in question must be prepared or obtained "because of the prospect of litigation." See, e.g., United States v. Rockwell Int'l., 897 F.2d 1255, 1266 (3d Cir. 1990), cert. denied, 466 U.S. 944 (1984). But see, Grumman Aerospace Corp. v. Titanium Metals Corp., 91 F.R.D. 84, 89 (E.D.N.Y. 1981) (litigation must be imminent for privilege to apply). The second factor requires that preparation for litigation be the "primary motivating purpose behind the creation of the document." United States v. Davis, 636 F.2d 1028, 1040 (5th Cir. 1981), cert. denied, 454 U.S. 862 (1981).[5]

Reports and attorney memoranda prepared in connection with internal investigations have been afforded protection from discovery under the work-product doctrine. See, e.g., In re Grand Jury Subpoena (John Doe), 599 F.2d 504, 511 and n.5 (2d Cir. 1979) (interview notes and memoranda, questionnaires, and summaries compiled by outside counsel pursuant to a legal audit of possible illegal foreign payments were prepared in anticipation of litigation).

---

[5]The substance of an interview with a former employee conducted in anticipation of a litigation is generally privileged under the work-product doctrine. See In re Gulf Oil/Cities Service Tender Offer Litigation, Nos. 82 Civ. 5253, 87 Civ. 8992, 1990 WL 108352 (S.D.N.Y. July 20, 1990).

C. The Self-Evaluative Analysis Privilege

The self-evaluative analysis privilege protects internal reports prepared from a review conducted to improve a procedure or product. See, Apex Oil Corp. v. De Mauro, 110 F.R.D. 490, 496 (S.D.N.Y. 1985). Thus, a report of an internal investigation may be privileged, independent of the attorney-client privilege or work-product doctrine.

No court has provided an exact definition of the self-evaluative analysis privilege, but, generally, three criteria must be met: (1) the information contained in the document must result from an internal investigation conducted to evaluate or improve a procedure or product; (2) the party must have intended that the information remain confidential and that there exists a strong interest in preserving the type of information sought; and (3) the information must be of a type whose flow would be hindered if discoverable. Etienne v. Mitre Corp., 146 F.R.D. 145 (E.D.Va. 1993); Flynn v. Goldman, Sachs & Co., 836 F. Supp. 152 (S.D.N.Y. 1993).

It has been argued that EEO-1's, or Equal Employment Opportunity Reports (Ethnic Composition Reports), are protected from discovery under the self-evaluative privilege. A majority of courts faced with this issue have ordered production of EEO-1's. Siskonen v. Stanadyne, 124 F.R.D. 610 (W.D. Mich. 1989); Capellupo v. FMC Corp., Civ. No. 4-85-1239, 1988 WL 41398 (D. Min. Apr. 1, 1990). However, at least one court has recognized the privilege. Roberts v. National Detroit Corp., 87 F.R.D. 30, 32 (E.D. Mich. 1980) (EEO-1's need not be produced "to the extent that they contain discussions of defendant's affirmative action plans (AAP) or similar 'self-critical analysis.'").

D. Preserving Confidentiality During An Internal Investigation

The preservation of confidentiality is of paramount importance. It must be constantly guarded -- prior to, during and after an investigation. The presence of an attorney throughout the investigation is required to maintain both the work-product and attorney-client privilege. The latter protects only against disclosure of communications to and from an attorney; the former protects only against disclosure of material prepared in anticipation of litigation.

Initially, a memorandum, or engagement letter if outside counsel is employed, should be prepared. It should detail the scope of the investigation, the intention that the work be privileged, and that all information is being developed in furtherance of rendering legal advice. Also, the number of individuals in a company with access to information should be limited. Finally, any writings from counsel summarizing investigations should contain both facts and legal analysis to ensure the applicability of the attorney-client privilege.[6] Moreover, preserving confidentiality will permit a company to maintain control of that decision.

VI. ETHICAL CONSIDERATIONS OF INTERNAL INVESTIGATIONS

A. The Joint Defense Privilege

An employee who seeks advice from the company's attorney must be informed that the attorney represents the company. Joint representation of an employee and a company gives

---

[6]It may later prove advantageous to produce the report of an internal investigation. As discussed above in Section I.B., a thorough investigation may prevent the imposition of liability on a company in a sexual harassment setting or on members of the board of directors in other settings. In these instances, and to establish a company's commitment to remedying a problem, the results of an investigation may be released.

rise to numerous problems and should generally be avoided. Steps should be taken to arrange for separate counsel where an obvious conflict exists.

When an employee chooses to hire a private attorney, an adversarial relationship is not inevitable. Confidential communications flowing from the employee to the company's attorney (or from the company to the employee's attorney) may still be protected under the joint defense privilege, also called the "common interest rule." Courts recognize that there may be a basis for a privilege claim where it is needed to protect "the free flow of information from client to attorney ... whenever multiple clients share a common interest about a legal matter." United States v. Schwimmer, 892 F.2d 237, 243-44 (2d Cir. 1989), cert. denied, 502 U.S. 810 (1991).

The assertion of the privilege has been upheld in virtually any litigation-related setting, provided that the parties share a common interest and that confidential information was exchanged to facilitate their legal representation. However, "the common interest doctrine does not encompass a joint business strategy which happens to include as one of its elements a concern about litigation." Bank Brussels Lambert v. Credit Lyonnais S.A., 160 F.R.D. 437, 447 (S.D.N.Y. 1995). It is not essential that the parties' joint efforts be evidenced by a formal written document, but some courts have noted the absence of an "informal agreement" in rejecting a privilege claim. See United States v. Sawyer, 878 F.Supp. 295, 297 (D. Mass. 1995).

Where an employee asks a company's attorney a specific question regarding his personal legal situation, that attorney is faced with a common ethical question. For, in effect, the employee is seeking legal representation from that attorney.

Rule 1.7 of the Model Code of Professional Conduct prohibits a lawyer from representing a new client with diverse interests from an existing client. Representation of both a company and employee may violate this rule. Joint representation is impermissible where two parties, here a company and an employee, have "directly adverse" interests. Only where each party can be represented fairly by counsel, and the employee consents to the representation after full disclosure of potential conflicts, may that attorney proceed in the representation. Model Code of Professional Conduct Rule 1.7 (1992). However, if the circumstances change, and a conflict between the company and employee becomes evident, the attorney should end his representation of the employee.

B. The Obligation to Disclose Corporate Wrongdoing

An internal investigation may uncover individual or corporate conduct that is criminal or which condones sexual harassment or race discrimination. The ethical issue facing the attorney-investigator is when and how he or she must report such wrongdoing.

Certain types of conduct clearly must be reported. Criminal conduct in the securities area by an employee of a publicly-traded company must be disclosed to the SEC. The release of hazardous substances by a company must be reported to the EPA. However, whether a company must disclose information relating to workplace discrimination or sexual harassment is unclear.

Under the 1934 Securities Exchange Act, a public company is required to disclose information concerning "materially important" events which the registrant deems to be of material importance to the security holders. The termination or resignation of a president or CEO is information always considered "materially important." See, e.g., 10K of Earl Scheib, Inc., Apr. 30, 1995 (Filing 95557261) (reporting that president resigned position). However, the reason a president or a unique employee (a software designer, for example) is terminated -- for sexual harassment or discrimination -- is not materially important, and it need not be disclosed.

Companies have consistently disclosed to the SEC widespread sexual harassment and gender and race discrimination that have led to full-scale EEOC investigations. See, e.g., 10K of Publix Supermarkets, Inc., Dec. 31, 1994 (Filing 9525759). However, even widespread discrimination that is being investigated internally does not pose the same problems for a company. Until an inquiry reveals the type of problems that could lead to liability, no "materially important" event has occurred, and no reporting requirement exists.

C. Spoliation Of Evidence

It is beyond dispute that an attorney may not destroy damaging or incriminating evidence he or she uncovers during an internal investigation. Model Code of Professional Conduct Rule 3.3(a) (1992). Attorneys risk being disbarred for aiding in or directly destroying documentary evidence. In re Glass, 399 N.Y.S.2d 6 (N.Y. App. Div. 1977).

Moreover, a similar issue is raised if an attorney becomes aware that potentially damaging or relevant evidence is scheduled to be destroyed pursuant to a long-standing document destruction program. Under these circumstances, an attorney is obligated to prevent the destruction of all relevant evidence.

VII. THE REPORT OF THE INVESTIGATION

A written report may be the most effective way to organize the investigator's conclusions and allow for a determination of appropriate remedial action. A thorough, non-privileged report should contain: (1) a description of the alleged wrongdoing; (2) a description of the documents, manuals and witnesses examined; (3) a summary of the information elicited;

(4) determinations as to credibility where there are "fact" conflicts; and, (5) findings of fact based on the credible evidence. This report should be shared with in-house or outside counsel who, based on the investigative findings, should render an opinion as to the potential legal liability and suggest actions to minimize any damage that may exist.

VIII. POTENTIAL CLAIMS BY THE ALLEGED HARASSER

There has been an increase in claims across the country, for example, wrongful discharge claims, by individuals who have been discharged for engaging in conduct the company determines violates its sexual harassment policy. These employees have asserted a number of different causes of action. For instance, many employees have claimed that their discharge amounted to a breach of an express contract, that it violated an implied contract that dismissal only could be for cause, or that it violated some public policy. Claims for discrimination and negligence (based on negligent investigation) also have been brought. There also have been defamation claims premised on the information disclosed to third parties about the allegations and/or the dismissal.

Some examples of these cases are as follows:

Kestenbaum v. Penzoil, 108 N.M. 20 (1988), cert. denied, 490 U.S. 1109 (1989). Employee alleged that his employment was not terminable at-will but was subject to an implied contract requiring a good reason to terminate him, and there was no good reason. [Held: for plaintiff.]

Ashway v. Ferrellgas, Inc., 1989 U.S. Dist. LEXIS 18315 (D. Arizona 1989), aff'd in part, rev'd in part, 945 F.2d 408 (9th Cir. 1991) cert. denied, 113 S.Ct. 72 (1992). Employee sued his former employer for negligently breaching its duty to investigate the sexual harassment charges against him prior to his termination. [Held: for defendant.]

Anderson v. Hewlett-Packard Corp., 694 F. Supp. 1294 (N.D. Ohio 1988). Employee sued former employer for breach of contract or, in the alternative, under theory of promissory estoppel. [Held: for defendant.]

Scherer v. Rockwell International Corp., 766 F. Supp. 593 (N.D. Ill. 1991), aff'd, 975 F.2d 356 (7th Cir. 1992). Employee sued former employer for breach of contract and defamation. [Held: for defendant.]

Elrod v. Sears Roebuck and Co., 939 F.2d 1466 (11th Cir. 1991). Employee claimed he was unlawfully discharged on the basis of age in violation of the Age Discrimination in Employment Act and that the stated reasons for his discharge, sexual harassment, were mere pretext. [Held: for defendant.] See also Crimm v Missouri Pacific Railroad Co., 750 F.2d 703 (8th Cir. 1984). [Held: for defendant.]

Nijjar v. Peterbilt Motors Co., 1993 U.S. Dist. LEXIS 619 (N.D. Calif. 1993), aff'd, 42 F.3d 1401 (9th Cir. 1994). Employee sued employer for breach of implied covenant of good faith and fair dealing, defamation, discrimination, and negligent infliction of emotional distress. [Held: for defendant.]

Coen v. Elco Chevrolet, Inc., 756 F. Supp. 414 (E.D.Mo.), aff'd, 950 F.2d 728 (8th Cir. 1991). Employee claimed his employer discriminated against him on the basis of sex when it discharged him after female employee accused him of sexual harassment. [Held: for defendant.]

The variety of claims asserted by employees terminated because of sexual harassment underscores the importance of conducting a thorough investigation and of keeping good records of that investigation. The outcomes of such cases have varied and depend on the law of the jurisdiction where the challenged acts occurred.

NOTES

6

HOW TO RESPOND EFFECTIVELY TO CHARGES OF SEXUAL HARASSMENT

Pamela S. Poff

HOW TO RESPOND EFFECTIVELY TO CHARGES OF SEXUAL HARASSMENT

I. AVOIDING LITIGATION IN THE WORKPLACE

Responding effectively to claims of sexual harassment is one of a number of ways to try to avoid potential litigation. Prior to discussing how to respond to sexual harassment claims, we would like to present some general rules for avoiding workplace litigation. The following is a ten point program for preempting outside interference at your company.

- The Preventative Employee Relations Audit: Conducting a Survey of Company Policies and Procedures to Expose and Correct Vulnerable Areas
  - Developing a system for preventing conflict through the comprehensive review of your organizations' legal concerns, recruitment and orientation practices, performance evaluations, disciplinary procedures, communications, complaint resolution procedure, compensation structure, and general overview of employee relations.
- Creating an Effective Employee Communications Program
  - The role of the supervisor, the art of communications, setting the stage for effective two-way communication, downward/upward communications, key points for effective communications, barriers to effective communications.
- Preempting Conflict Through the Employee Handbook
  - Effective issue avoidance through inclusion of personnel policies, organization's statement on employee relations, handbook receipt and disclaimer.
- Establishing Lawful and Effective Employee Participation Programs
  - Analysis of recent legal issues and specific recommendations for EPPs.
- Targeted Training for Supervisors and Managers to Avoid Conflicts
  - Operating the system for preventing conflict by training managers and supervisors through programs such as the Manager's Guide to EEO and Wage Hour Compliance, Managing Without Unions, Confronting Workplace Safety Issues, Eliminating Workplace Sexual Harassment, Meeting the Challenges of the Americans With Disabilities Act, Minimizing the Risk of Workplace Violence, Utilizing Alternative Dispute Resolution Techniques - The Role of the Manager.
- A Supervisor's Guide for Conflict Resolution
  - Equipping management with the tools to resolve conflict through the policy manual, guidelines for handling complaints and problems, and the role of the manager/supervisor in preserving union-free status.

- Effective Discipline and Termination Procedures to Minimize Conflict and Litigation
  - Spotting the issues and preparing the foundation
- Problem Solving and Compliant Resolution Procedures for Non-Union Employees
  - Empowering employees as a key element of the system for preventing conflict through complaint resolution procedures and peer review panels for grievances.
- Alternative Dispute Resolution: Its Value, Methods, and Results
  - Exploration of ADR as a method of preempting conflict and avoiding litigation through the use of agreements to arbitrate disputes.
- "How Are We Doing?"
  - Developing a System for Monitoring, Reporting, and Accountability in the Prevention and Resolution of Workplace Conflict.

II. UNDERSTANDING SEXUAL HARASSMENT

A. What is Sexual Harassment?

29 C.F.R. Section 1604.11 of the EEOC Guidelines defines Sexual Harassment as:

Unwelcome sexual advances, requests for sexual favors, and other verbal or physical conduct of a sexual nature when:

1. submission to such conduct is made either explicitly or implicitly a term or condition of an individual's employment;

2. submission to or rejection of such conduct by an individual is used as the basis for employment decisions affecting such individuals, or

3. such conduct has the purpose or effect of unreasonably interfering with an individual's work performance or creating an intimidating, hostile or offensive work environment.

There are two basic types of sexual harassment:

- quid pro quo

- hostile environment

B. Forms of Sexual Harassment

Sexual harassment occurs in various ways in the workplace. Some of the ways are:

1. VERBAL - Unwelcome words directed to another including:

- Lewd or suggestive remarks and conversation and sounds of a sexual nature or conversation with sexual overtones (ranging from subtle hints to direct, outright propositions).
- Jokes (a way to express hostility, put down a group, i.e. women).
- Comments on appearance. (A person's body, makeup, hair or dress have little to do with normal job duties).
- Invitations (for lunch, dinner, drinks, dates, sexual relations).
- Threats (hints to blatant intimidation).

2. PHYSICAL - Unwelcome contact with another by bumping, touching, stroking, cornering, mauling, grabbing, kissing, hugging, pinching and gesturing.

3. VISUAL - Unwelcome exposure to sexually-explicit photos, graffiti and staring.

C. Preventing Sexual Harassment

1. Guidelines

- conduct supervisory training
- develop an effective problem resolution procedure
- publish and implement a policy prohibiting sexual harassment
- encourage employees to report all incidents of sexual harassment and conduct investigations of complaints
- eliminate harassing conduct and abuses of power: treat co-workers respectfully

D. Examples of Sexual Harassment

Because of the inherent subjectivity of sexual harassment, it is impossible to define or identify each and every circumstance that represents a potential problem. However, there are certain categories of conduct that commonly do cause problems, and within each category it is possible to draw certain lines between conduct that is proper and that which is improper, recognizing that there are broad gray areas with no clear answers.

PRACTICAL HINTS:

1. **TOUCHING:** With the exception of handshaking, touching is not acceptable.

2. **JOKING:** Do not tell sexual jokes or make innuendoes. Harassment takes place not only for the parties involved in a conversation, but also for those who can hear the conversation.

3. **SUGGESTIVE REMARKS:** Avoid suggestive or targeted remarks about physical attributes, a person's sex life, or similar matters. Do not refer to female individuals as "girls" or male individuals as "boys". Avoid demanding or degrading comments targeted at one's sex or at persons of the other sex.

4. **FLIRTING/DATING:** While employees cannot be told who they can see while not at work, company policy can prohibit dating/flirting at work.

5. **GRAPHIC OR VISUAL HARASSMENT:** Avoid the display of pictures, posters, cartoons, drawings, or other printed materials that employees find offensive.

6. **INAPPROPRIATE GESTURES:** Leering, moaning, clutching are unacceptable behaviors.

7. **SEXUAL BRIBERY/COERCION:** "Sleep with me or else" threats, or promise of rewards for sexual favors, constitute harassment.

III. <u>EFFECTIVELY HANDLING A SEXUAL HARASSMENT COMPLAINT</u>

If a claim of sexual harassment does lead to litigation the EEOC will, in many cases, be investigating the complaint. Consequently, understanding how they believe sexual harassment claims should be handled would be beneficial. The EEOC's guidelines state:

A. A good policy statement and effective complaint resolution mechanism precludes liability if the complainant fails to resort to the mechanism within the requisite time frames.

B. Elements of a Good Policy Statement

1. Definition of sexual harassment.
2. Employer will not tolerate sexual harassment.
3. Non-compliance will be punished with effective sanctions.
4. Employees are encouraged to report violations.
5. Formal complaint procedure is established.

C. Sexual Harassment Grievance Mechanism

1. Grievance mechanism must provide an <u>adequate</u> and <u>effective</u> response to complaints of sexual harassment.
2. Mechanism must be publicized.
3. Elements of an effective grievance system.

(a) Encourage employees to come forward (provide confidential and "protective" avenue, e.g. do not require report to supervisor).

(b) Provide for investigation

- Promptly.
- Thoroughly (make victim whole and prevent occurrence).
- Confidentiality - be sensitive to both claimant and accused (a wrongly accused supervisor can also sue).
- When claim is made - take it seriously.

4. Provide for appropriate responsive action.

   (a) Where harassment occurred, take appropriate disciplinary action (sanctions must be effective) and reflect the severity of the allegations.

   (b) If claim unsupported, provide <u>positive reinforcement</u> to supervisor.

5. Provide for prompt and appropriate corrective action to alleviate abusive conditions.

D. Preventive Measures

   1. Training to affirmatively raise subject of sexual harassment.

   2. Educational programs for all employees to increase awareness of the problem and the employer's policy, disapproval and consequences for policy violations.

IV. THE ROLES OF IN-HOUSE AND OUTSIDE COUNSEL

After identifying the need for an investigation, the threshold issue for management is who will conduct the inquiry. Typically, attorneys are first considered. The skills required for an effective investigation - interviewing employees and non-company personnel, identifying and reviewing relevant documentation while determining how these facts relate to relevant law - are skills used every day by lawyers. Moreover, as discussed below, an attorney investigation may permit the results and supporting documentation of the investigation to be protected from disclosure as attorney work product and by the attorney-client privilege. If it is determined that an investigation should be conducted by an attorney, the selection of in-house or outside counsel to conduct the inquiry poses a separate issue for management.

With regard to investigations involving employees relations issues there is another choice - experienced human resources professionals. Both company employees and outside consultants are excellent fact finders and deciders of credibility.

A. In-House Counsel

1. The benefits of using in-house counsel

When a company initiates an internal investigation, a person that likely would be consulted is its in-house attorney. He or she is an employee of the company, and, therefore, is readily available.

An in-house attorney is probably familiar with the company, its business and operations. He or she will know the people, the organizational structure, and the shortcuts to conducting an efficient and thorough investigation. This knowledge often is crucial in saving time and expense.

In-house counsel's unique knowledge also is helpful when an investigation leads to litigation. During litigation, outside counsel's major focus will be on winning the case at hand. However, in-house counsel's knowledge of a company's operations, customers and suppliers will be important. The manner in which litigation is conducted, as well as winning or losing, may have greater ramifications after its conclusion than outside counsel would recognize initially. Thus having in-house counsel involved in an investigation at the point of an allegation may prove invaluable if a lawsuit ultimately is initiated.

Finally, the primary reason that companies elect to have their in-house counsel conducted internal investigations is cost. The use of outside counsel for an internal investigation typically is more costly in the short run than if in-house counsel conducted the same investigation. Moreover, if litigation does arise, the legal fees alone may be more disruptive to the company's business operations than would a quick settlement.

2. The downside to using in-house counsel

The use of in-house counsel in conducting an internal investigation should not be undertaken prior to evaluating the potential negative factors.

As discussed above, there is a presumption that an in-house attorney, as an employee of the company, has a better understanding of both the workings of the company and the nature of its business. This presumption is overcome, however, when an in-house attorney is asked to conduct an internal investigation of a subsidiary or separate division. Moreover, the attorney's expertise should be considered. A highly rated tax attorney, for example, may not have the necessary experience to conduct an investigation arising from a sexual harassment complaint. An in-house attorney also may have been the drafter of policies under review and, therefore, may lose his or her objectivity. Further, counsel's judgment may be affected by biases built up during his or her tenure, and previous confidences with witnesses may be threatened. In addition, there may be political considerations mitigating against the use of in-house counsel. For example, it may not be wise to ask an in-house attorney to investigate the conduct of his or her direct or indirect superiors. Finally, even if an investigation is protected by the attorney-client privilege, it may be best for the company if the investigation not remain privileged.

Accordingly, the size of a company, in-house counsel's role in that company, his or her professional and personal experiences while at the company, the political circumstances and the desire, if possible, to keep the investigation privileged must all be considered in choosing an appropriate investigator.

B. Outside Counsel

1. The benefits of using outside counsel

As an initial matter, hiring outside counsel to conduct an investigation may prove indicative of a high degree of commitment by a company. The importance of this is highlighted in the sexual harassment context and in satisfying the business judgment rule. An attorney experienced in conducting an investigation - interviewing witnesses, identifying and collecting documents and integrating facts with relevant law - is likely to be readily available. In addition, an outside attorney may be less influenced by political considerations.

2. The downside of using outside counsel

Outside counsel are not generally as familiar with company operations as in-house counsel. Further, they do not usually have the benefit of knowing the people involved in the investigation. Of course, use of outside counsel may prove to be more costly. Finally, if the company takes action based on the investigation, it may not be desirable to keep the investigation privileged. It may be necessary for the investigator to testify in a future action. If that investigator is your outside counsel, he or she may not be able to represent you in a subsequent litigation in which the company's actions and responsibilities are put in issue.

C. Human Resources Professionals

In employment situations, experienced human resources professionals are good alternatives to in-house or outside counsel as investigators. Human resources professionals often are knowledgeable in the law, are well-trained in talking to employees, and are careful fact gatherers. Further, juries may tend to give more credibility to a non-attorney investigation.

NOTES

7

EEOC ENFORCEMENT GUIDANCE ON THE EFFECT OF REPRESENTATIONS MADE IN APPLICATIONS FOR BENEFITS ON THE DETERMINATION OF WHETHER A PERSON IS A "QUALIFIED INDIVIDUAL WITH A DISABILITY UNDER THE AMERICANS WITH DISABILITIES ACT"

Presented by Paul Steven Miller

Table of Contents

Executive Summary: Enforcement Guidance on the Effect of Representations Made in Applications for Benefits on the Determination of Whether a Person Is a "Qualified Individual with a Disability" Under the Americans with Disabilities Act of 1990 (ADA or Act)

Introduction

This Enforcement Guidance explains why representations about the ability to work made in the course of applying for social security, workers' compensation, disability insurance, and other disability benefits do not bar the filing of an ADA charge. It provides instructions to EEOC investigators for assessing what weight, if any, to give to such representations in determining whether a charging party (CP) is a "qualified individual with a disability" for purposes of the ADA.

A "qualified individual with a disability" is "an individual with a disability who satisfies the requisite skill, experience, education and other job-related requirements of the employment position such individual holds or desires and who, with or without reasonable accommodation, can perform the essential functions of such position." Because of the fundamental differences in the definitions used in the ADA and the terms used in disability benefits programs, an individual can meet the eligibility requirements for receipt of disability benefits and still be a "qualified individual with a disability" for ADA purposes. Thus, a person's representations that s/he is "totally disabled" or "unable to work" for purposes of disability benefits are never an absolute bar to an ADA claim.

Americans with Disabilities Act

The definition of the term "qualified individual with a disability" reflects the ADA's broad remedial purpose to prohibit discrimination against individuals with disabilities who want to work and are qualified to work. Accordingly, the definition:

- requires an individualized assessment of a particular individual's capabilities;
- focuses on the essential functions of a particular position;
- looks at particular positions, not work in general; and
- considers whether a person can work with reasonable accommodation.

The ADA definition of "qualified individual with a disability" differs from the definitions used in the Social Security Act, state workers' compensation laws, disability insurance plans, and other disability benefits programs designed for different purposes.

Social Security Act

Disability programs established under the Social Security Act are designed to provide income to individuals with disabilities who generally are unable to work. Unlike the ADA definition of "qualified individual with a disability," the Social Security Administration (SSA) definition of "disability":

- permits general presumptions about an individual's ability to work;
- considers all tasks as jobs are customarily performed without focusing on the essential functions of a particular position;
- looks generally at whether an individual can do work which exists in the national economy rather than whether s/he can perform the essential functions of a particular position; and
- does not consider whether a person can work with reasonable accommodation.

Workers' Compensation Laws

The purpose of workers' compensation laws is to provide benefits to individuals whose earning capacity has been reduced because of a work-related injury or illness. Unlike the ADA definition of "qualified individual with a disability," the workers' compensation definitions of "disability" generally:

- permit generalized presumptions about an individual's ability to work;
- do not distinguish between marginal and essential functions;
- focus on whether an individual is unable to do any kind of work for which there is a reasonably stable employment market rather than whether s/he can perform the essential functions of a particular position; and
- do not consider whether an individual can work with reasonable accommodation.

Disability Insurance Plans

Disability insurance plans provide partial wage replacement when an employee becomes unable to work as a result of illness, injury, or disease. Frequently, the definitions of "disability" under such plans:

- do not distinguish between essential and marginal functions of a position; and
- make no allowance for an individual's ability to work with reasonable accommodation.

Relevant Factors for Determining Whether CP Is a "Qualified Individual with a Disability"

When assessing the effect of representations made in connection with an application for benefits on the determination of whether CP is a "qualified individual with disability," investigators should consider the following factors:

- the definitions of terms such as "disability," "permanent disability," "total disability," "inability to work," etc., under the relevant statute or contract pursuant to which CP applied for disability benefits (e.g., do they look at specific positions or general kinds of work? do these terms take into account reasonable accommodation?);
- the specific content of the representations, who made them, and the purpose for which they were made;
- whether the representations are in CP's own words;
- whether the representations about CP's inability to work are qualified in any way (e.g., "I am able to work with certain restrictions");
- when the representations were made, the period of time to which they refer, and whether CP's physical or mental condition has changed since the representations were made;
- whether CP was working during the period of time referred to as a period of total disability;
- whether the employer suggested that CP apply for benefits;
- whether CP asked for and was denied reasonable accommodation;

- when the employer learned of the representations; and
- other relevant factors, such as advances in technology or changes in the employer's operations that may have occurred since representations were made that may make it possible for CP to perform the essential functions of the position, with or without reasonable accommodation.

Enforcement Guidance: Effect of Representations Made in Applications for Disability Benefits on the Determination of Whether a Person Is a "Qualified Individual with a Disability" Under the Americans with Disabilities Act of 1990 (ADA)

Introduction

The Americans with Disabilities Act of 1990 (hereinafter ADA or Act)[1] prohibits employers from discriminating against qualified individuals with disabilities in all aspects of employment. To be protected by the ADA, a person must meet the definition of the term "qualified individual with a disability."[2] A "qualified individual with a disability" is "an individual with a disability who satisfies the requisite skill, experience, education and other job-related requirements of the employment position such individual holds or desires, and who, with or without reasonable accommodation, can perform the essential functions of such position."[3]

---

[1]Codified as amended at 42 U.S.C. §§ 12101-17, 12201-13 (1994).

[2]By including the phrase "qualified individual with a disability," Congress intended to reaffirm that the ADA "does not undermine an employer's ability to choose and maintain qualified workers." S. Rep. No. 101-116, at 26 (1989) [hereinafter Senate Report]; H.R. Rep. No. 101-485, pt. 2, at 55 (1990) [hereinafter House Education and Labor Report]. Rather, the ADA simply provides that employment decisions must not subject a "qualified individual with a disability" to discrimination on the basis of his/her disability. Id.

The ADA also protects individuals from discrimination on the basis of their relationship or association with a person with a disability and prohibits certain disability-related inquiries and medical examinations. 42 U.S.C. § 12112(b)(4), (d). Further, the Act prohibits retaliation or coercion against individuals because they have opposed any act that the ADA makes unlawful, have participated in the enforcement process, or have encouraged others to exercise their rights secured by the ADA. Id. § 12203. A person need not be a "qualified individual with a disability" to be protected by these sections of the Act.

[3]29 C.F.R. § 1630.2(m)(1996); see also 42 U.S.C. § 12111(8).

The issue of whether a person is a "qualified individual with a disability" arises when an individual brings an ADA claim alleging that s/he was subjected to an adverse employment action because of his/her disability. For example, in many charges received by the EEOC, individuals claim that they were not hired or were fired because of disability even though they were able to perform the essential functions of the position at issue. Often, the individual has requested but been denied a reasonable accommodation. Frequently, the individual also has filed for disability benefits, sometimes at the suggestion of the employer, and has represented that s/he meets the relevant eligibility requirements (e.g., that s/he is "totally disabled" or "unable to work"). In such cases, questions may arise as to whether the individual is barred from claiming that s/he is a "qualified individual with a disability" under the ADA.[4]

This enforcement guidance explains why representations made in other contexts about the ability to work are not necessarily a bar to an ADA claim.[5] In this regard, the guidance:

- analyzes the differences between the ADA's purposes and standards and those of other statutory schemes, disability benefits programs, and contracts;
- discusses recent and significant court decisions that have addressed this issue;
- explains why the doctrine of judicial estoppel and summary judgment procedures should not be used to bar the ADA claims of individuals who have applied for disability benefits;

---

[4]Similar questions also arise where individuals have filed claims for state disability, disability retirement, Railroad Retirement Board, and Federal Employee Compensation Act benefits. The analysis in this guidance also applies to representations concerning the ability to work made in other situations, such as applications for scholarships or admission to education programs and exemptions from, or deferments of, student loan repayments.

[5]The analysis in this guidance also applies to federal sector complaints of non-affirmative action employment discrimination arising under section 501 of the Rehabilitation Act of 1973, 29 U.S.C. § 791(g) (1994), and to complaints of non-affirmative action employment discrimination arising under sections 503 and 504 of the Rehabilitation Act of 1973, 29 U.S.C. §§ 793(d), 794(d) (1994).

- delineates why public policy supports the Commission's position; and
- explains how to assess what weight, if any, to give to such representations in determining whether an individual is a "qualified individual with a disability" for purposes of the ADA.

I. The ADA's Purposes and Standards Are Fundamentally Different from the Purposes and Standards of Other Statutory Schemes and Contractual Rights.

The primary purposes underlying the ADA are the elimination of barriers that prevent individuals with disabilities from participating in "the economic and social mainstream of American life"[6] and the provision of equal employment and other opportunities for persons with disabilities. In addition, Congress enacted the ADA to provide legal remedies to individuals who have experienced discrimination on the basis of disability.[7] Consistent with these goals, the ADA establishes specific standards for assessing whether an individual has a disability and whether s/he is a "qualified individual with a disability."

Because the ADA definitions of the terms "disability" and "qualified individual with a disability" are tailored to the broad remedial purposes of the Act, they differ from the definitions of the same or similar terms used in other laws and benefits programs designed for other purposes. The definitions of the terms used in the Social Security Act, state workers' compensation laws, disability insurance plans, and other disability benefits programs are tailored to the purposes of those laws and programs. Therefore, representations made under those laws and programs are not determinative of coverage under the ADA. Although representations made in connection with an application for disability benefits may be relevant to such a determination, they are never an absolute bar to a finding that a person is a "qualified individual with a disability" for purposes of the ADA.

---

[6]Senate Report at 20; House Education and Labor Report at 50.

[7]See 42 U.S.C. § 12101(a)(3).

A. Americans with Disabilities Act

1. Purposes

The ADA is a sweeping civil rights law designed "to provide a clear and comprehensive national mandate for the elimination of discrimination against individuals with disabilities."[8] It also is designed "to provide clear, strong, consistent, enforceable standards addressing discrimination against individuals with disabilities."[9]

In enacting the ADA, Congress made clear that "the Nation's proper goals regarding individuals with disabilities are to assure equality of opportunity, full participation, independent living, and economic self-sufficiency for such individuals."[10] Congress found that many of the more than 43 million Americans with disabilities "continually encounter various forms of discrimination" and that this invidious discrimination "persists in such critical areas as employment. . . ."[11] Unlike other discrete and insular minorities, however, individuals with disabilities "have often had no legal recourse to redress such discrimination."[12] As a result, this discrimination and denial of equal employment opportunity have "cost[] the United States billions of dollars in unnecessary expenses resulting from dependency and nonproductivity."[13]

Accordingly, Congress passed the ADA to enable individuals with disabilities to participate fully in all aspects of society, particularly employment. Underlying the ADA is the recognition that equal employment opportunity is the only way that this country can accomplish its "proper goal" of ensuring economic self-sufficiency for individuals with disabilities. It is this fundamental principle -- that individuals with disabilities who want to work and are qualified to work must have an equal

---

[8] 42 U.S.C. § 12101(b)(1).

[9] Id. § 12101(b)(2).

[10] Id. § 12101(a)(8).

[11] Id. § 12101(a)(5),(3).

[12] Id. § 12101(a)(4).

[13] Id. § 12101(a)(9).

opportunity to work -- that guides the Title I employment provisions of the ADA.[14]

The definition of the term "qualified individual with a disability" reflects this principle and the broad remedial purposes of the ADA. It focuses on what an individual with a disability can do, rather than on what s/he cannot do.[15] In addition, reflecting the Act's focus on individual rather than group characteristics,[16] the definition requires an individualized assessment of a person's abilities. Moreover, the definition looks at whether an individual with a disability is qualified for the specific position at issue, not at whether s/he is qualified for work in general.

2. Standards

Under the ADA, a "qualified individual with a disability" is

> an individual with a disability[17] who satisfies the requisite skill, experience, education and other job-related requirements of the employment position such individual holds or desires, and, who, with or without reasonable accommodation, can perform the essential functions of such position.[18]

---

[14]See id. § 12101(a)(9) (noting that discrimination "denies people with disabilities the opportunity to compete on an equal basis and to pursue those opportunities for which our free society is justifiably famous").

[15]See 135 Cong. Rec. S10,711 (daily ed. Sept. 7, 1989) (statement of Sen. Harkin).

[16]See 42 U.S.C. § 12101(a)(7) (denouncing "stereotypic assumptions not truly indicative of the individual ability of [people with disabilities] to participate in, and contribute to, society") (emphasis added).

[17]The ADA defines "disability" as:

> (1) a physical or mental impairment that substantially limits one or more of the major life activities of [an] individual; (2) a record of such an impairment; or (3) being regarded as having such an impairment.

Id. § 12102(2); 29 C.F.R. § 1630.2(g).

[18]29 C.F.R. § 1630.3(m); see also 42 U.S.C. § 12111(8).

The determination of whether an individual with a disability is "qualified" should be made in two steps.[19] The first step is to determine if the individual has the education, training, skills, experience, and other job-related credentials for the position. The second step is to determine whether the individual can perform the essential functions of the position held or desired, with or without accommodation.[20] The purpose of this second step is to ensure that individuals with disabilities who can perform a position's essential or fundamental functions are not denied employment opportunities simply because they are not able to perform the position's marginal or peripheral functions.[21]

The determination of whether a person is a "qualified individual with a disability" requires an individualized, case-by-case assessment of the specific abilities of the person, the specific requirements of the position that the person holds or desires, and the manner in which the person may be able or enabled to meet those requirements.[22] The issue is whether a particular individual with a disability is qualified for a particular position, not whether the individual or a group of individuals with a disability is qualified for a class of positions.[23]

Further, the definition of the term "qualified individual with a disability" expressly requires consideration of whether the individual can perform essential functions with reasonable accommodation. The ADA requires employers to provide reasonable

---

[19] 29 C.F.R. pt. 1630 app. § 1630.2(m) (Interpretive Guidance on Title I of the Americans with Disabilities Act).

[20] Id.

[21] See generally id. app. § 1630.2(n); Senate Report at 26; House Education and Labor Report at 55; H.R. Rep. No. 101-485, pt. 3, at 33 (1990)[hereinafter House Judiciary Report].

[22] See School Bd. of Nassau County v. Arline, 480 U.S. 273, 287 (1987) (noting that an individualized inquiry into whether a person is "otherwise qualified" for purposes of section 504 of the Rehabilitation Act is essential to the goal of protecting individuals with disabilities "from deprivations based on prejudice, stereotypes, or unfounded fear").

[23] See 29 C.F.R. pt. 1630 app. (noting in "Background" section that "the determination of whether an individual is qualified for a particular position must necessarily be made on a case-by-case basis" and that a "case-by-case approach is essential if qualified individuals of varying disabilities are to receive equal opportunities to compete for an infinitely diverse range of jobs").

accommodation to the known physical or mental limitations of otherwise qualified individuals with disabilities unless doing so would result in undue hardship.[24] This reasonable accommodation requirement is critical to achieving the goals of the ADA.[25]

In general, a reasonable accommodation is any change in the work environment or in the way things are customarily done that enables an individual with a disability to enjoy equal employment opportunities.[26] Some of the most common accommodations an employer may be required to provide are job restructuring, part-time or modified work schedules, modifications of equipment or devices, and other similar accommodations.[27]

The assessment of whether an individual with a disability is qualified should be based on the capabilities of the individual with a disability at the time of the employment decision. It should not be based on speculation that the individual may become incapacitated in the future.[28]

B. Other Statutory Schemes and Contractual Rights

1. Social Security Act

The Social Security Act establishes a social insurance program designed to provide guaranteed income to individuals with disabilities when they are found to be generally incapable of gainful employment. Its purpose is to provide a basic level of financial support for people who, because of disability, cannot support themselves. In adding disability as a basis for benefits

---

[24]42 U.S.C. § 12112(b)(5)(A); 29 C.F.R. § 1630.9.

[25]See Senate Report at 10 ("the provision of all types of reasonable accommodations is essential to accomplishing the critical goal of this legislation -- to allow individuals with disabilities to be part of the economic mainstream of our society"); House Education and Labor Report at 34 (same); House Judiciary Report at 39 (the "reasonable accommodation requirement is central to the non-discrimination mandate of the ADA").

[26]29 C.F.R. pt. 1630 app. § 1630.2(o).

[27]29 C.F.R. § 1630.2(o).

[28]29 C.F.R. pt. 1630 app. § 1630.2(m); see also Senate Report at 26; House Education and Labor Report at 55.

administered by the Social Security Administration (SSA) in 1956, Congress recognized society's obligation to provide assistance to people whose disabilities prevent them from achieving economic self-sufficiency.[29]

The SSA definition of the term "disability," therefore, reflects the obligation to provide benefits to people who generally are unable to work. As a result, the definition focuses on what a person cannot do and on whether s/he cannot find work in the national economy in general.

To receive SSA disability benefits, an individual must prove that s/he is disabled under the Social Security Disability Insurance (SSDI) or the Supplemental Security Income (SSI) program.[30] The essential requirement for both programs is that the claimant be unable to engage in "any substantial gainful activity by reason of any medically determinable physical or mental impairment which can be expected to result in death or which has lasted or can be expected to last for a continuous period of not less than 12 months."[31] Under the statute, a person is entitled to disability benefits if his/her impairment is "of such severity that [s/he] is not only unable to do [his/her] previous work but cannot, considering [his/her] age, education, and work experience, engage in any other kind of substantial gainful work which exists in the national economy."[32]

---

[29]See generally 42 U.S.C. §§ 1381, 1382c(a)(3)(B).

[30]The Social Security Act provides for several disability benefit programs administered by the SSA, including the SSDI and SSI programs. The SSDI program provides benefits to disabled workers, dependents, and widows/widowers if the worker is insured under the provisions of the program. The SSI program provides benefits to disabled individuals whose incomes and assets fall below a specified level. See 42 U.S.C. §§ 413-15, 1381-83. Although the eligibility criteria under the two programs are different (i.e., SSDI is insurance based and SSI is based on need), the determinations of disability are virtually identical. For purposes of this guidance, the phrase "social security disability benefits" or "SSA benefits" refers to both the SSDI and SSI programs.

[31]42 U.S.C. § 423(d)(1)(A); 20 C.F.R. § 404.1505 (1996).

[32]Id. § 423(d)(1)(A), (d)(2)(A); 20 C.F.R. § 404.1505. "Work which exists in the national economy" means work which exists in significant numbers, either in the region where such individual lives or in several regions of the country. Id. § 423(d)(2)(A).
(continued...)

The SSA itself, however, recognizes that an individual may be found to be unable to engage in substantial gainful activity and yet still may be able to work in a particular position. Although the SSA program is designed to provide a guaranteed income to individuals who are found to meet SSA disability eligibility criteria, Congress has recognized the importance of encouraging individuals with disabilities to work whenever possible.[33] Accordingly, the Social Security Act contains numerous work incentive provisions. For example, the SSA has a trial work period that allows beneficiaries to work for nine months while their benefit entitlement and payment levels remain unchanged.[34] Similarly, the SSA has an extended period of eligibility that provides individuals who return to work with benefits in any month in which earnings fall below a statutory level.[35] Thus, even the SSA does not view a person who meets its definition of "disability" as someone who is totally unable to work.

To determine if an individual meets the SSA definition of "disability," the SSA uses a sequential evaluation process.[36] This five-step process requires the SSA to ask the following questions:

(1) Is the claimant currently engaging in "substantial gainful activity"?[37] (If the answer is yes, the claim is

---

[32](...continued)
Isolated jobs which exist only in limited numbers in relatively few locations outside the region where the claimant lives are not considered "work which exists in the national economy." Id.

[33]Id. § 422(c); see also Mohamed v. Marriott, 1996 WL 631687, at *7 (S.D.N.Y. Oct. 30, 1996)(noting that "the Social Security Act shares the goal of encouraging individuals to engage in remunerative employment, because it permits an individual to receive benefits while working").

[34]Under SSA regulations, a beneficiary may evaluate whether his/her condition has improved by doing some work without fear of losing disability benefits. 20 C.F.R. § 404.1592(a).

[35]Id.

[36]Id. §§ 404.1520, 404.920.

[37]Substantial gainful activity refers to work activity that is both substantial and gainful. Id. §§ 404.1572, 416.972. Work activity is substantial if it requires the performance of significant physical and mental activities. Id. §§ 404.1572(a), 416.972(a). Work activity is gainful if it is engaged in for (continued...)

denied; if the answer is no, the claim continues to the next step.)

(2) Does the claimant have a "severe" impairment? (If the answer is no, the claim is denied; if the claimant has an impairment that significantly limits his/her ability to work -- that is, it is "severe" -- the claim continues to step 3.)

(3) Does the claimant have an impairment that is equivalent to any impairment the SSA has listed as so severe that it automatically precludes substantial gainful activity? (If the claimant has an impairment that is medically the equivalent of a listed impairment, the claimant is presumed disabled by the SSA and benefits are granted; if the claimant does not have a listed impairment, the claim proceeds to step 4.)

(4) Does the impairment prevent the claimant from performing his/her "past relevant work"?[38] (If the claimant can perform his/her past relevant work, the claim is denied; if the claimant cannot perform such work, the claim continues to step 5.)

(5) Does the impairment prevent the claimant from performing any other type of work? (If the SSA determines that the claimant is able to perform other work which exists in the national economy,[39] the claim is denied; if the SSA

---

[37](...continued)
profit. Id. §§ 404.1572(b), 416.972(b). In determining whether work actually performed is substantial gainful activity, the SSA considers factors such as the nature of the work performed, how well the claimant performs that work, whether the work is performed under special conditions, and the amount of time spent working. Id. §§ 404.1573, 416.973.

[38]"Past relevant work" is substantial gainful activity which was performed within the 15 years prior to the claim for benefits. See generally id. §§ 404.1560-61.

[39]To determine whether a claimant can perform any work which exists in the national economy, the SSA considers what the individual still can do, given his/her functional limitations and vocational capabilities (age, education, and past work experience). Id. § 404.1520(f)(1). Individuals who have marginal education, long work experience (i.e., 35 years or more) in only arduous unskilled physical labor, and can no longer do this kind of work may have a (continued...)

determines that the claimant is unable to perform any work, considering his/her age, education, and past work experience, benefits are granted.)

The SSA acknowledges the differences between its standards and those of other statutory schemes. In that regard, SSA regulations note that a decision by any other entity about whether an individual is disabled is based on the other entity's rules and may not be the same as the SSA's determination, which is based on social security law.[40]

The SSA definition of "disability" is inherently different from the ADA definition of "qualified individual with a disability." First, whereas the ADA always requires an individualized inquiry into the ability of a particular person to meet the requirements of a particular position, the SSA permits general presumptions about an individual's ability to work. In that regard, the SSA considers some conditions to be presumptively disabling. If a claimant has an impairment that is medically the equivalent of a listed impairment, then the SSA presumes that the disorder is so severe as to prevent the claimant from doing any substantial gainful activity, without considering his/her age, education, and past work experience.[41] Thus, an individual can

---

[39](...continued) disability for SSA purposes and be eligible for benefits even though they are capable of performing sedentary work. Id. §§ 404.1520(f)(2), .1562.

[40]Id. § 404.1504.

[41]See id. § 404.1520(d); 20 C.F.R. pt. 404, subpt. p, app. 1 (listings of impairments). The listings consist of medical criteria for specified disorders for each of the major body systems (e.g., musculoskeletal system, respiratory system, immune system). 20 C.F.R. § 404.1525(d). Most of the listed impairments are permanent or expected to result in death. For all others, the evidence must show that the impairment has lasted or is expected to last for a continuous period of at least 12 months. Id. The listings contain more than 150 categories of medical conditions that, according to the SSA, are severe enough ordinarily to prevent an individual from engaging in substantial gainful activity. For example, listed impairments under the musculoskeletal system include the loss of both hands or feet. 20 C.F.R. pt. 404, subpt. p, app. 1 § 1.09(A), (B). Under the ADA, however, a person with no hands or feet may well be a "qualified individual with a disability" who is able to work with or without reasonable accommodation.

(continued...)

have a "disability" under the SSA definition and yet in fact still be able to work.

Second, in determining whether a person meets the SSA definition of disability, the SSA looks at the customary requirements of jobs as usually performed in the national economy without focusing on the essential functions of a particular position.[42] All tasks required to perform the job are considered with no distinction made between fundamental and peripheral functions.[43] Thus, a person who is able to perform the essential functions of a particular position, but not the marginal functions, may be found to be unable to work and eligible for disability benefits. Accordingly, the SSA's determination that a person is unable to engage in any substantial gainful activity in the national economy does not mean that there is no job the person can perform. The person still may be able to perform the essential functions of a particular position.

Third, unlike the ADA definition, the SSA definition does not consider whether the individual can work with reasonable accommodation. An SSA interpretative guidance addressing the effect of the ADA on SSA's disability determination process states,

---

[41](...continued)

In addition, the Social Security Act provides a special disability eligibility for individuals who are blind. Any claimant age 55 or older who has a visual impairment that meets the statutory definition of blindness (i.e., central visual acuity of 20/200 or less in the better eye with use of correcting lens) is presumed to be incapable of engaging in substantial gainful activity and is deemed eligible for disability benefits. See 20 C.F.R. §§ 404.1581, .1583. Again, under the ADA, many persons who are blind are qualified to perform the essential functions of numerous positions with or without reasonable accommodation.

[42]See Eback v. Chater, 94 F.3d 410, 412 (8th Cir. 1996)(the inquiry into whether an individual with a disability can engage in substantial gainful activity "is based on the functional demands and duties of jobs as ordinarily required by employers throughout the national economy" and not on the requirements of a particular position); Overton v. Reilly, 977 F.2d 1190, 1196 (7th Cir. 1992)(a determination of disability for SSA purposes cannot be construed as a judgment that an individual cannot do a particular job).

[43]See generally 70A Am. Jur. 2d Social Security § 984 (all tasks required in the job must be considered).

> The fact that an individual may be able to return to a past relevant job, provided that the employer makes accommodations, is not relevant to the issue(s) to be resolved. . . . [H]ypothetical inquiries about whether an employer would or could make accommodations that would allow return to a prior job would not be appropriate.[44]

Thus, the SSA may find that a person is unable to do any work which exists in the national economy even though s/he can work with a reasonable accommodation.[45] In those instances, the person is both a person with a "disability" under SSA and a "qualified individual with a disability" under the ADA. Accordingly, a person claiming to be disabled or found to be disabled under SSA programs still may be entitled to protection under the ADA.

2. Workers' Compensation

The workers' compensation definitions of "disability" reflect the purposes of workers' compensation laws. Those laws provide a system for securing prompt and fair settlement of employees' claims against employers for occupational injury and illness.[46] In that regard, the laws generally require employers to compensate employees who are injured in the course of employment for the resulting loss of earning capacity and for medical care.[47] Thus, workers' compensation provides benefits to individuals whose earning capacity has been reduced because of a work-related injury.

---

[44]See "Americans with Disabilities Act of 1990 -- INFORMATION," Memorandum from the Associate Commissioner, Social Security Administration 1 (June 2, 1993).

[45]See Eback v. Chater, 94 F.3d at 412 (since the ADA and Social Security Act have different purposes, the SSA's determination whether there are available jobs that the claimant can do is based on broad vocational patterns and not on an assumption that an employer would be willing to make accommodations under the ADA); Mohamed v. Marriott, 1996 WL 631687 at *6 (S.D.N.Y. Oct. 30, 1996)(an individual may be "disabled" for purposes of receiving SSA benefits because few jobs which s/he might be able to perform are currently structured to accommodate his/her disability, but still be within the ADA's protected class because a particular position in which s/he has an interest could be modified to accommodate his/her disability).

[46]See generally 1 Arthur Larson, The Law of Workmen's Compensation, § 1-1.10 (1994).

[47]Id.

Because of the emphasis on lost earning capacity, the workers' compensation definitions of disability generally focus on what a person can no longer do rather than on what s/he still is capable of doing with or without reasonable accommodation.

To receive workers' compensation benefits, an employee generally must prove that s/he has a compensable "disability" as defined by the applicable workers' compensation statute.[48] The term "disability" in this context most commonly means loss or reduction of earning power that results from a work-related injury.[49]

Some statutes, however, do not define "disability" in terms of lost earning capacity. Instead, under these statutes, an injured worker has a "disability" if his/her physical efficiency has been substantially reduced, or if s/he is unable to perform the same work with the same ease as before the injury or is unable to do heavy work that s/he could do before the injury.[50] Under these statutes, the worker has a "disability" even if s/he is employed at the same work and at the same wages as before the injury.

Although workers' compensation laws vary from state to state, the typical statute ordinarily provides the following four classifications of disability, determined by duration (i.e., permanent or temporary) and severity or extent (i.e., partial or total): temporary partial, temporary total, permanent partial, and permanent total.[51] Generally, a disability is partial rather than total where the claimant is still capable of gainful employment, even though the disability is found to prevent the claimant from returning to his/her former employment. Conversely, a worker generally is considered "totally disabled" when the injury is found to render the worker temporarily or permanently unable to do any kind of work for which there is a reasonably stable employment market.[52]

---

[48]See id.

[49]82 Am. Jur. 2d Workers' Compensation § 380.

[50]Id.; see, e.g., W. Va. Code § 23-4-6(n).

[51]For the purposes of workers' compensation statutes, a disability is permanent if it appears to be of lasting or indefinite duration, as distinguished from a temporary condition from which a person usually recovers after normal healing. 82 Am. Jur. 2d Workers' Compensation § 381.

[52]Id.

Unlike the ADA, which always requires an individualized inquiry into the ability of a particular person to meet the requirements of a particular position, some workers' compensation statutes presume that some conditions are so severe as to prevent the claimant from doing any kind of work. In such instances, a claimant does not have to make any representations about ability to work and need not show a loss of earning capacity to prove permanent total disability. For example, under some workers' compensation statutes, a person who has lost vision in both eyes or has lost both arms or legs may have a "permanent total disability" and be deemed to be unable to work.[53] Such a person, however, clearly can perform the essential functions of many positions with or without reasonable accommodation.

Moreover, unlike the ADA definition of "qualified individual with a disability," the workers' compensation definitions of "disability" do not distinguish between marginal and essential functions and do not consider whether an individual can work with reasonable accommodation. In many workers' compensation cases, a person has a "total disability" when s/he is unable to do certain tasks, even if those tasks are marginal functions or if s/he could perform them with reasonable accommodation. Thus, a person may be "totally disabled" for workers' compensation purposes and yet still be able to perform a position's essential functions with or without reasonable accommodation.

Similarly, a person can receive workers' compensation benefits for a temporary total disability from which she is expected to recover if, during the time of incapacitation, s/he is unable to perform his/her duties in the occupation in which s/he was employed at the time of injury.[54] The person is found to have a "temporary total disability" even if the duties s/he cannot perform are marginal functions or s/he could perform duties with reasonable accommodation.

Further, some statutes permit a finding of "total disability" where a person can work but the work that s/he can do is of such limited availability that a reasonably stable and continuous market for such labor does not exist.[55] Thus, a determination under a workers' compensation statute that a person cannot do any kind of

---

[53]See generally 82 Am. Jur. 2d Workers' Compensation §§ 379-80.

[54]Temporary total disability benefits are designed to provide compensation to an injured or ill employee for the economic losses incurred during recuperation. 99 C.J.S. Workers' Compensation § 304.

[55]Id.

work for which a reasonably stable employment market exists, and therefore is totally disabled, does not necessarily mean that there is no job that the person can perform. Accordingly, an individual receiving workers' compensation benefits still may be entitled to protection under the ADA.

3. Disability Insurance Plans

Many employers offer disability insurance plans to their employees as benefits of employment.[56] Receipt of benefits pursuant to such plans is a contractual, rather than a statutory, right. The purpose of disability insurance plans is to provide partial wage replacement when an employee becomes unable to work as a result of illness, injury, or disease.[57] As a result, the plans' definitions of "disability" focus on individuals' inabilities rather than abilities.

To receive disability benefits, an individual must meet the eligibility requirements outlined by the terms of the contract (i.e., insurance policy). Disability insurance plans usually require that an individual have been employed for a set period and that s/he be "disabled." Disability benefits often are paid on a "residual" basis, meaning that they are payable in proportion to the earnings lost as a result of the disability. Benefits may be limited to "total disability," meaning generally that the insured is unable to perform any of the duties of his/her own occupation or any other type of remunerative work, or may be payable for "partial disability," where the insured is unable to perform one or more functions of his/her regular job.

The definition of "disability" depends on what the contract states and varies from contract to contract. Generally, "disability" is defined as the incapacity to perform one or more duties of the insured's regular occupation.

When assessing an individual's ability to perform job duties, disability insurance plans frequently do not distinguish between essential and marginal functions. For example, under one typical contract, an employee may be considered "totally disabled" if s/he

---

[56]Short-term disability (STD) plans pay benefits for disability up to a specified period, generally not exceeding two years; long-term disability (LTD) plans pay extended benefits, generally until retirement age, but may require a higher showing of disability. Employment Benefits Law 947 (ABA Section of Labor & Employment Law) (Steven J. Sacher et al. eds. 1991).

[57]See id.

is "unable to perform the duties of the job [s/he] held when [s/he] became disabled or any comparable job within [the company]."[58] Under this definition, an individual who could perform the essential, but not all the marginal, functions of a position would be considered "totally disabled." Some plans, however, may acknowledge the relative importance of different duties. Thus, one plan defined "total disability" as the inability of an individual "to perform the material and substantial duties of his or her own job during the Benefit Waiting Period plus the next 24 months . . . due to Injury or Sickness which requires regular care of a Physician."[59] Whether a contract's definition of "disability" distinguishes between essential and marginal functions is a key consideration when comparing a plan's definition of "disability" to the ADA definition of "qualified individual with a disability."

Another important consideration is whether the contract's definition of "disability" takes into account whether an individual can work with reasonable accommodation. Frequently, the definition makes no allowance for an individual's ability to work with reasonable accommodation.[60] In some cases, the definition expressly eliminates consideration of reasonable accommodations, such as modified or part-time work schedules.[61] For example, one disability plan defined a "totally disabled" individual as an employee "who is unable to perform the material duties of his/her job for the entire regularly scheduled work week as the result of illness or injury and requires the ongoing care of a physician. . . ."[62] Under such a plan, an individual with a disability who is able to work only part time may be both "totally disabled" under the plan and a "qualified individual with a disability" under the ADA. Accordingly, an individual receiving disability insurance benefits still may be entitled to protection under the ADA.

---

[58] See Miller v. U.S. Bancorp, 926 F. Supp. 994, 998, 5 AD Cas. (BNA) 968, 971 (D. Or. 1996).

[59] See Reiff v. Interim Personnel, Inc., 906 F. Supp. 1280, 1289, 5 AD Cas. (BNA) 740, 745 (D. Minn. 1995).

[60] See, e.g., Miller v. U.S. Bancorp, 926 F. Supp. at 998, 5 AD Cas. at 971.

[61] A part-time or modified work schedule is a form of reasonable accommodation under the ADA. 42 U.S.C. § 12111(9)(B); 29 C.F.R. § 1630.2(o).

[62] See D'Aprile v. Fleet Services Corp., 92 F.3d 1, 4-5 (1st Cir. 1996) (emphasis added).

C. Analysis

Several important elements distinguish the definition of the term "qualified individual with a disability" under the ADA from the definitions of "disability" under other statutory schemes and contracts. Because of these inherent differences, an individual may be able to meet the eligibility requirements for receipt of disability benefits and still be a "qualified individual with a disability" for ADA purposes. That is, an individual may be "unable to work" for the purposes of a disability benefits program and yet still be able to perform the essential functions of a particular position with or without reasonable accommodation.[63]

An individual's representations in connection with an application for disability benefits, therefore, do not preclude a determination that the individual is a "qualified individual with a disability." Although the representations that an individual has made in support of his/her application for benefits may be relevant to such a determination, they are never an absolute bar to a finding that the individual is a "qualified individual with a disability."

1. The ADA Definition of "Qualified Individual with a Disability" Always Requires an Individualized Assessment of the Particular Individual and the

---

[63]See, e.g., Robinson v. Neodata Services, Inc., 94 F.3d 499, 502 n. 2, 5 AD Cas. (BNA) 1441, 1442 n.2 (8th Cir. 1996)(SSA determinations of disability "are not synonymous with a determination of whether a plaintiff is a 'qualified person' for purposes of the ADA"); Overton v. Reilly, 977 F.2d 1190, 1196, 2 AD Cas. 254, 260 (7th Cir. 1992)(SSA's finding that a person is disabled "is consistent with a claim that the disabled person is 'qualified' to do his job under the Rehabilitation Act"); Pegues v. Emerson Electric Co., 913 F. Supp. 976, 980, 5 AD Cas. 376, 379 (N.D. Miss. 1996)(a finding of disability by a state workers' compensation commission or the SSA does not necessarily foreclose an ADA claim); Palmer v. Circuit Court of Cook County, Soc. Serv. Dep't, 905 F. Supp. 499, 508 n.10 (N.D. Ill. 1995)(citing Overton v. Reilly and Smith v. Dovenmuehle) (determinations made by the SSA concerning disability "are not dispositive findings for claims arising under the ADA"); Smith v. Dovenmuehle Mortgage, Inc., 859 F. Supp. 1138, 1141-42, 4 AD Cas. 132, 135 (N.D. Ill. 1994)(citing Overton v. Reilly)(a finding of disability by the SSA "cannot be construed as a judgment that the plaintiff is unable to do his job").

Particular Position; Other Definitions Permit Generalized Inquiries and Presumptions.

Unlike the definitions under other statutory and contractual schemes, which permit generalized inquiries, the definition of "qualified individual with a disability" under the ADA always requires an individualized inquiry into the ability of a particular person to meet the requirements of a particular position.[64] The ADA inquiry into whether a person is a "qualified individual with a disability" looks at whether an individual can perform the essential functions of a particular position, not whether s/he is able to work in general. Further, unlike the SSA and other statutory and contractual schemes, the ADA never presumes that some impairments are so severe as to prevent an individual from working. To the contrary, the ADA presumes that individuals with disabilities can work.[65]

The Seventh Circuit recognized this obvious and significant distinction in Overton v. Reilly, 977 F.2d 1190, 2 AD Cas. (BNA) 254 (7th Cir. 1992), when it ruled that a person could have a disability for SSA purposes and still be a "qualified individual with a disability" for Rehabilitation Act purposes. The SSA had granted benefits to the Overton plaintiff, who had an emotional disability, on a trial basis shortly after he began working for the defendant. The court made clear that the plaintiff's Rehabilitation Act claim of discriminatory discharge was not precluded by the SSA's decision to award him disability benefits.

In refusing to find that the plaintiff's receipt of benefits precluded his claim, the Seventh Circuit relied heavily on the fact that the SSA definition of disability permits generalized presumptions. First, the court noted that "the SSA may award disability benefits on a finding that the claimant meets the criteria for a listed disability, without inquiring into his ability to find work within the economy." 977 F.2d at 1196, 2 AD Cas. at 260. This, the court found, was the basis for the plaintiff's receipt of benefits. In addition, the Seventh Circuit emphasized that, "even if the SSA had looked into [the plaintiff's] ability to find work in the national economy, its inquiry would necessarily have been generalized." Id. Such a general inquiry, the court noted, may determine that a claimant is unlikely to find

---

[64]See School Bd. of Nassau County v. Arline, 480 U.S. 273, 287 n.17 (1987).

[65]See 42 U.S.C. § 12101(a)(9) (noting that discrimination "denies people with disabilities the opportunity to compete on an equal basis and to pursue those opportunities for which our free society is justifiably famous").

a job, but that does not mean that there is no work the claimant can do. Thus, a determination of disability for SSA purposes "can hardly be construed as a judgment that [the plaintiff] could not do [the particular job at issue]." Id.

Rather than be swayed by generalized presumptions, the Seventh Circuit looked specifically at the plaintiff's particular situation. In so doing, the circuit court found that the plaintiff's actual, adequate performance of work for the defendant refuted the district court's assertion that the plaintiff had not offered evidence that he could perform substantial gainful activity. The Seventh Circuit therefore concluded that the plaintiff had presented a genuine issue of material fact whether he was a "qualified individual with a disability." Id. By refusing to bar the plaintiff's claim of disability discrimination, the Seventh Circuit recognized that the individualized inquiry mandated by the definition of "qualified individual with a disability" differs significantly from the generalized inquiry permitted under the SSA definition of "disability." Id.; see also Smith v. Dovenmuehle Mortgage, Inc., 859 F. Supp. 1138, 1141, 4 AD Cas. (BNA) 132, 135 (N.D. Ill. 1994) (holding that the SSA's decision to award disability benefits, based on its determination that the plaintiff could not find work in the economy, did not mean that he was not a "qualified individual with a disability" under the ADA, particularly since he found another position after being terminated by the defendant).

Similarly, a district court in the Second Circuit recognized the fundamental differences between the ADA's individualized approach and the SSA assessment. In refusing to grant the defendant's motion for summary judgment, the court in Mohamed v. Marriott, 1996 WL 631687 (S.D.N.Y. Oct. 30, 1996), emphasized that the SSA awarded the plaintiff benefits based on a "listed disability" (profound deafness) and did not inquire into his capability to work. Id. at *6. In that regard, the court noted that the plaintiff did not make any specific representations about his ability to perform the essential functions of the job from which he was terminated and, in fact, represented to the SSA that he continued to seek work. Id. Like the Seventh Circuit, the Mohamed court refused to be swayed by generalized presumptions and looked at the plaintiff's particular situation. Noting that the plaintiff consistently had received positive evaluations and had no record of disciplinary actions prior to his termination, the court found that there was "ample evidence" that the plaintiff was capable of performing the essential functions of the job from which he was discharged. Id. at *5. The court further concluded that barring the plaintiff's ADA claim based on the SSA's determination that he was eligible for benefits "would undermine the legislative policy of providing [persons with disabilities] with both protection against destitution and a genuine opportunity to participate fully in the job market." Id. at *7.

The Third Circuit, in McNemar v. The Disney Store, Inc., 91 F.3d 610, 5 AD Cas.(BNA) 1227 (3d Cir. 1996), however, ignored this fundamental difference between the ADA and SSA and failed to conduct the individualized inquiry mandated by the ADA definition of "qualified individual with a disability." The McNemar plaintiff, who had AIDS, applied for and received SSA and state disability benefits after he was fired from his position of assistant manager. He certified on his benefits application that he had become unable to work approximately five weeks before his discharge. In affirming the district court's grant of summary judgment for the defendant, the Third Circuit found that it was irrelevant that AIDS is a presumptive disability that automatically renders a person "unable to work" for purposes of SSA benefits, since the plaintiff claimed that he was physically unable to work. The court also rejected the argument that the ADA's standards and purposes are fundamentally different from the SSA's. In reaching these conclusions, the court overlooked the fact that "unable to work" for SSA purposes does not mean unable to perform the essential functions of a particular position with or without reasonable accommodation.

The court's failure to acknowledge these inherent differences between the ADA definition of "qualified individual with a disability" and the SSA definition of "disability" is especially troubling here, where it is undisputed that the plaintiff was performing the essential functions of his assistant manager's position at the time of his discharge. It therefore also should have been undisputed that the plaintiff met the ADA definition of "qualified individual with a disability" at the time of the alleged discrimination. See Daffron v. McDonnell Douglas Corp., 874 S.W. 2d 482, 486, 3 AD Cas. (BNA) 183, 187 (Mo. Ct. App. 1994)(based on the plaintiff's assertions that he was capable of performing his job duties and was, in fact, performing those duties until the day he was laid off, the court found that there was evidence that could establish that the plaintiff was capable of performing his duties, even though he filed an application for disability benefits).

Moreover, the McNemar defendant's asserted reason for the discharge was unrelated to the issues raised by the benefits application. At the time of the discharge, the defendant maintained that the plaintiff was fired for theft; the defendant did not claim that the plaintiff's disability prevented the plaintiff from performing the essential functions of his position with or without reasonable accommodation. McNemar, 91 F.3d at 614, 5 AD Cas. at 1229. In fact, the defendant consistently disavowed any reliance on the plaintiff's disability. Since the plaintiff applied for disability benefits after his termination, the defendant obviously was unaware of the application when it decided to terminate him. Accordingly, under these circumstances, the defendant should not have been permitted to use benefits information acquired after the adverse action to challenge whether the plaintiff was a "qualified individual with a disability." Cf. McKennon v. Nashville Banner Pub. Co., 115 S. Ct. 879, 885 (1995)(employer liability is determined solely by information available to employer "'at the time of the decision'"). For all these reasons, the Commission believes that McNemar was wrongly decided.[66]

Other courts have recognized that the ADA's focus on a particular individual's ability to perform the essential functions of a particular position is different from disability benefits programs' definitions of "disability." For example, in Pressman v. Brigham Medical Group Foundation, Inc., 919 F. Supp. 516, 5 AD Cas. (BNA) 609 (D. Mass. 1996), the court concluded that a physician who consistently claimed that he was "totally disabled" under his private disability insurance plan still could be a "qualified individual with a disability" with respect to the particular internist position for which he had applied. In that case, the plaintiff, who had a heart disability, maintained that he was capable of performing the essential functions of the internist position even though he had a "total disability" for purposes of the insurance plan. 919 F. Supp. at 523, 5 AD Cas. at 613. According to the plaintiff, the plan permitted him to receive total disability benefits as long as there were restrictions on his ability to practice his sub-specialty of cardiology. 919 F. Supp. at 522, 5 AD Cas. at 613. Since there were genuine issues of material fact whether the definition of "total disability" under the plaintiff's disability plan meant that he generally was unable to practice medicine, or whether it meant that he specifically was unable "to conduct a solo practice with emergency room duties," the court denied the defendant's motion for summary judgment. Id.

As Pressman, Mohamed, Smith, and Overton illustrate, the definitions under the SSA and other statutory and contractual schemes do not focus on whether a particular person can meet the requirements of a particular position. As a result, an individual can both meet the requirements for disability benefits and be a "qualified individual with a disability" for purposes of the ADA.

---

[66]Further, although the Third Circuit used the doctrine of judicial estoppel to reject the plaintiff's claim, it stressed that judicial estoppel is a discretionary doctrine. The court also emphasized that "each case must be decided upon its own particular facts and circumstances." McNemar, 91 F.3d at 617, 5 AD Cas. at 1232.

2. The ADA Definition of "Qualified Individual with a Disability" Requires Consideration of Reasonable Accommodation; Other Definitions Do Not Consider Whether an Individual Can Work with Reasonable Accommodation.

Assessing whether a person can work with reasonable accommodation is a key part of determining if the person meets the ADA definition of the term "qualified individual with a disability." Unlike the ADA definition, however, the definitions of disability under the SSA, workers' compensation laws, and disability insurance plans do not consider whether a person can work with reasonable accommodation.[67] Thus, a person may be deemed unable to work and be awarded disability benefits even though s/he can perform the essential functions of a particular position with reasonable accommodation.

Courts have recognized this important difference between the ADA definition of "qualified individual with a disability" and other definitions of "disability" or "totally disabled." For example, in D'Aprile v. Fleet Services Corp., 92 F.3d 1 (1st Cir. 1996), the First Circuit reversed a district court's grant of summary judgment where the plaintiff had sought disability benefits after the defendant refused her request to work on a part-time basis.[68] In D'Aprile, the plaintiff had unofficially worked part time (through the use of accrued vacation leave) for two months after the defendant denied her request to be converted to a part-time status. After the plaintiff exhausted her vacation time, she submitted a doctor's note "stating that she was 'unable to work at this time and should be placed on disability.'" Id. at 3. The plaintiff then received disability benefits under an insurance plan that defined a "totally disabled" individual as an employee "who is unable to perform the material duties of his/her job for the entire regularly scheduled work week as the result of injury or illness . . . ." Id. at 4-5.

---

[67]See, e.g., Eback v. Chater, 94 F.3d 410, 412 (8th Cir. 1996)(since the ADA and Social Security Act have different purposes, the SSA's determination whether there are available jobs that the claimant can do is based on broad vocational patterns and not on an assumption that an employer would be willing to make accommodations under the ADA).

[68]The D'Aprile decision interpreted the Rhode Island Fair Employment Practices Act, R.I. Gen. Laws § 28-5-1, et seq., which includes a reasonable accommodation requirement. D'Aprile, 92 F.3d at 2. (The defendant removed the case to federal district court based on diversity of jurisdiction.)

The First Circuit found that the plaintiff's contention that she was unable to work because her employer had refused her request for a modified schedule was "entirely consistent with her claim to have been 'totally disabled' within the meaning of the policy." Id. at 5. Noting that the plaintiff asserted that she could work on a part-time basis and that she in fact had worked part time, the court found that there existed a genuine issue of material fact whether the plaintiff could have worked with reasonable accommodation. In so doing, the court expressly ruled that the plaintiff's application for benefits "sheds no light on how [the plaintiff] would have fared had the accommodation been made." Id. In addition, the D'Aprile court explicitly stated that August v. Offices Unlimited, Inc., 981 F.2d 576, 2 AD Cas. (BNA) 401 (1st Cir. 1992), does not stand for the broad proposition that a plaintiff who claims that s/he is "totally disabled" within the context of applying for disability benefits is barred from bringing an ADA claim but, rather, "stands for the narrow proposition that the plaintiff's ability to work with reasonable accommodation" is key in determining whether a person meets the ADA definition of "qualified individual with a disability." Id. at 3.[69] The Commission believes that D'Aprile is correct in recognizing that an individual can meet a disability benefits program definition of "totally disabled" and still be able to perform the essential functions of a particular position with reasonable accommodation.

Similarly, in Anzalone v. Allstate Ins. Co., 5 AD Cas. (BNA) 223 (E.D. La. 1995), the court correctly recognized the differences between the ADA definition of "qualified individual with a disability" and a disability insurance plan's definition of "total

---

[69]In August, a furniture salesperson applied for disability insurance benefits after his employer refused his request to return to work on a part-time basis following an extended leave of absence for severe depression. The First Circuit affirmed the district court's grant of summary judgment on the grounds that the plaintiff could not show that he was a "qualified individual with a disability" because he had conceded that he was totally disabled. 981 F.2d at 581, 2 AD Cas. at 406. The dissent, however, pointed out the weakness in the majority's reasoning, noting that it was not clear how "total disability" was defined in the plaintiff's insurance policy. Thus, the dissent correctly concluded that the plaintiff's inability to return to work after the employer denied his request for a part-time schedule "only demonstrates that, absent accommodations by [the employer, the plaintiff] could not work. It does not prove that he would have been incapable of working had his request[] been granted." August, 981 F.2d at 586, 2 AD Cas. at 408.

disability" in refusing to grant defendant's motion for summary judgment. The plaintiff in Anzalone applied for and received LTD benefits after the defendant had refused his request to work at home. Noting that the plaintiff had consistently stated that he could perform the essential functions of his claims adjuster position with certain modifications, the court found that his receipt of disability benefits did not bar his ADA claim. According to the court, the plaintiff's receipt of benefits was relevant -- but not dispositive -- evidence of whether the plaintiff could perform essential functions with or without reasonable accommodation. Anzalone, 5 AD Cas. at 225.[70] See also

[70] Compare Anzalone with Kennedy v. Applause Inc., 90 F.3d 1477, 5 AD Cas. (BNA) 1249 (9th Cir. 1996), where the court looked not only at the plaintiff's statements in support of her application for disability benefits but at all of the relevant evidence in assessing whether the plaintiff was a "qualified individual with a disability." In Kennedy, a sales representative who had returned to work after a three-month leave of absence was discharged after she submitted a doctor's note stating that she could not work and needed another leave of absence. She then applied for state disability benefits, stating that her symptoms forced her to stop working. She also stated in a subsequent SSA "Daily Activities Questionnaire" that she barely could get out of bed. In her deposition on her ADA claim, however, the plaintiff testified that she could have continued to perform her job duties on a part-time or adjusted work schedule.

In affirming the district court's grant of summary judgment, the Ninth Circuit based its holding on the fact that there was no evidence, other than the plaintiff's "self-serving" deposition testimony that she was capable of continuing to work, to show that she could have performed the essential functions of her job. 90 F.3d at 1481, 5 AD Cas. at 1251. Although the court cited to the plaintiff's application for disability benefits, it did so only to point out that the plaintiff's statements "corroborate[d]" her treating physician's assessment that she was totally unable to perform her job. Id. But see Garcia-Paz v. Swift Textiles, 873 F. Supp. 547, 3 AD Cas. (BNA) 1844 (D. Kan. 1995)(in granting the defendant's motion for summary judgment, the court failed to consider whether the plaintiff could have done her job with reasonable accommodation).

Thus, Kennedy supports the Commission's view that the plaintiff's statements might be relevant to -- but not dispositive of -- whether s/he was qualified for the job at issue. Such statements alone cannot defeat the plaintiff's case, especially where countervailing evidence otherwise supports a finding that the plaintiff is a "qualified individual with a disability."

Ward v. Westvaco Corp., 859 F. Supp. 608, 615, 3 AD Cas. (BNA) 739, 745 (D. Mass. 1994) (in denying the employer's motion for summary judgment, the court found that there was a genuine issue of material fact whether the plaintiff would have been able to perform his job duties with reasonable accommodation); Patel v. Everett Industries, No. 88-BEM-0451 (Mass. Comm'n Against Discrimination Sept. 18, 1996)(injured employee who received workers' compensation benefits was not precluded from proving that she was a "qualified individual with a disability" under state law where she did not claim that she was disabled from all work but only that she could not perform the heavy tasks to which she was assigned).[71]

As Patel, Ward, Anzalone, and D'Aprile demonstrate, an individual can meet the eligibility requirements for disability benefits and still be able to perform the essential functions of particular positions with reasonable accommodation.

II. Because of the Fundamental Differences Between the ADA and Other Statutory and Contractual Disability Benefits Programs, Representations Made in Connection with an Application for Benefits May Be Relevant to -- but Are Never Determinative of -- Whether a Person Is a "Qualified Individual with a Disability."

A. Representations Made in Connection with an Application for Disability Benefits Are Not Determinative of Whether a Person Is a "Qualified Individual with a Disability."

Because of the inherent differences in the definitions of the term "qualified individual with a disability" under the ADA and the terms used in the SSA, state workers' compensation laws, disability insurance plans, and other disability benefits programs, and because the ADA considers whether a person can work with reasonable accommodation, an individual can meet both the eligibility requirements for receipt of disability benefits and the definition of a "qualified individual with a disability" for ADA purposes. Thus, a person's representations that s/he is "disabled" or "totally disabled" for purposes of disability benefits are not necessarily inconsistent with his/her representations that s/he is

[71]The Patel decision interpreted the Massachusetts discrimination statute, Mass. Gen. Laws ch. 151B, §1(16), which defines a "qualified individual with a disability" in language nearly identical to the ADA.

a "qualified individual with a disability."[72] Accordingly, they should never be an automatic bar to an ADA claim. Thus, for example, the doctrine of judicial estoppel should not be used to bar the ADA claim of an individual who has applied for disability benefits. Similarly, granting summary judgment to bar such claims also is inappropriate.[73]

1. Judicial Estoppel

The common law doctrine of judicial estoppel prevents a party who has successfully maintained a position in one judicial proceeding from asserting a contrary position in another proceeding. It is a "principle of fairness" designed to preserve the integrity of the judicial process. 18 C. WRIGHT, A. MILLER & E. COOPER, FEDERAL PRACTICE AND PROCEDURE § 4477 at, 779-88 (1981). "Judicial estoppel applies where a party tries to contradict in a second lawsuit his sworn statement in previous litigation." Grant v. Lone Star Co., 21 F.3d 649, 651 n.2 (5th Cir. 1994). The doctrine protects the integrity of the judicial process by "minimiz[ing] the danger of a party contradicting a court's determination based on the party's prior position," thereby resulting in "inconsistent court determinations." United States ex. rel. Am. Bank v. C.I.T. Constr. Inc., 944 F.2d 253, 258 (5th Cir. 1991).[74]

---

[72]Further, representations made in the context of applying for disability benefits should not be construed as an evidentiary admission that a person is not a "qualified individual with a disability" for purposes of coverage under the ADA (i.e., an individual who represents that s/he meets the eligibility requirements for disability benefits is not necessarily admitting that s/he cannot perform the essential functions of a particular position with or without accommodation).

[73]EEOC investigators should note that, while the doctrine of judicial estoppel and summary judgment procedures are relevant to litigating civil lawsuits, they are not relevant to Commission charge processing.

[74]The doctrine of judicial estoppel has not been universally embraced. At least two circuit courts have refused to recognize the doctrine. See United Mine Workers of America 1974 Pension v. Pittston Co., 984 F.2d 469, 477 (D.C. Cir.), cert. denied, 113 S. Ct. 3039 (1993); Chrysler Credit Corp. v. Country Chrysler, Inc., 928 F.2d 1509, 1520 n.10 (10th Cir. 1991). Other courts have warned that the doctrine should be "applied with caution to avoid impugning on the truth-seeking function of the court." Teledyne Indus., Inc. v. NLRB, 911 F.2d 1214, 1218 (6th Cir. 1990).

As explained above, an individual who asserts that s/he is both "totally disabled" and a "qualified individual with a disability" has not necessarily made inconsistent representations. Accordingly, the doctrine of judicial estoppel should not be used to prevent the individual from raising an ADA claim. Thus, courts that have recognized the inherent differences between the definitions of "qualified individual with a disability" and "totally disabled" or "disabled" have refused to apply this doctrine to bar claims of disability discrimination. See, e.g., Smith v. Dovenmuehle Mortgage Co., 859 F. Supp. 1138, 4 AD Cas. (BNA) 132 (N.D. Ill. 1994) (judicial estoppel inappropriate where genuine issue of material fact whether position that plaintiff with AIDS took before SSA is inconsistent with assertion that plaintiff is a "qualified individual with a disability"); Mohamed v. Marriott, 1996 WL 631687, at *6 (S.D.N.Y. Oct. 30, 1996)("it would be inappropriate to invoke the fact-sensitive and limited doctrine of judicial estoppel to erect a per se bar to ADA protection for individuals who have also applied for and/or received [SSA] benefits").

Generally, the doctrine of judicial estoppel applies only when an individual took his/her earlier position in a prior judicial proceeding. See, e.g., Shell Oil Co. v. Trailer & Truck Repair Co., 828 F.2d 205, 209-210 (3d Cir. 1987); Smith v. Travelers Ins. Co., 438 F.2d 373, 377 (6th Cir.), cert. denied, 404 U.S. 832 (1971). However, in many cases, the individual has not made his/her representations before a judicial forum. Accordingly, courts that have recognized the significant differences in judicial proceedings and administrative determinations have declined to apply judicial estoppel to bar claims of disability discrimination. See, e.g., Mohamed v. Marriott, 1996 WL 631687, at *7 (S.D.N.Y. Oct. 30, 1996)("[t]he streamlined procedures giving rise to the SSA's determination of disability should, at a minimum, give pause to a court considering barring the courtroom door to a plaintiff alleging employment discrimination"); see also EEOC v. MTS Corp. d/b/a Supercuts, No. 94-1473 LH/WWD (D.N.M. July 26, 1996)(the court noted that, even if the Tenth Circuit recognized judicial estoppel, it would not apply the doctrine to the facts of this case where the plaintiff completed his SSA application over the telephone).[75]

---

[75]Other courts, however, have ignored this difference and have inappropriately applied the doctrine to dismiss ADA claims. See, e.g., McNemar v. The Disney Stores, 91 F.3d 610, 5 AD Cas.(BNA) 1227 (3d Cir. 1996)(discussed supra § I.C.1); August v. Offices, Unlimited, Inc., 981 F.2d 576 (1st Cir. 1992)(discussed supra § I.C.2).

Public policy considerations also preclude the application of judicial estoppel in the types of cases to which this guidance applies. See Marvello v. Chemical Bank, 923 F. Supp. 487, 491-92, 5 AD Cas. (BNA) 1400, 1403 (S.D.N.Y. 1996)(applying judicial estoppel to bar the ADA claim of individuals who have applied for disability benefits could undermine the policy goals of the ADA without advancing the separate goals of the Social Security Act); Mohamed v. Marriott, 1996 WL 531687, at *7 (S.D.N.Y. Oct. 30, 1996)(the ADA's overriding purpose of encouraging individuals with disabilities to seek employment would be thwarted by the application of judicial estoppel to the facts of this case). Because "[j]udicial estoppel is a technical rule designed to meet the needs of broad public policy," Johnson Serv. Co. v. Transamerica Ins. Co., 485 F.2d 164, 175 (5th Cir. 1973), courts have been reluctant to apply the doctrine where doing so would undermine the public policy goals of a federal statute. See City of Alma v. United States, 744 F. Supp. 1546, 1556 (S.D. Ga. 1990). In fact, some courts have declined to apply the doctrine where barring the plaintiff's suit "implicates not only the relevant interests of the litigating parties, but also the public's interest in promoting the underlying statute." Matter of Morristown & Erie R.R. Co., 677 F.2d 360, 368 n.10 (3d Cir. 1982); cf. McKennon v. Nashville Banner Co., 115 S. Ct. 879, 885 (1995)(the Supreme Court noted that "the broader objectives of [the anti-discrimination statutes] are furthered when even a single employee establishes that an employer has discriminated against him or her").

2. Summary Judgment

The inherent differences between the definitions of the term "qualified individual with a disability" under the ADA and the terms used in other statutory and contractual schemes also make summary judgment inappropriate. Granting summary judgment is only proper when there is no genuine issue of material fact and the moving party is entitled to judgment as a matter of law. Fed. R. Civ. P. 56(c). In deciding whether a factual dispute is "genuine," the court must determine whether the evidence is such that a reasonable jury could return a verdict for the nonmoving party." Anderson v. Liberty Lobby, Inc., 477 U.S. 242, 248 (1986). A court must review the facts in the light most favorable to the nonmoving party and accord the nonmoving party the benefit of all reasonable inferences to be drawn from the evidence. See, e.g., United States v. O'Block, 788 F.2d 1433 (10th Cir. 1986)(stating that "[t]he court must consider factual inferences tending to show triable issues in the light most favorable to the existence of those issues"). The court's function is not to weigh the evidence but, rather, merely to determine whether there is sufficient evidence favoring the nonmoving party for a finder of fact to return a verdict in that party's favor. Anderson, 477 U.S. at 249.

Essentially, the court performs the threshold inquiry of determining whether a trial is necessary. Id. at 250.

As discussed in detail in this guidance, because the ADA's purposes and standards are fundamentally different from those of disability benefits programs, an individual's representations made in connection with an application for disability benefits do not mean that the individual cannot perform the essential functions of the position held or desired with or without reasonable accommodation. Accordingly, the application for disability benefits does not mean that there does not exist a genuine issue of material fact concerning whether a person is a "qualified individual with a disability." Thus, for example, in Overton, the court held that summary judgment was inappropriate. Overton, 977 F.2d at 1194. See also Smith v. Dovenmuehle Mortgage Co., 859 F. Supp. 1138, 4 AD Cas. (BNA) 132 (N.D. Ill. 1994) (genuine issue of material fact whether position that plaintiff with AIDS took before SSA is inconsistent with assertion that plaintiff is a "qualified individual with a disability"); Oswald v. Larouche Chemicals, Inc., 894 F. Supp. 988 (E.D. La. 1995)(genuine issue of material fact whether the doctor, whose conclusion that the plaintiff could not perform any jobs formed the basis of the grant of disability retirement benefits to the plaintiff, properly assessed the plaintiff's ability to perform the essential functions of the modified position); Kupperschmidt v. Runyon, 827 F. Supp. 570, 3 AD Cas. (BNA) 52 (E.D. Wis. 1993)(genuine issue of material fact whether plaintiff, who received SSA and federal employee retirement system disability benefits, was a "qualified individual with a disability" for purposes of the Rehabilitation Act); EEOC v. MTS Corp. d/b/a Supercuts, No. 94-1473 LH/WWD (D.N.M. July 26, 1996)(genuine issue of material fact regarding when plaintiff with AIDS, who applied for SSA disability benefits, became incapable of performing the essential functions of his position).

B. A Determination of What, if Any, Weight to Give to Representations Made in Support of Applications for Disability Benefits Depends on the Context and Timing of the Representations.

In assessing the extent to which representations made in connection with an application for disability benefits are relevant to a determination of whether a person is a "qualified individual with a disability" under the ADA, it is necessary to look at the context and timing of the representations. Often, applications for disability benefits do not use precise terminology and do not clearly define terms such as "total disability."[76] In addition, these forms or applications may require an individual merely to check off boxes and not allow him/her to fully describe his/her disabling condition or may be taken over the telephone. Even during depositions or hearings, questions concerning an individual's disability and/or ability to work are not always posed with precision. Accordingly, courts declining to dismiss the ADA claims of individuals who have applied for disability benefits have looked behind the "labels" or terms used in various forums and have considered other factors (e.g., the content of the representations, who made them, the purpose for which they were made, when the representations were made, the period of time to which they refer, and any changes in the individual's physical or mental condition between the time of his/her application for benefits and the time of the adverse employment action at issue) in determining that a genuine issue of material fact exists as to whether an individual is a "qualified individual with a disability" for purposes of the ADA.

1. Context

Representations on a benefits application should not be viewed in a vacuum but, rather, considered in the context of all other relevant documents (e.g., disability reports, doctors' reports, depositions). In addition, the circumstances under which the individual applied for benefits should be considered (e.g., did the individual apply for benefits because s/he could not work because the employer denied reasonable accommodation?; did the individual maintain, at the time of application for benefits, that s/he could perform the essential functions of the position in question with accommodation?; did the individual apply for benefits based on a doctor's assessment that s/he was totally disabled?; did the individual apply for benefits at the suggestion of the employer?;[77] did the individual apply for benefits because s/he believed s/he was unable to work because of discrimination?).

---

[76]See, e.g., August v. Offices Unlimited, Inc., 981 F.2d 576, 586, 2 AD Cas. (BNA) 401, 408 (1st Cir. 1992)(Pettine, J., dissenting) (noting that the "disability insurance forms [at issue] are not legally or medically precise").

[77]See, e.g., Muellner v. Mars, Inc., 714 F. Supp. 351 (N.D. Ill. 1989)(in conjunction with the plaintiff's application for benefits under the employer's disability insurance plan, the employer and the insurer instructed the plaintiff to apply for SSA benefits because any such benefits would be set off against the disability insurance payments).

For example, in Anzalone v. Allstate Ins. Co., 5 AD Cas. (BNA) 223 (E.D. La. 1995), the plaintiff applied for disability benefits only after the defendant refused to allow him to return to work with certain restrictions. The court reviewed the context in which the plaintiff's statements were made and found that he did not unambiguously characterize himself as totally and completely disabled; rather, the plaintiff consistently took the position that he was capable of working under certain restrictions (i.e., with reasonable accommodation). Anzalone, 5 AD Cas. at 225. Similarly, in Ward v. Westvaco Corp., 859 F. Supp. 608, 614-15, 3 AD Cas. (BNA) 738, 744-45 (D. Mass. 1994), although the plaintiff applied for disability retirement benefits under the SSA and his company's disability insurance plan, stating on the applications that he was "totally and permanently disabled," he explained that he would have been able to perform his job had his employer made reasonable accommodations.[78] The court held that the plaintiff's testimony, in the context of his ADA claim, was not inherently inconsistent with his former statements made in the course of obtaining disability benefits.

In addition, in some cases, the plaintiff applies for disability benefits based on a doctor's assessment that s/he is disabled, although the plaintiff believes that s/he can still work with reasonable accommodation. Doctors, however, can be wrong in assessing a person's condition and/or ability to work. For example, in Oswald v. Larouche Chemicals, Inc., 894 F. Supp. 988 (E.D. La. 1995), the plaintiff, as well as his physical therapist, believed that he could perform the essential functions of a modified position, but the defendant's medical review officer determined that he could not. The court held that, because the employer's medical review officer's conclusion that the plaintiff could not perform any available jobs was the basis for the grant of disability benefits, there was a genuine issue of material fact whether the medical review officer properly assessed the plaintiff's abilities. Oswald, 894 F. Supp. at 996. Accordingly, it was possible that the plaintiff was a "qualified individual with a disability" capable of performing the essential functions of one or more positions with accommodation despite the medical review officer's determination that he was totally disabled.

In other cases, the plaintiff applies for disability benefits because the employer's alleged discriminatory conduct causes

---

[78]The plaintiff also attached a letter to his application for disability retirement, stating that his submission of his application and statements made on it were not intended as a waiver of his position that he would have been able to continue to perform his duties with reasonable accommodation. Ward, 859 F. Supp. at 614, 3 AD Cas. at 745.

him/her to be unable to work or to believe that s/he cannot work because of discrimination. For example, in EEOC v. MTS Corp. d/b/a Supercuts, No. 94-1473 LH/WWD (D.N.M. July 26, 1996), after other employees became concerned about working with the plaintiff who had AIDS, the defendant excluded the plaintiff from a meeting at which his condition was discussed, denied his request to return to his "home base" salon, refused to pay his travel expenses to an annual company convention, and, after terminating him, informed him that he was no longer permitted on the premises. The defendant moved for summary judgment on the plaintiff's ADA claim, arguing that he was not a "qualified individual with a disability" because he applied for and received SSA benefits. In declining to grant the defendant's motion, the court noted that the plaintiff had completed "the application over the phone, outside of judicial machinery, without the benefit of counsel, and arguably under a great deal of emotional distress." MTS Corp. d/b/a Supercuts, No. 94-1473 LH/WWD at 2. Moreover, crediting the EEOC's version of the facts, the court noted that the defendants had forced the plaintiff "into the unenviable position of being unemployed . . . and emotionally devastated by their discriminatory conduct." Id.

Similarly, in EEOC v. AIC Security, 820 F. Supp. 1060, 2 AD Cas. (BNA) 561 (N.D. Ill. 1993), the plaintiff, who had cancer, maintained that he was qualified to perform the essential functions of the position from which he was terminated. The plaintiff's doctor also agreed that the plaintiff still could perform his job and explained that the information he supplied to the SSA, in support of the plaintiff's application for disability benefits, "was premised on the fact that [the plaintiff] had been fired from his job and that he should be able to get some compensation because no one [was] going to hire him." AIC Security, 820 F. Supp. at 1066-67, 2 AD Cas. at 567; see also Mohamed v. Marriott, 1996 WL 631687, at *2 (S.D.N.Y. Oct. 30, 1996) (in response to a question on the SSA application requesting an explanation of how his condition prevented him from working, the plaintiff, who was deaf, stated that he had tried to get another job but had been "frustrated" any place he looked because there were not "enough jobs open").

2. Timing

It is possible that an individual can be "totally disabled" at one point and can later be able to return to work or become totally disabled after a period of being able to work. It is therefore necessary to review what the person said about his/her condition at the time of his/her application for disability benefits and what s/he maintained his/her condition was at the time of the alleged discrimination (i.e., was the condition at time to which the application refers different from condition at time of alleged discrimination?).[79]

For example, in Lundstedt v. City of Miami, 5 AD Cas. (BNA) 568 (S.D. Fla. 1995), the plaintiff applied for and was granted disability retirement benefits in 1980, based on his work-related accident in 1978 and subsequent related physical problems. The plaintiff also began receiving workers' compensation benefits in 1982 and received a lump sum payment in 1988 based on his total permanent disability. In 1992, the plaintiff requested to be reinstated to his former firefighter position, but the defendant denied his request.[80] In refusing to grant the defendant's motion for summary judgment with respect to the plaintiff's ADA claim, the court held that it was "perfectly consistent for [p]laintiff to assert that he was disabled in the past, but after time he became rehabilitated and is now able to return to work." Lundstedt, 5 AD Cas. at 577-78.

Similarly, in Smith v. Dovenmuehle Mortgage Co., 859 F. Supp. 1138, 4 AD Cas. (BNA) 132 (N.D. Ill. 1994), the plaintiff, who had AIDS, claimed that, about one month after his discharge, he improved enough to perform the functions of his position (although he was receiving SSA benefits). The court found that, because the plaintiff's condition had improved, his position with respect to his ADA claim was not inconsistent with his position before the SSA. Smith, 859 F. Supp. at 1142, 4 AD Cas. at 136.

In addition, in Lawrence v. United States I.C.C., 629 F. Supp. 819 (E.D. Pa. 1985), the plaintiff completed a disability retirement application, stating that he was "totally disabled" and "unable to carry out the vigorous activity required by [his] position"; later, he filed an ADA claim alleging that he was currently able to work. Since 22 months had lapsed between the plaintiff's application for SSA benefits and the filing of his ADA

---

[79]Moreover, some individuals with disabilities who have applied for disability benefits later seek employment when they learn of jobs that they can do with reasonable accommodation. Where such individuals believe that they were not hired for such positions because of discrimination, they should not be precluded from bringing an ADA claim merely because they previously applied for disability benefits stating that they were "totally disabled" or "unable to work."

[80]The defendant's Fire Fighters' and Police Officers' Retirement Trust Board of Trustees had the authority to recommend to the defendant that any retiree who is no longer incapacitated for service be returned to his former classification. Lundstedt, 5 AD Cas. at 571.

claim, the court reasoned that the plaintiff's claim that he was now able to work did not contradict his position at the time he applied for disability benefits. Lawrence, 629 F. Supp. at 822.[81]

III. Public Policy Supports the Conclusion that Representations Made in Connection with an Application for Disability Benefits Are Never an Absolute Bar to an ADA Claim.

A. Permitting Individuals to Go Forward with Their ADA Claims Is Critical to the ADA's Goal of Eradicating Discrimination Against Individuals with Disabilities.

The ADA's essential goal is "to provide a clear and comprehensive national mandate for the elimination of discrimination against individuals with disabilities."[82] Recognizing that individuals who have experienced discrimination on the basis of a disability "have often had no legal recourse to redress such discrimination,"[83] Congress enacted the ADA to provide legal remedies for the pervasive discrimination that "persists in such critical areas as employment . . . ."[84] Private lawsuits, therefore, play a critical role in the enforcement of the ADA.[85]

---

[81]Compare Lawrence with McNeill v. Atchison, Topeka, and Santa Fe Railway Co., 4 AD Cas. (BNA) 300 (S.D. Tex. 1995). In McNeill, eight days after receiving a $305,000 award under the Federal Employer's Liability Act for a back injury that allegedly prevented him from working, the plaintiff filed an ADA suit against the defendant for failure to reinstate him. "[A]stonished by the audacity of the plaintiff in asserting that he was 'rehabilitated' from a 'permanent disability' within eight days," the court granted the defendant's motion for summary judgment. Id. at 303. The court stated, however, that if the plaintiff had filed his ADA claim "after a protracted period of convalescence, or vigorous and successful rehabilitation," or if his condition had changed because of new medical treatments or scientific technology, it would have considered the merits of his claim. Id.

[82]42 U.S.C. § 12101(b)(1).

[83]Id. § 12101(a)(4).

[84]Id. § 12101(a)(3).

[85]Id. § 12117(a).

An individual who brings an employment discrimination case "acts not only to vindicate his or her personal interests in being made whole, but also acts as a 'private attorney general' to enforce the paramount public interest in eradicating invidious discrimination." Mardell v. Harleysville Life Ins. Co., 31 F.3d 1221, 1235 (3d Cir. 1994), vacated, 115 S. Ct. 1397 (1995), modified on other grounds, 65 F.3d 1072 (3d Cir. 1995). Accordingly, when the EEOC acts on allegations of discrimination, at the behest of and for the benefit of specific individuals, it also acts to vindicate the public interest in preventing employment discrimination. Barring individuals who apply for disability benefits from pursuing ADA claims would impede EEOC's enforcement of the ADA and deny individuals the right to have the court hear the merits of their claims. Moreover, it also would permit the continuation of the invidious discrimination that the ADA is designed to eradicate.

The Supreme Court has made clear that general equitable doctrines, such as judicial estoppel, cannot be applied as absolute bars to suits brought under the federal anti-discrimination statutes, given the important "'public purposes' furthered when even a single [person] establishes that an employer has discriminated against him or her." McKennon v. Nashville Banner Publishing Co., __U.S.__, 115 S. Ct. 879, 885 (1995). This is so because "[t]he private litigator who seeks redress for his injuries vindicates both the deterrence and compensation objectives of [the Act in question]." Id.

In addition, as the McKennon court explained:

> The disclosure through litigation of incidents or practices which violate national policies respecting nondiscrimination in the work force is itself important, for the occurrence of violations may disclose patterns of noncompliance resulting from a misappreciation of the Act's operation or entrenched resistance to its commands, either of which can be of industry-wide significance.

Id. at 885.

Thus, if an individual is prevented from bringing an ADA claim because s/he has applied for disability benefits, discrimination is not deterred and the plaintiff's interests are not vindicated. Instead, "patterns of noncompliance" and pervasive discrimination against people with disabilities continue. See also Smith v. Dovenmuehle Mortgage Co., 859 F. Supp. 1138, 1142, 4 AD Cas. (BNA) 132, 135 (N.D. Ill. 1994) (barring ADA claim of individual who received disability benefits would conflict with ADA's stated purpose "to combat the 'continuing existence of unfair and unnecessary discrimination and prejudice [which denies] people with disabilities the opportunity to compete on an equal basis'") (quoting 42 U.S.C. § 12101(a)(9)).

B. Individuals Should Not Have to Choose Between Applying for Disability Benefits and Vindicating Their Rights Under the ADA.

All persons have a right to be free from discrimination. In addition, each individual who meets the eligibility requirements for disability benefits has a right to receive such benefits. Barring an individual who applies for disability benefits from bringing a claim under the ADA would "place [him/her] in the untenable position of choosing between his right to seek disability benefits and his right to seek redress for an alleged violation of the ADA." Smith v. Dovenmuehle Mortgage Co., 859 F. Supp. 1138, 1142, 4 AD Cas. (BNA) 132, 135 (N.D. Ill. 1994).

Moreover, an individual who applies for SSA, workers' compensation, and/or disability insurance benefits is not knowingly relinquishing his/her right to bring an ADA claim but, rather, is exercising independent rights. Cf. Alexander v. Gardner-Denver, 415 U.S. 36, 94 S. Ct. 1011 (1974)(the court held that an employee who had pursued a discrimination claim through union arbitration could not be prevented by the arbitrator's decision from bringing an independent cause of action under Title VII). The ADA was passed with the assumption that individuals with disabilities who want to work and are qualified to work must have an equal opportunity to work. The SSA operates from the same presumption by providing work incentive programs for disability beneficiaries that permit individuals to retain benefits while transitioning into employment. Accordingly, both the ADA and the SSA seek to promote the employment of individuals with disabilities whenever possible. See Mohamed v. Marriott, 1996 WL 631687, at *6 (S.D.N.Y. Oct. 30, 1996)(noting that since the Social Security Act itself permits individuals to receive benefits and work at the same time, "the classes of individuals entitled to protection under the [Social Security Act and the ADA] are not mutually exclusive"). Thus, because neither the ADA nor the SSA assumes that individuals are either totally able or unable to work, a person should not have to choose between applying for disability benefits or challenging an alleged adverse employment action under the ADA.

IV. Instructions to Investigators

As explained above, representations made in connection with an application for disability benefits are not dispositive of whether a person is a "qualified individual with a disability" for purposes of the ADA. Therefore, those representations, and the application for disability benefits, do not bar the filing of an ADA charge, nor should they prevent an investigator from recommending a cause determination if the evidence supports such a determination.

When determining whether a charging party (CP) is a "qualified individual with a disability," the investigator must conduct an individualized, case-by-case inquiry into whether CP can perform the essential functions of the position held or desired with or without reasonable accommodation. This inquiry must focus on the particular individual and the particular position at issue.

Although applying for disability benefits does not preclude CP from bringing an ADA claim, the representations made while pursuing such benefits may be relevant -- but not dispositive -- evidence of whether CP is a "qualified individual with a disability." As explained in this guidance, it is essential to look not only at CP's application for disability benefits but at all of the relevant evidence (e.g., the facts surrounding the alleged discrimination, disability reports, doctors' reports, depositions) when determining whether CP meets this definition.

When assessing the effect that representations made in the context of applying for disability benefits may have on this determination, it is crucial to focus on the exact definition used by the benefits program, the precise content of the individual's representations, and the specific circumstances surrounding the application for disability benefits. It also is important to look at whether CP was "a qualified individual with a disability" at the time of the alleged discrimination and whether s/he maintained that s/he was still able to perform the essential functions of his/her position, with or without reasonable accommodation, at the time of the application for benefits. When deciding what, if any, weight to give to CP's representations made while pursuing disability benefits, investigators should consider the following factors:[86]

- the definitions of terms such as "disability," "permanent disability," "total disability," "inability to work," etc. under the relevant statute or contract pursuant to which CP applied for disability benefits (e.g., do they look at specific positions or general kinds of work? do these terms take into account reasonable accommodation?);

- the specific content of the representations, who made them, and the purpose for which they were made;

---

[86]No one factor is necessarily determinative of whether CP is a "qualified individual with a disability." Rather, the investigator should consider all relevant evidence.

- whether the representations are in CP's own words;
- whether the representations about CP's inability to work are qualified in any way (e.g., "I am able to work with certain restrictions");
- when the representations were made, the period of time to which they refer, and whether CP's physical or mental condition has changed since the representations were made;
- whether CP was working during the period of time referred to as a period of total disability;
- whether the employer suggested that CP apply for benefits;
- whether CP asked for and was denied a reasonable accommodation;
- when the employer learned of the representations; and
- other relevant factors, such as advances in technology or changes in the employer's operations that may have occurred since representations were made that may make it possible for CP to perform the essential functions of the position, with or without reasonable accommodation.

NOTES

8

EEOC ENFORCEMENT GUIDANCE: WORKERS' COMPENSATION AND THE ADA

Presented by Paul Steven Miller

EEOC Enforcement Guidance: Workers' Compensation and the ADA

TABLE OF CONTENTS

EEOC Enforcement Guidance: Workers' Compensation and the ADA

INTRODUCTION

This enforcement guidance concerns the interaction between Title I of the Americans with Disabilities Act of 1990 (ADA)[1] and state workers' compensation laws.[2] The purpose of Title I of the ADA is to prohibit employers from discriminating against qualified individuals because of disability in all aspects of employment.[3] On the other hand, the purpose of a workers' compensation law is to provide a system for securing prompt and fair settlement of employees' claims against employers for occupational injury and illness.[4] While the purposes of the two laws are not in conflict, the simultaneous application of the laws has raised questions for EEOC investigators, for employers, and for individuals with disabilities in a number of areas.[5] In this document, the Commission provides guidance concerning the following issues:

- whether a person with an occupational injury has a disability as defined by the ADA;

- disability-related questions and medical examinations relating to occupational injury and workers' compensation claims;

- hiring of persons with a history of occupational injury, return to work of persons with occupational injury, and application of the direct threat standard;

---

[1]Codified as amended at 42 U.S.C. §§ 12101-12117, 12201-12213 (1994).

[2]The analysis in this guidance also applies to federal sector complaints of non-affirmative action employment discrimination arising from the interaction between the Federal Employee's Compensation Act, 5 U.S.C. §§ 8101-8193 (1994), and section 501 of the Rehabilitation Act of 1973, 29 U.S.C. § 791(g) (1994), and to complaints of non-affirmative action employment discrimination arising from the interaction between sections 503 and 504 of the Rehabilitation Act of 1973, 29 U.S.C. §§ 793(d), 794(d) (1994), and state workers' compensation laws.

[3]42 U.S.C. § 12112(a); 29 C.F.R. § 1630.4.

[4]Workers' compensation laws generally require employers to compensate employees who are injured or become ill in the course of employment for the resulting loss of earning capacity and for medical care. See 1 Arthur Larson, The Law of Workmen's Compensation, § 1-1.10 (1994).

[5]Basic information on this topic may be found in EEOC: Technical Assistance Manual on the Employment Provisions (Title I) of the Americans with Disabilities Act at 9.0, 8 FEP Manual (BNA) 405:7055 (1992) [hereinafter Technical Assistance Manual].

• reasonable accommodation for persons with disability-related occupational injuries;

• light duty issues; and

• exclusive remedy provisions in workers' compensation laws.

DISABILITY

The Commission has provided general guidance on the definition of the term "disability" under the ADA in EEOC: Definition of the Term "Disability," 8 FEP Manual (BNA) 405:7251 (1995). This section applies that guidance in the context of occupational injury and workers' compensation. The definition of "disability" under the ADA is no different in the workers' compensation context than in any other context.

1. Does **everyone with an occupational injury** have a disability within the meaning of the ADA?

No. Even if an employee with an occupational injury has a "disability" as defined by a workers' compensation statute, s/he may not have a "disability" for ADA purposes.

The ADA defines "disability" as: (1) a physical or mental impairment that substantially limits a major life activity, (2) a record of such an impairment, or (3) being regarded as having such an impairment. Impairments resulting from occupational injury may not be severe enough to substantially limit a major life activity, or they may be only temporary, non-chronic, and have little or no long term impact.

2. Does every person who has filed a workers' compensation claim have a disability under the **"record of"** portion of the ADA definition?

No. A person has a disability under the "record of" portion of the ADA definition only if s/he has a history of, or has been misclassified as having, a mental or physical impairment that substantially limits one or more major life activities.

3. When does a person with an occupational injury have a disability under the **"regarded as"** portion of the ADA definition?

A person with an occupational injury has a disability under the "regarded as" portion of the ADA definition if s/he: (1) has an impairment that does not substantially limit a major life activity but is treated by an employer as if it were substantially limiting, (2) has an impairment that substantially limits a major life activity because of the attitude of others towards the impairment, or (3) has no impairment but is treated as having a substantially limiting impairment.[6]

Example A: An employee has an occupational injury that has resulted in a temporary back impairment that does not substantially limit a major life activity. However, the employer views her as not being able to lift more than a few pounds and refuses to return her to her position. The employer regards her as having an impairment that substantially limits the major life activity of lifting. The employee has a disability as defined by the ADA.

Example B: An employer refuses to allow an employee whose occupational injury results in a facial disfigurement to return to his position because the employer fears negative reactions by co-workers or customers. The employer regards him as having an impairment that substantially limits the major life activities of interacting with others and working. The employee has a disability as defined by the ADA.

Example C: An employee is fully recovered from an occupational injury that resulted in a temporary back impairment. The employer fires the employee because it believes that, if he returns to his heavy labor job, he will severely injure his back and be totally incapacitated. The employer regards the employee as having an impairment that disqualifies him from a class of jobs (heavy labor) and therefore as substantially limited in the major life activity of working. The employee has a disability as defined by the ADA.

[6] For a detailed discussion of whether an individual is covered under the "regarded as" portion of the ADA definition of disability, see EEOC: Definition of the Term "Disability" at 902.8(a), 8 FEP Manual (BNA) 405:7278-405:7286 (1995).

QUESTIONS AND EXAMINATIONS

The Commission has provided general guidance on disability-related questions and medical examinations in ADA Enforcement Guidance: Preemployment Disability-Related Questions and Medical Examinations, 8 FEP Manual (BNA) 405:7191 (1995). The guidance provided here pertains particularly to disability-related questions and medical examinations related to workers' compensation and occupational injuries.

4. When may an employer **ask questions** about an applicant's **prior workers' compensation claims or occupational injuries**?

> An employer may ask questions about an applicant's prior workers' compensation claims or occupational injuries after it has made a conditional offer of employment, but before employment has begun, as long as it asks the same questions of all entering employees in the same job category.

5. When may an employer **require a medical examination** of an applicant to obtain information about the existence or nature of prior occupational injuries?

> An employer may require a medical examination to obtain information about the existence or nature of an applicant's prior occupational injuries, after it has made a conditional offer of employment, but before employment has begun, as long as it requires all entering employees in the same job category to have a medical examination. Where an employer has already obtained basic medical information from all entering employees in a job category, it may require specific individuals to have follow-up medical examinations only if they are medically related to the previously obtained medical information.

6. Before making a conditional offer of employment, may an employer **obtain information** about an applicant's **prior workers' compensation claims or occupational injuries** from **third parties**, such as former employers, state workers' compensation offices, or a service that provides workers' compensation information?

No. At the pre-offer stage, as at any other time, an employer may not obtain from third parties any information that it could not lawfully obtain directly from the applicant.

7. May an employer ask disability-related **questions** or require a medical **examination** of an employee either **at the time s/he experiences an occupational injury** or **when s/he seeks to return to the job** following such an injury?

Yes, in both instances, provided that the disability-related questions or medical examinations are job-related and consistent with business necessity. This requirement is met where an employer reasonably believes that the occupational injury will impair the employee's ability to perform essential job functions or raises legitimate concerns about direct threat. However, the questions and examinations must not exceed the scope of the specific occupational injury and its effect on the employee's ability, with or without reasonable accommodation, to perform essential job functions or to work without posing a direct threat.[7]

8. May an employer ask disability-related **questions** or require a medical **examination** of an employee with an occupational injury in order to ascertain the extent of its **workers' compensation liability**?

Yes. The ADA does not prohibit an employer or its agent from asking disability-related questions or requiring medical examinations that are necessary to ascertain the extent of its workers' compensation liability.[8]

[7]If, as a result of an examination or inquiry, an employer refuses to return an employee to work because of a disability, the reason for doing so must be job-related and consistent with business necessity. See 29 C.F.R. § 1630.10 and Appendix (1995). Where safety considerations are implicated, the employer can only refuse to return the employee to work where his/her employment in the position would pose a "direct threat." Direct threat is discussed in questions 11, 12, 14, and 15, below.

[8]This is because the ADA does not invalidate the procedures of any federal, state, or local law "that provides greater or equal protection for the rights of individuals with disabilities" than is provided by the ADA. 42 U.S.C. § 12201(b) (1994). Those portions of state workers' compensation laws that protect the rights of individuals to be compensated for work-related injury provide such greater or equal protection. The same is true for the analogous portions of the Federal Employee's Compensation Act, 5 U.S.C. §§ 8101-8193 (1994).

However, the questions and examinations must be consistent with the state law's intended purpose of determining an employee's eligibility for workers' compensation benefits. An employer may not use an employee's occupational injury as an opportunity to ask far-ranging disability-related questions or to require unrelated medical examinations. Examinations and questions must be limited in scope to the specific occupational injury and its impact on the individual and may not be required more often than is necessary to determine an individual's initial or continued eligibility for workers' compensation benefits. Excessive questioning or imposition of medical examinations may constitute disability-based harassment which is prohibited by the ADA.

9. If an employee with a disability-related occupational injury **requests a reasonable accommodation**, may the employer **ask for documentation** of his/her disability?

Yes. If an employee with a disability-related occupational injury[9] requests reasonable accommodation and the need for accommodation is not obvious, the employer may require reasonable documentation of the employee's entitlement to reasonable accommodation. While the employer may require documentation showing that the employee has a covered disability and stating his/her functional limitations, it is not entitled to medical records that are unnecessary to the request for reasonable accommodation.

CONFIDENTIALITY OF MEDICAL INFORMATION

10. Do the ADA's **confidentiality requirements** apply to **medical information regarding** an applicant's or employee's **occupational injury or workers' compensation claim**?

Yes. Medical information regarding an applicant's or employee's occupational injury or workers' compensation claim must be collected and maintained on separate forms and kept in a separate medical file along

[9]An individual with a disability may have an occupational injury that has nothing to do with the disability. The term "disability-related occupational injury" is used herein when the ADA and workers' compensation statutes apply simultaneously, i.e., where there is a connection between an occupational injury and a disability as defined by the ADA.

with other information required to be kept confidential under the ADA. An employer must keep medical information confidential even if someone is no longer an applicant or an employee.

The ADA allows disclosure of this information only in the following circumstances:

- supervisors and managers may be told about necessary restrictions on the work or duties of the employee and about necessary accommodations;[10]

- first aid and safety personnel may be told, when appropriate, if the disability might require emergency treatment;[11]

- government officials investigating compliance with the ADA must be given relevant information on request;[12]

- employers may give information to state workers' compensation offices, state second injury funds, and workers' compensation insurance carriers in accordance with state workers' compensation laws;[13] and

- employers may use the information for insurance purposes.[14]

HIRING DECISIONS

11 May an employer **refuse to hire** a person with a disability simply because it assumes, correctly or incorrectly, that s/he **poses some increased risk of occupational injury** and increased workers' compensation costs?

---

[10]42 U.S.C. § 12112(d)(3)(B)(i) (1994); 29 C.F.R. § 1630.14(b)(1)(i), (c)(1)(i) (1995).

[11]42 U.S.C. § 12112(d)(3)(B)(ii); 29 C.F.R. § 1630.14(b)(1)(ii), (c)(1)(ii).

[12]42 U.S.C. § 12112(d)(3)(B)(iii); 29 C.F.R. § 1630.14(b)(1)(iii), (c)(1)(iii).

[13]See 42 U.S.C. § 12201(b); 29 C.F.R. pt. 1630 app. § 1630.14(b).

[14]See 42 U.S.C. § 12201(c); 29 C.F.R. pt. 1630 app. §§ 1630.14(b) and 1630.16(f). For example, an employer may submit medical information to the company's health insurance carrier if the information is needed to administer a health insurance plan in accordance with § 501(c) of the ADA.

No, unless the employer can show that employment of the person in the position poses a "direct threat." In enacting the ADA, Congress sought to address stereotypes regarding disability, including assumptions about workers' compensation costs.[15] Where an employer refuses to hire a person because it assumes, correctly or incorrectly, that, because of a disability, s/he poses merely **some** increased risk of occupational injury (and, therefore, increased workers' compensation costs), the employer discriminates against that person on the basis of disability. The employer can refuse to hire the person **only** if it can show that his/her employment in the position poses a "direct threat." This means that an employer may not "err on the side of safety" simply because of a potential health or safety risk. Rather, the employer must demonstrate that the risk rises to the level of a direct threat.

"Direct threat" means a significant risk of substantial harm to the health or safety of the individual or others that cannot be eliminated or reduced by reasonable accommodation.[16] The determination that a direct threat exists must be the result of a fact-based, individualized inquiry that takes into account the specific circumstances of the individual with a disability.

In determining whether employment of a person in a particular position poses a direct threat, the factors to be considered are:

- the duration of the risk;
- the nature and severity of the potential harm;
- the likelihood that the potential harm will occur; and
- the imminence of the potential harm.[17]

Some state health or safety laws may permit or require an employer to exclude a person with a disability from employment in cases where the

[15]H.R. Rep. No. 485 pt. 3, 101st Cong., 2d Sess. 31 (1990).

[16]29 C.F.R. § 1630.2(r) (1995).

[17]"Direct threat" is discussed more fully in the Commission's ADA regulations and interpretive guidance, 29 C.F.R. § 1630.2(r) and Appendix (1995), and in the Technical Assistance Manual at 4.5, 8 FEP Manual (BNA) 405:7022-405:7026 (1992).

ADA would not permit exclusion because employment of the person in the position does not pose a direct threat. Because the ADA supersedes such state laws, an employer may not defend its exclusion of a person with a disability on the basis of such a law.

12. May an employer **refuse to hire** a person with a disability simply because s/he sustained **a prior occupational injury**?

No. The mere fact that a person with a disability experienced an occupational injury in the past does not, by itself, establish that his/her current employment in the position in question poses a direct threat, i.e., a significant risk of substantial harm that cannot be lowered or eliminated by a reasonable accommodation. However, evidence about a person's prior occupational injury, in some circumstances, may be relevant to the direct threat analysis discussed in question 11, above.

An investigator should consider the following factors regarding a prior occupational injury in applying the direct threat analysis set forth in question 11, above:

• whether the prior injury is related to the person's disability (e.g., if employees without disabilities in the person's prior job had similar injuries, this may indicate that the injury is not related to the disability and, thus, is irrelevant to the direct threat inquiry);

• the circumstances surrounding the prior injury (e.g., the actions of others in the workplace or the lack of appropriate safety devices or procedures may have caused or contributed to the injury);

• the similarities and differences between the position in question and the position in which the prior injury occurred (e.g., the prior position may have involved hazards not present in the position under consideration);

• whether the current condition of the person with a disability is similar to his/her condition at the time of the prior injury (e.g., if the person's condition has improved, the prior injury may have little significance);

• the number and frequency of prior occupational injuries;

• the nature and severity of the prior injury (e.g., if the injury was minor, it may have little or no significance);

• the amount of time the person has worked in the same or a similar position since the prior injury without subsequent injury; and

• whether the risk of harm can be lowered or eliminated by a reasonable accommodation.

Example A: CP applies for a position operating a large saw with R, a lumber mill. After making a conditional job offer, R discovers that CP, who has insulin-dependent diabetes, was seriously injured while operating a similar saw for another lumber mill. The injury was caused by the failure of a safety device and was unrelated to CP's diabetes. R assumes, however, that the injury was related to the diabetes and refuses to hire CP for safety reasons. CP's prior occupational injury, which was unrelated to her disability, does not constitute evidence that she poses a direct threat in the saw operator position because of her disability.

Example B: CP, who has a shoulder disability, applies to R restaurant for the position of bus person which requires frequent carrying of basins full of dirty dishes weighing 40-45 pounds. After a conditional job offer, R discovers that CP has had five serious injuries to his left shoulder while carrying basins full of dirty dishes in other bussing jobs over the past four years. A medical examination and physical fitness test show that the condition of CP's shoulder has significantly deteriorated with each injury. They also show that, if CP carries heavy basins, there is a high probability that his left shoulder will be immediately and permanently injured to the point where his left arm will be useless. Assume that there is no reasonable accommodation that will enable CP to perform the essential functions of the bussing position. The objective medical and other evidence (the number, frequency, nature, and severity of the prior injuries; the similarity of the position at issue to the positions in which the injuries occurred; the progressive deterioration of CP's shoulder with each injury; and the evidence that a further injury will render CP's arm useless) supports a finding that CP's employment in the position of bus person poses a significant risk of substantial harm. The evidence further shows that the risk cannot be lowered or eliminated through a reasonable accommodation. Therefore, CP's employment in the position of bus person poses a direct threat.

Example C: CP applies for a position as a laborer with R, a construction company. The position requires lifting equipment and other items weighing up to 100 pounds. After making a conditional offer of employment to CP, R requires him to undergo its standard medical examination. As a result, R discovers that CP previously injured his back while working for an automotive repair shop. CP's prior on-the-job injury, which occurred when CP was helping a co-worker push a stalled vehicle, was not serious. CP has completely recovered from the back injury. Nevertheless, R rescinds its offer of employment because it is worried about increased workers' compensation costs and considers CP to be a poor risk for heavy labor.[18] CP's prior occupational injury, which was not serious and which occurred in a position involving hazards not present in R's position, does not constitute evidence that employment of CP in the laborer position would pose a direct threat.

RETURN TO WORK DECISIONS

13. May an employer **require** that an employee with a disability-related occupational injury be able to **return to "full duty"** before allowing him/her to return to work?

No. The term "full duty" may include marginal as well as essential job functions or may mean performing job functions without any accommodation. An employer may **not** require that an employee with a disability-related occupational injury who can perform essential functions be able to return to "full duty" **if**, because of the disability, s/he is unable to perform marginal functions of the position[19] or requires a reasonable accommodation that would not impose an undue hardship.

14. May an employer **refuse to return to work** an employee with a disability-related occupational injury simply because it assumes, correctly or incorrectly,

---

[18]CP has a disability as defined by the ADA because R regards CP as having a substantially limiting impairment. R, which disqualified CP from the heavy laborer position because it believed that CP was a poor risk for heavy labor, treated CP as unsuitable for the class of heavy labor jobs. Accordingly, R regards CP as substantially limited in the major life activity of working. See EEOC: Definition of the Term "Disability" at 902.8(f), 8 FEP Manual (BNA) 405:7282 (1995).

[19]The employer can reallocate or redistribute to other employees the marginal functions that the employee is unable to perform because of the disability.

that s/he **poses some increased risk of reinjury** and increased workers' compensation costs?

No, unless an employer can show that employment of the person in the position poses a "direct threat." Where an employer refuses to return an employee to work because it assumes, correctly or incorrectly, that his/her disability-related occupational injury creates merely **some** increased risk of further occupational injury and increased workers' compensation costs, it discriminates on the basis of disability. The employer may not refuse to return to work an employee who is able to perform the essential functions of the job, with or without a reasonable accommodation, unless it can show that returning the person to the position poses a "direct threat." (See the discussion of direct threat in questions 11 and 12, above.)

The fact that an employee has had a disability-related occupational injury does not, by itself, indicate that s/he is unable to perform the essential functions of the job or that returning him/her to work poses a direct threat. In some circumstances, evidence about an employee's disability-related occupational injury may be relevant to whether s/he can perform the essential functions of the job, with or without a reasonable accommodation, or it may be relevant to the direct threat analysis. An employer should consider the pertinent factors listed in questions 11 and 12, above, in applying the direct threat analysis in this context.

Example A: CP, a clerk/typist, breaks her wrist while trying to move heavy office equipment with a co-worker. CP is unable to work for six weeks and receives workers' compensation. After CP's wrist completely heals, she asks to return to work. A physician indicates that there is little risk that repetitive motion will damage CP's wrist. However, R refuses her request to return to the clerk/typist position because it believes that any repetitive motion will cause serious and permanent reinjury of her wrist.[20] The following objective evidence supports a finding that returning CP to the clerk/typist position does not pose a significant risk of substantial harm (i.e., direct threat): (1) her injury was not caused by repetitive motion, (2) her wrist has completely healed, and (3) there is little risk that she will reinjure her wrist through repetitive motion. R has violated the ADA by not returning CP to her clerk/typist position.

---

[20]CP has a disability because R regards her as having an impairment that disqualifies her from a class of jobs (clerk/typist) and therefore as substantially limited in the major life activity of working. See EEOC: Definition of the Term "Disability" at 902.8(f), 8 FEP Manual (BNA) 405:7282 (1995).

Example B: CP, a maintenance worker, badly fractures both ankles in a workplace accident. She is unable to work for six months and receives workers' compensation. Although CP's ankles partially heal, she is unable to walk and stand for more than short periods of time. CP's maintenance job requires extensive walking and standing on cement floors. The report from CP's most recent medical examination shows that there is a high probability of immediate, severe, and permanent damage to CP's ankles if she walks or stands for more than short periods of time, especially on hard surfaces. Assume that there is no accommodation that will lower the risk of harm. R may refuse to return CP to her maintenance position because there is sufficient evidence to support a finding that her employment in the position poses a direct threat, i.e., a significant risk of substantial harm that cannot be eliminated or reduced through a reasonable accommodation. (However, R must reassign CP, as set forth in question 22, below, absent undue hardship.)

15. May an employer **refuse to return to work** an employee with a disability-related occupational injury simply because of a **workers' compensation determination** that s/he has a **"permanent disability"** or is **"totally disabled"**?

No. Workers' compensation laws are different in purpose from the ADA and may utilize different standards for evaluating whether an individual has a "disability" or whether s/he is capable of working. For example, under a workers' compensation statute, a person who loses vision in both eyes or has loss of use of both arms or both legs may have a "permanent total disability," although s/he may be able to work. A workers' compensation determination also may relate to a different time period. Such a determination is **never dispositive** regarding an individual's ability to return to work, although it may provide relevant evidence regarding an employee's ability to perform the essential functions of the position in question or to return to work without posing a direct threat.

16. Under the ADA, **is a rehabilitation counselor, physician, or other specialist responsible for deciding** whether an employee with a disability-related occupational injury is **ready to return to work**?

No. The employer bears the ultimate responsibility for deciding whether an employee with a disability-related occupational injury is ready to return to work. Therefore, the employer, rather than a rehabilitation counselor, physician, or other specialist, must determine whether the employee can perform the essential functions of the job, with or without reasonable accommodation, or can work without posing a direct threat.

On the other hand, the employer may find it helpful to seek information from the rehabilitation counselor, physician, or other specialist regarding the employee's specific functional limitations, abilities, and possible reasonable accommodations.

In order to obtain useful and accurate information from a rehabilitation counselor, physician, or other specialist in making a return to work decision, an employer may wish to provide him/her with specific information about the following:

• the essential functions of the employee's position and the nature of the work to be performed;

• the work environment and the employer's operations, including any unavoidable health or safety hazards which may exist; and

• possible reasonable accommodations.

An employer also may obtain useful information from others who are not experts but who are knowledgeable about the employee's current abilities, limitations, and possible reasonable accommodations. Such information will enable the employer to make an independent and accurate determination about the employee's ability to return to work.

REASONABLE ACCOMMODATION

The ADA requires that an employer make reasonable accommodation to the known physical or mental limitations of an otherwise qualified individual with a disability, unless the employer can demonstrate that the accommodation would impose an undue hardship. The general principles regarding reasonable accommodation and undue hardship are discussed in the Commission's ADA regulations and interpretive guidance (29 C.F.R. §§ 1630.2, 1630.9 and Appendix (1995)), and in the Technical Assistance Manual at 3.0, 8 FEP Manual (BNA) 405:6998 (1992). This section provides specific guidance regarding reasonable accommodation in the context of workers' compensation.

17. Does the ADA require an employer to provide **reasonable accommodation** for an employee with **an occupational injury who does not have a disability** as defined by the ADA?

No. The ADA does not require an employer to provide a reasonable accommodation for an employee with an occupational injury who does not have a disability as defined by the ADA.

18. May an employer **discharge** an employee who is **temporarily unable to work** because of a disability-related occupational injury?

No. An employer may not discharge an employee who is temporarily unable to work because of a disability-related occupational injury where it would not impose an undue hardship to provide leave as a reasonable accommodation.[21]

19. What are the **reinstatement rights** of an employee with a disability-related occupational injury?

An employee with a disability-related occupational injury is entitled to return to his/her same position unless the employer demonstrates that holding open the position would impose an undue hardship.

In some instances, an employee may request more leave even after the employer has communicated that it would impose an undue hardship to hold open the employee's position any longer. In this situation, the employer must consider whether it has a vacant, equivalent position for which the employee is qualified and to which the employee can be reassigned without undue hardship to continue his/her leave for a specific period of time. For example, suppose that an employee needs six months to recover from a disability-related occupational injury, but holding his/her original position open for more than four months will impose an undue hardship. The employer must consider whether it has a vacant equivalent

[21] Under the ADA, permitting the use of accrued paid leave or providing additional unpaid leave for treatment and/or recovery are forms of reasonable accommodation that an employer must provide, absent undue hardship. See 29 C.F.R. pt. 1630 app. § 1630.2(o) (1995); Technical Assistance Manual at 3.10(4), 8 FEP Manual (BNA) 405:7011 (1992). In addition, an injured employee may be entitled to leave under the Family and Medical Leave Act of 1993, 29 U.S.C. §§ 2601-2654 (1994), which is enforced by the United States Department of Labor.

position to which the employee can be reassigned for the remaining two months of leave. If an equivalent position is not available, the employer must look for a vacant position at a lower level. Continued leave is not required as a reasonable accommodation if a vacant position at a lower level is also unavailable.[22]

20. Must an employer, as a **reasonable accommodation**, **reallocate job duties** of an employee with a disability-related occupational injury?

Yes, if the duties to be reallocated are marginal functions[23] of the position that the employee cannot perform because of the disability. Reasonable accommodation includes restructuring a position by reallocating or redistributing the marginal functions that the employee cannot perform because of the disability. However, an employer need not eliminate essential functions of the position.

21. May an employer **unilaterally reassign** an employee with a disability-related occupational injury to a **different position** instead of first trying to **accommodate** the employee in the **position s/he held at the time the injury occurred**?

No. An employer must first assess whether the employee can perform the essential functions of his/her original position, with or without a reasonable accommodation. Examples of reasonable accommodation include job restructuring, modification of equipment, or a part-time work schedule. Reassignment should be considered only when accommodation within the employee's original position is not possible or would impose an undue hardship.[24]

---

[22]For further information on an employer's obligations regarding reassignment, see questions 21 and 22, below.

[23]For a discussion of essential and marginal job functions see 29 C.F.R. § 1630.2(n) and Appendix (1995) and the Technical Assistance Manual at 2.3(a)-(c), 8 FEP Man. (BNA) 405:6993-405:6998 (1992).

[24]29 C.F.R. pt. 1630 app. § 1630.2(o); Technical Assistance Manual at 3.10(5), 8 FEP Manual (BNA) 405:7011-405:7012 (1992). Note, however, that the ADA does not prohibit an employer and an employee from choosing reassignment rather than accommodation in the original position, if both parties voluntarily agree that reassignment is preferable.

22. Must an employer **reassign** an employee who is **no longer able to perform the essential functions** of his/her **original position**, with or without a reasonable accommodation, because of a disability-related occupational injury?

> Yes. Where an employee can no longer perform the essential functions of his/her original position, with or without a reasonable accommodation, because of a disability-related occupational injury, an employer must reassign him/her to an equivalent vacant position for which s/he is qualified, absent undue hardship.[25] If no equivalent vacant position (in terms of pay, status, etc.) exists, then the employee must be reassigned to a lower graded position for which s/he is qualified, absent undue hardship.

23. If there is no vacancy for an employee who can no longer perform his/her original position because of a disability-related occupational injury, **must an employer create a new position** or **"bump" another employee** from his/her position?

> No. The ADA does not require an employer to create a new position or to bump another employee from his/her position in order to reassign an employee who can no longer perform the essential functions of his/her original position, with or without a reasonable accommodation.

24. When an employee **requests leave as a reasonable accommodation** under the ADA because of a disability-related occupational injury, may an employer **provide an accommodation that requires him/her to remain on the job instead**?

> Yes. An employer need not provide an employee's preferred accommodation as long as the employer provides an effective accommodation -- one that is sufficient to meet the employee's job-related needs.

---

[25] Id. Note, however, that the ADA does not prohibit an employer from removing an essential function that an employee is no longer able to perform, in lieu of reassignment, if removing the essential function does not result in a diminution of an employment opportunity or status. Where removing an essential function results in a diminution of an employment opportunity or status, an employer may remove the essential function in lieu of reassignment only if both parties voluntarily agree that it is preferable to reassignment. Of course, the ADA does not require an employer to remove an essential job function as a reasonable accommodation.

Accordingly, an employer may provide a reasonable accommodation that requires an employee to remain on the job, in lieu of providing leave (e.g., reallocating marginal functions, or providing temporary reassignment).

The employer is obligated, however, to restore the employee's full duties or to return the employee to his/her original position once s/he has recovered sufficiently to perform its essential functions, with or without a reasonable accommodation.

However, if an employee with a disability-related occupational injury does not request a reasonable accommodation, but simply requests leave that is routinely granted to other employees (e.g., accrued paid leave or leave without pay), an employer may not require him/her to remain on the job with some type of adjustment unless it also requires employees without disabilities who request such leave to remain on the job with some type of adjustment.

(Note that, if an employee qualifies for leave under the Family and Medical Leave Act, an employer may not require him/her to remain on the job with an adjustment in lieu of taking a leave of absence. 29 C.F.R. § 825.702(d)(1) (1995).)

25. May an employer satisfy its ADA **obligation to provide reasonable accommodation** for an employee with a disability-related occupational injury by **placing him/her in a workers' compensation vocational rehabilitation program**?

No. An employer cannot substitute vocational rehabilitation services in place of a reasonable accommodation required by the ADA for an employee with a disability-related occupational injury. An employee's rights under the ADA are separate from his/her entitlements under a workers' compensation law. The ADA requires employers to accommodate an employee in his/her current position through job restructuring or some other modification, absent undue hardship.[26] If it would impose an undue hardship to accommodate an employee in his/her current position, then the

[26] 29 C.F.R. pt. 1630 app. § 1630.2(o) (1995); Technical Assistance Manual at 3.10(5), 8 FEP Manual (BNA) 405:7011-405:7012 (1992).

ADA requires that an employer reassign the employee to a vacant position s/he can perform, absent undue hardship.[27] (See question 22, above.)

26. May an employer make a **workplace modification that is not a required form of reasonable accommodation** under the ADA in order to **offset workers' compensation costs**?

Yes. Nothing in the ADA prohibits an employer from making a workplace modification that is not a required form of reasonable accommodation under the ADA for an employee with an occupational injury in order to offset workers' compensation costs. For example, the ADA does not require employers to lower production standards to accommodate individuals with disabilities. However, an employer is clearly permitted to lower production standards for an occupationally injured employee as a way of returning him/her to work more quickly.

LIGHT DUTY

The term "light duty" has a number of different meanings in the employment setting. Generally, "light duty" refers to temporary or permanent work that is physically or mentally less demanding than normal job duties. Some employers use the term "light duty" to mean simply excusing an employee from performing those job functions that s/he is unable to perform because of an impairment. "Light duty" also may consist of particular positions with duties that are less physically or mentally demanding created specifically for the purpose of providing alternative work for employees who are unable to perform some or all of their normal duties. Further, an employer may refer to any position that is sedentary or is less physically or mentally demanding as "light duty."

In the following questions and answers, the term "light duty" refers only to particular positions created specifically for the purpose of providing work for employees who are unable to perform some or all of their normal duties.

27. Does the ADA prohibit an employer from **creating a light duty position for an employee when s/he is injured on the job**?

[27]However, the ADA does not prohibit an employer and an employee from choosing vocational rehabilitation as an alternative to accommodating the employee in his/her current position, if both parties voluntarily agree that vocational rehabilitation is preferable.

No, in most instances. An employer may recognize a special obligation arising out of the employment relationship to create a light duty position for an employee when s/he has been injured while performing work for the employer and, as a consequence, is unable to perform his/her regular job duties. Such a policy, on its face, does not treat an individual with a disability less favorably than an individual without a disability; nor does it screen out an individual on the basis of disability.[28]

Of course, an employer must apply its policy of creating a light duty position for an employee when s/he is occupationally injured on a non-discriminatory basis. In other words, an employer may not use disability as a reason to refuse to create a light duty position when an employee is occupationally injured.

An employer need not create a light duty position for a non-occupationally injured employee with a disability as a reasonable accommodation. The principle that the ADA does not require employers to create positions as a form of reasonable accommodation applies equally to the creation of light duty positions. However, an employer must provide other forms of reasonable accommodation required under the ADA. For example, subject to undue hardship, an employer must: (1) restructure a position by redistributing marginal functions which an individual cannot perform because of a disability, (2) provide modified scheduling (including part time work), or (3) reassign a non-occupationally injured employee with a disability to an equivalent existing vacancy for which s/he is qualified. Accordingly, an employer may not avoid its obligation to accommodate an individual with a disability simply by asserting that the disability did not derive from an occupational injury.

In some cases, the only effective reasonable accommodation available for an individual with a disability may be similar or equivalent to a light duty position. The employer would have to provide that reasonable accommodation unless the employer can demonstrate that doing so would impose an undue hardship.

---

[28]A policy of creating light duty jobs for employees when they are occupationally injured in some instances may disproportionately exclude a class of individuals with disabilities. Where this is established by appropriate evidence of adverse impact, an employer must show that the policy is job-related and consistent with business necessity. Similarly, where such a policy has a disparate impact on a protected class under Title VII of the Civil Rights Act of 1964, as amended, 42 U.S.C. §§ 2000e-2000e-17 (1994), or the Age Discrimination in Employment Act of 1967, 29 U.S.C. §§ 621-634 (1994), the employer must show that the policy is job-related and consistent with business necessity.

Example: R creates light duty positions for employees when they are occupationally injured if they are unable to perform one or more of their regular job duties. CP can no longer perform functions of her position because of a disability caused by an off-the-job accident. She requests that R create a light duty position for her as a reasonable accommodation. R denies CP's request because she has not been injured on the job. R has not violated the ADA. However, R must provide another reasonable accommodation, absent undue hardship. If it is determined that the only effective accommodation is to restructure CP's position by redistributing the marginal functions, and the restructured position resembles a light duty position, R must provide the reasonable accommodation unless it can prove that it imposes an undue hardship.

28. If an employer **reserves light duty positions for employees with occupational injuries**, does the ADA require it to consider **reassigning an employee with a disability** who is not occupationally injured to such positions as a **reasonable accommodation**?

Yes.[29] If an employee with a disability who is not occupationally injured becomes unable to perform the essential functions of his/her job, and there is no other effective accommodation available, the employer must reassign him/her to a vacant reserved light duty position as a reasonable accommodation if (1) s/he can perform its essential functions, with or without a reasonable accommodation; and (2) the reassignment would not impose an undue hardship. This is because reassignment to a vacant position and appropriate modification of an employer's policy are forms of reasonable accommodation required by the ADA, absent undue hardship.[30] An employer cannot establish that the reassignment to a vacant reserved light duty position imposes an undue hardship simply by showing that it would have no other vacant light duty positions available if an employee became injured on the job and needed light duty.

---

[29]If it is established by appropriate evidence that a policy of reserving light duty jobs for employees who have been occupationally injured has an adverse impact on a protected class under any of the laws enforced by the EEOC, an employer must show that the policy is job-related and consistent with business necessity. See footnote 28, above. Of course, an employer may not apply the policy in a discriminatory manner.

[30]29 C.F.R. § 1630.2(o)(2)(ii) (1995).

Example: R has light duty positions which it reserves for employees in its manufacturing department when they are unable to perform their regular job duties because of on-the-job injuries. CP, an assembly line worker, has multiple sclerosis (MS) which substantially limits a number of major life activities. Eventually CP is unable to perform the essential functions of her position, with or without a reasonable accommodation, because of the MS. As a reasonable accommodation, CP requests that she be reassigned to a vacant light duty position for which she is qualified. R says that the vacant light duty position is reserved for employees who are injured on the job and refuses to reassign CP, although it would not impose an undue hardship to do so. R has violated the ADA by refusing to reassign her to the vacant light duty position.

29. If an employer has only **temporary light duty positions**, must it still provide a **permanent light duty position** for an employee with a disability-related occupational injury?

No. The ADA typically does not limit an employer's ability to establish or change the content, nature, or functions of its positions. So, for example, an employer is free to determine that a light duty position will be temporary rather than permanent.[31] Thus, if an employer provides light duty positions only on a temporary basis, it need only provide a temporary light duty position for an employee with a disability-related occupational injury.

EXCLUSIVE REMEDY PROVISIONS

30. Do **exclusive remedy provisions** in workers' compensation laws **bar employees from pursuing ADA claims**?

No. The purpose of workers' compensation exclusivity clauses is to protect employers from being sued under common law theories of personal injury for occupational injury. Courts have generally held that the exclusive remedy provisions of state workers' compensation laws cannot bar claims

[31]Technical Assistance Manual at 9.4, 8 FEP Manual (BNA) 405:7057-405:7058 (1992).

arising under federal civil rights laws,[32] even where a state workers' compensation law provides some relief for disability discrimination. Applying a state workers' compensation law's exclusivity provision to bar an individual's ADA claim would violate the Supremacy Clause of the U.S. Constitution and seriously diminish the civil rights protection Congress granted to persons with disabilities.

---

[32]The only federal court to have addressed the issue under the ADA has held that an individual's ADA rights are not precluded by a state workers' compensation exclusive remedy provision. Wood v. County of Alameda, 875 F. Supp. 659, 664, 4 AD Cas. (BNA) 43 (N.D. Cal. 1995). Prior to enactment of the ADA, it was well established that the exclusive remedy provisions of state workers' compensation laws could not bar claims arising under federal civil rights laws, including the Rehabilitation Act. See, e.g., Lopez v. S.B. Thomas, Inc., 831 F.2d 1184, 1190 (2d Cir. 1987) (while workers' compensation law might bar plaintiff's state common law claim, it cannot bar relief under 42 U.S.C. § 1981 for discriminatory discharge); Rosa v. Cantrell, 705 F.2d 1208, 1221 (10th Cir. 1982), cert. denied, 464 U.S. 821 (1983) (state statute's exclusivity provision does not bar a federal civil rights claim under 42 U.S.C. § 1983); Smith v. Lake City Nursing Home, 771 F. Supp. 985, 987, 1 AD Cas. (BNA) 1874 (D. Minn. 1991) (federal remedy under section 504 of Rehabilitation Act for disability discrimination cannot be limited by a state workers' compensation act).

INDEX

NOTES

NOTES

9

ADA ENFORCEMENT GUIDANCE: PREEMPLOYMENT DISABILITY-RELATED QUESTION AND MEDICAL EXAMINATIONS

Presented by Paul Steven Miller

ADA Enforcement Guidance: Preemployment Disability-Related Questions and Medical Examinations

Introduction

Under the Americans with Disabilities Act of 1990 (the "ADA"),[1] an employer may ask disability-related questions and require medical examinations of an applicant only after the applicant has been given a conditional job offer. This Enforcement Guidance explains these ADA provisions.[2]

Background

In the past, some employment applications and interviews requested information about an applicant's physical and/or mental condition. This information was often used to exclude applicants with disabilities before their ability to perform the job was even evaluated.

For example, applicants may have been asked about their medical conditions at the same time that they were engaging in other parts of the application process, such as completing a written job application or having references checked. If an applicant was then rejected, s/he did not necessarily know whether s/he was rejected because of disability, or because of insufficient skills or experience or a bad report from a reference.

As a result, Congress established a process within the ADA to isolate an employer's consideration of an applicant's non-medical qualifications from any consideration of the applicant's medical condition.

---

[1] Codified as amended at 42 U.S.C. §§ 12101-17, 12201-13 (Supp. V 1994).

[2] The analysis in this guidance also applies to federal sector complaints of non-affirmative action employment discrimination arising under section 501 of the Rehabilitation Act of 1973. 29 U.S.C.A. § 791(g) (West Supp. 1994). In addition, the analysis applies to complaints of non-affirmative action employment discrimination arising under section 503 and employment discrimination under section 504 of the Rehabilitation Act. 29 U.S.C.A. §§ 793(d), 794(d) (West Supp. 1994).

The Statutory and Regulatory Framework

Under the law, an employer may not ask disability-related questions and may not conduct medical examinations until *after* it makes a conditional job offer to the applicant.[3] This helps ensure that an applicant's possible hidden disability (including a prior history of a disability) is not considered before the employer evaluates an applicant's non-medical qualifications. An employer may not ask disability-related questions or require a medical examination pre-offer *even if* it intends to look at the answers or results only at the post-offer stage.

Although employers may not ask disability-related questions or require medical examinations at the pre-offer stage, they *may* do a wide variety of things to evaluate whether an applicant is qualified for the job, including the following:

- Employers *may* ask about an applicant's ability to perform specific job functions. For example, an employer may state the physical requirements of a job (such as the ability to lift a certain amount of weight, or the ability to climb ladders), and ask if an applicant can satisfy these requirements.

- Employers *may* ask about an applicant's non-medical qualifications and skills, such as the applicant's education, work history, and required certifications and licenses.

- Employers *may* ask applicants to describe or demonstrate how they would perform job tasks.

Once a conditional job offer is made, the employer may ask disability-related questions and require medical examinations as long as this is done for all entering employees in that job category. If the employer rejects the applicant after a disability-related question or medical examination, investigators will closely scrutinize whether the rejection was based on the results of that question or examination.

If the question or examination screens out an individual because of a disability, the employer must demonstrate that the reason for the rejection is "job-related and consistent with business necessity."[4]

---

[3] 42 U.S.C. § 12112(d)(2); 29 C.F.R. §§ 1630.13(a), 1630.14(a),(b).

[4] 42 U.S.C. § 12112(b); 29 C.F.R. §§ 1630.10, 1630.14(b)(3).

In addition, if the individual is screened out for safety reasons, the employer must demonstrate that the individual poses a "direct threat." This means that the individual poses a significant risk of substantial harm to him/herself or others, and that the risk cannot be reduced below the direct threat level through reasonable accommodation.[5]

Medical information must be kept confidential.[6] The ADA contains narrow exceptions for disclosing specific, limited information to supervisors and managers, first aid and safety personnel, and government officials investigating compliance with the ADA. Employers may also disclose medical information to state workers' compensation offices, state second injury funds, or workers' compensation insurance carriers in accordance with state workers' compensation laws[7] and may use the medical information for insurance purposes.[8]

---

[5] 42 U.S.C. § 12113(b); See 29 C.F.R. pt. 1630 app. § 1630.2(r).

[6] 29 C.F.R. § 1630.14(b)(1)(i-iii).

[7] See 42 U.S.C. § 12201(b); 29 C.F.R. pt. 1630 app. § 1630.14(b).

[8] See 42 U.S.C. § 12201(c); 29 C.F.R. pt. 1630 app. § 1630.14(b). For example, an employer may submit medical information to the company's health insurance carrier if the information is needed to administer a health insurance plan in accordance with § 501(c) of the ADA.

The Pre-Offer Stage

What is a Disability-Related Question?

Definition: "Disability-Related Question" means a question that is *likely to elicit* information about a disability.

At the pre-offer stage, an employer cannot ask questions that are *likely to elicit* information about a disability. This includes directly asking whether an applicant has a particular disability. It also means that an employer cannot ask questions that are *closely related* to disability.[9]

On the other hand, if there are many possible answers to a question and only some of those answers would contain disability-related information, that question is not "disability-related."[10]

Below are some commonly asked questions about this area of the law.

- May an employer ask **whether an applicant can perform the job?**

  Yes. An employer may ask whether applicants can perform any or all job functions, including whether applicants can perform job functions "with or without reasonable accommodation."[11]

---

[9] Of course, an employer can always ask about an applicant's ability to perform the job.

[10] Sometimes, applicants disclose disability-related information in responding to an otherwise lawful pre-offer question. Although the employer has not asked an unlawful question, it still cannot refuse to hire an applicant based on disability unless the reason is "job-related and consistent with business necessity."

[11] However, an employer cannot ask a question in a manner that requires the individual to disclose the need for reasonable accommodation. For example, as described later in this guidance, an employer may not ask, "Can you do these functions with ___ without ___ reasonable accommodation? (Check One)"

• May an employer ask applicants to **describe or demonstrate how they would perform the job** (including any needed reasonable accommodations)?

Yes. An employer may ask applicants to describe how they would perform any or all job functions, as long as all applicants in the job category are asked to do this.

Employers should remember that, if an applicant says that s/he will need a reasonable accommodation to do a job demonstration, the employer must either:

• provide a reasonable accommodation that does not create an undue hardship; or

• allow the applicant to simply describe how s/he would perform the job function.

• May an employer ask a **particular applicant to describe or demonstrate how s/he would perform the job**, if other applicants aren't asked to do this?

When an employer could reasonably believe that an applicant will not be able to perform a job function because of a known disability, the employer may ask that particular applicant to describe or demonstrate how s/he would perform the function. An applicant's disability would be a "known disability" either because it is obvious (for example, the applicant uses a wheelchair), or because the applicant has voluntarily disclosed that s/he has a hidden disability.

• May an employer ask applicants **whether they will need reasonable accommodation for the hiring process**?

Yes. An employer may tell applicants what the hiring process involves (for example, an interview, timed written test, or job demonstration), and may ask applicants whether they will need a reasonable accommodation for this process.

• May an employer ask an applicant for **documentation of his/her disability when the applicant requests reasonable accommodation for the hiring process?**

Yes. If the need for accommodation is not obvious, an employer may ask an applicant for *reasonable* documentation about his/her disability if the applicant requests reasonable accommodation for the hiring process (such as a request for the employer to reformat an examination, or a request for an accommodation in connection with a job demonstration). The employer is entitled to know that the applicant has a covered disability and that s/he needs an accommodation.

So, the applicant may be required to provide documentation from an appropriate professional, such as a doctor or a rehabilitation counselor, concerning the applicant's disability and functional limitations.

• May an employer ask applicants **whether they will need reasonable accommodation to perform the functions of the job?**

In general, an employer may not ask questions on an application or in an interview about whether an applicant will need reasonable accommodation for a job. This is because these questions are likely to elicit whether the applicant has a disability (generally, only people who have disabilities will need reasonable accommodations).

Example: An employment application may not ask, "Do you need reasonable accommodation to perform this job?"

Example: An employment application may not ask, "Can you do these functions with ___ without ___ reasonable accommodation? (Check One)"

Example: An applicant with no known disability is being interviewed for a job. He has not asked for any reasonable accommodation, either for the application process or for the job. The employer may not ask him, "Will you need reasonable accommodation to perform this job?"

However, when an employer could reasonably believe that an applicant will need reasonable accommodation to perform the functions of the job, the employer may ask that applicant certain limited questions. Specifically, the employer may ask *whether s/he needs reasonable accommodation* and *what type of reasonable accommodation* would be needed to perform the functions of the job.[12] The employer could ask these questions if:

- the employer reasonably believes the applicant will need reasonable accommodation because of an obvious disability;

- the employer reasonably believes the applicant will need reasonable accommodation because of a hidden disability that the applicant has voluntarily disclosed to the employer; or

- an applicant has voluntarily disclosed to the employer that s/he needs reasonable accommodation to perform the job.

Example: An individual with diabetes applying for a receptionist position voluntarily discloses that she will need periodic breaks to take medication. The employer may ask the applicant questions about the reasonable accommodation such as how often she will need breaks, and how long the breaks must be. Of course, the employer may not ask any questions about the underlying physical condition.

Example: An applicant with a severe visual impairment applies for a job involving computer work. The employer may ask whether he will need reasonable accommodation to perform the functions of the job. If the applicant answers "no," the employer may not ask additional questions about reasonable accommodation (although, of course, the employer could ask the applicant to describe or demonstrate performance). If the applicant says that he *will* need accommodation, the employer may ask questions about the type of required accommodation such as, "What will you need?" If the applicant says he needs software that increases the size of text on the computer screen, the employer may ask questions such as, "Who makes that software?" "Do you need a particular brand?" or "Is that software compatible with our computers?" However, the employer may not ask questions about the applicant's underlying condition. In addition, the employer may not ask reasonable accommodation questions that are unrelated to job functions such as, "Will you need reasonable accommodation to get to the cafeteria?"

---

[12] It should be noted that an employer might lawfully ask questions about the need for reasonable accommodation on the job and then fail to hire the applicant. The rejected applicant may then claim that the refusal to hire was based on the need for accommodation. Under these facts, the EEOC will consider the employer's pre-offer questions as evidence that the employer *knew* about the need for reasonable accommodation, and will carefully scrutinize whether the need to provide accommodation was a reason for rejecting the applicant.

An employer may only ask about reasonable accommodation that is needed now or in the near future. An applicant is not required to disclose reasonable accommodations that may be needed in the more distant future.

• May an employer ask **whether an applicant can meet the employer's attendance requirements**?

Yes. An employer may state its attendance requirements and ask whether an applicant can meet them. An employer also may ask about an applicant's prior attendance record (for example, how many days the applicant was absent from his/her last job). These questions are not likely to elicit information about a disability because there may be many reasons unrelated to disability why someone cannot meet attendance requirements or was frequently absent from a previous job (for example, an applicant may have had day-care problems).

An employer also may ask questions designed to detect whether an applicant abused his/her leave because these questions are not likely to elicit information about a disability.

Example: An employer may ask an applicant, "How many Mondays or Fridays were you absent last year on leave other than approved vacation leave?"

However, at the pre-offer stage, an employer may not ask how many days an applicant was *sick*, because these questions relate directly to the *severity of an individual's impairments*. Therefore, these questions are likely to elicit information about a disability.

• May an employer ask applicants about their **certifications and licenses**?

Yes. An employer may ask an applicant at the pre-offer stage whether s/he has certifications or licenses required for any job duties. An employer also may ask an applicant whether s/he intends to get a particular job-related certification or license, or why s/he does not have the certification or license. These questions are not likely to elicit information about an applicant's disability because there may be a number of reasons unrelated to disability why someone does not have -- or does not intend to get -- a certification/license.

• May an employer ask applicants about their **arrest or conviction records**?

Yes. Questions about an applicant's arrest or conviction records are not likely to elicit information about disability because there are many reasons unrelated to disability why someone may have an arrest/conviction record.[13]

• May an employer ask questions about an **applicant's impairments**?

Yes, if the particular question is not likely to elicit information about whether the applicant has a disability. It is important to remember that not all impairments will be disabilities; an impairment is a disability *only* if it substantially limits a major life activity. So, an employer may ask an applicant with a broken leg how she broke her leg. Since a broken leg normally is a temporary condition which does not rise to the level of a disability, this question is not likely to disclose whether the applicant has a disability. But, such questions as "Do you expect the leg to heal normally?" or "Do you break bones easily?" *would* be disability-related. Certainly, an employer may not ask a broad question about impairments that is likely to elicit information about disability, such as, "What impairments do you have?"

• May an employer ask **whether applicants can perform major life activities**, such as standing, lifting, walking, etc.?

Questions about whether an applicant can perform major life activities are almost always disability-related because they are likely to elicit information about a disability. For example, if an applicant cannot stand or walk, it is likely to be a result of a disability. So, these questions are prohibited at the pre-offer stage *unless* they are specifically about the ability to perform

---

[13] However, investigators should be aware that Title VII of the Civil Rights Act of 1964, as amended, applies to such questions and that nothing in this Enforcement Guidance relieves an employer of its obligations to comply with Title VII. The Commission has previously provided guidance for investigators to follow concerning an employer's use of arrest/conviction records. See Policy Guidance No. N-915-061 (9/7/90) ("Policy Guidance on the Consideration of Arrest Records in Employment Decisions under Title VII of the Civil Rights Act of 1964, as amended, 42 U.S.C. § 2000e et seq. (1982)"); EEOC Compliance Manual, Vol. II, Appendices 604-A ("Conviction Records") and 604-B ("Conviction Records - Statistics").

job functions.

• May an employer ask applicants about their **workers' compensation history**?

No. An employer may not ask applicants about job-related injuries or workers' compensation history. These questions relate directly to the *severity of an applicant's impairments*. Therefore, these questions are likely to elicit information about disability.

• May an employer ask applicants about their **current illegal use of drugs**?

Yes. An employer may ask applicants about current illegal use of drugs[14] because an individual who currently illegally uses drugs is not protected under the ADA (when the employer acts on the basis of the drug use).[15]

• May an employer ask applicants about their **lawful drug use**?

No, if the question is likely to elicit information about disability. Employers should know that many questions about current or prior lawful drug use *are* likely to elicit information about a disability, and are therefore impermissible at the pre-offer stage. For example, questions like, "What medications are you currently taking?" or "Have you ever taken AZT?" certainly elicit information about whether an applicant has a disability.

However, some innocuous questions about lawful drug use are not likely to elicit information about disability.

Example: During her interview, an applicant volunteers to the interviewer that she is coughing and wheezing because her allergies are acting up as a result of pollen in the air. The interviewer, who also has allergies, tells the applicant that he finds "Lemebreathe" (an over-the-counter antihistamine) to be effective, and asks the applicant if she has tried it. There are many reasons why someone might have tried "Lemebreathe" which have nothing to do with disability. Therefore, this question is not

---

[14] "Drug" means a controlled substance, as defined in schedules I through V of Section 202 of the Controlled Substances Act (21 U.S.C. § 812). 29 C.F.R. § 1630.3(a)(1).

[15] 42 U.S.C. § 12114(a); 29 C.F.R. § 1630.3(a).

likely to elicit information about a disability.

• May an employer ask applicants about their **lawful drug use** if the employer is administering a test for illegal use of drugs?

Yes, *if* an applicant tests positive for illegal drug use. In that case, the employer may validate the test results by asking about lawful drug use or possible explanations for the positive result other than the illegal use of drugs.

Example: If an applicant tests positive for use of a controlled substance, the employer may lawfully ask questions such as, "What medications have you taken that might have resulted in this positive test result? Are you taking this medication under a lawful prescription?"

• May an employer ask applicants about their **prior illegal drug use**?

Yes, provided that the particular question is not likely to elicit information about a disability. It is important to remember that past *addiction* to illegal drugs or controlled substances is a covered disability under the ADA (as long as the person is not a current illegal drug user), but past *casual* use is not a covered disability. Therefore, the question is fine as long as it does not go to past drug *addiction*.

Example: An employer may ask, "Have you ever used illegal drugs?" "When is the last time you used illegal drugs?" or "Have you used illegal drugs in the last six months?" These questions are not likely to tell the employer anything about whether the applicant was addicted to drugs.

However, questions that ask how much the applicant used drugs in the past are likely to elicit information about whether the applicant was a past drug addict. These questions are therefore impermissible at the pre-offer stage.

Example: At the pre-offer stage, an employer may not ask an applicant questions such as, "How often did you use illegal drugs in the past?" "Have you ever been addicted to drugs?" "Have you ever been treated for drug addiction?" or "Have you ever been treated for drug abuse?"

• May an employer ask applicants about their **drinking habits**?

Yes, unless the particular question is likely to elicit information about alcoholism, which is a disability. An employer may ask an applicant whether s/he drinks alcohol, or whether s/he has been arrested for driving under the influence because these questions do not reveal whether someone has alcoholism. However, questions asking *how much* alcohol an applicant drinks or whether s/he has participated in an alcohol rehabilitation program *are* likely to elicit information about whether the applicant has alcoholism.

• May an employer ask applicants to **"self-identify"** as individuals with disabilities for purposes of the **employer's affirmative action program?**

Yes. An employer may invite applicants to voluntarily self-identify for purposes of the employer's affirmative action program *if*:

• the employer is undertaking affirmative action because of a federal, state, or local law (including a veterans' preference law) that requires affirmative action for individuals with disabilities (that is, the law requires some action to be taken on behalf of such individuals); *or*

• the employer is *voluntarily* using the information to benefit individuals with disabilities.

Employers should remember that state or local laws sometimes permit or encourage affirmative action. In those cases, an employer may invite voluntary self-identification *only* if the employer uses the information to benefit individuals with disabilities.

• Are there any **special steps an employer should take** if it asks applicants to **"self-identify"** for purposes of the **employer's affirmative action program?**

Yes. If the employer invites applicants to voluntarily self-identify in connection with providing affirmative action, the employer *must* do the following:

• state clearly on any written questionnaire, or state clearly orally (if no written questionnaire is used), that the information requested is used solely in connection with its affirmative action obligations or efforts; and

• state clearly that the information is being requested on a voluntary basis, that it will be kept confidential in accordance with the ADA, that refusal to provide it will not subject the applicant to any adverse treatment, and that it will be used only in accordance with the ADA.

In order to ensure that the self-identification information is kept confidential, the information must be on a form that is kept separate from the application.

• May an employer ask **third parties questions it could not ask the applicant directly?**

No. An employer may not ask a third party (such as a service that provides information about workers' compensation claims, a state agency, or an applicant's friends, family, or former employers) any questions that it could not directly ask the applicant.

What is a Medical Examination?

Definition: A "Medical Examination" is a procedure or test that seeks information about an individual's physical or mental impairments or health.

At the pre-offer stage, an employer cannot require examinations that seek information about physical or mental impairments or health. It is not always easy to determine whether something is a *medical* examination. The following factors are helpful in determining whether a procedure or test is *medical*:

- Is it administered by a health care professional or someone trained by a health care professional?

- Are the results interpreted by a health care professional or someone trained by a health care professional?

- Is it designed to reveal an impairment or physical or mental health?

- Is the employer trying to determine the applicant's physical or mental health or impairments?

- Is it invasive (for example, does it require the drawing of blood, urine or breath)?

- Does it measure an applicant's performance of a task, *or* does it measure the applicant's physiological responses to performing the task?

- Is it normally given in a medical setting (for example, a health care professional's office)?

- Is medical equipment used?

In many cases, a combination of factors will be relevant in figuring out whether a procedure or test is a *medical* examination. In some cases, one factor may be enough to determine that a procedure or test is medical.

> Example: An employer requires applicants to lift a thirty pound box and carry it twenty feet. This is not a medical examination; it is just a test of whether the applicant can perform this task. But, if the employer takes the applicant's blood pressure or heart rate after the lifting and carrying, the test *would* be a medical examination because it is measuring the applicant's physiological response to lifting and carrying, as opposed to the applicant's ability to lift and carry.

Example: A psychological test is designed to reveal mental illness, but a particular employer says it does not give the test to disclose mental illness (for example, the employer says it uses the test to disclose just tastes and habits). But, the test also is interpreted by a psychologist, and is routinely used in a clinical setting to provide evidence that would lead to a diagnosis of a mental disorder or impairment (for example, whether an applicant has paranoid tendencies, or is depressed). Under these facts, this test is a medical examination.

Below are some commonly asked questions about the ADA's restrictions on pre-offer medical examinations.

- May an employer require applicants to take **physical agility tests**?

  Yes. A physical agility test, in which an applicant demonstrates the ability to perform actual or simulated job tasks, is not a medical examination under the ADA.[16]

  Example: A police department tests police officer applicants' ability to run through an obstacle course designed to simulate a suspect chase in an urban setting. This is not a medical examination.

- May an employer require applicants to take **physical fitness tests**?

  Yes. A physical fitness test, in which an applicant's performance of physical tasks -- such as running or lifting -- is measured, is not a medical examination.[17]

  However, if an employer measures an applicant's *physiological or biological responses* to performance, the test would be medical.

---

[16] Of course, an employer cannot use a test in violation of other federal civil rights statutes. For example, if a test has an adverse impact under Title VII of the Civil Rights Act of 1964, as amended, 42 U.S.C. § 2000e et seq., it must be shown to be job-related and consistent with business necessity.

[17] Although physical agility tests and physical fitness tests are not "medical" examinations, these tests are still subject to other parts of the ADA. For example, if a physical fitness test which requires applicants to run one mile in ten minutes screens out an applicant on the basis of disability, the employer must be prepared to demonstrate that the test is "job-related and consistent with business necessity."

Example: A messenger service tests applicants' ability to run one mile in 15 minutes. At the end of the run, the employer takes the applicants' blood pressure and heart rate. Measuring the applicant's physiological responses makes this a medical examination.

• May an employer ask an applicant to provide **medical certification that s/he can safely perform a physical agility or physical fitness test**?

Yes. Although an employer cannot ask disability-related questions, it may give the applicant a description of the agility or fitness test and ask the applicant to have a private physician simply state whether s/he can safely perform the test.

• May an employer ask an applicant to **assume liability for injuries incurred in performing a physical agility or physical fitness test**?

Yes. An employer may ask an applicant to assume responsibility and release the employer of liability for injuries incurred in performing a physical agility or fitness test.

• May an employer give **psychological examinations** to applicants?

Yes, unless the particular examination is *medical*. This determination would be based on some of the factors listed above, such as the purpose of the test and the intent of the employer in giving the test. Psychological examinations are medical if they provide evidence that would lead to identifying a mental disorder or impairment (for example, those listed in the American Psychiatric Association's most recent Diagnostic and Statistical Manual of Mental Disorders (DSM)).

Example: An employer gives applicants the RUOK Test (hypothetical), an examination which reflects whether applicants have characteristics that lead to identifying whether the individual has excessive anxiety, depression, and certain compulsive disorders (DSM-listed conditions). This test is medical.

On the other hand, if a test is designed and used to measure only things such as honesty, tastes, and habits, it is not *medical*.

Example: An employer gives the IFIB Personality Test (hypothetical), an examination designed and used to reflect only whether an applicant is likely to lie. This test, as used by the employer, is not a medical examination.

• May an employer give **polygraph examinations** to applicants?

Although most employers are prohibited by federal and state laws from giving polygraph examinations, some employers are not prohibited from giving these examinations. Under the ADA, polygraph examinations are not medical examinations.[18] Many times, however, polygraph examinations contain disability-related questions, such as questions about what lawful medications the applicant is taking. Employers cannot ask disability-related questions as part of a pre-offer examination, even if the examination is not itself "medical."

• May an employer give **vision tests** to applicants?

Yes, unless the particular test is *medical.* Evaluating someone's ability to read labels or distinguish objects as part of a demonstration of the person's ability to do the job is not a medical examination. However, an ophthalmologist's or optometrist's analysis of someone's vision *is* medical. Similarly, requiring an individual to read an eye chart would be a medical examination.

• May an employer give applicants **tests to determine illegal use of controlled substances**?

Yes. The ADA specifically states that, for purposes of the ADA, tests to determine the current illegal use of controlled substances are not considered medical examinations.

• May an employer give **alcohol tests** to applicants?

No. Tests to determine whether and/or how much alcohol an individual has consumed are medical, and there is no statutory exemption.

---

[18] A polygraph examination purportedly measures whether a person believes s/he is telling the truth in response to a particular inquiry. The examination does not measure health or impairments. Rather, it just measures relative *changes* in physiological responses of the test taker.

The Post-Offer Stage

After giving a job offer to an applicant, an employer may ask disability-related questions and perform medical examinations. The job offer may be conditioned on the results of post-offer disability-related questions or medical examinations.

At the "post-offer" stage, an employer may ask about an individual's workers' compensation history, prior sick leave usage, illnesses/diseases/impairments, and general physical and mental health. Disability-related questions and medical examinations at the post-offer stage do not have to be related to the job.[19]

If an employer asks post-offer disability-related questions, or requires post-offer medical examinations, it must make sure that it follows certain procedures:

- all entering employees in the same job category must be subjected to the examination/inquiry, regardless of disability;[20] and

- medical information obtained must be kept confidential.[21]

Below are some commonly asked questions about the post-offer stage.

- What is considered a ***real*** **job offer**?

  Since an employer can ask disability-related questions and require medical examinations after a job offer, it is important that the job offer be *real*. A job offer is real if the employer has evaluated all relevant non-medical information which it reasonably could have obtained and analyzed prior to giving the offer. Of course, there are times when an employer cannot reasonably obtain and evaluate *all* non-medical information at the pre-offer stage. If an employer can show that is the case, the offer would still be considered a real offer.

  Example: It may be too costly for a law enforcement employer wishing to administer a polygraph examination to administer a pre-offer examination asking non-disability-related questions, and a post-offer examination asking

---

[19] But, if an individual is screened out because of disability, the employer must show that the exclusionary criterion is job-related and consistent with business necessity. 42 U.S.C. § 12112(b); 29 C.F.R. §§ 1630.10, 1630.14(b)(3).

[20] 42 U.S.C. § 12112(d)(3); 29 C.F.R. § 1630.14(b)(1),(2).

[21] Id.

disability-related questions. In this case, the employer may be able to demonstrate that it could not reasonably obtain and evaluate the non-medical polygraph information at the pre-offer stage.

Example: An applicant might state that his current employer should not be asked for a reference check until the potential employer makes a conditional job offer. In this case, the potential employer could not reasonably obtain and evaluate the non-medical information from the reference at the pre-offer stage.

• Do offers have to be limited to **current vacancies**?

No. An employer may give offers to fill current vacancies *or* reasonably anticipated openings.

• May an employer give **offers that exceed the number of vacancies or reasonably anticipated openings**?

Yes. The offers will still be considered *real* if the employer can demonstrate that it needs to give more offers in order to actually fill vacancies or reasonably anticipated openings. For example, an employer may demonstrate that a certain percentage of the offerees will likely be disqualified or will withdraw from the pool.

Example: A police department may be able to demonstrate that it needs to make offers to 50 applicants for 25 available positions because about half of the offers will likely be revoked based on post-offer medical tests and/or security checks, and because some applicants may voluntarily withdraw from consideration

Of course, an employer must comply with the ADA when taking people out of the pool to fill actual vacancies. The employer must *notify* an individual (orally or in writing) if his/her placement into an actual vacancy is in any way adversely affected by the results of a post-offer medical examination or disability-related question.

If an individual alleges that disability has affected his/her placement into an actual vacancy, the EEOC will carefully scrutinize whether disability was a reason for any adverse action. If disability was a reason, the EEOC will determine whether the action was job-related and consistent with business necessity.

• After an employer has obtained basic medical information from all individuals who have been given conditional offers in a job category, may it ask **specific individuals for more medical information?**

Yes, if the follow-up examinations or questions are medically related to the previously obtained medical information.[22]

Example: At the post-offer stage, an employer asks new hires whether they have had back injuries, and learns that some of the individuals have had such injuries. The employer may give medical examinations designed to diagnose back impairments to persons who stated that they had prior back injuries, as long as these examinations are medically related to those injuries.

• At the post-offer stage, may an employer ask all individuals **whether they need reasonable accommodation to perform the job?**

Yes.

• If, at the post-offer stage, someone requests **reasonable accommodation to perform the job**, may the employer ask him/her for **documentation of his/her disability**?

Yes. If someone requests reasonable accommodation so s/he will be able to perform a job and the need for the accommodation is not obvious, the employer may require *reasonable* documentation of the individual's entitlement to reasonable accommodation. So, the employer may require documentation showing that the individual has a *covered disability*, and stating his/her *functional limitations*.

Example: An entering employee states that she will need a 15-minute break every two hours to eat a snack in order to maintain her blood sugar level. The employer may ask her to provide documentation from her doctor showing that: (1) she has an impairment that substantially limits a major life activity; and (2) she actually needs the requested breaks because of the impairment.

---

[22] Once again, if an examination or inquiry screens out someone *because of disability*, the exclusionary criteria must be "job-related and consistent with business necessity." Where safety considerations are the reason, the individual can only be screened out because s/he poses a "direct threat."

Confidentiality

An employer must keep *any* medical information on applicants or employees confidential, with the following limited exceptions:

- supervisors and managers may be told about necessary restrictions on the work or duties of the employee and about necessary accommodations;

- first aid and safety personnel may be told *if* the disability might require emergency treatment;

- government officials investigating compliance with the ADA must be given relevant information on request;[23]

- employers may give information to state workers' compensation offices, state second injury funds or workers' compensation insurance carriers in accordance with state workers' compensation laws;[24] and

- employers may use the information for insurance purposes.[25]

Below are some commonly asked questions about the ADA's confidentiality requirements.

- May **medical information** be given to **decision-makers involved in the hiring process**?

  Yes. Medical information may be given to -- and used by -- appropriate decision-makers involved in the hiring process so they can make employment decisions consistent with the ADA. In addition, the employer may use the information to determine reasonable accommodations for the individual. For example, the employer may share the information with a third party, such as a health care professional, to determine whether a reasonable accommodation is possible for a particular individual. The information certainly must be kept confidential.

---

[23] 29 C.F.R. § 1630.14(b)(1)(i-iii).

[24] See 42 U.S.C. § 12201(b); 29 C.F.R. pt. 1630 app. § 1630.14(b).

[25] See 42 U.S.C. § 12201(c); 29 C.F.R. pt. 1630 app. § 1630.14(b). For example, an employer may submit medical information to the company's health insurance carrier if the information is needed to administer a health insurance plan in accordance with § 501(c) of the ADA.

Of course, the employer may only share the medical information with individuals involved in the hiring process (or in implementing an affirmative action program) who *need to know* the information. For example, in some cases, a number of people may be involved in evaluating an applicant. Some individuals may simply be responsible for evaluating an applicant's references; these individuals may have no need to know an applicant's medical condition and therefore should not have access to the medical information.

• Can an individual **voluntarily disclose his/her own medical information** to persons beyond those to whom an employer can disclose such information?

Yes, as long as it's *really* voluntary. The employer cannot request, persuade, coerce, or otherwise pressure the individual to get him/her to disclose medical information.

• Does the employer's confidentiality obligation extend to **medical information that an individual voluntarily tells the employer?**

Yes. For example, if an applicant voluntarily discloses bipolar disorder and the need for reasonable accommodation, the employer may not disclose the condition or the applicant's need for accommodation to the applicant's references.

• Can **medical information be kept in an employee's regular personnel file?**

No. Medical information must be collected and maintained on separate forms and in separate medical files.[26] An employer should not place any medical-related material in an employee's non-medical personnel file. If an employer wants to put a document in a personnel file, and that document happens to contain some medical information, the employer must simply remove the medical information from the document before putting it in the personnel file.

---

[26] A notation that an individual has taken sick leave or had a doctor's appointment is not confidential medical information. Of course, documentation of the individual's diagnosis or symptoms would be medical information.

• Does the **confidentiality obligation end when the person is no longer an applicant or employee?**

No, an employer must keep medical information confidential *even if* someone is no longer an applicant (for example, s/he wasn't hired) or is no longer an employee.

• Is an employer required to **remove from its personnel files medical information obtained before the ADA's effective date?**

No.

INDEX

APPENDIX TO ENFORCEMENT GUIDANCE

1. SUBJECT: Enforcement Guidance: Preemployment Disability-Related Questions and Medical Examinations.

2. PURPOSE: This document provides the EEOC's position under the Americans with Disabilities Act of 1990, on preemployment disability-related questions and medical examinations.

3. EFFECTIVE DATE: Upon receipt.

4. EXPIRATION DATE: As an exception to EEOC Order 205.001, Appendix B, Attachment 4, § a(5), this Notice will remain in effect until rescinded or superseded.

5. ORIGINATOR: ADA Division, Office of Legal Counsel.

6. INSTRUCTIONS: File after Section 902 of Volume II of the Compliance Manual.

10/10/95
Date

Gilbert F. Casellas
Chairman

DISTRIBUTION: CM Holders

26

NOTES

NOTES

10

EEOC COMPLIANCE MANUAL

Presented by Paul Steven Miller

Executive Summary: Compliance Manual Section 902, Definition of the Term "Disability"

Introduction

Compliance Manual section 902 provides guidance and instructions for determining whether an individual has a "disability" as defined by the Americans with Disabilities Act of 1990 (ADA or Act). It has been issued for use by EEOC investigators when investigating charges of discrimination under the ADA.

Rationale and Legal Framework

The definition of "disability" under the ADA reflects Congressional intent to prohibit the specific forms of discrimination that people with disabilities face. Since the definition is tailored to the purpose of eliminating discrimination prohibited by the ADA, it may differ from the definition of "disability" under other statutes. A determination of whether a charging party has a "disability" turns on whether he or she meets the ADA definition of that term.

A charging party has a "disability" for purposes of the ADA if she or he (1) has a physical or mental impairment that substantially limits a major life activity, (2) has a record of such an impairment, or (3) is regarded as having such an impairment. A charging party must satisfy at least one of these three parts of the definition to be considered an individual with a "disability." To determine whether a charging party has a "disability," the investigator first should determine whether the charging party satisfies the first part of the definition of the term. If the charging party does not satisfy the first part of the definition of "disability," or if the investigator after attempting an analysis is unsure whether the charging party meets the first part, then the investigator should determine whether he or she satisfies the second or third part of the definition.

When determining whether a charging party satisfies the definition of "disability," the investigator should remember that the concepts of "impairment," "major life activity," and "substantially limits" are relevant to all three parts of the definition of "disability." The investigator also should remember that the "disability" determination should be made without regard to the availability of mitigating measures. Further, the investigator should remember that certain conditions are specifically excluded from the definition of "disability."

Application of the Definition of "Disability"

Below is a brief summary of some topics relevant to the determination of whether a charging party satisfies the ADA definition of "disability."

Impairment

- An impairment is a physiological disorder affecting one or more of a number of body systems or a mental or psychological disorder.
- The following conditions are not impairments:
    - environmental, cultural, and economic disadvantages
    - homosexuality and bisexuality
    - pregnancy
    - physical characteristics
    - common personality traits
    - normal deviations in height, weight, or strength.

Major Life Activities

- Examples of major life activities listed in the Title I regulations include caring for oneself, performing manual tasks, walking, seeing, hearing, speaking, breathing, learning, and working.
- Other examples of major life activities include sitting, standing, lifting, and mental and emotional processes such as thinking, concentrating, and interacting with others.

Substantially Limits

- An impairment is substantially limiting if it prohibits or significantly restricts an individual's ability to perform a major life activity as compared to the ability of the average person in the general population to perform the same activity.

- The determination of whether an impairment substantially limits a major life activity depends on the nature and severity of the impairment, the duration or expected duration of the impairment, and the permanent or long-term impact of the impairment.

- An impairment substantially limits an individual's ability to work if it prevents or significantly restricts the individual from performing a class of jobs or a broad range of jobs in various classes.

- Although very short-term, temporary restrictions generally are not substantially limiting, an impairment does not have to be permanent to rise to the level of a disability. Temporary impairments that take significantly longer than normal to heal, long-term impairments, or potentially long-term impairments of indefinite duration may be disabilities if they are severe.

- Chronic or episodic disorders that are substantially limiting when active or have a high likelihood of recurrence in substantially limiting forms may be disabilities.

- An individual who has two or more impairments that are not substantially limiting by themselves but that together substantially limit one or more major life activities has a disability.

<u>Record</u>

- An individual has a record of a substantially limiting impairment if she or he

    - has a history of a substantially limiting impairment or

    - has been misclassified as having a substantially limiting impairment.

<u>Regarded</u>

- An individual is regarded as having a substantially limiting impairment if he or she

    - has an impairment that does not substantially limit major life activities but is treated by a covered entity as constituting such limitation,

- has an impairment that substantially limits major life activities only as a result of the attitudes of others toward such impairment, or

- has no impairment but is treated by a covered entity as having a substantially limiting impairment.

- An employer regards an individual as having an impairment that substantially limits the major life activity of working if it treats the individual as having an impairment that disqualifies or significantly restricts the individual from working in a class of jobs or a broad range of jobs in various classes.

Illegal Use of Drugs

- The statute and regulations exclude from the definition of "disability" an individual currently engaging in the illegal use of drugs when the covered entity acts on the basis of the use. This exclusion, however, does not apply to an individual who has a record of illegal use of drugs but no longer uses drugs illegally or who is erroneously regarded as engaging in such use.

- An individual does not automatically satisfy the definition of "disability" simply because she or he has a record of the illegal use of drugs or is erroneously regarded as engaging in such use. The record or perception must pertain to a record or perception that the individual is or was addicted to drugs. A record or perception of occasional, casual use of drugs does not constitute a disability.

SECTION 902

DEFINITION OF THE TERM "DISABILITY"

Table of Contents

SECTION 902

DEFINITION OF THE TERM "DISABILITY"

902.1 Introduction and Summary

(a) General -- Title I of the Americans with Disabilities Act, 42 U.S.C. §§ 12101-17 (Supp. IV 1992) [hereinafter ADA or Act], prohibits employment discrimination on the basis of disability.[1] The ADA protects a qualified individual with a "disability" from discrimination in job application procedures; hiring; advancement; discharge; compensation; job training; and other terms, conditions, and privileges of employment. 42 U.S.C. § 12112(a). To be protected by the ADA, a person must meet the definition of the term "qualified individual with a disability" as defined by the Act and implementing regulations.[2] This Compliance Manual section discusses the ADA definition of the term "disability."[3] The

[1] The ADA uses the terms "disability" and "individual with a disability" rather than the terms "handicap" and "handicapped person" or "individual with handicaps." The use of these terms "represents an effort by [Congress] to make use of up-to-date, currently accepted terminology." The change in phraseology does not reflect a change in definition or substance. S. Rep. No. 116, 101st Cong., 1st Sess. 21 (1989) [hereinafter Senate Report]; H.R. Rep. No. 485 pt. 2, 101st Cong., 2d Sess. 50-51 (1990) [hereinafter House Education and Labor Report].

[2] The ADA also protects individuals from discrimination on the basis of their relationship or association with a person with a disability. 42 U.S.C. § 12112(b)(4); 29 C.F.R. § 1630.8; see also Senate Report at 30; House Education and Labor Report at 61-62; H.R. Rep. No. 485 pt. 3, 101st Cong., 2d Sess. 38-39 (1990) [hereinafter House Judiciary Report]. Further, the Act prohibits retaliation or coercion against individuals because they have opposed any act that the ADA makes unlawful, have participated in the enforcement process, or have encouraged others to exercise their rights secured by the ADA. 42 U.S.C. § 12203; 29 C.F.R. § 1630.12; see also Senate Report at 86; House Education and Labor Report at 138; House Judiciary Report at 72.

[3] The Rehabilitation Act Amendments of 1992 amended the Rehabilitation Act of 1973, 29 U.S.C. §§ 701-97 (1988 & Supp. IV (continued...)

definition of the term "qualified individual with a disability" and the appropriate analysis for determining whether a person meets that definition will be discussed in a separate forthcoming Compliance Manual section.

A major part of the inquiry in an ADA charge often will be the determination of whether the charging party is protected by the Act. This determination frequently requires more extensive analysis than does the determination of whether a person is protected by other nondiscrimination statutes. For example, it is generally clear whether a person is of a particular race, national origin, age, or sex that is alleged to be the basis of discrimination. By contrast, it often is less clear whether a person's physical or mental condition constitutes an impairment of sufficient degree to establish that the person meets the statutory definition of an individual with a "disability."

The definition of "disability" under the ADA reflects the intent of Congress to prohibit the specific forms of discrimination that persons with disabilities face. While individuals with disabilities may experience the types of discrimination that confront other groups, they also may encounter unique forms of discrimination because of the nature of their disabilities and the effect that their present, past, or perceived conditions have on other persons. The purpose of the ADA is to eliminate discrimination that confronts individuals with disabilities.

Since the definition of the term "disability" under the ADA is tailored to the purpose of eliminating discrimination prohibited by the ADA, it may differ from the definition of "disability" in other laws drafted for other purposes. For example, the definition of a "disabled veteran" is not the same as the definition of an individual with a disability under the ADA.[4]

---

[3](...continued)
1992), to apply the substantive standards of Title I of the ADA to sections 501, 503, and 504 of the Rehabilitation Act for non-affirmative action employment discrimination cases. Pub. L. No. 102-569, 106 Stat. 4344 at 4424, 4428 (1992) (codified at 29 U.S.C. §§ 791(g), 793(d), 794(d) (Supp. IV 1992)). (Sections 501, 503, and 504 of the Rehabilitation Act prohibit federal agencies, federal contractors, and programs receiving federal financial assistance from discriminating on the basis of disability.) The ADA definition of the term "disability," therefore, also applies to those sections of the Rehabilitation Act.

[4]The Vietnam Era Veterans Readjustment Assistance Act of 1974 defines a disabled veteran as

> (A) a veteran who is entitled to compensation (or who but for the receipt of military retired pay would be entitled

(continued...)

Similarly, an individual might be eligible for disability retirement but not be an individual with a disability under the ADA. Conversely, a person who meets the ADA definition of "disability" might not meet the requirements for disability retirement.

(b) Statutory Definition -- With respect to an individual, the term "disability" means

(A) a physical or mental impairment that substantially limits one or more of the major life activities of such individual;

(B) a record of such an impairment; or

(C) being regarded as having such an impairment.

42 U.S.C. § 12102(2); see also 29 C.F.R. § 1630.2(g). A person must meet the requirements of at least one of these three criteria to be an individual with a disability under the Act.

The first part of the definition covers persons who actually have physical or mental impairments that substantially limit one or more major life activities. The focus under the first part is on the individual, to determine if (s)he has a substantially limiting impairment. To fall under the first part of the definition, a person must establish three elements:

(1) that (s)he has a physical or mental impairment

(2) that substantially limits

(3) one or more major life activities.

The second and third parts of the definition cover persons who may not have an impairment that substantially limits a major life activity but who have a history of, or have been misclassified as having, such a substantially limiting impairment, or who are perceived as having such a substantially limiting impairment. The focus under the second and third parts is on the reactions of other persons to a history of an impairment or to a

---

[4](...continued)
to compensation) under laws administered by the Secretary, or (B) a person who was discharged or released from active duty because of a service-connected disability.

38 U.S.C. § 4211(3) (Supp. III 1991).

perceived impairment. A history or perception of an impairment that substantially limits a major life activity is a "disability." These parts of the definition reflect a recognition by Congress that stereotyped assumptions about what constitutes a disability and unfounded concerns about the limitations of individuals with disabilities form major discriminatory barriers, not only to those persons presently disabled, but also to those persons either previously disabled, misclassified as previously disabled, or mistakenly perceived to be disabled. To combat the effects of these prevalent misperceptions, the definition of an individual with a disability precludes discrimination against persons who are treated as if they have a substantially limiting impairment, even if in fact they have no such current incapacity.

(c) <u>Summary</u> -- To determine whether a charging party is protected by the ADA, the EEOC investigator initially should determine why the charging party believes that the respondent has discriminated against him/her on the basis of disability. The charging party's response usually will provide the investigator with a starting point for analysis by identifying the type of condition at issue. For example, if the charging party replies that the respondent refused to hire him/her because it learned that the charging party had received psychiatric treatment, then the investigator will know to investigate whether the charging party has, has a record of, or is regarded as having a psychiatric disability. (Of course, further investigation may reveal other disabilities that may constitute the reason for the challenged employment action.)

The investigator then should determine whether the charging party meets the first part of the definition of "disability"; that is, the investigator should determine whether the charging party actually has a physical or mental impairment that substantially limits a major life activity. In that regard, the investigator should determine whether the charging party's condition is an impairment. <u>See</u> § 902.2, <u>infra</u>. If the condition is an impairment, then the investigator should determine whether the charging party's impairment substantially limits a major life activity other than working. <u>See</u> § 902.4(c)(1), <u>infra</u>. If the impairment does not, then the investigator should determine whether the charging party is substantially limited in the ability to work. <u>See</u> § 902.4(c)(2), <u>infra</u>.

If the charging party does not meet the first part of the definition of "disability," or if the investigator after attempting an analysis is unsure whether the charging party meets the first part, then the investigator should determine whether the charging party meets the second or third part of the definition. <u>See</u> §§ 902.7, .8 <u>infra</u>. With respect to the second part, the investigator should determine whether the charging party has a history of, <u>see</u> § 902.7(b), <u>infra</u>, or has been misclassified as having, <u>see</u> § 902.7(c), <u>infra</u>, an impairment that substantially limited a major life activity. With respect to the third part, the investigator should determine whether the charging party is regarded as having an impairment that substantially limits a major life activity. In that regard, the investigator should determine whether the charging party (1) has an impairment that does not substantially limit a major life activity but that is regarded as being substantially limiting, _see_ § 902.8(c), _infra_, (2) has an impairment that is substantially limiting only as a result of the attitudes of others, _see_ § 902.8(d), _infra_, or (3) has no impairment but is regarded as having a substantially limiting impairment, _see_ § 902.8(e), _infra_.

902.2 Impairment

(a) General -- The person claiming to be an individual with a disability as defined by the first part of the definition must have an actual impairment. If the person does not have an impairment, (s)he does not meet the requirements of the first part of the definition of disability. Under the second and third parts of the definition, the person must have a record of a substantially limiting impairment or be regarded as having a substantially limiting impairment.[5]

A person has a disability only if his/her limitations are, were, or are regarded as being the result of an impairment. It is essential, therefore, to distinguish between conditions that are impairments and those that are not impairments. Not everything that restricts a person's major life activities is an impairment. For example, a person may be having financial problems that significantly restrict what that person does in life. Financial problems or other economic disadvantages, however, are not impairments under the ADA. Accordingly, the person in that situation does not have a "disability" as that term is defined by the ADA. On the other hand, an individual may be unable to cope with everyday stress because (s)he has bipolar disorder. Bipolar disorder is an impairment. In that situation, the analysis proceeds to whether the individual's impairment substantially limits a major life activity.

---

[5]This section frequently refers to the term "impairment" in the present tense. These references are not meant to imply that the determination of whether a condition is an impairment is relevant only to whether an individual meets the first part of the definition of "disability," i.e., actually has a physical or mental impairment that substantially limits a major life activity. This determination also is relevant to whether an individual has a record of such an impairment or is regarded as having such an impairment.

The determination of whether a condition constitutes an impairment should be made without regard to mitigating measures. _See_ § 902.5, _infra_.

(b) Regulatory Definition -- A physical or mental impairment means

(1) [a]ny physiological disorder, or condition, cosmetic disfigurement, or anatomical loss affecting one or more of the following body systems: neurological, musculoskeletal, special sense organs, respiratory (including speech organs), cardiovascular, reproductive, digestive, genito-urinary, hemic and lymphatic, skin, and endocrine; or

(2) [a]ny mental or psychological disorder, such as mental retardation, organic brain syndrome, emotional or mental illness, and specific learning disabilities.

29 C.F.R. § 1630.2(h); see also S. Rep. No. 116, 101st Cong., 1st Sess. 22 (1989) [hereinafter Senate Report]; H.R. Rep. No. 485 pt. 2, 101st Cong., 2d Sess. 51 (1990) [hereinafter House Education and Labor Report]; H.R. Rep. No. 485 pt. 3, 101st Cong., 2d Sess. 28 (1990) [hereinafter House Judiciary Report].

This regulatory definition does not set forth an exclusive list of specific impairments covered by the ADA. Instead, the definition describes the type of condition that constitutes an impairment.

The first step in investigating whether a charging party has a disability is investigating whether (s)he has an impairment, has a record of an impairment, or is regarded as having an impairment. In many cases, it is obvious that a condition is an impairment. In other cases, however, it is not obvious. When it is unclear whether a charging party has an impairment, the investigator should ask the charging party for medical documentation that describes his/her condition. Medical documentation that describes the charging party's condition or that contains a diagnosis of the condition will help to determine if the charging party has an impairment.[6] In addition, the investigator

---

[6]A diagnosis is relevant to determining whether a charging party has an impairment. It is important to remember, however, that a diagnosis may be insufficient to determine if the charging party has a disability. An impairment rises to the level of a disability when it substantially limits one or more major life activities. The investigator, therefore, also should obtain available medical or other documentation that describes the extent to which the impairment limits the charging party's major life activities. See §§ 902.3, 902.4, infra.

should ask the respondent to provide copies of relevant medical documentation concerning the charging party's condition that the respondent has in his/her possession. Such documentation should include the results of any medical examination conducted or ordered by the respondent as well as copies of medical documentation that the charging party provided to the respondent. If the investigator requests the information directly from a third party, rather than from the charging party or the respondent, then the investigator first should obtain a signed medical release from the charging party and should submit the release with the request. Other information, such as the charging party's description of his/her condition or statements from the charging party's friends, family, or co-workers, also may be relevant to determining whether the charging party has an impairment.

(c) Conditions That Are Not Impairments

(1) Statutory and Legislative History Exceptions -- The statute and the legislative history specifically state that certain conditions are not impairments under the ADA.[7] The term "impairment" does not include homosexuality and bisexuality. 42 U.S.C. § 12211(a); see also 29 C.F.R. § 1630.3(e); H.R. Rep. No. 596, 101st Cong., 2d Sess. 88 (1990) [hereinafter Conference Report]; House Education and Labor Report at 142; House Judiciary Report at 75. Further, environmental, cultural, and economic disadvantages such as a prison record or a lack of education are not impairments. Senate Report at 22; House Education and Labor Report at 51-52; House Judiciary Report at 28. In addition, age, by itself, is not an impairment. See Senate Report at 22; House Education and Labor Report at 52; House Judiciary Report at 28. A person who has a medical condition (such as hearing loss, osteoporosis[8], or arthritis) often associated with age has an impairment on the basis of the medical condition. A person does not have an impairment, however, simply because (s)he is advanced in years. 29 C.F.R. pt. 1630 app. § 1630.2(h).

Example 1 -- CP has been unemployed for two years. Although she has actively sought work, CP has not been able to find a job. CP asserts that employers will not hire her because she is a convicted felon who served three years in prison for

[7]The statute also specifies that certain conditions, even though they may be impairments, are not disabilities covered by the ADA. See § 902.6, infra.

[8]Osteoporosis is a "[r]eduction in the quantity of bone or atrophy of skeletal tissue." Stedman's Medical Dictionary 1110 (25th ed. 1990).

armed robbery. CP argues that her prison record is a disability because it prevents her from getting a job. CP, however, does not have a disability because she does not have a physical or mental impairment as defined by the ADA. A prison record is not an impairment for ADA purposes.

Example 2 -- CP applies for a job as a cashier at his neighborhood supermarket. The store manager speaks with CP briefly and then asks CP to fill out a written job application form. CP does not complete the form because he cannot read it. CP, who has the equivalent of a second-grade education, was never taught to read. CP does not have a physical or mental impairment as defined by the ADA. A lack of education is not an impairment for ADA purposes.

Example 3 -- Same as Example 2, above, except CP cannot read because he has a severe form of dyslexia. CP has an impairment as defined by the ADA. Dyslexia, a learning disability, is an impairment for ADA purposes.

Example 4 -- CP, who is sixty-three, has osteoporosis. The osteoporosis, a reduction in bone quantity, is an impairment as defined by the ADA. CP's age, sixty-three, is not a physical or mental impairment as defined by the ADA.

(2) Physical Characteristics -- Simple physical characteristics are not impairments under the ADA. For example, a person cannot claim to be impaired because of blue eyes or black hair. Senate Report at 22; House Education and Labor Report at 51; House Judiciary Report at 28. Similarly, a person does not have an impairment simply because (s)he is left-

handed. de la Torres v. Bolger, 781 F.2d 1134, 39 EPD ¶ 35,883, 1 AD Cas. (BNA) 852 (5th Cir. 1986).[9]

Further, a characteristic predisposition to illness or disease is not an impairment. 29 C.F.R. pt. 1630 app. § 1630.2(h). A person may be predisposed to developing an illness or a disease because of factors such as environmental, economic, cultural, or social conditions. This predisposition does not amount to an impairment.

(3) Pregnancy -- Because pregnancy is not the result of a physiological disorder, it is not an impairment. 29 C.F.R. pt. 1630 app. § 1630.2(h); see also Byerly v. Herr Foods, Inc., 61 EPD ¶ 42,226, 2 AD Cas. (BNA) 666 (E.D. Pa. 1993). Complications resulting from pregnancy, however, are impairments.[10]

> Example 1 -- CP is in the third trimester of her pregnancy. Her pregnancy has proceeded well, and she has developed no complications. CP does not have an impairment. Pregnancy, by itself, is not an impairment.
>
> Example 2 -- Same as Example 1, above, except CP has developed hypertension. CP has an impairment, hypertension. (Remember that the mere presence of an impairment does not automatically mean that CP has a disability. Whether the hypertension rises to the level of a disability will turn on whether the

---

[9]The ADA definition of "disability" is similar to the definition of "individual with a disability" that has been applied to Title V of the Rehabilitation Act of 1973, 29 U.S.C. § 706(8)(B), (C) (Supp. IV 1992). See Senate Report at 21; House Education and Labor Report at 50; House Judiciary Report at 27. Since both Acts use the same three-part definition, this manual section draws on case law applying the Rehabilitation Act where appropriate.

[10]Although other statutes may use the term "disability" when referring to pregnancy, pregnancy is not a "disability" for purposes of the ADA. Note, however, that allegations of employment discrimination based on pregnancy are covered by Title VII of the Civil Rights Act of 1964, 42 U.S.C. § 2000e. The appropriate analysis for assessing a charge of pregnancy-based employment discrimination is discussed in a separate Compliance Manual section. See § 626, supra.

impairment substantially limits, or is regarded as substantially limiting, a major life activity.)

(4) Common Personality Traits -- Like physical characteristics, common personality traits also are not impairments. In Daley v. Koch, 892 F.2d 212, 214, 52 EPD ¶ 39,534 at 60,471, 1 AD Cas. (BNA) 1549, 1550 (2d Cir. 1989), a psychological profile of an applicant for a police officer position determined that the applicant "showed 'poor judgment, irresponsible behavior and poor impulse control'" but did not have "any particular psychological disease or disorder." The court ruled that the applicant's personality traits did not constitute an impairment. 892 F.2d at 215, 52 EPD at 60,473, 1 AD Cas. at 1551.

Example 1 -- CP is a lawyer who is impatient with her co-workers and her boss. She often loses her temper, frequently shouts at her subordinates, and publicly questions her boss's directions. Her colleagues think that she is rude and arrogant, and they find it difficult to get along with her. CP does not have an impairment. Personality traits, such as impatience, a quick temper, and arrogance, in and of themselves are not impairments.

Example 2 -- Same as Example 1, above, except CP's behavior results from bipolar disorder. CP has an impairment, bipolar disorder.[11]

Example 3 -- CP is an account manager who is in charge of developing a major advertising campaign for his firm's biggest client. Although he used to be easygoing and relaxed in the office, CP has become very irritable at work. He has twice lost his temper

[11]Note, however, that CP's employer does not have to excuse CP's misconduct, even if the misconduct results from an impairment that rises to the level of a disability, if it does not excuse similar misconduct from its other employees. See 56 Fed. Reg. 35,733 (1990) (referring to revisions that "clarify that employers may hold all employees, disabled (including those disabled by alcoholism or drug addiction) and nondisabled, to the same performance and conduct standards").

with his assistant, and he recently engaged in a shouting match with one of his superiors. CP has consulted a psychiatrist, who diagnosed a recurrence of the post-traumatic stress disorder for which CP was treated several years ago. CP has an impairment. CP's post-traumatic stress disorder, a mental disorder, is a mental impairment.[12]

(5) Normal Deviations in Height, Weight, or Strength -- Similarly, normal deviations in height, weight, or strength that are not the result of a physiological disorder are not impairments.[13] 29 C.F.R. pt. 1630 app. § 1630.2(h); see also Jasany v. United States Postal Service, 755 F.2d 1244, 1249, 36 EPD ¶ 35,070 at 36,835, 1 AD Cas. (BNA) 706, 709 (6th Cir. 1985). At extremes, however, such deviations may constitute impairments. Further, some individuals may have underlying physical disorders that affect their height, weight, or strength.

(i) For example, a four foot, ten inch tall woman who was denied employment as an automotive production worker because the employer thought she was too small to do the work does not have an impairment. See American Motors Corp. v. Wisconsin Labor and Industry Review Commission, 119 Wis. 2d 706, 350 N.W.2d 120, 36 EPD ¶ 34,936, 1 AD Cas. (BNA) 611 (1984) (interpreting state law). The woman's height was below the

---

[12]As in Example 2, CP's employer does not have to excuse CP's misconduct, even if the misconduct results from an impairment that rises to the level of a disability, if it does not excuse similar misconduct from its other employees. See 56 Fed. Reg. 35,733 (1990) (referring to revisions that "clarify that employers may hold all employees, disabled (including those disabled by alcoholism or drug addiction) and nondisabled, to the same performance and conduct standards").

[13]Note, however, that persons who have normal deviations in height or weight may allege that height or weight standards violate Title VII of the Civil Rights Act of 1964, 42 U.S.C. § 2000e. See Dothard v. Rawlinson, 433 U.S. 321, 14 EPD ¶ 7,632 (1977) (minimum height/weight requirement for correctional counselor position had adverse impact on women and was not job related and consistent with business necessity); Gerdom v. Continental Airlines, 692 F.2d 602, 30 EPD ¶ 33,156 (9th Cir. 1982) (en banc), cert. dismissed, 460 U.S. 1074 (1983) (maximum weight standards that were applied to exclusively female position of flight hostess constituted disparate treatment based on sex where no such weight policy was applied to similar but exclusively male position of director of passenger service).

norm, but her small stature was not so extreme as to constitute an impairment and was not the result of a defect, disorder, or other physical abnormality. On the other hand, a four feet, five inches tall man with achondroplastic dwarfism[14] does have an impairment. See Dexler v. Tisch, 660 F. Supp. 1418, 1425, 43 EPD ¶ 37,280 at 48,207, 1 AD Cas. (BNA) 1086, 1092 (D. Conn. 1987). The man's stature was the result of an underlying disorder, achondroplastic dwarfism, which is an impairment.

(ii) Being overweight, in and of itself, generally is not an impairment. See 29 C.F.R. pt. 1630 app. § 1630.2(h) (noting that weight that is "within 'normal' range and not the result of a physiological disorder" is not an impairment); see also id. § 1630.2(j) (noting that, "except in rare circumstances, obesity is not considered a disabling impairment"). Thus, for example, a flight attendant who, because of avid body building (which resulted in a low percentage of body fat and a high percentage of muscle), exceeds the airline's weight guidelines does not have an impairment. See Tudyman v. United Airlines, 608 F. Supp. 739, 746, 38 EPD ¶ 35,674 at 40,015, 1 AD Cas. (BNA) 664, 669 (C.D. Cal. 1984). Similarly, a mildly overweight flight attendant who has not been clinically diagnosed as having any medical anomaly does not have an impairment. Underwood v. Trans World Airlines, 710 F. Supp. 78, 83-84, 51 EPD ¶ 39,297 at 59,106-07 (S.D.N.Y. 1989) (plaintiff's state action preempted by federal law where plaintiff failed to establish that being mildly overweight brought her within class protected by state human rights law with broad definition of disability).

On the other hand, severe obesity,[15] which has been defined as body weight more than 100% over the norm, see The Merck Manual of Diagnosis and Therapy 981 (Robert Berkow ed., 16th ed. 1992), is clearly an impairment. See Cook v. Rhode Island Dep't of Mental Health, Retardation and Hosp., 10 F.3d 17, 63 EPD ¶ 42,673, 2 AD Cas. (BNA) 1476 (1st Cir. 1993). In addition, a person with obesity may have an underlying or resultant physiological disorder,

---

[14] "Achondroplastic dwarfism is a growth disorder that affects all four extremities and results in short limbs and short stature." Dexler v. Tisch, 660 F. Supp. 1418, 1419, 43 EPD ¶ 37,280 at 48,202, 1 AD Cas. (BNA) at 1086 (D. Conn. 1987).

[15] Investigators should be aware that medical experts sometimes use the term "morbid obesity" or "gross obesity" to mean the same thing as "severe obesity," i.e., body weight more than 100% over the norm.

The term "obesity" has been defined as "[t]he excessive accumulation of body fat. Except for heavily muscled persons, a body weight 20% over that in standard height-weight tables is arbitrarily considered obesity." The Merck Manual of Diagnosis and Therapy 981 (Robert Berkow ed., 16th ed. 1992).

such as hypertension or a thyroid disorder. A physiological disorder is an impairment. See 29 C.F.R. § 1630.2(h).[16]

(6) Persons with One of These Conditions and an Impairment -- A person who has one or more of these characteristics or traits also may have other conditions that are physical or mental impairments. See Senate Report at 22; House Education and Labor Report at 52; House Judiciary Report at 28. Thus, a left-handed individual who has a heart condition has an impairment. Although left-handedness is not an impairment, heart disease is an impairment.

(d) Contagion -- A contagious disease is an impairment.[17] The contagious nature of the disease does not, by itself, remove that condition from the protection of the ADA. In School Bd. of Nassau County v. Arline, 480 U.S. 273, 42 EPD ¶ 36,791, 1 AD Cas. (BNA) 1026 (1987), the United States Supreme Court considered the case of an elementary school teacher who had been discharged because she had experienced a recurrence of tuberculosis. The Supreme Court found that the tuberculosis, which had affected the teacher's respiratory system, constituted an impairment. 480 U.S. at 281, 42 EPD at 45,635, 1 AD Cas. at 1029. In so doing, the Court rejected the argument that the contagious effects of a condition (i.e., the effects of the condition on others) could be distinguished from the effects of the condition on the carrier. 480 U.S. at 282, 42 EPD at 45,636, 1 AD Cas. at 1029-30.

The legislative history to the ADA expressly provides that infection with the Human Immunodeficiency Virus (HIV) is an impairment under the Act. Senate Report at 22; House Education and Labor Report at 51; House Judiciary Report at 28. Thus, for the

---

[16]The mere presence of an impairment does not automatically mean that an individual has a disability. Whether severe obesity rises to the level of a disability will turn on whether the obesity substantially limits, has substantially limited, or is regarded as substantially limiting, a major life activity. "[E]xcept in rare circumstances, obesity is not considered a disabling impairment." 29 C.F.R. pt. 1630 app. § 1630.2(j).

[17]The fact that a contagious disease is an impairment does not automatically mean that it is a disability. To be a disability, an impairment must substantially limit (or have substantially limited or be regarded as substantially limiting) one or more major life activities. See 29 U.S.C. § 12102(2); see also 29 C.F.R. § 1630.2(g).

purposes of the ADA, an individual with HIV infection has an impairment.[18]

(e) Voluntariness -- Voluntariness is irrelevant when determining whether a condition constitutes an impairment. For example, an individual who develops lung cancer as a result of smoking has an impairment, notwithstanding the fact that some apparently volitional act of the individual may have caused the impairment. The cause of a condition has no effect on whether that condition is an impairment. See House Judiciary Report at 29 (noting that "[t]he cause of a disability is always irrelevant to the determination of disability"); see also Cook v. Rhode Island Dep't of Mental Health, Retardation and Hosp., 10 F.3d 17, 63 EPD ¶ 42,673, 2 AD Cas. (BNA) 1476 (1st Cir. 1993). Further, the voluntary use of a prosthetic device or other mitigating measure to correct or to lessen the effects of a condition also has no bearing on whether that condition is an impairment. See § 902.5, infra.

902.3 Major Life Activities

(a) General -- For an impairment to rise to the level of a disability, it must substantially limit, have previously substantially limited, or be perceived as substantially limiting, one or more of a person's major life activities. There has been little controversy about what constitutes a major life activity. In most cases, courts have simply stated that an impaired activity is a major life activity. In general, major life activities "are those basic activities that the average person in the general population can perform with little or no difficulty." 29 C.F.R. pt. 1630 app. § 1630.2(i).

(b) Regulatory Definition -- Commission regulations define the term "major life activities" to mean "functions such as caring for oneself, performing manual tasks, walking, seeing, hearing, speaking, breathing, learning, and working." 29 C.F.R. § 1630.2(i); see also Senate Report at 22; House Education and Labor Report at 52; House Judiciary Report at 28.

---

[18]An individual who has HIV infection, including asymptomatic HIV infection, has a disability covered under the ADA. See § 902.4(c)(1), infra; see also Doe v. Kohn Nast & Graf, 862 F. Supp. 1310, 1321, 3 AD Cas. (BNA) 879, 885 (E.D. Pa. 1994); Doe v. District of Columbia, 796 F. Supp. 559, 59 EPD ¶ 41,656, 2 AD Cas. (BNA) 197 (D.D.C. 1992); Senate Report at 22; House Education and Labor Report at 52; House Judiciary Report at 28 n.18; Memorandum from Douglas W. Kmiec, Acting Assistant Attorney General, to Arthur B. Culvahouse, Jr., Counsel to President Reagan, 8 Fair Empl. Prac. Manual (BNA) No. 641, at 405:1 (Sept. 27, 1988); Federal Contract Compliance Manual App. 6D, 8 Fair Empl. Prac. Manual (BNA) No. 694, at 405:352 (Dec. 23, 1988).

This list is not an exhaustive list of all major life activities. Instead, it is representative of the types of activities that are major life activities. Specific activities that are similar to the listed activities in terms of their impact on an individual's functioning, as compared to the average person, also may be major life activities. Thus, as the interpretive appendix to the regulations notes, "other major life activities include, but are not limited to, sitting, standing, lifting, [and] reaching." 29 C.F.R. pt. 1630 app. § 1630.2(i). Mental and emotional processes such as thinking, concentrating, and interacting with others are other examples of major life activities.[19]

(c) Judicial Interpretations -- Courts interpreting the Rehabilitation Act of 1973 also have found that other activities constitute major life activities. Such major life activities include sitting and standing, Oesterling v. Walters, 760 F.2d 859, 861, 36 EPD ¶ 35,201 at 37,485, 1 AD Cas. (BNA) 722, 723 (8th Cir. 1985); and reading, Pridemore v. Rural Legal Aid Society, 625 F. Supp. 1180, 1183-84, 40 EPD ¶ 36,184 at 42,659, 2 AD Cas. (BNA) 382, 384 (S.D. Ohio 1985) (mild cerebral palsy affected, but did not substantially limit, plaintiff's ability to read); see also DiPompo v. West Point Military Academy, 708 F. Supp. 540, 549, 50 EPD ¶ 39,182 at 58,435 (S.D.N.Y. 1989).

902.4 Substantially Limits

(a) General -- Unlike the term "major life activities," the term "substantially limits" frequently requires extensive analysis. The term "substantially limits" is a comparative term that implies a degree of severity and duration. The primary focus here is on the extent to which an impairment restricts one or more of an individual's major life activities. A secondary factor that may affect the analysis is the duration of the impairment.[20]

---

[19]Note, however, that an individual is not substantially limited in a major life activity unless (s)he is unable to perform the activity or is significantly restricted in performing the activity as compared to the average person in the general population. See 29 C.F.R. § 1630.2(j); see also § 902.4, infra.

[20]This section frequently refers to the term "substantially limits" in the present tense. These references are not meant to imply that the determination of whether an impairment is substantially limiting is relevant only to whether an individual meets the first part of the definition of "disability," i.e., actually has a physical or mental impairment that substantially limits a major life activity. This determination also is relevant to whether an individual has a record of such an impairment or is regarded as having such an impairment.

(continued...)

When analyzing the degree of limitation, one must remember that the determination of whether an impairment substantially limits a major life activity can be made only with reference to a specific individual. The issue is whether an impairment substantially limits any of the major life activities of the person in question, not whether the impairment is substantially limiting in general. Thus, one must consider the extent to which an impairment restricts a specific individual's activities and the duration of that individual's impairment.

(b) Regulatory Definition -- Commission regulations define the term "substantially limits" and outline factors to consider when determining whether an impairment substantially limits any of an individual's major life activities. In that respect, the regulations state,

> (1) The term "substantially limits" means:
>
> (i) Unable to perform a major life activity that the average person in the general population can perform; or
>
> (ii) Significantly restricted as to the condition, manner or duration under which an individual can perform a particular major life activity as compared to the condition, manner, or duration under which the average person in the general population can perform that same major life activity.
>
> (2) The following factors should be considered in determining whether an individual is substantially limited in a major life activity:
>
> (i) The nature and severity of the impairment;
>
> (ii) The duration or expected duration of the impairment; and
>
> (iii) The permanent or long term impact, or the expected permanent or long term impact of or resulting from the impairment.

29 C.F.R. § 1630.2(j).

---

[20](...continued)
The determination of whether an impairment is substantially limiting should be made without regard to mitigating measures. See § 902.5, infra.

As the regulations make clear, a determination of whether an impairment substantially limits any of an individual's major life activities depends upon the extent, duration, and impact of the impairment. The factors to consider when making this determination will be discussed in more detail below.

(c) Extent to Which an Impairment Restricts a Major Life Activity -- An impairment is substantially limiting when it prevents an individual from performing a major life activity or when it significantly restricts the condition, manner, or duration under which an individual can perform a major life activity. 29 C.F.R. § 1630.2(j). The individual's ability to perform the major life activity must be restricted as compared to the ability of the average person in the general population to perform the activity. *Id.* The reference to the "average person" does not "imply a precise mathematical 'average.'" 29 C.F.R. pt. 1630 app. § 1630.2(j).

> Example 1 -- CP has a permanent knee impairment that causes him pain when he walks for extended periods. He can walk for ten miles at a time without discomfort, but he experiences pain on the eleventh mile. CP's knee impairment does not substantially limit his ability to walk. The average person in the general population would not be able to walk for eleven miles without experiencing some discomfort.
>
> Example 2 -- CP, who has sickle cell anemia, frequently experiences severe back and joint pain. As a result of the sickle cell disease, CP often cannot walk for more than very short distances. CP's impairment (sickle cell anemia) substantially limits his ability to walk. The average person in the general population can walk for more than very short distances. (Note that allegations of employment discrimination based on sickle cell anemia also may be covered by Title VII of the Civil Rights Act of 1964, 42 U.S.C. § 2000e. *See* EEOC Dec. No. 81-8, 1983 EEOC Decisions (CCH) ¶ 6764 (Nov. 18, 1980).)

Further, the limitation must be substantial, rather than minor. Not every impairment affects an individual's life to the extent that it is a substantially limiting impairment. A minor impairment, such as an infected finger, is not a disability. Senate Report at 23; House Education and Labor Report at 52.

Most of the discussion and analysis of the concept of substantial limitation has focused on its meaning as applied to the major life activity of working. This is largely because there has been little dispute about what is meant by such terms as "breathing," "walking," "hearing," or "seeing" but much dispute about what is meant by the term "working." Consequently, the determination of whether a person's impairment is substantially limiting should first address major life activities other than working. If it is clear that a person's impairment substantially limits a major life activity other than working, then one need not determine whether the impairment substantially limits the person's ability to work. See 29 C.F.R. pt. 1630 app. § 1630.2(j). On the other hand, if an impairment does not substantially limit any of the other major life activities, then one must determine whether the person is substantially limited in working. See id.

For example, if an individual's arthritis makes it unusually difficult (as compared to most people or to the average person in the general population) to walk, then the individual is substantially limited in the ability to walk. In that case, one would not need to ascertain whether the individual is also substantially limited in working. If, however, it was not clear whether the person's impairment substantially limited his/her ability to walk (or to perform other major life activities), then one would have to analyze whether the impairment substantially limited the person's ability to work.

(1) Substantial Limitation of Major Life Activities Generally -- In most cases, a careful, case-by-case analysis is necessary to determine whether an impairment substantially limits any of a person's major life activities. This analysis focuses on the individual in question and analyzes whether the individual's impairment is substantially limiting for that individual.

The key here is the extent to which the impairment restricts a major life activity. If there is no showing that the impairment significantly restricts a major life activity, then the impairment is not a disability. Thus, an individual who alleged that he had asthma but did not even assert that the asthma substantially limited a major life activity did not establish that he was an individual with a disability. Harris v. Adams, 873 F.2d 929, 933, 50 EPD ¶ 38,973 at 57,217, 1 AD Cas. (BNA) 1475, 1477 (6th Cir. 1989). Similarly, an employee failed to establish that he was an individual with a disability when he presented no credible evidence to establish that his sinusitis and hypertension substantially limited major life activities. Thomas v. General Services Administration, 49 Fair Empl. Prac. Cas. (BNA) 1602, 1607, 51 EPD ¶ 39,221 at 58,685 (D.D.C. 1989).

The investigator, therefore, should conduct a careful analysis of whether a charging party's impairment substantially limits one or more major life activities. The investigator should conduct this analysis even if the charging party does not make a specific allegation that his/her impairment is substantially limiting. (For guidance on how to conduct this analysis, refer to the suggestions for investigators at the end of this subsection, infra.)

> Example -- CP alleges that her employer discriminated against her on the basis of disability. She defines her disability as a "knee injury." When the investigator asks how the injury affects her, CP responds, "I don't know." She provides no information in response to the investigator's inquiries about the extent to which the injury restricts her ability to walk or to perform any other activities. There is no showing that the knee injury limits CP in any way. As a result, there is no evidence that CP's knee injury substantially limits one or more of her major life activities.

To rise to the level of a disability, an impairment must significantly restrict an individual's major life activities. Impairments that result in only mild limitations are not disabilities. Thus, a mild case of varicose veins that moderately affect an individual's ability to stand and to sit is not a disability. Oesterling v. Walters, 760 F.2d 859, 861, 36 EPD ¶ 35,201 at 37,485, 1 AD Cas. (BNA) 722, 723-24 (8th Cir. 1985). Similarly, a "borderline" case of cerebral palsy that only slightly interferes with an individual's ability to read (because of poor control over ocular muscles) and to speak also is not a disability. Pridemore v. Rural Legal Aid Society, 625 F. Supp. 1180, 1183-84, 40 EPD ¶ 36,184 at 42,659, 2 AD Cas. (BNA) 382, 384 (S.D. Ohio 1985). In both instances, impairments may affect major life activities, but they do not substantially restrict those activities.

One of the reasons an individualized approach is necessary is because the same types of impairments often vary in severity and often restrict different people to different degrees or in different ways.

> The determination of whether an individual has a disability is not necessarily based on the name or diagnosis of the impairment the person has, but rather on the effect of that impairment on the life of the individual. Some impairments may be disabling for

> particular individuals but not for others, depending on the stage of the disease or disorder, the presence of other impairments that combine to make the impairment disabling or any number of other factors.

29 C.F.R. pt. 1630 app. § 1630.2(j). For example, the plaintiff in Perez v. Philadelphia Housing Authority, 677 F. Supp. 357, 1 AD Cas. (BNA) 1170 (E.D. Pa. 1987), aff'd, 841 F.2d 1120, 2 AD Cas. (BNA) 1104 (3d Cir. 1988), sustained a back injury that resulted in considerable pain. The evidence indicated that the plaintiff's back pain restricted "her ability to walk, sit, stand, drive, care for her home and child, and engage in leisure pastimes." 677 F. Supp. at 360, 1 AD Cas. at 1173. As a result, the court found that the plaintiff was an individual with a disability. 677 F. Supp. at 360-61, 1 AD Cas. at 1173. In another case, however, a court determined that a general laborer who had sustained a back injury was not an individual with a disability. Fuqua v. Unisys Corp., 716 F. Supp. 1201 (D. Minn. 1989) (applying state law similar to Rehabilitation Act). The plaintiff in that case had been able to continue an active life that included weight lifting and other recreational activities. Id. at 1203. In addition, he had obtained alternative employment as a security guard and had not been significantly restricted in employment. Id. Accordingly, the court found that the plaintiff's back injury did not rise to the level of a disability. Id. at 1206.

> Example 1 -- CP has a mild form of Type II, non-insulin-dependent diabetes. She does not need to take insulin or other medication, and her physician has placed no significant restrictions on her activities. Instead, her physician simply has advised CP to maintain a well balanced diet and to reduce her consumption of foods that are high in sugar or starch. Although diabetes often substantially limits an individual's major life activities, CP's diabetes does not substantially limit any of her major life activities. It has only a moderate effect on what she eats, and it does not restrict her in any other way.

> Example 2 -- Same as Example 1, above, except CP's condition requires CP to follow a strict regimen. She must adhere to a stringent diet, eat meals on a regular schedule, and ensure a proper balance between her caloric

> intake and her level of physical activity. A change of routine, such as a high-calorie meal or unexpected strenuous exercise, could result in blood-sugar levels that are dangerously high or low. CP's condition significantly restricts how she functions in her day-to-day life. CP, therefore, has an impairment (diabetes) that substantially limits one or more of her major life activities.

In very rare instances, impairments are so severe that there is no doubt that they substantially limit major life activities. In those cases, it is undisputed that the complainant is an individual with a disability. Thus, courts accepted without discussion that a person was an individual with a disability when the impairment was insulin-dependent diabetes, Bentivegna v. United States Department of Labor, 694 F.2d 619, 621, 30 EPD ¶ 33,211 at 27,791, 1 AD Cas. (BNA) 403, 405 (9th Cir. 1982); legal blindness, Norcross v. Sneed, 755 F.2d 113, 36 EPD ¶ 35,006, 1 AD Cas. (BNA) 689 (8th Cir. 1985); deafness, Davis v. Frank, 711 F. Supp. 447, 453, 50 EPD ¶ 39,157 at 58,339 (N.D. Ill. 1989), manic depressive syndrome, Gardner v. Morris, 752 F.2d 1271, 35 EPD ¶ 34,906, 1 AD Cas. (BNA) 673 (8th Cir. 1985), and alcoholism, Whitlock v. Donovan, 598 F. Supp. 126, 129, 35 EPD ¶ 34,815 at 35,533, 1 AD Cas. (BNA) 630, 632 (D.D.C. 1984), aff'd sub nom. Whitlock v. Brock, 790 F.2d 964, 1 AD Cas. (BNA) 1050 (D.C. Cir. 1986). Further, according to the legislative history, an individual who has HIV infection (including asymptomatic HIV infection) is an individual with a disability. Senate Report at 22; House Education and Labor Report at 52; House Judiciary Report at 28 n.18; see also Doe v. Kohn Nast & Graf, 862 F. Supp. 1310, 1321, 3 AD Cas. (BNA) 879, 885 (E.D. Pa. 1994); Doe v. District of Columbia, 796 F. Supp. 559, 59 EPD ¶ 41,656, 2 AD Cas. (BNA) 197 (D.D.C. 1992); Memorandum from Douglas W. Kmiec, Acting Assistant Attorney General, to Arthur B. Culvahouse, Jr., Counsel to President Reagan, 8 Fair Empl. Prac. Manual (BNA) No. 641, at 405:1 (Sept. 27, 1988); Federal Contract Compliance Manual App. 6D, 8 Fair Empl. Prac. Manual (BNA) No. 694, at 405:352 (Dec. 23, 1988).

Just as medical documentation submitted by a charging party is relevant to determining whether the charging party has an impairment, see supra § 902.2(b), it also is a good starting point for determining the extent to which a physical or mental impairment limits any of the charging party's major life activities. Such documentation often describes the restrictions that the impairment places on the charging party. For example, the documentation may state that the charging party cannot lift objects weighing more than a few pounds, cannot walk unassisted, or cannot hear at all. On the other hand, the documentation may state that the charging party's impairment results in only minimal limitations. The investigator should ask the charging party for copies of medical statements that describe the charging party's restrictions. In addition, the investigator should ask the respondent for copies of relevant medical documentation in the respondent's possession. Such documentation may include medical information that accompanied a request for light or limited duty as well as information obtained through fitness-for-duty examinations conducted or ordered by the respondent. If the investigator requests the information directly from a third party, rather than from the charging party or the respondent, then the investigator should obtain a signed medical release from the charging party and should submit the release with the request.

Although medical documentation can provide important information about the restrictions that an impairment places on an individual, the investigator should not rely solely on this information. The investigator should obtain other available relevant information that describes the restrictions resulting from the impairment. In this regard, it is essential that the investigator obtain a statement in which the charging party describes the nature of his/her condition and explains how the condition limits his/her performance of major life activities. In addition, the investigator should obtain statements from other persons who have direct knowledge of the individual's restrictions. For example, persons such as friends and family members, supervisors, rehabilitation counselors, and occupational or physical therapists may be able to describe the restrictions that the individual's impairment places on the individual. Further, the investigator's own observations of the charging party may supply or confirm information about the charging party's restrictions.

The information that the investigator obtains should be specific. For example, it is insufficient for the charging party merely to state that his/her condition interferes with the ability to walk. The charging party should explain the extent of the interference; that is, the charging party should provide such information as whether the condition prevents him/her from walking at all, whether (s)he can walk under certain conditions, and whether (s)he can walk for short or long distances and periods.

(2) Substantial Limitation of Major Life Activity of Working -- As noted previously, supra, one need not determine whether an impairment substantially limits an individual's ability to work if the impairment substantially limits another major life activity. If the individual is not substantially limited with respect to any other major life activity, then one should consider whether the individual is substantially limited in working.

The Commission has provided regulatory guidance for determining whether an impairment substantially limits an individual in the major life activity of working. The regulation states,

> (3) With respect to the major life activity of working--
>
> (i) The term substantially limits means significantly restricted in the ability to perform either a class of jobs or a broad range of jobs in various classes as compared to the average person having comparable training, skills and abilities. The inability to perform a single, particular job does not constitute a substantial limitation in the major life activity of working.
>
> (ii) In addition to the factors listed in paragraph (j)(2) of this section, the following factors may be considered in determining whether an individual is substantially limited in the major life activity of "working":
>
> (A) The geographical area to which the individual has reasonable access;
>
> (B) The job from which the individual has been disqualified because of an impairment, and the number and types of jobs utilizing similar training, knowledge, skills or abilities, within that geographical area, from which the individual is also disqualified because of the impairment (class of jobs); and/or
>
> (C) The job from which the individual has been disqualified because of an impairment, and the number and types of other jobs not utilizing similar training, knowledge, skills or abilities, within that geographical area, from which the individual is also disqualified because of the impairment (broad range of jobs in various classes).

29 C.F.R. § 1630.2(j)(3) (emphasis in the original).

As the regulation makes clear, an impairment that prevents an individual from working at one particular job, because of circumstances or materials unique to that job, does not substantially limit that individual's ability to work. See House Judiciary Report at 29. A person is not substantially limited in the ability to work simply because (s)he cannot perform one particular job for one particular employer. See E.E. Black, Ltd. v. Marshall, 497 F. Supp. 1088, 1099, 24 EPD ¶ 31,260 at 17,650, 1 AD Cas. (BNA) 220, 229 (D. Hawaii 1980). Rather, an individual is substantially limited in working if (s)he is prevented or significantly restricted (when compared to the average person having similar qualifications) from performing a class of jobs or a wide range of various jobs. See id.; see also 29 C.F.R. § 1630.2(j)(3).

In E.E. Black, an apprentice carpenter was denied employment after a preemployment physical examination disclosed a congenital back anomaly. The court held that the term "substantial limitation" means more than an inability to perform one particular job but less than a general inability to work. It suggested that the evaluation of whether an individual is substantially limited in working focus on such factors as the number and type of jobs from which the individual is disqualified and the geographical area to which the individual has reasonable access. 497 F. Supp. at 1099-1101, 24 EPD at 17,650-52, 1 AD Cas. at 229-30.

These criteria, when read together, indicate that an impairment is a substantial limitation to working if it disqualifies an individual from a class of jobs or a broad range of jobs in various classes. For example, a charging party is substantially limited in working if (s)he has a back impairment that precludes him/her from heavy lifting and, therefore, from the class of heavy labor jobs. See 497 F. Supp. at 1102, 24 EPD at 17,652, 1 AD Cas. at 231. Conversely, a postal clerk with a mild case of crossed eyes that caused him to develop eye strain and headaches after operating a particular machine that required detailed eye work was not substantially limited in working. Jasany v. United States Postal Service, 755 F.2d 1244, 1250, 36 EPD ¶ 35,070 at 36,835, 1 AD Cas. (BNA) 706, 710 (6th Cir. 1985). Unlike the charging party in the first example, this complainant did not have an impairment that precluded him from performing any other job or duty within a class of jobs. In fact, the parties agreed that his impairment had not affected his past work history or his ability to perform other duties at the post office. Id. The impairment had limited only his ability to perform this one particular job and perhaps a narrow range of like jobs. For the same reason, an individual whose vision impairment and high-tone hearing loss disqualified him from a position as a detention deputy but did not disqualify him from other positions (e.g., corrections officer) was not substantially limited in working. See State v. Hennepin County, 441 N.W.2d 106, 51 EPD ¶ 39,383, 1 AD Cas. (BNA) 1490 (Minn. 1989) (applying state law with same definition of "disability").

> Example 1 -- CP is a computer programmer. She develops a vision impairment that does not substantially limit her ability to see but does prevent her from distinguishing characters on computer screens (without reasonable accommodation). As a result, she cannot perform any work that

requires her to read characters on computer screens. Her vision impairment prevents her from working as a computer programmer, a systems analyst, a computer instructor, and a computer operator. CP is substantially limited in working because her impairment prevents her from working in the class of jobs requiring use of a computer.

Example 2 -- Same as Example 1, above, except CP's vision impairment does not interfere with her ability to distinguish characters on most computer screens. It does prevent her, however, from distinguishing characters on the peculiar type of computer screens that R uses. Although CP cannot work with the unique screens that R uses, she can work with other computer screens. CP, therefore, is not substantially limited in working. Her impairment prevents her from being a computer programmer for one particular employer (R), but it does not prevent her from performing similar jobs for other employers.

Impairments that preclude an individual from performing a broad range of jobs in various classes also may substantially limit the major life activity of working. For example, an individual could be substantially limited in working if (s)he has a severe allergy to a substance found in many high-rise office buildings. If the allergy prevents the individual from working in many of the high-rise office buildings in the geographical area to which the individual has reasonable access, then the individual is substantially limited in working. This is so because a great number of positions within many classes of jobs would be performed in those buildings. 29 C.F.R. pt. 1630 app. § 1630.2(j).

By contrast, a severe allergy to the peculiar type or amount of dust found within one office is not an impairment that substantially limits the ability to work. Wright v. Tisch, 45 Fair Empl. Prac. Cas. (BNA) 151, 1 AD Cas. (BNA) 1157 (E.D. Va. 1987). In Wright, the court determined that a complainant's inability to tolerate the dusty environment in the unit where she worked did not constitute a disability. 45 Fair Empl. Prac. Cas. at 152-53, 1 AD Cas. at 1158. The court noted that none of the complainant's other work activities was affected by her allergy. 45 Fair Empl. Prac. Cas. at 152, 1 AD Cas. at 1158. It also noted that the complainant's allergy did not restrict her from working in other offices with dust and that she had, in fact, worked in the presence of dust in other offices within the agency. Id.

> Example 1 -- CP has a hearing impairment that only mildly affects his ability to hear. The impairment, however, makes CP extremely sensitive to very loud noises. CP experiences severe pain when he is exposed to loud noises for more than a brief period. Because of this sensitivity, CP cannot work in environments where noise levels routinely exceed a certain decibel level. As a result, R refused to hire CP for a welder's position. Further, CP could not work in carpentry or auto repair shops and could not be a heavy equipment operator, a demolitions expert, or a member of an airport ground crew. CP's impairment, therefore, prevents CP from working in a broad range of jobs in various classes. Accordingly, CP has an impairment that substantially limits his ability to work.

> Example 2 -- CP has a hearing impairment that does not significantly restrict his ability to hear but does make him very sensitive to sound at one particular pitch. CP works on an assembly line at an automobile plant in an area that has several such plants. His employer has installed a new conveyor belt that has a unique whistle that sounds approximately every ten minutes, every time the conveyor belt stops and starts. CP experiences severe pain in his ears whenever the whistle sounds. As a result, CP can no longer work at that plant. CP's impairment, however, does not substantially limit his ability to work. Although the impairment prevents him from performing this particular job for this particular employer, it does not prevent him from performing similar jobs for other employers in his geographical area.

> <u>Example 3</u> -- CP has an impairment that requires radiation therapy, which results in an abnormal rate or degree of exhaustion. CP becomes very tired very easily and cannot engage in continuous activity for long periods. Assume that CP's impairment does not substantially limit her ability to perform any major life activity other than working. As a result of the impairment, however, CP cannot work more than four hours per day. This prevents CP from working in all jobs requiring full-time work. Since those jobs constitute a wide range of jobs in various classes, CP is substantially limited in working. (A reasonable accommodation of a part-time or modified work schedule might enable CP to work in a number of jobs from which she otherwise would be excluded. When determining whether an impairment is substantially limiting, however, one does not consider the ameliorative effects of reasonable accommodation or other mitigating measures. <u>See</u> § 902.5, <u>infra</u>.)

As the Commission's regulation notes, a number of factors may help to determine whether an individual is substantially limited in working. 29 C.F.R. § 1630.2(j)(3)(ii). Although a showing with respect to each factor is not a required element of proof, information relating to the factors is relevant to whether an individual is significantly restricted in the ability to perform a class of jobs or a broad range of jobs in various classes. Thus, information about the geographical area to which an individual has access and the number and types of jobs from which an individual is disqualified because of his/her impairment may be considered when determining whether an impairment substantially limits the individual's ability to work. <u>See id.</u>

The reference to the "number and types" of jobs is not meant to require an onerous evidentiary showing. 29 C.F.R. pt. 1630 app. § 1630.2(j). The reference does not mean that an individual must identify the exact number of jobs using similar or dissimilar skills in a certain geographic area. Further, the reference does not mean that an individual must count positions or otherwise present a precise number of jobs from which (s)he is disqualified because of an impairment. Instead, the reference to the "number and types" of jobs "only require[s] the presentation of evidence of general employment demographics and/or of recognized occupational classifications that indicate the approximate number of jobs (e.g., 'few,' 'many,' 'most') from which an individual would be excluded because of an impairment." Id. Furthermore, in cases where it is clear that an individual is excluded from a class of jobs or a broad range of jobs in various classes, only minimal evidence will be required.

An assessment of whether an impairment substantially limits an individual's ability to work focuses on whether the individual is significantly restricted in the ability to perform a class of jobs or a broad range of jobs in various classes as compared to the average person having comparable training, skills, and abilities. 29 C.F.R. § 1630.2(j)(3)(i). For example, suppose that an individual has an impairment that interferes with his/her ability to work in the class of clerical jobs. The individual is substantially limited in working if (s)he is significantly restricted in performing clerical work as compared to the average person having comparable clerical skills. Thus, if the individual has clerical skills and training and the impairment prevents him/her from performing many of the clerical jobs that the average person with comparable clerical skills can perform, then the individual is substantially limited in working. On the other hand, if the individual wants to work as a clerk but has no clerical skills or training, then (s)he is substantially limited in working only if the impairment significantly restricts his/her ability to work in the clerical class as compared to the ability of the average person with a similar lack of clerical skills. (It is likely in that case that the average person with a lack of clerical skills can perform only a limited number of clerical jobs and that the individual is not significantly restricted when compared to the average person.)

The investigator often can begin to obtain information relevant to a determination of whether the charging party's impairment significantly restricts his/her ability to perform either a class of jobs or a broad range of jobs in various classes from: a position description of the job at issue, the respondent's explanation of the requirements of the job, and the charging party's description of his/her qualifications and his/her experience in similar positions. This information, which helps to identify the skills relevant to the job, may be useful in identifying other jobs using similar or dissimilar skills. In addition, the investigator should attempt to determine the number and types of jobs in the geographical area from which the charging party is disqualified because of the impairment. Information about other jobs where the charging party has worked, or for which the charging party has or has not applied, may be relevant to this inquiry. For example, other employers may have refused to employ the charging party because of his/her impairment, or the charging party may not have applied for certain jobs because the impairment disqualified him/her from those jobs. Similarly, an employment agency or an employment counselor may have told the charging party that the impairment prevents him/her from working in certain jobs.

On the other hand, the fact that the charging party performed certain jobs successfully may indicate that the impairment -- if it existed at the time that the charging party performed those jobs -- does not disqualify him/her from that type of work.[21]

(d) Duration and Impact of Impairment -- One of the factors that may be relevant to whether an impairment is substantially limiting is the duration of the impairment. The length of time that an impairment affects major life activities may help to determine whether the impairment substantially limits those activities. As with all other matters, the determination must be made on a case-by-case basis. There are no set time limits for determining whether an impairment is of sufficient duration to be considered substantially limiting. There are, however, a few basic guidelines.

Generally, conditions that last for only a few days or weeks and have no permanent or long-term effects on an individual's health are not substantially limiting impairments. Examples of such transitory conditions are common colds, influenza, and most broken bones and sprains. The mere fact that an individual may have required absolute bed rest or hospitalization for such a condition does not alter the transitory nature of the condition. Even the necessity of surgery, without more, is not sufficient to raise a short-term condition to the level of a disability. Thus, for example, an employee who had an undisclosed temporary illness that required exploratory surgery but who was expected to recover completely in six to eight weeks did not have an impairment that substantially limited major life activities. Stevens v. Stubbs, 576 F. Supp. 1409, 1 AD Cas. (BNA) 546 (N.D. Ga. 1983). In that case, a temporary illness with no permanent effects on the individual's health was not a substantially limiting impairment. 576 F. Supp. at 1414, 1 AD Cas. at 549-50. Similarly, an employee who incurred a knee injury that required surgery was not an individual with a disability. Evans v. City of Dallas, 861 F.2d 846, 49 EPD ¶ 38,674, 1 AD Cas. (BNA) 1394 (5th Cir. 1988). Although the injury may have limited the employee's major life activities during his recuperation, it did not continue to do so after his recuperation. See 861 F.2d at 852-53, 49 EPD at 55,700, 1 AD Cas. at 1398-99 (quoting district court opinion). For the same reason, an attack of appendicitis accompanied by a "routine" appendectomy would not constitute a disability. The condition

[21]If the charging party does not have an impairment that substantially limits his or her ability to work (or to perform any other major life activity), then the investigator should determine whether the charging party has a record of such an impairment (see § 902.7, infra) or is regarded as having such an impairment (see § 902.8, infra). An individual who in fact does not have an impairment that substantially limits the major life activity of working nonetheless may be regarded as having such an impairment (see § 902.8(f), infra).

might restrict an individual's activities for a few days or weeks, but the restrictions would be only temporary.

> Example 1 -- CP has laryngitis. It is very painful for her to speak, and she cannot talk above a whisper when she does speak. Her physician has prescribed medication for her, has instructed her to drink plenty of fluids, and has advised her to stay home from work. She should be fully recovered within seven to ten days. CP does not have a disability. Although the laryngitis significantly restricts her ability to speak, it does so only on a very short-term basis and has no long-lasting or permanent effects on CP.

> Example 2 -- CP sustains a compound fracture of her arm and must undergo surgery to set the bone. She is hospitalized for one week and will have a cast on her arm for five additional weeks. During these six weeks, CP must wear a sling and must keep her arm immobilized. She will have full use of her arm after the cast is removed. CP's broken arm is not a disability. Instead, it is a short-term, temporary impairment with no long-lasting or permanent effects.

Although short-term, temporary restrictions generally are not substantially limiting, an impairment does not necessarily have to be permanent to rise to the level of a disability. Some conditions may be long-term, or potentially long-term, in that their duration is indefinite and unknowable or is expected to be at least several months. Such conditions, if severe, may constitute disabilities. Thus, a person who has been blinded or paralyzed but is expected to recover fully "eventually" is an individual with a disability, despite the prognosis for full recovery at some indeterminable time in the future.

> Example 1 -- CP has nodes on his vocal chords. His doctor has told CP that he must rest his vocal chords and that he will lose his ability to speak unless he refrains from talking for more than one hour per day for the next one-and-one-half years. If CP follows his

doctor's advice, his vocal chords will heal and he will have full use of his voice. CP, whose impairment will last for many months and will significantly restrict his ability to speak during that time, has a disability.

Example 2 -- CP recently was released from the hospital following a ten-month stay for treatment for a mood disorder. The disorder significantly restricted CP's ability to interact with people and to care for herself. She will require two months of daily treatment, on an out-patient basis, to ensure that she can deal with people on a day-to-day basis and then four to six months of less intensive out-patient treatment. Her doctor anticipates that CP will be fully recovered when she completes her treatment. CP has a disability. Although her impairment (a mood disorder) is not permanent, it is long lasting and has significantly restricted her major life activities for an extended period (at least ten months during her hospitalization and possibly for the two months of intensive out-patient treatment).

Example 3 -- CP recently was diagnosed as having Guillain-Barre syndrome, a neurological disorder of unknown origin. As a result of the condition, she cannot walk. Her doctor has told her that she must undergo extensive rehabilitation and that the rehabilitation period will last for several months. The doctor tells CP that there is a good chance that she will regain total use of her legs after she completes her rehabilitation. CP has a disability because she has an impairment (Guillain-Barre syndrome) that substantially limits her ability to walk. The impairment prevents CP from walking, and it will be at least several months before she will be able to walk again. Although CP is expected to recover at some point in the future, her restrictions are significant and long-lasting.

Example 4 -- CP fractured her left ankle as the result of a skiing accident. Immediately after the accident, she underwent surgery on her ankle. She was hospitalized for one week and has been using crutches for two weeks. Her physician has directed her to use crutches for another two weeks, after which time she should be able to walk unaided. Her prognosis for a full recovery is excellent. CP does not have an impairment that substantially limits her major life activities. Although her ankle injury has restricted her ability to walk, it has done so for only a relatively short time (five weeks). The injury is a transitory impairment that has no long-term effects on CP.

Example 5 -- Same as Example 4, above, except the surgery was not successful. Although CP can now walk unaided, she can do so only for three to five minutes without experiencing excruciating pain. Her physician predicts that CP's condition, which may improve at some point in the future, will remain like this indefinitely. CP has an ankle impairment that substantially limits her ability to walk. Most people can walk for three to five minutes without pain. Although the condition may not be permanent, it is long-term. CP is an individual with a disability.

Sometimes a temporary impairment that usually is not substantially limiting because it generally heals within a few weeks will take longer than the normal healing period to heal. In that case, the impairment may be substantially limiting if it goes on for a long period and significantly restricts the performance of a major life activity during that time. Thus, an impairment that takes significantly longer than the normal healing period to heal and prevents or significantly restricts the performance of a major life activity for an extended time during the healing process is a disability.

> Example -- CP sustains a broken leg. Although broken legs generally heal within a few months, CP's leg will require eleven months to heal. CP will be unable to walk without the use of crutches during the eleven-month healing period. CP, whose impairment will take significantly longer than the normal healing period to heal and will significantly restrict CP's ability to perform a major life activity (walking) during the healing period, has a disability.

In some cases, an impairment that appears to be temporary may have residual effects. That is, the impairment may have a long-term impact on an individual's ability to perform one or more major life activities. For example, a person may sustain an injury that heals but nonetheless leaves a permanent or long-term residual effect. Although a short-term impairment that does not have a long-lasting impact is not a disability, an impairment that results in a long-term, substantial limitation is a disability.

> Example 1 -- CP sustained a head injury in an automobile accident. He felt dizzy and disoriented immediately after the accident and was hospitalized overnight for observation. His doctor told him that x-rays revealed a slight concussion but no permanent injury. He was released from the hospital the next day, and he has experienced no side effects from the injury. CP's head injury was not substantially limiting. The impairment lasted for only a brief time and had no permanent or long-term impact on CP's major life activities. CP, therefore, does not have a disability.

> Example 2 -- Same as Example 1, above, except CP sustained a serious concussion that resulted in permanent brain damage. Because of this, CP has a short-term memory deficit, has trouble processing information, cannot concentrate, and

> has great difficulty learning. CP's concussion resulted in long-term, significant restrictions on his major life activities. CP, therefore, has a disability.

Further, some chronic conditions may constitute substantially limiting impairments. Such conditions may be substantially limiting when active or may have a high likelihood of recurrence in substantially limiting forms. In addition, such conditions may require a substantial limitation of a major life activity to prevent or to lessen the likelihood or severity of recurrence. Some severe back problems and most forms of heart disease and cancer fall into this category. This category also includes illnesses, such as tuberculosis, that may lay dormant for long periods but can reemerge at any time in a substantially limiting manner. Similarly, episodic disorders, such as bipolar disorder, which remit and then intensify also fall into this category.

Finally, the duration of an impairment does not, by itself, determine whether the impairment substantially limits an individual's major life activities. It is just one factor to be considered with all of the other relevant information. An impairment may be long lasting or permanent but still not constitute a substantial limitation to major life activities. For example, a permanently injured finger is not substantially limiting if it does not significantly restrict an individual's ability to perform a major life activity such as performing manual tasks or caring for oneself. Thus, when determining whether an impairment substantially limits a major life activity, one must consider the severity of the limitation caused by the impairment as well as the duration of the limitation. An impairment is substantially limiting if it lasts for more than several months and significantly restricts the performance of one or more major life activities during that time. It is not substantially limiting if it lasts for only a brief time or does not significantly restrict an individual's ability to perform a major life activity.

In sum, relatively brief and transitory illnesses or injuries that have no permanent or long-term effects on an individual's major life activities are not disabilities. Temporary impairments may be disabilities if they take significantly longer than normal to heal and significantly restrict the performance of major life activities during the healing period. Similarly, long-term impairments, or potentially long-term impairments of indefinite duration, may be disabilities if they are severe. Chronic conditions that are substantially limiting when active, and conditions with a high likelihood of recurrence in substantially limiting form, also are disabilities.

Because the duration of an impairment may be relevant to determining whether the impairment is a disability, the investigator should ask the charging party how long (s)he has had the impairment at issue. In addition, the investigator should obtain copies of any available medical documentation that indicates the length of time the charging party has had the impairment, describes the long-term effects of the impairment, or gives a prognosis for recovery.

(e) Multiple Impairments -- An individual may have two or more impairments that are not substantially limiting by themselves but that together substantially limit one or more major life activities. In that situation, the individual has a disability. "Multiple impairments that combine to substantially limit one or more of an individual's major life activities also constitute a disability." 29 C.F.R. pt. 1630 app. § 1630.2(j).

> Example -- CP has a mild form of arthritis in her wrists and hands and a mild form of osteoporosis (a reduction in bone quantity). Neither impairment, by itself, would significantly restrict any of CP's major life activities. Together, however, the two impairments affect CP's manual dexterity to such an extent that they significantly restrict her ability to perform manual tasks. Thus, the combination of the two impairments substantially limits one or more of CP's major life activities. CP, therefore, has a disability.

902.5 Mitigating Measures -- The determination of whether a condition constitutes an impairment must be made without regard to mitigating measures. 29 C.F.R. pt. 1630 app. § 1630.2(h). The availability of reasonable accommodation or auxiliary aids such as hearing aids to alleviate the effects of a condition has no bearing on whether the condition is an impairment. It is the scope or perceived scope of the condition itself, not its origin or capacity for being corrected, that determines whether a particular condition is an impairment.

Further, the extent to which the impairment limits the individual's major life activities should be assessed without regard to the availability of mitigating measures. 29 C.F.R. pt. 1630 app. § 1630.2(j); see also Senate Report at 23; House Education and Labor Report at 52; House Judiciary Report at 28. Thus, an individual who has experienced a significant loss of hearing is substantially limited in his/her ability to hear, even if the use of a hearing aid would improve the individual's level of hearing. House Education and Labor Report at 52; see also House Judiciary Report at 28-29. Similarly, individuals with impairments (such as epilepsy or diabetes) that substantially limit major life activities are individuals with disabilities, even if medication controls the effects of the impairments. House Education and Labor Report at 52; see also House Judiciary Report at 28-29. Accordingly, an individual who received dialysis treatments for polycystic kidney disease had a substantially limiting impairment, even though the disease was adequately treated through dialysis. Gilbert v. Frank, 949 F.2d 637, 641, 57 EPD ¶ 41,106 at 68,909, 2 AD Cas. (BNA) 60, 63 (2d Cir. 1991) ("We are inclined to view persons whose kidneys would cease to function without mechanical assistance, or whose kidneys do not function sufficiently to rid their bodies of waste matter without regular dialysis, as substantially limited in their ability to care for themselves.")

> Example 1 -- CP, who has schizophrenia, takes medication to control the disorder. With medication, CP can function well in his everyday life. Without medication, however, CP cannot care for himself. CP has an impairment, schizophrenia, that substantially limits his major life activities. Although CP can function well with medication, he cannot care for himself without medication.
>
> Example 2 -- CP has systemic lupus, which often results in acute anemia and arthritis-like symptoms. CP's physician has prescribed medication to control the effects of the disease. Without medication, CP is very lethargic, develops a skin rash, and experiences severe swelling and stiffness in her joints. With medication, CP experiences none of these symptoms. CP has a disability. Her impairment, when evaluated without regard to the effects of medication, substantially limits her major life activities.
>
> Example 3 -- CP's right leg was amputated below the knee. Using a prosthesis, he can walk for a long distance without discomfort. CP has an impairment that substantially limits his ability to walk, even though he can walk with the use of a prosthesis. CP is an individual with a disability.

Note, finally, that the mere use of a mitigating measure does not automatically indicate the presence of a disability. Some individuals may use medication, prosthetic devices, or auxiliary aids to alleviate impairments that are not substantially limiting. For example, an individual who uses a hearing aid to correct a slight hearing impairment may not have a disability under the first part of the definition of the term "disability." The individual's impairment may only mildly affect his/her hearing and may not substantially limit the individual's ability to hear.

902.6 Statutory Exceptions to the Definition of "Disability" -- The statute specifies that certain conditions are not disabilities covered by the ADA. Since homosexuality and bisexuality are not impairments, those conditions are not disabilities. 42 U.S.C. § 12211(a); see also 29 C.F.R. § 1630.3(e). In addition, "the term 'individual with a disability' does not include an individual who is currently engaging in the illegal use of drugs, when the covered entity acts on the basis of such use." 42 U.S.C. § 12210(a); see also 29 C.F.R. § 1630.3(a). Further, the term "disability" does not include

> (1) transvestism, transsexualism, pedophilia, exhibitionism, voyeurism, gender identity disorders not resulting from physical impairments, or other sexual behavior disorders;
>
> (2) compulsive gambling, kleptomania, or pyromania; or
>
> (3) psychoactive substance use disorders resulting from current illegal use of drugs.

42 U.S.C. § 12211(b); see also 29 C.F.R. § 1630.3(d).

The term "illegal use of drugs" refers to drugs whose possession or distribution is unlawful under the Controlled Substances Act, 21 U.S.C. § 812.[22] It "does not include the use of a drug taken under supervision by a licensed health care professional, or other uses authorized by the Controlled Substances Act or other provision of Federal law." 42 U.S.C. §§ 12111(6)(A), 12110(d)(1); see also 29 C.F.R. § 1630.3(a)(2). The term does include, however, the unlawful use of prescription controlled substances. 29 C.F.R. pt. 1630 app. § 1630.3(a)-(c).

---

[22]Medications required by law to be prescribed by licensed health care professionals are not necessarily "controlled substances." "Controlled substances" are those which are addictive or have potential for abuse and which are listed on Schedules I-V of the Controlled Substances Act. Many prescription medications, therefore, are not "controlled substances."

The reference to a person "currently engaging" in the illegal use of drugs does not mean that this exclusion is limited to a person who illegally used drugs "on the day of, or within a matter of days or weeks before, the employment action in question." Id. Rather, the exclusion applies to any individual whose "illegal use of drugs . . . has occurred recently enough to indicate that the individual is actively engaged in such conduct." Id. If an individual tests positive on a test for the illegal use of drugs, the individual will be considered a current drug user under the ADA where the test correctly indicates that the individual is engaging in the current illegal use of a controlled substance.

Although the ADA excludes individuals currently engaging in the illegal use of drugs, it does not exclude individuals who have a record of such use or who are erroneously regarded as engaging in such use. 42 U.S.C. § 12110(b); see also 29 C.F.R. § 1630.3(b). It is important to remember, however, that an individual who has a record of the illegal use of drugs or who is erroneously regarded as engaging in such use is not automatically an individual with a disability. One still must evaluate whether the record or erroneous perception pertains to a substantially limiting impairment. Only addiction or perceived addiction to a controlled substance meets this standard. Occasional, casual illegal use of drugs does not constitute a disability. Similarly, a record or perception of such casual use does not constitute a disability. See Hartman v. City of Petaluma, 841 F. Supp. 946, 949, 2 AD Cas. (BNA) 1860, 1862-63 (N.D. Cal. 1994) (ADA provisions "require some indicia of dependence sufficient to substantially limit a major life activity").

> Example 1 -- Several years ago, CP was hospitalized for treatment for a cocaine addiction. He has been rehabilitated successfully and has not engaged in the illegal use of drugs since receiving treatment. CP, who has a record of an impairment that substantially limited his major life activities, is covered by the ADA.

> Example 2 -- Three years ago, CP was arrested and convicted of the possession of cocaine. He had used the substance occasionally, perhaps three or four times over a sixteen-month period. CP has not used cocaine or any other illegal drug since his arrest. CP is not covered by the ADA. Although CP has a record of cocaine use, the use was not an addiction and did not

substantially limit any of CP's major life activities.

Example 3 -- CP applies for a job with R, which requires job applicants to undergo a test to determine the current illegal use of drugs. CP's drug test falsely indicates that CP is using cocaine. R's personnel manager informs CP that the test came back positive for cocaine use and that R will not hire CP because "we don't want drug addicts working here." CP is not currently using cocaine and does not use any other drug illegally. R, which erroneously regards CP as being addicted to cocaine, erroneously regards CP as having a substantially limiting impairment. CP, therefore, meets the definition of "disability."

Example 4 -- Same as Example 3, above, except the personnel manager tells CP that the test came back showing marijuana use and that R will not hire CP because "we don't hire anybody who uses drugs illegally." The personnel manager tells the EEOC investigator that she did not hire CP because of R's strict policy against hiring anyone who tests positive for the illegal use of drugs and that she had not considered or been concerned about the extent of CP's use. "All I know is that his test showed marijuana use. I didn't think about anything beyond that." Since there is no evidence that R regarded CP as being addicted to marijuana, there is no evidence that R erroneously regarded CP as having a substantially limiting impairment. CP, therefore, does not meet the definition of disability.

A person who alleges disability based on one of the excluded conditions is not an individual with a disability under the ADA. Note, however, that a person who has one of these conditions is an individual with a disability if (s)he has another condition that rises to the level of a disability. See House

Education and Labor Report at 142. Thus, a compulsive gambler who has a heart impairment that substantially limits his/her major life activities is an individual with a disability. Although compulsive gambling is not a disability, the individual's heart impairment is a disability.

902.7 Record of an Impairment that Substantially Limits Major Life Activities

(a) General -- The second part of the statutory definition of the term "disability" applies to persons who have a record of a substantially limiting impairment. This part covers persons who have a history of, or have been classified or misclassified as having, a physical or mental impairment that substantially limits one or more major life activities. It includes persons who have had a disabling impairment but have recovered in whole or in part and are not now substantially limited. It also includes persons who have been incorrectly classified as having a disability. See 29 C.F.R. § 1630.2(k).

The legislative history of the ADA emphasizes that this part of the definition is intended to prevent discrimination against individuals who have been classified or labeled, correctly or incorrectly, as having a disability. It also makes clear that the coverage of the Act extends to persons who have recovered, in whole or in part, from a disability but are subjected to discrimination because of their history of a substantially limiting impairment. Senate Report at 23; House Education and Labor Report at 52-53; House Judiciary Report at 29.

When determining whether an individual is covered by this part of the definition of the term "disability," one must remember that the record at issue must be a record of an impairment that substantially limited a major life activity. A record of a condition that is not an impairment, or of an impairment that was not substantially limiting, does not satisfy this part of the definition. See Byrne v. Board of Educ., 979 F.2d 560, 566-67, 60 EPD ¶ 41,862 at 73,020-21, 2 AD Cas. (BNA) 284, 289-90 (7th Cir. 1992) (single hospital stay for administration of allergy tests is not a record of a such an impairment). Further, a record of a condition, such as transvestism or compulsive gambling, that is specifically excluded from ADA coverage also does not satisfy this part of the definition. (Note, however, that a record of addiction to the illegal use of drugs is a disability, even though current illegal use of drugs is specifically excluded from ADA coverage. See § 902.6, supra.)

Example 1 -- For several years, CP was twenty-to-thirty pounds beyond the target weight for men of his height and bone structure. His condition did not rise to the level of morbid obesity and did not cause or result from a physiological disorder. Further, his condition did not restrict any of his activities. CP recently completed a weight-loss program and is now at his target weight. CP does not have a record of a disability. He has a history of obesity, but his obesity was not an impairment and did not substantially limit any of his major life activities.

Example 2 -- CP was recently hospitalized for appendicitis. She underwent a routine appendectomy, was hospitalized for one week, and recovered fully within the normal healing period. Although CP has a hospital record of treatment for appendicitis, she does not have a record of a disability. The appendicitis restricted CP's activities for only a brief period and had no long-term or permanent effects on CP. The impairment, therefore, did not substantially limit any of CP's major life activities. As a result, CP does not have a history of a disability and the hospital record does not constitute a record of a disability.

Example 3 -- CP was convicted several times of shoplifting. He received treatment for kleptomania and has recovered from the condition. CP has a record of kleptomania, but he does not have a record of a disability. Kleptomania is specifically excluded from the statutory definition of the term "disability."

An individual who has a record of a disability under other laws or regulations does not necessarily have a record of a disability for purposes of the ADA. Other laws may define the term "disability" differently from the way the ADA defines the term. See § 902.1(a), supra. The investigator, therefore, should not assume that an individual who has been certified as having a disability or a handicap for other purposes, such as veterans programs, state vocational rehabilitation programs, or disability retirement programs, also has a disability under the ADA. The investigator, however, should obtain a copy of the certification and other similar available documents. Such certification is not dispositive for the purposes of the ADA, but it may provide relevant information. For example, medical information supporting the certification may be relevant to whether the charging party has a "disability" under the ADA. Further, the respondent's knowledge of and attitude toward the certification may be relevant to whether the respondent regarded the charging party as having a substantially limiting impairment. See § 902.8, infra.

(b) History of Such an Impairment -- The term "disability" covers persons who have recovered from substantially limiting physical or mental impairments. Examples of persons who would fall under this part of the definition of the term "disability" include individuals who have histories of substantially limiting forms of heart disease or mental or emotional illness. Senate Report at 23; House Education and Labor Report at 52-53.

In School Bd. of Nassau County v. Arline, 480 U.S. 273, 281, 42 EPD ¶ 36,791 at 45,635, 1 AD Cas. (BNA) 1026, 1029 (1987), the United States Supreme Court stated that the plaintiff's hospitalization for an acute form of tuberculosis, an illness that had substantially limited one or more of the plaintiff's major life activities, sufficed to establish a record of a substantially limiting impairment.[23] Similarly, a district court found that an individual who had incurred four or five shoulder dislocations prior to undergoing corrective surgery had a "history" of a substantially limiting impairment. Mahoney v. Ortiz, 645 F. Supp. 22, 24, 1 AD Cas. (BNA) 924, 925 (S.D.N.Y. 1986).

> Example -- CP, who is thirty, had a severe form of depression when he was in his early twenties. He lost his appetite, could not sleep, was always tired, and rarely left his home. The depression became so serious that he could not function in day-to-day life. CP was hospitalized for four months and then received therapy on an out-patient basis for six months. The treatment was successful, and CP has had no recurrence of the depression. Although CP does not currently have

---

[23]The plaintiff had been hospitalized for tuberculosis from May 1957 until August 1958. Arline v. School Board of Nassau County, 692 F. Supp. 1286, 1289, 48 EPD ¶ 38,397 at 54,248, 1 AD Cas. (BNA) 1345, 1348 (M.D. Fla. 1988). The plaintiff's tuberculosis, which required lengthy hospitalization, was a substantially limiting impairment. See § 902.4(d), supra.

an impairment that substantially limits a major life activity, he has a history of such an impairment. CP, therefore, falls under the second part of the definition of the term "disability."

(c) Misclassified as Having Such an Impairment -- The term "disability" covers persons who are not, and may have never actually been, impaired but nonetheless have been misclassified as having a disability. Thus, school or other institutional documents labeling or classifying an individual as having a substantially limiting impairment would establish a "record" of a disability. Individuals who have been misclassified by a school or a hospital as having mental retardation or a substantially limiting learning disability would be covered by this part of the definition of the term "disability." See Senate Report at 23; House Education and Labor Report at 52-53; House Judiciary Report at 29.

902.8 Regarded as Having a Substantially Limiting Impairment

(a) General -- The third part of the statutory definition of the term "disability" applies to individuals who are regarded as having impairments that substantially limit one or more major life activities. This part covers persons who have impairments that do not substantially limit major life activities but are treated by covered entities as constituting substantially limiting impairments. It also covers persons whose impairments are substantially limiting only as the result of the attitudes of others toward the impairment and persons who have no impairments but nonetheless are treated as having substantially limiting impairments. 29 C.F.R. pt. 1630 app. § 1630.2(l); see also Senate Report at 23; House Education and Labor Report at 53.

The inclusion of persons regarded as having a substantially limiting impairment reflects Congressional intent to protect all persons who are subjected to discrimination based on disability, even if they do not in fact have a disability. It also reflects a recognition by Congress that the reactions of others to an impairment or a perceived impairment can be just as disabling as the limitations caused by an actual impairment. See House Judiciary Report at 30. As noted in the legislative history of the ADA (see Senate Report at 23-24; House Education and Labor Report at 53; House Judiciary Report at 30), the United States Supreme Court effectively explained the rationale for this aspect of the definition of the term "disability" in School Bd. of Nassau County v. Arline, 480 U.S. 273, 42 EPD ¶ 36,791, 1 AD Cas. (BNA) 1026 (1987). The Court stated,

> By amending the definition of "handicapped individual" to include not only those who are actually physically

> impaired, but also those who are regarded as impaired and who, as a result, are substantially limited in a major life activity, Congress acknowledged that society's accumulated myths and fears about disability and disease are as handicapping as are the physical limitations that flow from actual impairment.

480 U.S. at 284, 42 EPD at 45,637, 1 AD Cas. at 1030 (footnote omitted).

This aspect of the definition of the term "disability," therefore, is designed to protect against myths, fears, stereotypes, and other attitudinal barriers about disability. Common attitudinal barriers include, but are not limited to, "concerns about productivity, safety, insurance, liability, attendance, cost of accommodation and accessibility, and acceptance by co-workers and customers." House Judiciary Report at 30. Quite often, employers will assume, without any objective evidence, that a person's physical or mental condition will cause problems in these areas. The ADA is designed to prevent employment discrimination based on mere speculation and unfounded fears about disability. Thus, the third part of the definition is designed to protect individuals who experience employment discrimination because of myths, fears, and stereotypes associated with disabilities, even if the individuals' physical or mental conditions do not meet the criteria of the first or second part of the definition. Id.

In contrast to the first two parts of the statutory definition of the term "disability," this part of the definition is directed at the employer rather than at the individual alleging discrimination. The issue is whether the employer treats the individual as having an impairment that substantially limits major life activities. Thus, as the legislative history to the ADA notes, "[t]he perception of the covered entity is a key element of this test." House Judiciary Report at 30. Because it is the employer's perception that is at issue, it is not necessary that the individual alleging discrimination actually have a disability or an impairment. It also is not necessary that the employer's perception of the individual be shared by other employers. The individual is covered by this part of the definition if (s)he can show that the employer "made an employment decision because of a perception of disability based on 'myth, fear or stereotype'. . . . If the employer cannot articulate a non-discriminatory reason for the employment action, an inference that the employer is acting on the basis of 'myth, fear or stereotype' can be drawn." 29 C.F.R. pt. 1630 app. § 1630.2(l); see also House Judiciary Report at 30-31.

The legislative history to the Act makes clear that the individual does not have to demonstrate that the employer's perception is wrong. As the legislative history notes,

> A person who is covered because of being regarded as having an impairment is not required to show that the employer's perception is inaccurate, e.g., that he will be accepted by others, or that insurance rates will not increase, in order to be qualified for the job.
>
> For example, many people are rejected from jobs because a back x-ray reveals some anomaly, even though the person has no symptoms of a back impairment. The reasons for the rejection are often the fear of injury, as well as increased insurance or worker's compensation costs. These reasons for rejection rely on common barriers to employment for persons with disabilities and therefore, the person is perceived to be disabled under the third test.

House Judiciary Report at 31.

This part of the definition of "disability" applies to individuals who are subjected to discrimination on the basis of genetic information relating to illness, disease, or other disorders. Covered entities that discriminate against individuals on the basis of such genetic information are regarding the individuals as having impairments that substantially limit a major life activity. Those individuals, therefore, are covered by the third part of the definition of "disability." *See* 136 Cong. Rec. H4623 (daily ed. July 12, 1990) (statement of Rep. Owens); *id.* at H4624-25 (statement of Rep. Edwards); *id.* at H4627 (statement of Rep. Waxman).

> *Example* -- CP's genetic profile reveals an increased susceptibility to colon cancer. CP is currently asymptomatic and may never in fact develop colon cancer. After making CP a conditional offer of employment, R learns about CP's increased susceptibility to colon cancer. R then withdraws the job offer because of concerns about matters such as CP's productivity, insurance costs, and attendance. R is treating CP as having an impairment that substantially limits a major life activity. Accordingly, CP is covered by the third part of the definition of "disability."

To determine whether an employer regards an individual as having an impairment that substantially limits major life activities, one must examine the employer's perception and treatment of the charging party. Toward that end, the investigator may obtain a statement in which the respondent explains his/her perceptions of the charging party's physical or mental condition. The statement should describe the type of condition that the respondent perceives the charging party to have and the extent to which the respondent believes the condition to limit the charging party's major life activities. Further, if the charging party has been classified as having a disability or handicap under another law or benefit program, then the investigator may determine if the respondent was aware of the classification and, if so, how the respondent interpreted the classification. For example, if the charging party has a veterans' disability rating, then the investigator may determine whether the respondent was aware of that rating. The investigator also may determine whether the respondent viewed the rating as indicative of an impairment that substantially limited a major life activity. A respondent might, for example, believe that all individuals who have ten-percent veterans' disability ratings are substantially limited in a major life activity. In addition, the investigator may ascertain the information that the employer had about the charging party's condition at the time of the employment action at issue. Other information, such as statements from other individuals in the work place or evidence that the employer has a pattern of not hiring individuals with the same or similar impairment, also may help to determine how the employer perceived the charging party.

Further, the investigator should examine carefully the employer's treatment of the charging party. An employer may claim that it does not perceive an individual as having an impairment that substantially limits a major life activity but nonetheless may treat the individual as having such an impairment. In such a case, actions may speak louder than words. For example, an employer may assert that it does not regard an individual as substantially limited in working but nonetheless may treat an individual as having an impairment that disqualifies him or her from a class of jobs or a broad range of jobs in various classes. The employer in that case regards the individual as substantially limited in the major life activity of working. See § 902.8(f), infra.

The investigator should remember that a determination that an employer regarded a charging party as having an impairment that substantially limits a major life activity does not automatically require a finding of discrimination. The determination of whether the charging party is covered by the third part of the definition of "disability" and the determination of whether the respondent discriminated against the charging party are two separate determinations. In each charge involving the third part of the definition of "disability," the investigator should engage in a careful evidentiary analysis to determine whether the respondent (1) regarded the individual as having a substantially limiting impairment and (2) acted on that basis in violation of the ADA. Although the same facts may be relevant to both determinations, a finding of coverage does not necessarily lead to a finding of liability. An employer that erroneously regards an individual as having a substantially limiting impairment may nonetheless take an employment action for a legitimate reason. For example, evidence may show that an employer that gave an employee a low performance rating erroneously regarded the employee as having AIDS. The evidence also may show, however, that the employee's work objectively warranted the rating, that other employees with comparable performances received comparable ratings, and that the employer has had employees who actually had AIDS and has never discriminated against them on that basis. In that situation, there is coverage but no liability.

(b) Regulatory Definition -- An individual is covered by this part of the definition if (s)he

> (1) [h]as a physical or mental impairment that does not substantially limit major life activities but is treated by a covered entity as constituting such limitation;
>
> (2) [h]as a physical or mental impairment that substantially limits major life activities only as a result of the attitudes of others toward such impairment; or
>
> (3) [h]as none of the impairments defined in [the definition of the term "impairment"] but is treated by the covered entity as having a substantially limiting impairment.

29 C.F.R. § 1630.2(l). Each of these three subparts of the third part of the definition of the term "disability" is discussed below in detail.

(c) Persons with Impairments Regarded as Substantially Limiting -- This subpart of the regulatory definition covers individuals who have impairments that do not substantially limit major life activities but who are perceived as being substantially limited. For example, an individual who has a slight limp that does not substantially limit any major life activities but who is rejected for employment because the employer believes that the limp significantly restricts the individual's ability to walk is covered by this part of the definition. Although the individual's limp does not in fact substantially limit major life activities, the employer perceives the limp as substantially limiting the individual's ability to walk. The individual meets the definition of an individual with a disability because (s)he is regarded as having an impairment that substantially limits his/her major life activity of walking.

> Example -- CP has a mild form of strabismus (crossed eyes). The impairment only slightly affects CP's ability to see. CP's employer, however, thinks that the impairment

> prevents CP from seeing all printed material. As a result, the employer refuses to promote CP to a supervisory position that would require CP to review the written work of others. Although CP does not actually have a disability, she is regarded as having an impairment that substantially limits her ability to see. CP, therefore, is covered by the third part of the definition of "disability."

(d) Persons Who Are Substantially Limited as a Result of Others' Attitudes -- This subpart covers individuals who have stigmatic conditions that constitute physical or mental impairments but that do not by themselves substantially limit a major life activity. The impairments become substantially limiting only because of the negative reactions of others toward the impairments. For example, a person who has experienced severe burns may have an impairment that is substantially limiting solely because of the attitudes of others. Similarly, a person who has a cosmetic disfigurement may be continuously refused employment because of employers' fears about the negative reactions of co-workers or clients. These persons would be covered under the third part of the definition of the term "disability." *See* Senate Report at 24; House Education and Labor Report at 53; House Judiciary Report at 30-31.

> Example -- CP, who has a facial scar that runs from the base of his left ear to his chin, applies for a job as a sales representative in a home appliance store. The sales manager of the store refuses to consider CP for the position because she fears that CP's presence on the showroom floor will dissuade customers from shopping at the store. CP is covered by the third part of the definition of the term "disability." He has an impairment, a facial scar, that is substantially limiting only as a result of the negative attitudes of others.

(e) Unimpaired Persons Regarded as Having Substantially Limiting Impairments -- This subpart covers persons who have no actual physical or mental impairments but nonetheless are treated as having substantially limiting impairments. For example, an individual who is rejected for employment because the employer erroneously believes that the individual is infected with the Human Immunodeficiency Virus is an individual with a disability. Even though the individual has no impairment, (s)he is regarded as having a substantially limiting impairment.

Similarly, in a nonemployment case under the Rehabilitation Act, a court ruled that a parent whose children had been erroneously placed in a class for mentally retarded students had standing to sue. Although the children had no actual impairments, they were regarded as having disabilities. Carter v. Orleans Parish Pub. Sch., 725 F.2d 261, 262-63 (5th Cir. 1984).

Example 1 -- R refuses to consider CP for a position as a lifeguard because R believes that CP has a serious heart condition that significantly restricts her ability to engage in physical activity. CP, in fact, has no heart condition. Although CP does not have an impairment, CP is regarded as having an impairment that substantially limits her major life activities. CP, therefore, is covered by this part of the definition of the term "disability."

Example 2 -- CP and her spouse have recently completed couples counseling by a clinical psychologist in an effort to remedy problems in their marriage. Neither CP nor her spouse has any psychological disabilities. CP's employer, however, believes that anyone who sees or has seen a psychologist "must be crazy." He finds a pretext under which to fire her. CP, therefore, is covered by the third part of the definition of "disability," because she is being treated by her employer as though she has a substantially limiting impairment although, in fact, she does not.

Example 3 -- CP has high normal blood pressure. Her blood pressure is within "normal" range, and she does not have hypertension. Nonetheless, R fires CP because R thinks this means that CP cannot perform everyday activities without risking a massive stroke. Although

CP does not have an impairment, she is regarded as having an impairment that substantially limits major life activities. CP, therefore, is covered by the third part of the definition of "disability."

Example 4 -- CP had abdominal surgery a few years ago to treat a hernia. The hernia was fully corrected, and CP has no residual effects. R, however, thinks that this means that CP cannot lift anything weighing more than a few pounds and refuses to hire CP. R regards CP as having an impairment that substantially limits the major life activity of lifting. CP, therefore, is covered by this part of the definition of the term "disability."

(f) Regarded as Substantially Limited in the Major Life Activity of Working -- If an individual is not regarded as having an impairment that substantially limits any other major life activities (and does not fall under either of the first two parts of the definition of "disability"), then the investigator should consider whether (s)he is regarded as having an impairment that substantially limits the major life activity of working. An employer regards an individual as substantially limited in the ability to work if, as the result of myths, fears, stereotypes, or other attitudinal barriers commonly associated with disability, it treats the individual as having an impairment that disqualifies or significantly restricts him or her from working in a class of jobs or in a broad range of jobs in various classes. An employer does not regard an individual as substantially limited in the ability to work simply because it finds the individual unsuitable for one particular job. Forrisi v. Bowen, 794 F.2d 931, 934, 40 EPD ¶ 36,307 at 43,277-78, 1 AD Cas. (BNA) 921, 923 (9th Cir. 1986); see also E.E. Black, Ltd. v. Marshall, 497 F. Supp. 1088, 24 EPD ¶ 31,260, 1 AD Cas. (BNA) 220 (D. Hawaii 1980). Rather, an employer regards an individual as substantially limited in working if it perceives the individual to have an impairment that "foreclose[s] generally the type of employment involved." Forrisi, 794 F.2d at 935, 40 EPD ¶ at 43,278, 1 AD Cas. at 923.

In Forrisi, an employer discharged a newly hired utility systems repairer who had acrophobia (fear of heights). The condition had not previously interfered with the individual's employability. It did, however, prevent the individual from performing the job at issue, a utility systems repairer position at the employer's plant, which required work at high elevations. The employer viewed the individual as qualified for and generally capable of doing utility systems repair work but as unable to perform one particular job. Noting that the individual "was seen as unsuited for one position in one plant--and nothing more," the court found that he was not regarded as substantially limited in working. Id.

To determine whether an employer regards an individual as substantially limited in working, one must determine whether the employer (1) perceives the individual as having an impairment that precludes or significantly restricts work only in a particular job or a narrow range of jobs or (2) perceives the individual as having an impairment that disqualifies or significantly restricts the individual from a class of jobs or a broad range of jobs. This means that one must determine what the employer thinks about the impairment and how the employer believes the impairment affects the individual's ability to work. That is, one must identify the work limitations that the employer believes result from the impairment.

To do this, one first should identify the qualification standard or other criterion that the employer has used to disqualify or restrict the individual from employment. For example, the Forrisi employer disqualified the plaintiff because he could not perform utility systems repair work at certain heights, 794 F. 2d at 933, 40 EPD at 43,276, 1 AD Cas. at 922, and the E.E. Black employer disqualified the plaintiff because he had a congenital back anomaly that the employer thought made him "a poor risk for heavy labor," 497 F. Supp. at 1091, 24 EPD at 17,644, 1 AD Cas. at 222. Other disqualifying criteria include such requirements as a certain level of hearing or vision, an ability to carry objects for a certain distance, an ability to lift a certain amount of weight, an ability to work with a certain substance, and an ability to handle particularly stressful situations.

Next, one should determine whether the criterion pertains uniquely to the peculiar job or work site of one particular employer. If the criterion pertains only to the peculiar job or work site, then an employer who refuses to employ an individual who does not meet the criterion regards the individual as disqualified only from work in that particular job or at that particular work site. The employer, who perceives the individual to be unsuited for one particular job, does not regard the individual as substantially limited in working.

For example, the Forrisi criterion, an ability to perform utility systems repair work at certain heights, was unique to that employer's job. The criterion did not measure the employee's ability to perform a class of jobs; rather, the criterion measured the employee's ability to perform utility repair work at the employer's plant, which exposed the employee to certain heights. See 794 F.2d at 935, 40 EPD at 43,278, 1 AD Cas. at 923 (employer doubted plaintiff's ability to perform utility repair work above certain heights in employer's plant, not plaintiff's ability to perform such work in general). The Forrisi employer did not regard the plaintiff as substantially limited in the ability to work. Instead, the employer regarded the plaintiff as unable to meet a unique criterion that pertained to the location of one specific job for one specific employer.

If the criterion does not pertain to the peculiar job or work site of one particular employer, then the investigator should determine whether the criterion pertains to a class of jobs or a broad range of jobs in various classes. To do this, the investigator should look at the number and types of jobs, in the geographical area to which the individual has reasonable access, that use similar training, knowledge, skills, and abilities (a class of jobs) and that do not use similar training, knowledge, skills, and abilities (a broad range of jobs). 29 C.F.R. § 1630.2(j)(3)(ii). If the criterion pertains to a class of jobs or to a broad range of jobs, then the employer that applied the criterion has treated the individual as having an impairment that disqualifies or restricts him or her from a class of jobs or from a broad range of jobs in various classes. The employer's actions, therefore, demonstrate that the employer regards the individual as having an impairment that precludes or significantly restricts work in a class of jobs or a broad range of jobs in various classes. Accordingly, the employer regards the individual as substantially limited in working.

For example, the E.E. Black criterion that the plaintiff could not meet because of a back anomaly did not pertain uniquely to the peculiar job or work site of one particular employer. Instead, the requirement that employees not be "a poor risk for heavy labor" pertained to the plaintiff's ability to perform all jobs involving heavy labor and not just to a particular job of the employer. See 497 F. Supp. at 1091, 24 EPD at 17,644, 1 AD Cas. at 222 (noting that plaintiff was disqualified from employment because he "was a poor risk for heavy labor"). The criterion, therefore, pertained to a class of jobs, heavy labor jobs. By applying the criterion to exclude the plaintiff from employment, the employer treated the plaintiff as having an impairment that disqualified him from a class of jobs. As a result, the employer demonstrated that it regarded the plaintiff as having an impairment that disqualified him from a class of jobs and, therefore, as substantially limited in the ability to work.

On the other hand, an employer that disqualifies an individual from employment on the basis of a criterion that does not pertain to a class of jobs or a broad range of jobs (for example, a criterion that pertains only to a narrow range of jobs) does not regard the individual as substantially limited in working. See 29 C.F.R. pt. 1630 app. § 1630.2(j). An employer that applies such a criterion to disqualify an individual because of an impairment is treating the individual as having an impairment that disqualifies him or her only from a narrow range of jobs. The employer, therefore, regards the individual as having an impairment that precludes work only in a narrow range of jobs (rather than in a class of jobs or a broad range of jobs). Accordingly, the employer, which does not regard the individual as disqualified from a class of jobs or a broad range of jobs, does not regard the individual as substantially limited in working.

In summary, an employer that disqualifies an individual from a job on the basis of a criterion that pertains to a unique aspect of the job at issue does not regard the individual as substantially limited in the ability to work. Instead, the employer merely regards the individual as unsuitable for one particular job. The individual, therefore, does not meet the third, "regarded as" part of the definition of the term "disability" with respect to the major life activity of working. On the other hand, an employer that disqualifies an individual on the basis of a criterion that does not pertain to a unique aspect of one particular job does regard the individual as substantially limited in working if the criterion pertains to a class of jobs or to a broad range of jobs. In that case, the individual is covered by the third part of the definition of "disability."

> Example 1 -- CP is an industrial painter who has extensive experience painting factories, warehouses, aircraft hangars, and other large structures. He applies for a position with R, a company with a contract to paint all of the buildings at a nuclear power facility. R plans to paint the buildings with a unique type of paint that contains a substance designed to help insulate buildings from radiation. R erroneously believes that CP is allergic to that substance and cannot use paint that contains it. As a result, R does not hire CP. In this case, the exclusionary criterion -- the requirement that employees be able to work with paint that contains a certain substance -- is unique to this job. The criterion pertains specifically to R's work site. By disqualifying CP from employment on the basis of a criterion that pertains to a unique aspect of R's job, R has shown that it finds CP to be unsuitable only for one particular job for one particular employer. R, therefore, does not regard CP as substantially limited in working.

Example 2 -- CP is a warehouse worker whose duties include loading and unloading vehicles, moving heavy boxes from one part of the warehouse to another, and keeping an inventory of the items stored in one section of the warehouse. R requires its warehouse workers to be able to lift packages weighing up to seventy pounds, to carry those packages for up to one hundred yards, to bend repeatedly, and to climb up and down ladders several times each day. CP recently learned that she has arthritis in her left knee. The arthritis does not significantly restrict her in any way, and her physician has placed no limitations on her activities. Nevertheless, R believes that the arthritis prevents CP from meeting the lifting, carrying, bending, and climbing requirements of the warehouse position. R has no objective evidence about any limitations that CP might have but instead bases its belief on its views about arthritis in general. R fires CP on the grounds that she can no longer meet the climbing, lifting, bending, and carrying requirements of her warehouse job. The exclusionary criteria -- R's climbing, lifting, bending, and carrying requirements -- do not apply to some unique aspect of R's warehouse. Instead, the criteria apply to the class of jobs that involve manual labor. By disqualifying CP from employment on the basis of criteria that apply to manual labor jobs, R has shown that it finds CP to be unsuitable for work in a class of jobs. R, therefore, regards CP as substantially limited in the ability to work.

Example 3 -- CP, a bank teller, has a mild form of clinically diagnosed depression. The depression does not substantially limit any of CP's major life activities. R, CP's employer, learns of CP's clinically diagnosed depression and assumes that the depression will prevent CP from working well with customers and other members of the public. There is no factual basis to R's assumption. Nevertheless, R reassigns CP to a clerical position in a back office. In this case, the exclusionary criterion -- the requirement that employees be able to work well with members of the public -- does not pertain to a unique aspect of the job or work site. Rather, since a wide variety of jobs involves working with the public, the exclusionary criterion applies to a broad range of jobs. By disqualifying CP from the teller position on the basis of a criterion that applies to a broad range of jobs in various classes, R has demonstrated that it finds CP to be unsuitable for work in a broad range of jobs. Accordingly, R regards CP as substantially limited in the ability to work.

Example 4 -- CP applies for a job as a laborer at R's construction site. A post-offer medical examination reveals that CP has a congenital back anomaly. CP is asymptomatic; the back anomaly does not limit any of her activities. Nonetheless, R withdraws the job offer because it believes that the back anomaly makes CP a poor risk for heavy labor jobs. That is, R thinks that CP will injure her back on the job and will increase R's workers' compensation costs. The criterion -- a requirement that employees not pose a risk of injury in heavy labor jobs -- does not apply to a unique aspect of R's job or work site. Instead, the criterion applies to a class of jobs -- heavy labor jobs. By disqualifying CP from employment on the basis of a criterion that applies to all heavy labor jobs, R has shown that it finds CP to be unsuitable for work in a class of jobs. R, therefore, regards CP as substantially limited in working.

To determine whether a respondent regards a charging party as having an impairment that substantially limits the major life activity of working, the investigator should take the following steps:

(1) identify the impairment that CP has or is regarded as having;

(2) identify the criterion that disqualifies or significantly restricts CP because of the impairment;

(3) determine whether the criterion pertains uniquely to the peculiar job or work site of R;

(a) if the criterion pertains uniquely to the peculiar job or work site of R, then R does not regard CP as substantially limited in working; instead, R regards CP as unsuitable for one particular job for one particular employer;

(b) if the criterion does not pertain uniquely to the peculiar job or work site of R, then

(4) determine whether the criterion pertains to a class of jobs or a broad range of jobs in various classes;

(a) if the criterion pertains to a class of jobs or a broad range of jobs in various classes, then R regards CP as substantially limited in working;

(b) if the criterion does not pertain to a class of jobs or a broad range of jobs in various classes, then R does not regard CP as substantially limited in working.

902.9 Cross References

(a) How to Investigate, § 602

(b) Definition of the Term "Qualified Individual with a Disability," § ___

INDEX

NOTES

NOTES

11

AVOIDING WORKPLACE LITIGATION: WHEN YOU WRITE, YOU MAY BE WRONG

Alan M. Koral

TABLE OF CONTENTS

PRACTISING LAW INSTITUTE

AVOIDING WORKPLACE LITIGATION: WHEN YOU WRITE, YOU MAY BE WRONG

By Alan M. Koral

I. HANDBOOK PROCEDURES

Plaintiffs may claim that a handbook or manual, and the disciplinary procedures set forth therein, create a contract. However, New York is among the most conservative states in the Northeast, and among the more conservative states in the nation, on the question of abrogating the traditional common law presumption of employment at will.

A. State Courts

In Weiner v. McGraw-Hill, Inc., 57 N.Y.2d 458, 457 N.Y.S.2d 193 (1982), the New York Court of Appeals allowed a cause of action for breach of what appeared to be an at-will employment arrangement under the following circumstances: Weiner alleged that McGraw-Hill representatives induced him to leave his previous employment with a competitor by assuring him that he would have job security with McGraw-Hill, as it had a policy of not discharging employees without just cause and only after all reasonable efforts at rehabilitation had been tried. Weiner also claimed that the assurance of just cause discharge had been further alleged that after he was employed, when he had recommended termination of subordinates, he had been told by McGraw-Hill officials that failure to comply with the handbook provisions could expose McGraw-Hill to a lawsuit. Finally, Weiner alleged that he had been performing satisfactorily and nevertheless was terminated without warning for "lack of application." Under these circumstances, the Court of Appeals allowed a cause of action for a breach of contract.

Following Weiner, with the single exception of Tiranno v. Sears, Roebuck & Co., 99 A.D.2d 675, 472 N.Y.S.2d 49 (4th Dep't 1984), not one reported Appellate Division found that Weiner's exacting criteria--inducement, a written express limitation on the employer's otherwise unlimited right to terminate at will and clear evidence of reliance by plaintiff--were sufficiently evident to abrogate the employer's rights. The Court of Appeals' intent after Weiner decision was resolved in Sabetay v. Sterling Drug Inc., 69 N.Y.2d 329, 514 N.Y.S.2d 209 (1987), where the Court held that to come within the Weiner holding, a plaintiff must establish an express limitation on the employer's right to discharge the employee at will, and must meet the other Weiner elements, which would certainly include inducement and reliance, and would arguably include a written incorporation of that guarantee in an application form and probably in a personnel manual or employee handbook as well.

The lower courts have generally adhered strictly to the Sabetay teachings. For example, in Fiammeta v. St. Francis Hospital, 168 A.D.2d 556, 562 N.Y.S.2d 777 (2d Dep't 1990), the absence of an express clause in an employee policy manual was fatal to the plaintiff's case. Similarly, plaintiffs pointing to the existence of an internal grievance procedure or corrective action policies contained in a personnel manual fared poorly. See, e.g., Fischer-Jackson v. LaGuardia Hosp., 187 A.D.2d 696, 590 N.Y.S.2d 278 (2d Dep't 1992) (existence of internal grievance procedure in policy manual did not create limitation on employer's right to terminate employee); Preston v. Champion Home Builders, Inc., 187 A.D.2d 795, 589 N.Y.S.2d 940 (3d Dep't 1992) (accord).

The Court of Appeals recently addressed these issues in De Petris v. Union Settlement Association, Inc., 86 N.Y.2d 406, 633 N.Y.S.2d 274 (1995). It cited Sabetay for the proposition that absent an express agreement establishing a fixed duration, an employee is presumed to be at-will and may be terminated at any time, and cited Weiner for the proposition that a policy statement in an employer's manual restricting termination may be a contract, provided that the employee demonstrate that the employer made the employee aware of its express policy limiting its right of discharge and that the employee demonstrate that he "detrimentally relied on that policy in accepting the employment." In De Petris, the petitioner in the Article 78 proceeding claimed that his termination letter failed to state the reasons for the termination or provide the warnings that the employee manual required, i.e., that employees would be informed, in writing, of any job performance problems and given a period of time to improve. In dismissing petitioner's claim, the Court of Appeals held that the petitioner failed to prove detrimental reliance on the manual's representations because the employee been employed for several years prior to the distribution of the manual, and because the manual's introduction included a reservation of the employer's right to revise it any time.

Following De Petris, appellate courts have dismissed many claims based on a detrimental reliance theory. For example, in Murchison v. Community Counseling and Mediation Services, Inc., 646 N.Y.S.2d 10 (2d Dep't 1996), the court dismissed plaintiff's action for an injunction barring the employer from terminating plaintiff's employment. The plaintiff could not establish detrimental reliance because the plaintiff was not aware of the defendant's personnel manual when he was hired and had never discussed the reasons for which he could be terminated with the employer.

In Kelley v. Institute for Nonviolence, 644 N.Y.S.2d 862 (3d Dep't 1996), the plaintiff challenged her termination and sought reinstatement. In granting summary judgment for the employer, the court found that the plaintiff was not aware of the policy prior to being hired and that she had not relied on it in accepting employment. See, also, Tucker v. Battery Park City Parks Corp., 642 N.Y.S.2d 891 (1st Dep't 1996) (affirming grant of motion to dismiss where former employee failed to allege that he was induced to leave prior employment or otherwise suffered a detriment in reliance on any limitations in manual).

However, in Coclin v. Lane Press, Inc., 644 N.Y.S.2d 275 (1st Dep't 1996), the appellate division reversed a directed verdict in favor of the employer, stating that an issue of fact existed as to whether plaintiff's employer made her aware of its express written policy limiting its right to discharge and as to whether she detrimentally relied on the policy in accepting her employment.

However, states such as Connecticut and Illinois have taken a more liberal approach than that of New York.

In Torosyan v. Boehringer, 234 Conn. 1, 9, 662 A.2d 89, 94 (1995), the Connecticut Supreme Court held that a contractual commitment had been made to the plaintiff-biochemist who had been provided a 1981 manual by the defendant-employer which stated, "[t]he company recognizes its right and obligation to operate and manage its facilities. This includes the right to hire, discharge for cause, promote, demote, reclassify and assign work to employees" (emphasis added by the Court). The manual also encouraged employees to resolve problems at the immediate supervisory or management level whenever possible. The court found that the provisions in the manual were material to the plaintiff's decision to continue to work for the defendant. In 1984, the plaintiff was provided with an updated copy of the defendant's employee manual. However, the 1984 version stated, on its cover, that it was "subject to change without notice" and listed certain "unacceptable" practices which would subject employees to disciplinary action, including dismissal. 234 Conn. at 10, 662 A.2d at 95. The plaintiff did not believe that the new manual applied to him. Based on the foregoing, the trial court held that there was no express contract between the parties that termination could only be for cause. The Supreme Court reversed. The Court found that testimony from the plaintiff about oral statements made to him relating to job scrutiny, found credible by the trial court, coupled with the 1981 manual formed an implied contract, which was not modified by the 1984 manual.

In Duldulao v. Saint Mary of Nazareth Hospital Center, 115 Ill. 2d 482, 505 N.E.2d 314 (1987), the court held that "an employee handbook or other policy statement creates enforceable contractual rights if the traditional requirements for contract formation are present. "First, the language of the handbook or policy statement must contain a promise clear enough that an employee would reasonably believe that an offer had be made. Second, the statement must be disseminated to the employee so that the employee is aware of its contents and reasonably believes it to be an offer. Third, the employee must accept the offer by beginning or continuing to work after learning of the policy statement." 115 Ill. at 489, 505 N.E.2d at 318. Applying the above standard, the court in Duldulao held that an employee handbook which stated, inter alia, (i) "[a]t the end of 90 calendar days since employment the employee becomes a permanent employee and termination contemplated by the hospital cannot occur without proper notice and investigation;" and (ii) "permanent employees are never dismissed without prior written admonitions and/or an investigation that has been properly documented" created an enforceable right to the particular disciplinary procedures described in the handbook. The court pointed out that the handbook contained no disclaimers to negate he promises made, but instead stated in the introduction that the policies in the handbook "are designed to clarify your right and duties as employees." 115 Ill. at 489, 505 N.E.2d at 318.

B. Federal Courts

In Wolde-Meskel v. Tremont Commonwealth Council, 1994 WL 167977 (S.D.N.Y. 1994), the federal court denied an employer's motion to dismiss a terminated employee's breach of contract claim, despite the employee's failure to plead the Weiner elements with particularity. The employee had been terminated without reference to an employment manual providing termination procedures. The court refused to read Weiner as having enumerated the factors that must be met to establish an employment contract, and reaffirmed the Second Circuit's adherence to a "context-sensitive" approach, requiring an examination of the "totality of the circumstances" to determine whether an employer agreed to terminate only for cause.

Similarly, in Polakoff v. St. Lawrence University, No. 95 Civ. 1660, 1996 WL 481552 (N.D.N.Y. Aug. 19, 1996), plaintiff claimed that the University violated the handbook when it used improper criteria and procedures to deny her tenure. In stating that federal courts weigh the "totality of the circumstances" to determine whether or not a contractual imitation has arisen, the court found that it had to conduct a fact-specific analysis of the circumstances surrounding plaintiff's employment in order to make a judgment regarding the totality of the circumstances. The court then denied summary judgment for the employer on this cause of action on the ground that a factual dispute existed regarding whether plaintiff relied on the handbook.

But even the federal courts have had to yield to disclaimer language. In Awan v. Daya, No. 95 Civ. 6630, 1996 WL 284946 (S.D.N.Y. May 29, 1996), the plaintiff alleged that, in addition to oral assurances, the employee manual required the employer to implement progressive disciplinary procedures prior to discharging her and prohibited it from firing her without cause. In finding that the manual failed to provide a basis for plaintiff's claim, the court noted the manual's disciplinary provisions contained language stating that the steps were to be used only as a"guide," and that certain conduct may warrant termination without prior warnings. Furthermore, the plaintiff did not allege reliance upon the manual.

In Varrallo v. Hammond Inc., 94 F.3d 842 (3d Cir. 1996), the Third Circuit, applying New Jersey law, upheld the U.S. District Court for the District of New Jersey's grant of summary judgment to an employer on the issue of whether the two employee manuals at issue there created a contract. The Third Circuit cited to the New Jersey Supreme Court's ruling in Witkowski v. Thomas J. Lipton, Inc., 643 A.2d 546, 552-53 (N.J. 1994) that "an employee manual or handbook may constitute an offer of such a contract by the employer, which employees may accept by continuing in their jobs." However, the Third Circuit found that the two manuals before it failed to satisfy the test set forth in Witkowski that the effect of an employment manual depends on whether "when fairly read [it] 'gives rise to . . . reasonable expectations. . .that it confers enforceable obligations.' which are intended to displace the employers unfettered discretion concerning termination." Varrallo, 94 F.3d at 847 (quoting

Witkowski, 643 A.2d at 550). The factors to be considered in making this determination are those having to do with the "manual's specific provisions" and those involving the "context of its preparation and distribution." Id. In Varrallo, the Third Circuit found that these factors militated against finding that a contract existed: There was no express promise that termination of employment would occur only for specified causes and the manual did not contain specific provisions relating to job scrutiny so as to find that the employer intended that its provisions be regarded by its workforce as enforceable. Id. (distinguishing Fregara v. Jet Aviation Business Jets, 764 F. Supp 940, 949 (D.N.J. 1991), in which the employee handbook stated that "[d]uring the probation period, you are subject to termination without recourse to the grievance procedures afforded herein to regular employees.").

C. Disclaimers

A disclaimer contained in a handbook may be a way of avoiding litigation that is based on an employee handbook. Such disclaimers usually state that the employee's employment is at-will, that the employee can modify the terms and conditions in the handbook at any time and that the handbook does not create any contractual obligations but is provided solely as a guideline. A sample disclaimer is provided herein.

Oddly, there have been very few cases addressing the efficacy of a disclaimer in an employer's handbook or manual. One of the few is Charyn v. National Westminster Bank, 612 N.Y.S.2d 432 (2d Dep't 1994), in which the court affirmed summary judgment for an employer where the handbook contained a provision disclaiming any legal rights to employment on the basis of its provisions. And note that the employer's "reservation" of the right to revise policies was of importance in De Petris, above. But see Aharawna v. Trustees of Columbia Univ., 163 A.D.2d 8, 557 N.Y.S.2d 76 (1st Dep't 1990) (affirming denial of motion to dismiss based on disclaimer because of conflicting language between disclaimer and possible contractual obligation in handbook).

In Pisana v. Merrill Lynch & Co., 1995 U.S. Dist. LEXIS 10296 (S.D.N.Y. 1995), however, the court gave effect to a disclaimer in a handbook and held that plaintiff was an at-will employee who could be discharged for any or no reason, even thought the handbook contained a term possibly inconsistent with the disclaimer. The handbook contained a complaint procedure, which stated that employees would not be penalized for availing themselves of the procedure. The court found that in light of the unambiguous language of the disclaimer that was located on the first page of the handbook under the heading, in bold-face, "Employment At Will/No Contract", the language in the handbook regarding the complaint procedure did not create any contractual obligation

II. <u>Giving Job References</u>

Although job references are an important aspect of a prospective employer's hiring process, many prior employers provide only "name, rank and serial number" references to avoid a perceived risk of liability for defamation; indeed some, out of fear for the new doctrine of compelled self-publication will not even advise a terminated employee of the reasons for his/her termination. The need to get references, and to obtain truthful information from applicants about their reasons for leaving their prior employment is underscored, however, by the threat of a new kind of lawsuit--for negligent hiring. Paradoxically, employers may also risk liability for <u>not</u> saying anything negative in a reference, and even for keeping silent altogether. At the outset it should be said that the danger of losing a defamation suit arising out of giving a negative reference is very small; however, the cost of winning may be very great, and the desire to avoid litigation rather than the likelihood of losing is the motivation behind contemporary reticence in this area.

A. Defamation

1. Generally

Many employers today provide prospective employers with the "name, rank and serial number" type reference, which basically consists of confirming the former employee's dates of employment, job title and (with a release) salary. As a general rule, this limited reference will protect an employer from a defamation claim. For example, in Buffolino v. Long Island Savings Bank, 126 A.D.2d 508, 510 N.Y.S.2d 628 (2d Dep't 1987), the employer required all employees, including plaintiff, to undergo polygraph tests after a cash shortage was discovered. Plaintiff was discharged after failing two such tests. Plaintiff then sued for defamation, among other causes of action, claiming that the employer's reference letter, which provided only "name, rank and serial number," was defamatory. The court dismissed plaintiff's defamation claim because its contents could not reasonably be construed as impugning plaintiff's character or reputation. Indeed, the letter expressly stated that it was the Bank's policy to provide no other information to potential employers and specifically advised the recipient that "[the] failure to comment on the individual's character does not reflect on the individual." This statement, or some variant of it, is a good disclaimer to use in neutral letters of reference.

Employers frequently resort to such limited references, of course, because they fear a defamation lawsuit. A recent example of how liability can occur when references are given without strict accuracy is found in Purgess v. Sharrock, 33 F.3d 134 (2d Cir. 1994), in which a former anesthesiologist at the Hospital for Special Surgery ("HSS"), sued both HSS and its director of anesthesiology, Sharrock, for defamation. After HSS terminated its relationship with Dr. Purgess, HSS's president filed a report with the New York State Office of Professional Misconduct ("NYSOPM"), which stated that plaintiff's privileges at HSS had been "revoked" pursuant to Section 2803-e.1(a) of the Public Health Law. That statute requires a report of a physician's termination only if the individual is terminated for "reasons related in any way to alleged mental or physical impairment, incompetence, malpractice or misconduct or impairment of patient safety or welfare." HSS enclosed five medical charts relating to patient incidents with the report, but one of those cases involved a different doctor, and the person who prepared the records knew that it did not involve Dr. Purgess.

In addition to providing reports, HSS responded to inquiries from New York University Medical Center ("NYU"), a prospective employer, that plaintiff had been terminated "for alleged malpractice or misconduct." When NYU requested more details, HSS explained that Dr. Purgess had been involved in four quality of care incidents, two of which were "episodes of asystole." The term asystole refers to heart stoppages and implies that an anesthesiologist has done "something wrong." Although HSS reported two such incidents, it later admitted that there was only one such incident. As a result, plaintiff did not receive an offer from NYU.

The defamation claim was based on Sharrock's and other officials' communications to hospitals and the state medical examiners. Plaintiff was awarded $3.5 million for defamation. On appeal the court found that the statements were understood as defamatory and seriously damaged plaintiff's reputation as he was involved in only one heart stoppage. The hospital's report was based on false information, became a part of plaintiff's permanent record and affected his career. The qualified privilege defense was lost, the court found, because the statute[1] required the hospital to make reports and give references "in good faith," and a jury could find malicious intent on these facts.

What makes Purgess noteworthy is the combination of factors that led to liability. Given the importance to public health and safety of having hospitals provide frank and full disclosure of the competence and performance of medical personnel, an importance apparently reflected in the legislation that was partly at issue in Purgess, it is surprising and perhaps alarming that HSS was nailed with a huge judgment. But HSS relied on its own faulty records, and apparently harbored a rogue employee who either knew or should have known that some of the information disseminated about Dr. Purgess was false or exaggerated. While greater care in maintaining and checking records and references might have avoided the HSS disaster, it is understandable that employers are more inclined to avoid danger, when they have the choice, by saying nothing--who can be sure that records and evaluations completed by a variety of supervisors over the years are accurate or made in good faith? Who can be sure that employees charged with

---

[1] The public health field is one of the very few where substantive references are actually required by statute. See N.Y. Public Health Law § 2803-e.

compiling records for reference purposes don't harbor a private grudge, or are just indifferent to whether their analysis is accurate? Yet "good faith" is a defense in the context of references, and maintenance and dissemination of accurate records is an achievable goal for most organizations (and an essential one for those that are required to provide references and reports).

2. Elements

To state a cause of action for defamation, an employee must show:

(1) a defamatory statement;

(2) publication or communication to a third party;

(3) injury.[2]

Tischmann v. ITT/Sheraton Corp., 882 F. Supp. 1358, 1370 (S.D.N.Y. 1995).

---

[2] Injury is presumed when defamatory statements are slander per se. Weldy v. Piedmont Airlines, Inc., 985 F.2d 57, 62 (2d Cir. 1993). Injury is presumed if the defamation is libel per se. Nellis v. Miller, 101 A.D.2d 1002, 477 N.Y.S.2d 72, 73 (4th Dep't 1984). A "per se" defamatory writing or statement includes one that tends to disparage a person in the way of his office, his profession, or his trade. Tedeschi v. Smith Barney, Harris, Upham & Co., Inc., 548 F. Supp. 1172 (S.D.N.Y. 1982).

3. Defenses

Truth is always a defense to a defamation claim. Kovacs v. Briarcliffe Sch., 208 A.D.2d 686, 617 N.Y.S.2d 804 (2d Dep't 1994); Love v. William Morrow & Co., Inc., 193 A.D.2d 586, 597 N.Y.S.2d 424 (2d Dep't 1993). Thus "our records show that X was absent 10 times without a medical excuse in the last 6 months" is safer than "X was fired because of excessive absenteeism," which might put at issue the question of whether X's absences were in fact "excessive."

A statement of "pure opinion" is not actionable. Lowinger v. Jacques, 204 A.D.2d 175, 612 N.Y.S.2d 18 (1st Dep't 1994); Rinaldi v. Holt, Rinehart & Winston, Inc., 42 N.Y.2d 369, 397 N.Y.S.2d 943, 950, cert. denied, 434 U.S. 969 (1977). Thus "we believe that X requires close supervision" is better than "X is not a good worker unless closely supervised."

An absolute or qualified privilege also may be a defense. An absolute privilege exists in judicial proceedings, if the statements are material and pertinent, irrespective of the motive with which they are made. Herzfeld & Stern, Inc. v. Beck, 175 A.D.2d 689, 572 N.Y.S.2d 683, 685 (1st Dep't 1991); Weiner v. Weintraub, 22 N.Y.2d 330, 331, 292 N.Y.S.2d 667, 668

(1968). Statements to the unemployment insurance authorities have been held to enjoy an absolute privilege. Noble v. Creative Tech. Servs. Inc., 126 A.D.2d 611, 613, 511 N.Y.S.2d 51, 53 (2d Dep't 1987); Pappas v. Air France, 652 F. Supp. 198, 202 (E.D.N.Y. 1986).[3]

A qualified privilege applies to communications made by one person to another upon a subject in which both have an interest. Liberman v. Gelstein, 80 N.Y.2d 429, 590 N.Y.S.2d 857 (1992). Once a qualified privilege is established, a plaintiff must show that the

---

[3] Furthermore, if an employer provides a submission in response to a plaintiff's administrative complaint, which submission was prepared by the employer's counsel, the basis of the statements in the submission is protected by the attorney-client privilege. Accordingly the employer's counsel is not compelled to identify who gave him or her information, what documents (s)he reviewed, and who reviewed the submission before it was submitted to the administrative agency. Carter v. Rosenberg & Estis, P.C., 72 FEP Cas. (BNA) 1281 (S.D.N.Y. Dec. 4, 1996). The court added that the submission to the agency, even if made voluntarily, does not waive the attorney-client privilege for documents or communications underlying the disclosed document, especially since the employer did not use the documents or communications as both a "sword and a shield" and none of the factors militating access to such documents or communications were present. Id. at 1282. Furthermore, the court noted, in denying access to the information, that the plaintiff had conducted extensive discovery at trial and had access to the submission itself.

statement was motivated by actual malice, ill will, spite, or culpable recklessness or gross negligence. Weir v. Equifax Servs. Inc., 210 A.D.2d 944, 620 N.Y.S.2d 675 (4th Dep't 1994).

New York generally recognizes a qualified privilege attaching to references. In DeSapio v. Kohlmyer, 52 A.D.2d 780, 383 N.Y.S.2d 16 (1st Dep't 1976), the appellate division held that plaintiff's former employer had a qualified privilege in making known and transmitting derogatory information concerning the former employee to another employer. The court stated:

> A qualified privilege exists for the purpose of permitting a prior employer to give a prospective employer honest information as to the character of a former employee even though such information may prove ultimately to be inaccurate. (emphasis added)

In Khuri v. M.W. Kellog Co., 33 A.D.2d 736, 305 N.Y.S.2d 873 (1st Dep't 1969), a former employee of defendant brought a defamation claim based on defendant's reply to a professor's request for an evaluation of plaintiff. The court ruled that when a qualified privilege exists, it will not assume that there was malicious intent absent evidence of actual malice or evidence sufficient to raise an issue thereof. Because plaintiff failed to submit any such evidence, defendant's motion dismissing the cause of action was granted. Malice is difficult to prove ... but easy to allege, even if in a conclusory way.

In Buckley v. Litman, 57 N.Y.2d 516, 457 N.Y.S.2d 221 (1982), a doctor discovered that a large number of his patient files were missing and concluded that his former physician's assistant had the files. He then lodged a complaint with the State Physician's Assistant Licensure Board and sent a copy to the accused's new employer. The court found that both the letter to the Board and the copy to the doctor enjoyed a qualified privilege. As the plaintiff had no evidence of malice, the qualified privilege could not be overcome.

The privilege may also apply to an agency hired to investigate an employee's background. In Weir v. Equifax Servs., Inc., 210 A.D.2d 944, 620 N.Y.S.2d 675, 676 (4th Dep't 1994), plaintiff was employed by defendant Polish Union, an insurance company, until June 1989. In 1991, plaintiff applied for employment with Royal Neighbors of America ("Royal Neighbors"), another insurer, which engaged defendant Equifax Services, Inc. ("Equifax"), a retail credit investigating reporting company, to conduct a background check on plaintiff's employment and credit history. Equifax's report included information provided by Polish Union which stated that plaintiff left Polish Union owing it $6,000; that there were many chargebacks against plaintiff's account because of policies cancelled shortly after commissions were paid; plaintiff had falsified records on insurance applications for himself and his family; and that litigation was pending between plaintiff and Polish Union. Royal Neighbors did not employ plaintiff, based in part on the report. The court stated that "it is undisputed that both Polish Union and Equifax are cloaked with a qualified privilege." The court then granted summary judgment because defendant could not prove malice.

In Kaplan v. MacNamara, 116 A.D.2d 626, 497 N.Y.S.2d 710 (2d Dep't 1986), a teacher who was denied tenure brought a libel action against, among others, his departmental chairperson. The claim was based on a letter the chairperson had sent to the plaintiff and the Acting Dean which stated the plaintiff's application for tenure had been rejected based on the plaintiff's "[f]ailure to evidence satisfactory qualities of personality and character" and his "[f]ailure to evidence willingness to cooperate with others." Id. at 711. The court affirmed a finding of summary judgment for the defendant, finding the plaintiff did not show evidence of malice, which would be necessary because the Acting

Dean and the Chairperson shared a qualified privilege. The court found the plaintiff's allegation that he and the Chairperson had a "poor professional relationship characterized by competition and hostility" was not enough to show malice. Id. at 712.

The privilege may be lost if abused. An employee may demonstrate an abuse of the qualified privilege by showing: (1) the employer acted with common law malice (i.e. with an intent to cause harm); (2) acted outside the scope of the privilege; or (3) acted with knowledge that the statement was false or with a reckless disregard for the truth. Weldy v. Piedmont Airlines, Inc., 985 F.2d 57, 62 (2d Cir. 1993). Under common law, malice means spite or ill will, which refers to the speaker's motivation for making the statements. Liberman v. Gelstein, 80 N.Y.2d 429, 590 N.Y.S.2d 857, 862-63 (1992). The defense of qualified privilege may be invoked when a defendant's acts "were for a proper purpose and exercised in a reasonable manner; however, the privilege is forfeited if the defendant steps outside the scope of the privilege or abuses the occasion." Harris v. Hirsch, 161 A.D.2d 452, 555 N.Y.S.2d 735, 737 (1st Dep't 1990), aff'd, 83 N.Y.2d 734, 613 N.Y.S.2d 842 (1994). Moreover, a defendant exceeds the scope of the privilege if the defamatory statement is made "in furtherance of an improper purpose." Weldy, 985 F.2d at 62.

For example, in Konowitz v. Archway School Inc., 65 A.D.2d 752, 409 N.Y.S.2d 757 (2d Dep't 1978), plaintiff was fired after several months of working as a teaching assistant. She alleged that she was informed that she was fired for budgetary reasons. After her discharge, the Nassau Teacher's Registry wrote to the defendant school requesting that it provide the "reason for her dismissal." The letter was returned with a notation that the plaintiff was discharged because she was not effective enough with difficult children. Plaintiff then sued for defamation. The court found that the statement was subject to the general rule of qualified privilege, but that actual malice may be proved by a showing of culpable recklessness or gross negligence which constitutes a wanton disregard of the rights of others in addition to personal spite or ill will. Here, the discrepancy between the statement and the reason given to the plaintiff for her discharge was sufficient to raise a triable issue of malice. Clearly, consistency between the two statements would have avoided potential liability; nevertheless, this is an unusual result perhaps explained by the fact that the defendant was a school.

Where a comment about a former employee is made which does not relate to, or is not in reference to, the former employee's work abilities or job reputation, the comment has been deemed not actionable in defamation. For example, where five years after a faculty member's dismissal the faculty member challenged the present college faculty to a "teach-in" and offered $2,000 to anyone who could out-teach him, the Chairman of the English Department's comment to the student newspaper referring to the dismissed faculty member as a "clown" was deemed not actionable because it was not related to and was not made in reference to the dismissed faculty member's "abilities as a teacher or his reputation as a scholar." Depuy v. St. John Fisher College, 129 A.D.2d 972, 514 N.Y.S.2d 286, 287 (4th Dep't 1987).

In Anderson v. Vanden Dorpel et al., 172 Ill. 2d 399, 667 N.E.2d 1296, the Illinois Supreme Court applied an "innocent construction" standard to the plaintiff-employee's claim that her supervisor had made defamatory remarks about her to a prospective employer. Specifically, the plaintiff, alleged that the supervisor told the prospective employer that she could not get along with her co-workers and that she did not follow up on assignments. Since both the trial court and the appellate court agreed that the statement regarding the co-workers was subject to an "innocent construction" and, therefore, was not actionable, the Supreme Court had to decide whether the statement that the plaintiff did not follow up an assignments was defamatory per se. The Court concluded she was not. Id. at 413, 667 N.E.2d 1296, 1302. The court based its decision on its prior holding in Chapski v. Copley Press, 92 Ill. 2d 344, 352, 442 N.E.2d 195 (1982), in which the "innocent construction" rule was reaffirmed:

> We therefore hold that a written or oral statement is to be considered in context, with the words and implications therefrom given their natural and obvious meaning: if, as so construe, the statement may reasonably be innocently interpreted as referring to someone other than the plaintiff it cannot be actionable per se.

Applying this holding to the instant case, the Anderson Court agreed with the defendants that the remark, in context, could simply have meant that the plaintiff did not fit in with the particular organization of the employer making the assessment and failed to perform in the particular job setting and not as a comment on her ability to work in future positions. Id. at 413, 667 N.E.2d 1296, 1302.

In Randi W. v. Muroc Joint Unified School District, 929 P.2d 582, 60 Cal. Rptr. 2d 263 (Jan. 27, 1997), the California Supreme Court ruled that employers can be held liable for misrepresentations relating to a former employee's character and qualifications if those statements present a foreseeable risk of physical injury to others. There, the court held that school districts who had provided unqualified recommendations to the Livingston Union School District on behalf of a former teacher were negligent. The plaintiff, a 13-year-old girl who was a student in the Livingston Union School District, alleged that the teacher had sexually molested her and that the defendant school districts knew of charges of repeated sexual improprieties by the teacher. However, the Court ruled that in the absence of resulting physical injury, or some special relationship between the parties, "the writer of a letter of recommendation should have no duty of care extending to third persons for misrepresentations made concerning former employees." 929 P.2d at 591, 60 Cal. Rptr. 2d 263 at 272.

Interestingly, on May 24, 1996, the Illinois Legislature passed the Employment Record Disclosure Act. The Act is designed to shield businesses from liability when giving information about a current or former employee to a prospective employer. The employers retain this immunity provided they give "truthful" information, or information which they in good faith believe is "truthful." 103 Daily Labor Report (BNA) A10-11 (May 29, 1996). Illinois Governor Jim Edgar announced that he would sign the Act, which may encourage employers to furnish candid reference letters to other employers. The extent to which employers will be so encouraged remains to be seen, as does the extent to which artful pleading and pro-plaintiff judges can destroy the safe haven envisioned by the legislation.

Other states that have passed similar immunity laws include Alaska, Arizona, California, Florida, Georgia, Kansas, Louisiana, Maine, Maryland, New Mexico, Oklahoma, and Tennessee. For example, in Florida an employer who discloses information about a former employee's job performance to a prospective employer is presumed to be acting in good faith, and unless a lack of good faith is shown by clear and convincing evidence, the employer is immune from civil liability. Fl. St. § 768.095 (West 1996).[4]

---

[4] A defamation claim may also arise under the "compelled self-publication" concept. Under this claim, a discharged employee sues for defamation even if an employer made the defamatory statement to no one other than the employee, if the employer knows, or should know, of circumstances where the employee will be later put in a position in which he has no reasonable means of avoiding publication of the statement and must repeat it. In effect, the employer is presumed to furnish a constructive reference letter merely by telling the employee the reason for his termination.

New York and virtually all of the state courts that have considered the question have rejected this cause of action. E.g., Wieder v. Chemical Bank, 202 A.D.2d 168, 608 N.Y.S.2d 195, 196 (1st Dep't 1994); Weintraub v. Phillips, Nizer, Benjamin, Krimm &

B. Saying Nothing

An employer also may face liability by keeping silent in a reference. A highly publicized Florida lawsuit demonstrates an employer's potential liability for failing

Ballon, 172 A.D.2d 254, 568 N.Y.S.2d 84, 85 (1st Dep't 1991). See also Mendoza v. SSC & B Lintas, New York, 799 F.Supp. 1502, 1512 (S.D.N.Y. 1992)(stating that judge's "independent research [had] failed to uncover, any New York State court case recognizing [self-publication]."). However, Minnesota and Colorado have recognized the doctrine of compelled self-publication. E.g., Lewis v. Equitable Assur. Soc., 389 N.W.2d 876, 886-88 (Minn. 1986) (originator knew or should have known of "circumstances whereby the defamed person has no reasonable means of avoiding publication of the statement"); Churchey v. Adolph Coors Co., 759 P.2d 1336, 1343-45 (Colo. 1988) (ruling that originator is responsible for publication when the "originator of the defamatory statement has reason to believe that the person defamed will be under strong compulsion to disclose the contents of the defamatory statement to a third person")(internal citations omitted).

Despite the notable lack of enthusiasm in the state courts, some generous-minded federal judges have been more hospitable to the theory. E.g., Elmore v. Shell Oil Co., 733 F. Supp. 544 (E.D.N.Y. 1988)(stating that exception to the general rule was justified, particularly where plaintiff seeks new employment after being discharged for alleged wrongdoing, because a causal connection exists between the making of the statement and the "compelled" repetition).

to disclose negative aspects in an employment reference. In Jerner v. Allstate Insurance Co., 193 Daily Labor Report (BNA) D17 (Fla. Cir.Ct. October 5, 1995), Allstate Insurance Company ("Allstate") was sued for fraud, misrepresentation, and conspiracy, among other things, after ex-employee Paul Calden ("Calden") shot five co-workers in the cafeteria of his subsequent employer, Fireman's Fund Insurance Companies ("Fireman's Fund"). Plaintiffs claimed that because Allstate managers were afraid of Calden they provided him with a letter of recommendation that stated that his departure from Allstate was not related to job performance; however, Allstate terminated Calden for violating company policy by carrying a gun in his briefcase. Thus, Allstate allegedly "violated its duty to fully and truthfully disclose all of its knowledge regarding Calden's mental instability and dangerous propensity for violence." In addition to allegedly carrying a gun to work, Calden's immediate supervisor at Allstate indicated at deposition that he was aware that Calden had made threats against others. Moreover, Calden allegedly had told people at Allstate bizarre stories, including a claim that he was an alien from another planet; other behavior allegedly included devil worship on his computer and threatening behavior toward females Allstate employees.

After the judge ruled that plaintiffs could seek punitive damages against Allstate, plaintiffs and Allstate reached a confidential settlement agreement. See also Buffolino (p. 14, above), in which an employee attempted unsuccessfully to sue on the theory that the employer's refusal to provide a substantive reference was defamatory.

At least one court has held that an employee had no claim against an employer who disclosed information about an employee pursuant to a statutory duty to disclose such information.

In Picton v. Anderson Union High School District, 50 Cal. App. 4th 726, 57 Cal. Rptr. 829 (Cal. App. 3d 1996), the California Court of Appeal held that a high school teacher had no breach-of-contract claim based on disclosure to the state commission on teacher credentialing that the teacher had resigned after being accused of raping a female student. The Court rejected the teacher's reliance on the resignation agreement which prohibited disclosure in exchange for the resignation. The court stated that the school district had a statutory duty under Title 5, Section 80311 of the California Code of Regulation to notify the Commission of all facts involving disciplinary action and held that the nondisclosure provision was void as against public policy.

III. Getting References and Pre-Employment Screening

A. Negligent Hiring/Retention

Employers have an interest in attempting to obtain proper references regarding prospective employees, for numerous reasons. Among the less compelling is the avoidance of liability for negligent hiring. New York and New Jersey, like most jurisdictions, recognizes the tort of negligent hiring. See, e.g., Brown v. Bronx Cross County Medical Group, 834 F. Supp. 105, 110 (S.D.N.Y. 1993); Di Cosala v. Kay, 91 N.J. 159 (1982)(citing, inter alia, Evans v. Morsel, 284 M.D. 160 (1978), Williams v. Feather Sound Inc., 866 So. 2d 1238 (Fla. App. 1980), Coath v. Jones, 277 Pa. Super. 479 (Pa. Super. 1980)). Usually, it applies to employers whose services require a heightened screening of employees because they have access to peoples' homes (e.g. meter readers), persons (e.g. hospital staff) or children (e.g. childcare centers). The essence of the tort lies "in [the employer's] having placed the employee in a position to cause foreseeable harm, harm which would most probably have been spared the injured party had the employer taken reasonable care in making decisions respecting the hiring and retention of his employees."

Detone v. Bullit Courier Serv., Inc., 140 A.D.2d 278, 279, 528 N.Y.S.2d 575, 576 (1st Dep't 1988). See also Di Cosala, 91 N.J. at 173-74 (imposing liaibility for the "negligent hiring or the retention of an incompetent, unfit or dangerous employee and hold[ing] that one may be liable to third parties proximately caused by such negligence."). This theory allows an action against an employer for injuries caused by an employee acting outside the scope of employment. In order to prove this tort, plaintiff must show assault or professional incompetence on the part of the negligently hired and retained employee resulting in personal injury to the plaintiff. Brown, 834 F. Supp. at 110.

An employer may be negligent if (s)he hired an employee who was not qualified or competent. Whether an employee is "fit" depends on the type of employment. For example, in Annonio v. Balzano, 139 A.D.2d 943, 527 N.Y.S.2d 923 (4th Dep't 1988), plaintiff, a professional jockey, sued a fellow jockey and the owner of a horse ridden by the jockey for injuries in a horse race. In granting summary judgment to the horse's owner on a claim for negligent hiring of the jockey, the court stated that the owner had demonstrated that his jockey was skilled and experienced and that the owner had hired the jockey in reliance on such skills. Moreover, plaintiff failed to prove that defendant owner knew of any reason to doubt the jockey's competence or that the jockey in fact had been involved in any incident suggesting incompetence.

An employer may be liable where it had actual knowledge of an employee's dangerous tendencies or prior criminal record and a foreseeable risk of the employee's committing harmful acts exists. Di Cosala, 91 N.J. at 177. An employer may also be liable based on a "should have known" standard. For example, in Corbally v. Sikras, 161 A.D.2d 107, 554 N.Y.S.2d 839 (1st Dep't 1990), the court held that a question of fact existed as to whether the defendant realty company negligently hired an employee. The company had never explored the reasons for the employee's prior termination in even a routine background check at the time of hiring. Moreover, the employer had received complaints from tenants that the employee was "rude, uncooperative and at times scary," as well as information about the employee's affinity for Nazi memorabilia and knives.

If, however, an employer seeks references and conducts a background check and both fail to reveal dangerous information, the employer may avoid liability for negligent hiring. For example, in Mastroianni v.

Village of Hempstead, 166 A.D.2d 560, 560 N.Y.S.2d 843 (2d Dep't 1990), defendant Gregory was hired as a police officer by defendant village. On his day off, Gregory saw his wife with another man, which ended in an altercation between the two men. A few weeks later, Gregory again found his wife with the other man. A struggle between the two men ensued, and Gregory's gun went off and killed the other man. Plaintiff, the other man's survivor, sued the Village and Gregory. One of plaintiff's claims was for negligent hiring of Gregory. The court found that defendant Village's summary judgment motion should have been granted, stating that plaintiff failed to come forward with or suggest the existence of any facts to overcome those which established that Gregory's hiring, training and retention were in accordance with acceptable standards. See also Kirkman v. Astoria Gen. Hosp., 204 A.D.2d 401, 611 N.Y.S. 2d 615 (2d Dep't 1994) (granting summary judgment to defendant security company on plaintiffs' claim of negligent hiring where defendant's security guard raped minor plaintiff because Burns conducted thorough pre-employment check into employee's background and obtained confirmation that employee had no prior criminal history).[5]

A recent California case emphasizes the importance of a direct connection between the possible information about the employee that was available to the prospective employer and the particular risk of harm. In Roman Catholic Bishop v. Superior Court, 42 Cal. App. 4th 1556, 50 Cal. Rptr. 2d 399 (1996), a priest engaged in sexual misconduct with a member of his parish who was a minor. The minor sued the priest's church for negligent hiring claiming the church should have discovered the priest's unfitness prior to hiring him. The California Court of Appeal said the church was not negligent in hiring the priest because even if the church had discovered that the priest had several sexual

---

[5] One Connecticut case has held that even where the employer's job application form inquired as to whether the employee had any criminal convictions or charges pending, which the employee denied and was verified through a police fingerprint check, the employer may be liable for negligent hiring where it gives the employee access to female-plaintiff's apartment and the employee subsequently sexually assaults plaintiff. There, the court held that the question was for the jury to determine whether the assault was a foreseeable result of the employer's decision to give the employee keys to plaintiff's apartment. Gutierrez v. Thorne, 537 A.2d 527 (Conn. App. 1988).

relationships with adults, that did not indicate he would commit sexual crimes with a minor. The court also emphasized that the questioning into sexual activity by the prospective employer that the minor was seeking to impose would violate the priest's right to privacy under both the federal and California constitutions.

B. Pre-Employment Screening

Employers may be interested in conducting pre-employment screening in order to hire the best employees and to protect against a negligent hiring claim. The law provides guidelines in a number of areas as to how an employer may conduct pre-employment screening.

1. Disability

The Americans with Disabilities Act, 42 U.S.C. § 12101 et seq. ("ADA"), prohibits an employer from discriminating against qualified individuals with disabilities because of their disabilities. Therefore, an employer should not ask questions, including in an employment application, about a prospective employee's medical history because information about a qualified disability may be conveyed. The exception is where the inquiry is "job related and consistent with business necessity." The EEOC has taken the position that an inquiry is job related and consistent with business necessity when an employee suffers an illness or injury which appears to affect the employee's ability to perform essential job functions, requests an accommodation or is required to submit to an examination or screening required by other laws.

New York's Human Rights Law also prohibits discrimination based upon disability. N.Y. Exec. Law § 296.1. The NYS Division of Human Rights' guide on pre-employment screening states that there are no lawful questions that can be asked about a disability. An employer may only ask if an applicant can perform certain tasks in a reasonable manner.

The New York Human Rights Law, Section 296, also prohibits discriminating based on a number of other factors including age, race, creed, color, national origin, sex, marital status, arrest records and certain prior criminal convictions. N.Y. Exec. Law § 296.1 Section 296.1 prohibits an employer from making "any inquiry in connection with prospective employment, which expresses directly or indirectly, any limitation, specification or discrimination" as to any of the above factors (including disability).

In Connecticut, discrimination is prohibited on the basis of race, color, religious creed, age, sex, marital status, national origin, ancestry, past or present history of mental disorder, mental retardation or physical disability, except in the case of a bona fide occupational qualification. Conn. Gen. Stat. Ann. § 46a-60.

Similarly, in New Jersey, it is unlawful for an employer to discriminate on the basis of race, creed, color, national origin, ancestry, age, marital status, affectational or sexual orientation, sex or atypical hereditary cellular or blood trait of any individual, or because of the liability for service in the Armed Forces of the United States. N.J. Stat. § 10:5-12(a). However, it is not unlawful to refuse to hire someone who has received a notice of induction to report for active duty in the Armed Forces, or in the case of a bona fide occupational qualification. Id. It is unlawful to "make any inquiry in connection with prospective employment, which expresses, directly or indirectly, any limitation, specification or discrimination as to the above. N.J. Stat. § 10:5-12(c).

2. Criminal Record

In New York, an employer may inquire into past convictions of an applicant. In fact, in certain situations, an employer must inquire into an applicant's past convictions. For example, a day care center will not receive a license unless it has a procedure whereby it asks applicants if they have ever been convicted of a crime. N.Y. Soc. Serv. Law § 390-a(2)(a)

An employer may not inquire into past arrests. N.Y. Exec. Law § 296.16. Although an employer may not inquire into past arrests, it may consider independent evidence of conduct that led to an arrest. Matter of Skyline Inn Corp. v. State Liquor Auth., 44 N.Y.2d 695, 405 N.Y.S.2d 440 (1978). If an employer happens to legally find out about the prior arrest of an applicant, the employer may ask the applicant for proof of the disposition of the arrest. State Dep't of Mental Hyg. v. State Div. of Human Rights, 103 A.D. 546, 481 N.Y.S.2d 371 (2d Dep't 1984), aff'd, 497 N.Y.S.2d 361 (1985).

New York Correction Law § 752 further states that an applicant shall not be denied employment based on past convictions, unless "there is a direct relationship between one or more of the previous criminal offenses and the ... employment sought" or "the granting of the employment would involve an unreasonable risk to property or to the safety or welfare of specific individuals or the general public."

Connecticut law provides that a person shall not be disqualified from employment solely because of a prior conviction, unless the applicant is not suitable for the position. Conn. Gen. Stat. Ann. §§ 46a-80(a),(b). In determining suitability, an employer must consider: (1) the nature of the crime and its relationship to the job; (2) the degree of rehabilitation of the person; and (3) the time since the conviction or release. Id. If a conviction is used as a basis for rejection, a written rejection stating the evidence presented and the reasons for the rejection must be completed. Id. § 46a-80(c). Such a rejection must be sent via registered mail to the applicant. Id. As for arrest records, Connecticut law provides that the State may not provide the arrest records which were erased or not followed by a conviction in connection with an employment application. Conn. Gen. Stat. Ann. § 46a-80(d).

3. Workers' Compensation

New York Workers' Compensation Law § 125 states an employer may not inquire into or even consider whether a job applicant has previously filed for or received workers' compensation benefits. Therefore, an employer should not ask any questions regarding a prospective employee's filing of workers' compensation claims.

The EEOC Technical Assistance on Title I of ADA states that an employer may not inquire into an applicant's workers' compensation history before making a conditional offer of employment. The ADA does allow an employer to obtain information regarding an applicant's medical history only if the employer requires a medical examination from all applicants after offers of employment have been made and prior to the commencement of the employment duties, and has conditioned the offer on the result of the examination. 42 U.S.C. § 12112(d)(3). Thus, according to the EEOC, once a conditional offer is made, an employer is allowed to inquire about the applicant's workers' compensation history in a medical inquiry or examination that is required of all applicants in the same job category. However, the EEOC warns that "an employer may not base an employment decision on the speculation that an applicant may cause increased workers' compensation costs in the future."

4. Credit Checks

Under the Fair Credit Reporting Act, an employer can request a consumer report from a consumer reporting agency in reference to a prospective employee. The Act states that a consumer reporting agency may provide a consumer report "[t]o a person which it has reason to believe ... intends to use the information for employment purposes ... ." 15 U.S.C. § 1681b. The Act defines "employment purposes" as "for the purpose of evaluating a consumer for employment, promotion, reassignment or retention as an employee." 15 U.S.C. § 1681a(h). If, based on the prospective employee's consumer credit report, the employer decides not to hire the employee, § 1681b provides the employer "advise the consumer against whom such adverse action has been taken and supply the name and address of the consumer reporting agency making the report."

The Act defines an "investigative consumer report" as "a consumer report or portion thereof in which information on a consumer's character, general reputation, personal characteristics, or mode of living is obtained through personal interviews with neighbors, friends, or associates of the consumer reported on or with others with whom he is acquainted or who may have knowledge concerning any such items of information. 15 U.S.C. § 1681a(e). The Act does not allow a prospective employer to obtain an investigative consumer report on any prospective employee unless (1) it is first made clear in writing to the prospective employee that such a report may be made and the employee is informed of his right to a complete disclosure of the investigation (see following paragraph) or (2) "the report is to be used for employment purposes for which the consumer has not specifically applied." 15 U.S.C. § 1681d.

If an employer has an investigative consumer report made, the employer must make a complete disclosure of the nature and scope of the investigation if the employee makes a request for such information in writing. The employer's disclosure must be made in writing, no later than five days after the later of when the employee makes their request or the report was first requested by the employer. Id.

New York's Fair Credit Reporting Act also allows an employer to request a consumer report for a prospective employee. N.Y. Gen. Bus. Law § 380-b. However, the employer must first inform the employee that a report may be requested and "the applicant upon request will be informed whether or not a consumer report was requested, and if such report was requested, informed of the name and address of the consumer reporting agency that furnished the report." Id. New York law regarding investigative consumer reports is the same as the federal Act. Id. § 380-a,-c.

5. Polygraph Testing

The Employee Polygraph Protection Act of 1988 ("EPPA"), 29 U.S.C. § 2001-2009 (1988), basically eliminates the use of the polygraph as a screening device for job applicants, with a few exceptions. EPPA forbids employers to require, request, suggest or cause a job applicant to undergo a lie detector test. EPPA forbids employers to use, accept, refer to, or inquire about the results of any such test, or to discharge, discipline, or deny employment or promotion to, or even threaten to take such action, against a job applicant who refuses or fails a lie detector test. Security services and the drug industry are exempt, as are employers when investigating incidents involving economic loss or injury to the employer's business. Prospective employees with direct access to controlled substances may also be tested.

In New York it is unlawful for an employer to "knowingly administer" a polygraph test. N.Y. Lab. Law § 735.

In Connecticut, employees have an absolute right to refuse to submit to any type of truth verification test. Conn. Gen. Stat. Ann. § 31-51g(b)(1) prohibits any person from requesting or requiring prospective or current employees to submit to a polygraph examination as a condition of employment. Any dismissal or disciplinary action taken against an employee for failing a polygraph is forbidden. Id.

New Jersey law prohibits any employer from influencing, requesting, or requiring a prospective employee to submit to a lie detector test as a condition of employment. N.J. Stat. Ann. § 2C:40A-1. Employers who dispense, distribute or manufacture controlled substances are exempt from this law. Id.

C. How to Avoid Liability While Getting Real Information in References

There is no foolproof way to get truthful information from a prior employer in the absence of a statutory mandate to supply such information such as that found in N.Y. Public Health Law § 2803-e, discussed above in connection with the Purgess case. Apart from asking job-related questions on employment applications and then verifying the information (usually post-hire, with a statement on the application that misrepresentations will lead to immediate discharge) the following have been tried with mixed success:

1. Agreements Not to Sue and Waivers

Some employers include on their application forms a statement that the applicant acknowledges that the employer will seek references from prior employers and an agreement not to sue such employers regarding anything said in a reference. This may also be accomplished in a separate document. The difficulty with this strategy is that there is some doubt whether there is consideration to support the promise not to sue a third party, especially if the individual is not hired. However, the chilling effect of having signed may be useful, even if it is not legally enforceable.

Another strategy to avoid liability is the use of a waiver and release of claims with respect to recommendations from prior employers. The issue arises again whether there is sufficient consideration to support a waiver, to which is added an additional difficulty, which is that courts generally hold that a release of future claims (i.e. those not in existence at the time of the release) is not enforceable. A sample release in application form is attached herein.

2. Hold Harmless Agreements

An employer that is very anxious to obtain a candid reference may do so by agreeing to assume the liability of the prior employer in the event of a law suit. This may prove very costly, and is not recommended except in truly extraordinary circumstances. A sample hold harmless agreement is provided herein.

V. EMPLOYEE RELEASES

A valid employee release is a useful tool to shield an employer from liability. Releases can be obtained from an employee in a variety of circumstances, such as a reduction in force, a voluntary resignation program, or some other kind of termination, to preclude an employee from later raising a claim in connection with his or her termination, or to serve as a defense if the employee nevertheless brings a lawsuit.[6] As it is a fundamental principle of law that a release cannot cover future injury or claim, it is pointless to obtain such a release at the outset of employment, except to address specific issues such as obtaining references, taking samples for drug testing and other pre-employment activity.

A. Required Elements of a Release

1. Common Law "Totality of Circumstances" Test

To be enforceable, a waiver of the right to bring an action pursuant to Title VII must have been entered into knowingly and voluntarily. Evans v. Waldorf-

---

[6] A release does not preclude an employee's filing of charge with the EEOC or the New York Human Rights Commission, or prevent either agency from investigating such a complaint. E.E.O.C. v. Cosmair, Inc., 821 F.2d 1085, 1090 (5th Cir. 1987)("[A]n employer and an employee cannot agree to deny to the EEOC the information it needs to advance [the] public interest [in preventing employment discrimination]. A waiver of the right to file a charge is void as against public policy."). If the EEOC sues on behalf of an employee, a release would not be a bar to such suit, Isaacs v. Caterpillar, Inc., 765 F. Supp. 1359, 1371 (C.D. Ill. 1991) ("The EEOC's right to sue is independent of the employee's private action rights."), although it might limit a complainant's ability to collect damages, Cosmair, 821 F.2d at 1091. The Second Circuit has not made a specific ruling to this effect.

Astoria Corp., 827 F. Supp. 911, 913 (E.D.N.Y. 1993), aff'd, 33 F.3d 49 (2d Cir. 1994). In the Second Circuit, the courts look to the "totality of the circumstances" in determining whether a waiver was entered into knowingly and voluntarily. The factors to be considered are:

> 1) plaintiff's education and business experience; 2) the amount of time the plaintiff has access to the agreement before signing it; 3) the role of the plaintiff in deciding the terms of the agreement; 4) the clarity of the agreement; 5) whether the plaintiff was represented by or consulted with an attorney; and 6) whether the consideration given in exchange for the waiver exceeds employee benefits to which the employee was already entitled by contract or law [(i.e., whether there was adequate consideration)].

Id. (citing Bormann v. AT & T Communications, Inc., 875 F. 2d 399 (2d Cir.), cert. denied, 493 U.S. 924 (1989)). The court in Evans held that the waiver was made knowingly and voluntarily since plaintiff was represented by an attorney provided by her union; she had ample time to consider the waiver even though only for a few hours, since she had the assistance of counsel and was able to reject inadequate offers; she had a role in negotiating the terms of the agreement; and the language of the agreement was simple and unambiguous. Id.

If evidence shows that plaintiff knowingly and voluntarily entered into a release, plaintiff cannot thereafter obviate the terms of the agreement by conclusorily alleging unilateral mistake. A New York court thus rejected an attempt by plaintiff to repudiate a release by claiming to have misunderstood the terms of the agreement, and accordingly dismissed plaintiff's age discrimination claim. Koster v. Ketchum Communications, 204 A.D.2d 280, 611 N.Y.S.2d 298 (2d Dep't 1994).

The "totality" test applies to all matters affecting releases other than those subject to OWBPA, described below.

2. OWBPA Requirements for Waiving ADEA Claims

The Older Workers Benefit Protect Act ("OWBPA"), was enacted in 1990 to amend 29 U.S.C. § 626(f) of the Age Discrimination in Employment Act ("ADEA"), 29 U.S.C. § 621 et seq. The statute provides:

> (1) An individual may not waive any right or claim under this chapter unless the waiver is knowing and voluntary. . . . [A] waiver may not be considered knowing and voluntary unless at a minimum--
>
> (A) **the waiver is part of an agreement between the individual and the employer that is**

written in a manner calculated to be understood by such individual, or by the average individual eligible to participate;

(B) **the waiver specifically refers to rights or claims arising under this chapter**;

(C) **the individual does not waive rights or claims that may arise after the date the waiver is executed**;

(D) the individual waives rights or claims only in exchange for consideration in addition to anything of value to which the individual already is entitled;

(E) **the individual is advised in writing to consult with an attorney prior to executing the agreement**;

(F)(i) the individual is given a period of at least 21 days within which to consider the agreement; or

(ii) if a waiver is requested in connection with an exit incentive or other employment termination program offered to a group or class of employees, the individual is given a period of at least 45 days within which to consider the agreement;

(G) the agreement provides that for a period of at least 7 days following the execution of such agreement, the individual may revoke the agreement, and the agreement shall not become effective or enforceable until the revocation period has expired;

(H) if a waiver is requested in connection with an exit incentive or other employment termination program offered to a group or class of employees, the employer . . . informs the individual in writing in a manner calculated to be understood by the average individual eligible to participate as to--

> (i) any class, unit, or group of individuals covered by such program, any eligibility factors for such program, and any time limits applicable to such program; and
>
> (ii) the job titles and ages of all individuals eligible or selected for the program, and the ages of all individuals in the same job classification or organizational unit who are not eligible or selected for the program.

29 U.S.C. § 626(f)(1)(emphases added). Thus the statute provides a new and unprecedented definition of the traditional "knowing and voluntary" standard in federal age discrimination cases.

ADEA cases in the Second Circuit following the enactment of OWBPA apparently apply either the OWBPA requirements or the "totality of circumstances" test. E.g., Murphy v. International Business Machs. Corp., 810 F. Supp. 93, 96 (S.D.N.Y. 1992)("Mr. Murphy waived his right to sue IBM in a manner that was 'knowing and voluntary' whether analyzed in a line-by-line comparison with the minimum statutory factors in amended section 626(f) [of OWBPA], or under the Second Circuit totality of the circumstances' test adopted in Bormann . . . .") (citation omitted); Ross v. Arcata Graphics Co., 788 F. Supp. 1298 (W.D.N.Y. 1992) (applying Bormann totality of circumstances test). In Ross, the district court held that plaintiff did not voluntarily waive her right to file an ADEA suit since, among other factors, the release did not specifically refer to ADEA. 788 F. Supp. at 1303. OWBPA applies only to ADEA claims, and has no application to state and city claims or to other federal claims.

B. Claims Covered by a Release

If a claim exists and is contemplated by the parties at the time of the release, and is reflected in the language of the release, such claim will be covered by the release. In Baba v. Warren Management Consultants, Inc., 882 F. Supp. 339 (S.D.N.Y.), aff'd, 89 F.3d 826 (2d Cir. 1995, cert. denied, 117 S. Ct. 119 (1996), the court upheld a waiver signed by plaintiff and, accordingly, dismissed her Title VII suit. Plaintiff had previously brought suit in New York City Civil Court for unpaid wages and expenses. Both parties agreed to arbitrate, which resulted in an award of $513.86 to plaintiff. Unsatisfied, plaintiff demanded a trial de novo, and was successful at trial, winning an award of $3,007.29 for the unpaid wages claim. Thereafter, plaintiff signed a general release waiving all claims against defendant. Defendant claimed the release was in exchange for defendant's foregoing of any appeals of the judgment. Plaintiff was paid the award, but later filed a sex discrimination charge with the EEOC, followed by a federal lawsuit.

The court rejected plaintiff's argument that she understood the release to apply only to the unpaid wages claim and any further actions relating to that claim. The court found that the plain and unambiguous language of the general release outlined the breadth of the waiver. Furthermore, plaintiff was represented by counsel and was given valid consideration for the release (i.e., defendant's waiver of appeal and its payment of the award). Accordingly, the court held that the general release was made knowingly and voluntarily.

C. Release from Defamation Suits

In Thailer v. LaRocca, 174 A.D.2d 731, 571 N.Y.S.2d 569 (2d Dep't 1991), plaintiff had signed a "request for employment verification" when he applied for a position with the Bank of New York. The request for employment verification contained the following authorization and release:

> I authorize you to release to the Bank of New York the information requested on the reverse side of this form. I hereby agree to release your company, its officers, directors and employees from liability for any claim arising at any time as a result of its compliance with this request.

The Bank made an inquiry with plaintiff's former employer. Plaintiff thereafter brought a defamation suit against his former employer and argued that the release was unenforceable because he did not intend to release his former employer from liability for communicating statements that were allegedly false. The court found that plaintiff's subjective intent, uncommunicated at time of the execution of the release, was insufficient to invalidate the clear and unambiguous language of the waiver. Id.

VI. EMPLOYEE EVALUATIONS AND DISCIPLINE: PRACTICE POINTERS

Regular and periodic evaluations of employees can be vitally important in documenting the performance of an employee against established requirements. Such evaluations are often extremely important during a lawsuit, and accordingly, such evaluations must accurately reflect the employee's performance. Employers who either overstate or downplay performance issues can create problems that are not easily fixed after the fact. When conducting evaluations, supervisors must be honest with employees and treat similarly-situated employees equally. These evaluations should focus on objective data or carefully observed job-related behavior, and should not contain irrelevant comments and generalities.

Each warning, whether verbal or written, or other discipline imposed should be recorded in the employee's personnel file. Employers often allow employees to read, add comments to and signed disciplinary reports, but these procedures are not necessary at the time of making the records.

If suspension is one of the employer's progressive disciplinary measure, the employer may consider a policy statement indicating that suspended employees will not receive or continue to accrue any employee benefits, except pre-paid health insurance, during the suspension. "Suspension pending investigation" is becoming an increasingly popular form of protecting the employers' business while it is investigating a possible employee violation.

VII. TERMINATION LETTERS

An at-will employee can be "discharged for any reason or for no reason, but not for a statutorily impermissible reason." Cottongim v. Onondaga County Sheriff's Dep't, 71 N.Y.2d 623, 528 N.Y.S.2d 802, 804 (1988). New York's Human Rights Law states that it is a discriminatory practice for an employer to discharge an employee because of "age, race, creed, color, national origin, sex, or disability, or marital status." N.Y. Exec. Law § 296(1)(a). Though no reason is required for terminating an at-will employee, it is best have some reason in order to limit the risk of a wrongful discharge claim. In general, any ground is acceptable if it is not contrary to the law or to any promises made to the employee. Some typical legitimate reasons for discharge include: reduction in force because of business conditions, layoffs, reorganization or termination of a job position, poor performance, insubordination, misconduct.[7] Following are a sampling of cases where courts have found there to be sufficient evidence that the reason given for an employee's termination was a pretext for the real, discriminatory reason; often the basis for the determination is based on the discrepancy between what was said at the termination meeting or stated in a termination letter and other evidence of the reasons for termination.

---

[7] Any list of possible grounds for discharge in a handbook should include a disclaimer that the listed grounds for discharge are not exclusive and the company retains its rights to terminate employees for any reason. The termination policy, if any, also should establish that a certain number of days absent from work without notice to superior will be considered as resignation.

In Cottongim, the Onondaga County Sheriff's Department ("the Department") said, at an administrative hearing, that the reason a white, female employee (the plaintiff) had been advised either to resign or be fired was because she had abused sick time. When this reason proved baseless, the Department then said the plaintiff had been discharged (1) because she had failed to report another employee's abuse of sick time, (2) for violating a rule against conduct which would tend to bring discredit upon the Department, and (3) for an unsatisfactory work record. Cottongim, 528 N.Y.S.2d at 803. Based on the fact that (1) the Department had no written or oral rule requiring an employee to report a rule violation by another employee and that such a rule had never before been applied, (2) no disciplinary action had ever been taken against the plaintiff before her discharge and (3) the black, male employee who had actually abused sick time had not been charged either with conduct which would tend to discredit the Department or with any act of misconduct for having abused sick time, the Court of Appeals agreed with the State Division of Human Rights that the plaintiff had been discriminated against on the basis of race and sex. Id. at 804. The court found the Department's changing explanations for the plaintiff's termination alone, especially where the first offered explanation proved baseless, to be evidence allowing an inference that later justifications were pretextual. Id. The court also found that the specific reasons for the plaintiff's termination given by the Department could be pretextual.

A reduction in force may also be a basis for a discrimination claim, where the employee charges the termination of his or her position was a pretext for discrimination. For example, in Gallo v. Prudential Residential Servs., 22 F.3d 1219 (2d Cir. 1994), Gallo brought an age discrimination claim against Prudential based on her termination. Prudential offered affidavits by several of its officers stating the termination was due to a downturn in business. The court reversed a grant of summary judgement for Prudential because (1) 99% of Gallo's duties were transferred to another department, (2) Prudential refused to interview Gallo after she responded to a blind ad which listed several of her previous duties, although the Prudential policy manual stated employees whose jobs had been eliminated would be given priority when openings arose and (3) the effective decision maker in deciding to terminate Gallo subsequently hired four younger employees to perform duties similar to Gallo's former duties.

When false reasons are given, legal liability may arise because the reasons may be perceived as pretexts covering a discriminatory motive. Indeed, a jury that decides that the employee was lied to may not be overly careful in concluding that the real reason was discrimination: they will be angry enough so that they won't care.

Similarly, false reasons will often provoke a lawsuit. If any employee believes he has been lied to, he or she will be ready to believe that a more sinister reason underlies the decision.

A

SAMPLE DISCLAIMER

This Handbook is not a contract of employment and none of the provisions are to be construed as a promise of any kind. Your employment with the company is "at will." This means that you may leave the company at any time and the company may terminate your employment at any time with or without cause. The company must continue to have sole discretion with respect to decisions affecting staff employment and terminations. It intends to exercise that discretion in a manner consistent with its management philosophy of mutual respect, understanding and cooperation. Additionally, in order to adjust to changing circumstances, the company may modify the terms and conditions described in this Handbook.

Such released claims include, without limitation, any and all claims of defamation and self compelled publication.

Dated:

_______________ __________________

Signature Witnesses

B

SAMPLE RELEASE IN APPLICATION FORM

I hereby understand and agree that Prospective Employer may seek information and/or references from my prior employers. In consideration for my being able to apply for a position with Prospective Employer, and for other good and valuable consideration, I hereby release, acquit, and forever discharge any such former employer and all its subsidiaries and affiliated corporations, companies, divisions, subdivisions, and departments, its current and former officers, directors, agents, employees, insurers, plans, and attorneys, from any liability to me arising out of the provision of information and/or references.

Dated:

_________________ ___________________

Signature Witnesses

C

SAMPLE HOLD HARMLESS AGREEMENT

Prospective Employer [name] seeks to obtain information and/or references from Former Employer [name] concerning Prospective Employee [name]. Prospective Employer hereby agrees to indemnify and to hold harmless Former Employer from any claim, demand and/or lawsuit in law or in equity, including liability, damage, cost and expenses associated therewith (including, without limitation, reasonable attorneys' fees) made by Prospective Employee from or in connection with the information provided by Former Employer about the Prospective Employee to Prospective Employer.

This indemnification is expressly limited to activities related to the providing of information and/or references by Former Employer about Prospective Employee and this indemnification shall not apply to any claim, demand, lawsuit, liability, expense, damage and cost which is outside the scope of this limitation.

Former Employer agrees to give prompt, written notice to Prospective Employer of any actual or threatened claim which might give rise to a claim for indemnification hereunder. Any such written notice shall be sent via Federal Express Overnight Delivery Service, to the following address: [Prospective Employer's address]. Prospective Employer shall then be entitled (without prejudice to the right of Former Employer to participate at its own expense through counsel of its own choosing) to defend such claim in the name of Former Employer at the expense of Prospective Employer and through any counsel of Prospective Employer's choosing, if Prospective Employer gives written notice of its intention to defend such claim to Former Employer within 30 days after the receipt of the aforesaid written notice from Former Employer. Within 15 days after the receipt of the aforesaid written notice from Former Employer, Prospective Employer shall give written notice to Former Employer of whether or not Prospective Employer intends to defend and indemnify Former Employer for such claim. Any such written notice to Former Employer shall be sent via Federal Express Overnight Delivery Service to [Former Employer address]. Former Employer agrees to cooperate in the defense of any claim defended by Prospective Employer and shall furnish such records, information and testimony, and attend such conferences, discovery pleadings, hearings, trials and appeals, as may be reasonably required in connection therewith. With respect to any claim defended by Prospective Employer on behalf of Former Employer, Prospective Employer shall be entitled to settle any such claim without the consent of Former Employer, except for settlement terms that restrict or affect Former Employer's interests and as to such terms, Prospective Employer shall be required to request and obtain Former Employer's consent, which Former Employer agrees shall not be unreasonably withheld.

Dated:

_______________ _______________

Signature Signature

D

SAMPLE RELEASE

In consideration for information and/or references and other valuable consideration provided herein, Prospective Employee, for herself, her heirs, executors, administrators, successors, assigns, and insurers, does hereby **RELEASE, ACQUIT, and FOREVER DISCHARGE** Former Employer and all its subsidiary and affiliated corporations, companies, divisions, subdivisions, and departments, its current and former officers, directors, agents, employees, insurers, plans, attorneys, and all other persons, entities, firms, and corporations to whom or for whose conduct the parties hereby released may be liable (hereinafter "the Releasees"), of and from any and every action, cause of action, claim, demand, right, obligation, damages (including compensatory, liquidated, consequential and/or punitive damages), remedies, liability, complaint, cost, and/or expense (including attorneys' fees), arising out of events concerning the providing of information and/or references, including, but not limited to claims that Prospective Employee has or may have against the Releasees, of whatsoever kind or nature, whether legal or equitable, or administrative, and whether known or unknown, for any occurrence arising directly or indirectly or pertaining in any way to the provision of information and/or references about Prospective Employee.

E

Reference Inquiry

Date ______________________

Name ______________________

SSN ______________________

Date of Birth ______________________

Date of Employment/Attendance

from __________ to __________

____

____

____

Attn ______________________

I have made application to the above company for employment as ______________________
I would appreciate your verification of facts stated on my application and your help in completing the following inquiries. Please send this form to my prospective employer; a pre-stamped self-addressed envelope is enclosed for your convenience.

Name if different from above ______________________ Signature in full ______________________

A. To be completed by previous employer

Dates of employment: from: ________ to: ________ Position or title: ______________________

Last salary: ______________ per ________

Reason for termination: ______________________

Was employee recommended for rehire? ______________________

Date	Title or position	Signature

B. To be completed by School Registrar

Dates of attendance: from: ________ to: ________ Graduated? Yes ☐ No ☐

Major subject if any ______________________ Type of diploma or degree ______________________

Date	Title or position	Signature

NOTES

12

REDUCTIONS IN FORCE

Michael I. Bernstein
Scott A. Gold

REDUCTIONS IN FORCE

Michael I. Bernstein, Esq.
Scott A. Gold, Esq.

I. REDUCTIONS IN FORCE AND ALTERNATIVES: EVALUATION

A. Most Common Errors.

1. Failure to recognize the importance of first establishing, documenting and communicating the need for the reduction in force -- legally and as a matter of sound employee relations.

2. Failure to comprehend the need to consider alternative measures before implementing a reduction in force, and to document and communicate such -- legally and as a matter of sound employee relations.

3. Failure to take into account the fact that a reduction in force may be attributable to any one or more of a number of reasons, each of which may lead to different personnel rankings and selections and require a different rationale, supporting proof and documentation, *e.g.*, a reduction in force attributable to technological changes may well differ from a reduction in force attributable to a general decline in business.

4. Failure to appreciate that good faith intentions may not necessarily carry the day under a disparate impact analysis, if such is applied. Numerous courts have found disparate impact analysis applicable to ADEA claims. *See., e.g., Faulkner v. Super Valu Stores, Inc.*, 3 F.3d 1419 (10th Cir. 1993); *Abbott v. Federal Forge, Inc.*, 912 F.2d 867, 872 (6th Cir. 1990); *Lowe v. Commack Union Free Sch. Dist.*, 886 F.2d 1364, 1372-73 (2d Cir. 1989), *cert. denied*, 494 U.S. 1026 (1990); *Geller v. Markham*, 635 F.2d 1027, 1032 (2d Cir. 1980), *cert. denied*, 451 U.S. 945 (1981); *Martin v. Envelope Div. of Westvaco Corp.*, 850 F. Supp. 83, 90 (D. Mass. 1994) ("a reasonable jury" could conclude that evidence employees over age 50 were more likely to lose their jobs "suffices to create a presumption of age discrimination"); *Graffam v. Scott Paper Co.*, 848 F. Supp. 1, 4 (D. Me. 1994) ("A rule barring subgrouping in ADEA disparate impact cases would thus permit policies and practices that clearly have an adverse impact on individuals based on their age to escape judicial scrutiny"). On the other hand, it is still an unsettled question. *See Hazen Paper Co. v. Biggins*, 507 U.S. 604, 113 S. Ct. 1701, 1706 (1993) (majority and concurring opinions suggest disparate impact may not be applicable); *EEOC v. Francis W. Parker Sch.*, 41 F.3d 1073 (7th Cir. 1994) (salary limits legal notwithstanding their impact on older workers), *cert. denied*, 115 S. Ct. 2577 (1995); *Lubeck v. Comet Die & Engraving Co.*, 848 F. Supp. 783, 790 (N.D. Ill. 1994) (disparate impact analysis not applicable); *Martincic v. Urban Redevelopment Auth. of Pittsburgh*, 844 F. Supp. 1073, 1077 (W.D. Pa.), *aff'd without op.*, 43 F.3d 1461 (3d Cir. 1994) (same); *Leidig v. Honeywell, Inc.*, 850 F. Supp. 796, 801 (D. Minn. 1994) ("the Court expresses some doubt about the viability of an ADEA disparate impact claim").

5. Failure, prior to its implementation, to establish an internal audit procedure to review the proposed reduction, for potential legal problems. Failure to appreciate the fact that such an approach could avoid a finding of willfulness and double damages.

6. Failure, before implementation of any reduction in force, to review prior employee evaluations that, on their face, seemingly cannot be reconciled with the contemplated choices for layoff. If prior evaluations are to be disregarded, failure to lay a foundation for the new evaluations and rankings.

7. Failure to follow previous practice or policy -- written or verbal -- or to lay a foundation for changing the practice or policy.

8. Failure to recognize, flag or anticipate potentially explosive situations, and to deal with such appropriately (*e.g.*, where "smoking gun" statements have been made, statistical imbalances exist or certain patterns have evolved). *See*, in this connection, *Earley v. Champion Int'l Corp.*, 907 F.2d 1077, 1082 (11th Cir. 1990) ("Evaluations of the age of the work force as part of a restructuring and reduction-in-force plan are indicative of thorough business planning and are not direct evidence of discriminatory intent"), cited in *Armbruster v. Unisys Corp.*, 32 F.3d 768, 781 (3d Cir. 1994).

9. Failure to recognize that the manner in which a reduction in force is implemented (*e.g.*, sensitivity, compassion, communications) may be just as important, from a legal standpoint, as the decision itself.

10. Failure to coordinate and centralize decisionmaking and communication process.

11. Failure to consider voluntary measures before resorting to involuntary measures.

B. Identification, analysis and documentation of the problems and needs, the alternative solutions and the reasons less drastic alternatives are inadequate.

1. The fact that alternatives to a reduction in force were explored may be subject to discovery. *See*, however, two unpublished discovery orders -- *EEOC v. Consolidated Edison Co.*, 80 Civ. 1292 (S.D.N.Y. 1982); *Burns v. Equitable Life Assurance Soc'y*, 79 Civ. 4726 (S.D.N.Y. 1982) -- where the courts refused to permit discovery as to whether the employer considered alternatives to layoffs or terminations.

2. On the other hand, it generally is to the employer's advantage -- especially in a jury trial and as a matter of employee relations -- to establish it acted with compassion in that, before resorting to a reduction in force, it considered less drastic alternatives, but found them unacceptable, or that such measures, though adopted, proved inadequate. Moreover, absent evidence of pretext, courts often are reluctant to substitute their judgment for the employer's as to whether other alternatives were more viable, *e.g.*:

a. *Sahadi v. Reynolds Chemical*, 636 F.2d 1116 (6th Cir. 1980) (question not whether plaintiff treated fairly, but whether discrimination occurred).

b. *Parcinski v. Outlet Co.*, 673 F.2d 34 (2d Cir. 1982), *cert. denied*, 459 U.S. 1103 (1983) (failure to bump as an alternative not fatal).

c. *Wilbur v. Southern Galvanizing Co.*, 34 Fair Empl. Prac. Cas. (BNA) 1468 (D. Md. 1983) (failure by employer to achieve cost savings, but raises given to remaining employees were necessary to maintain competitive wages and to boost morale).

3. In certain situations a court may seek to determine if any of the options considered were less detrimental to the protected group and to hold the employer to a "least detrimental impact" standard. *Abbott v. Federal Forge, Inc.*, 912 F.2d 867, 876 & n.5 (6th Cir. 1990); *Metz v. Transit Mix, Inc.*, 828 F.2d 1202, 1208 (7th Cir. 1987) ("did not pursue obvious less-detrimental alternatives"); *EEOC v. Chrysler Corp.*, 733 F.2d 1183, 1186 (6th Cir. 1983), *reh'g denied*, 738 F.2d 167 (6th Cir. 1984); *see also Geller v. Markham*, 635 F.2d 1027 (2d Cir. 1980), *cert. denied*, 451 U.S. 945 (1981); *EEOC v. Francis W. Parker Sch.*, 1993 U.S. Dist. LEXIS 3600 (N.D. Ill. 1993), *summ. j. granted*, 1993 U.S. Dist. LEXIS 14909 (N.D. Ill. 1993), *aff'd*, 41 F.3d 1073 (7th Cir. 1994), *cert. denied*, 115 S. Ct. 2577 (1995).

4. Documentation is essential, both from the standpoint of employee communications and articulating, in the event of litigation, legitimate business reasons for the action in question. *See, e.g., Sorosky v. Burroughs Corp.*, 37 Fair Empl. Prac. Cas. (BNA) 1510 (C.D. Cal. 1985), *aff'd in relevant part*, 826 F.2d 794 (9th Cir. 1987); *Parcinski v. Outlet Co.*, 673 F.2d at 37; *Cooper v. Cook Paint & Varnish Co.*, 563 F. Supp. 1146 (W.D. Mo. 1983). Beware, however, of documentation prepared under circumstances suggesting they were merely "created for litigation" and are, therefore, indicative of discriminatory intent. *See, e.g., Hawks v. Ingersoll Johnson Steel Co.*, 38 Fair Empl. Prac. Cas. (BNA) 93 (S.D. Ind. 1984).

C. Even as to reductions in force, various approaches are possible and need to be explored, subject to certain considerations.

1. Employer can study the pension cost impact of various options without giving rise to an inference of discrimination. *See, e.g., Stanojev v. Ebasco Servs., Inc.*, 643 F.2d 914 (2d Cir. 1981).

2. Concern over potential liability under Age Discrimination in Employment Act, 29 U.S.C. § 626 ("ADEA"), is not necessarily evidence of age discrimination. *Morser v. AT&T Info. Sys.*, 703 F. Supp. 1072, 1083 (S.D.N.Y. 1989), *summ. j. granted on reh'g*, 715 F. Supp. 516 (S.D.N.Y. 1989) (employer reviewed RIF statistics to avoid disparate impact); *Marson v. Jones & Laughlin Steel Corp.*, 523 F. Supp. 503 (E.D. Wis. 1981).

3. Repeated "dry run" considerations of the impact of various options could be viewed as evidence of discrimination if the program ultimately implemented has greater adverse impact than one of its predecessor options. *Polstorff v. Fletcher*, 452 F. Supp. 17 (N.D. Ala. 1978). *But see Connell v. Bank of Boston*, 924 F.2d 1169, 1175-76 (1st Cir. 1991), *cert. denied*, 501 U.S. 1218 (1991) (employer's

consideration and rejection of early retirement program did not show age animus).

4. A model approach: Internal audit. *Stendebach v. CPC Int'l, Inc.*, 691 F.2d 735 (5th Cir. 1982), *cert. denied*, 461 U.S. 944 (1983). *But see EEOC v. Sandia Corp.*, 639 F.2d 600 (10th Cir. 1980).

D. A written plan, with input from counsel, is recommended and may be a useful exhibit in any later litigation. *See Astor v. International Business Machs. Corp.*, 7 F.3d 533 (6th Cir. 1993); *Gill v. Union Carbide Corp.*, 368 F. Supp. 364, 368 (E.D. Tenn. 1973); *Stringfellow v. Monsanto Co.*, 320 F. Supp. 1175, 1181 (W.D. Ark. 1970). The plan itself will not be privileged, but certain planning documents might be given such treatment. Consider impact on avoiding finding of willfulness under ADEA. 29 U.S.C. § 626(b); *Trans World Airlines, Inc. v. Thurston*, 469 U.S. 111, 105 S. Ct. 613 (1985).

II. LEGAL AND CONTRACTUAL FRAMES OF REFERENCE

A. Where applicable, collective bargaining agreements and practices thereunder.

B. Individual employment contracts, written and oral, express and implied, including personnel manuals and employee handbooks. *See, e.g., Weiner v. McGraw Hill*, Inc., 57 N.Y.2d 458, 475 N.Y.S.2d 193 (1982) (individual employment contract); *Novinger v. Eden Park Health Serv., Inc.*, 167 A.D.2d 590, 563 N.Y.S.2d 219 (3d Dept. 1990), *appeal denied*, 77 N.Y.2d 810, 571 N.Y.S.2d 913 (1991) (reliance on personnel policy manual); *but see Dickstein v. Del Labs., Inc.*, 145 A.D.2d 408, 535 N.Y.S.2d 92 (2d Dept. 1988), *appeal denied*, 73 N.Y.2d 709, 540 N.Y.S.2d 1004 (1989) (handbook insufficient to establish an employment contract). *See also Sabetay v. Sterling Drug, Inc.*, 69 N.Y.2d 329, 514 N.Y.S.2d 209 (1987); *Murphy v. American Home Prods. Corp.*, 58 N.Y.2d 293, 461 N.Y.S.2d 232 (1983).

C. Written or oral representations and inducements; fraud.

D. Statute of Frauds. General Obligations Law § 5-701. *See, e.g., D&N Boening, Inc. v. Kirsch Beverages, Inc.*, 63 N.Y.2d 449, 454, 483 N.Y.S.2d 164, 165 (1984) (applies "to those contracts only which by their very terms have absolutely no possibility in fact or in law of full performance within one year").

E. Federal, state and local anti-discrimination laws (*e.g.*, age, race, sex, pregnancy and other disability, national origin, religion, marital status, sexual preference).

F. ERISA and related benefits protection laws. 29 U.S.C. §§ 1001 *et seq.*

G. Wrongful terminations (contractual and tortious in nature).

H. Intentional infliction of emotional distress.

I. "Smoking gun" statements and documents. *See, e.g., Kirschner v. Office of Comptroller*, 973 F.2d 88, 92 (2d Cir. 1992); *Normand v. Research Inst. of Am., Inc.*, 927 F.2d 857, 863 (5th Cir. 1991); *Siegel v. Alpha Wire Corp.*, 894 F.2d 50, 54 (3d Cir.), *cert. denied*, 496 U.S. 906 (1990); *Naton v. Bank of Cal.*, 649 F.2d 691, 697-98 (9th Cir. 1981); *Stendebach v. CPC Int'l, Inc.*, 691 F.2d at 738; *EEOC v. Sandia Corp.*, 639 F.2d at 612-

13; *Polstorff v. Fletcher*, 452 F. Supp. at 25. *See also Price Waterhouse v. Hopkins*, 490 U.S. 228, 277 (1989) ("stray remarks in the workplace" do not establish employer liability, nor do "statements by nondecisionmakers, or statements by decisionmakers unrelated to the decisional process itself").

J. Defamation; privileged communications.

K. Older Workers Benefit Protection Act ("OWBPA"), Pub. L. No. 101-433; 29 U.S.C. §§ 623, 626, 630.

L. Worker Adjustment and Retraining Notification Act ("WARN"), 29 U.S.C. §§ 2101 *et seq.*

III. EMPLOYEE COMMUNICATIONS

A. The nature, scope and magnitude of the problems, the solution adopted and the reasons therefor, including the number by which the workforce must be reduced. The importance not only of why, but the manner in which the reduction in force is implemented.

B. If possible, the use of voluntary reductions first; involuntary reductions only as a last resort and to the extent necessary. *See Vega v. Kodak Caribbean Ltd.*, 807 F. Supp. 872, 874 (D.P.R. 1992), *aff'd*, 3 F.3d 476 (1st Cir. 1993) (okay to inform employees that "only in the event that not enough employees joined the voluntary program would the involuntary plan be put into effect").

C. Timetable.

D. Voluntary separation incentive plan.

E. Involuntary separation pay plan.

F. Consideration of a "priority placement" list of surplus employees when filling open positions, *i.e.*, before resorting to transfer of other employees or outside hiring. (Employer may require surplus employees to identify the particular jobs for which they want to be considered, the geographic areas they will consider, and whether they will accept downgrades.)

G. Outplacement counseling.

IV. VOLUNTARY SEPARATION INCENTIVE PLANS

A. Permissible under the ADEA. 29 U.S.C. § 623(f)(2)(B)(ii); 29 C.F.R. § 1625.2(b) (1985). *See, e.g., Coburn v. Pan Am. World Airways, Inc.*, 711 F.2d 339, 344 (D.C. Cir.), *cert. denied*, 464 U.S. 944 (1983), describing such voluntary plans as common corporate practices utilized to prevent individual hardship: "It is a humane practice well accepted by both employers and employees and is purely voluntary . . . . [The employer] was justified in attempting to reduce its costs, and voluntary retirement was clearly a fair attempt to do so. It supports not a hint of age discrimination." *See also Gustovich v. AT&T Communications, Inc.*, 972 F.2d 845, 850 (7th Cir. 1992); *Bowman v. Firestone Tire & Rubber Co.*, 724 F. Supp. 493, 506 (N.D. Ohio 1989); *Wingfield v. United Technologies Corp.*, 678 F. Supp. 973, 981 (D. Conn. 1988).

B. The key to any such plan is in its voluntariness. *See, e.g.*, *Vega v. Kodak Caribbean, Ltd.*, 3 F.3d at 480 (voluntary where employees had six weeks to consider and offer was "cast as one to be accepted or rejected at an employee's will"); *Henn v. National Geographic Soc'y*, 819 F.2d 824, 826 (7th Cir.), *cert. denied*, 484 U.S. 964 (1987) (early retirement plans are presumptively lawful; plaintiff claiming coercion must show he was forced to quit, was not provided with full information about the plan or had an unreasonably short time to make the decision); *Ackerman v. Diamond Shamrock Corp.*, 670 F.2d 66 (6th Cir. 1982); *Allen v. Colgate-Palmolive Co.*, 539 F. Supp. 57 (S.D.N.Y. 1981). *See generally* OWBPA.

1. Managers and supervisors must be informed of the details of the plan and of their obligation to avoid even the appearance of coercion, intimidation or pressure. This does not preclude, within limits, frank discussion of the company's future prospects and the likelihood of the need for additional steps if the voluntary approach proves inadequate. *See Vega v. Kodak Caribbean Ltd.*, 807 F. Supp. at 874 (employees informed that "only in the event that not enough employees joined the voluntary program would the involuntary plan be put into effect"). It does not contemplate, however, a message to the employee that "if you don't leave voluntarily, you'll be fired." *See Hebert v. Mohawk Rubber Co.*, 872 F.2d 1104, 1112-13 (1st Cir. 1989); *Tribble v. Westinghouse Elec. Co.*, 669 F.2d 1193 (8th Cir. 1982), *cert. denied*, 460 U.S. 1080 (1983); *and see Downey v. Southern Natural Gas Co.*, 649 F.2d 302 (5th Cir.), *reh'g denied*, 656 F.2d 704 (5th Cir 1984); *Marshall v. Arlene Knitwear, Inc.*, 454 F. Supp. 715 (E.D.N.Y. 1978), *aff'd in part mem.*, 608 F.2d 1369 (2d Cir. 1979). At the same time, and under certain circumstances (*e.g.*, in response to the employee's pointed inquiry), a properly phrased statement informing an employee of his "precarious" position may be permissible. *See Ackerman v. Diamond Shamrock Corp.*, 670 F.2d at 68; *Sutton v. Atlantic Richfield Corp.*, 646 F.2d 407 (9th Cir. 1981); *Toussaint v. Ford Motor Co.*, 581 F.2d 812, 815 (10th Cir. 1978); *Weidman v. Western Elec. Co.*, 527 F. Supp. 263 (M.D.N.C. 1981). [NOTE: This should only be done with careful guidance and centralized review and control.]

2. Employees' departure due to uncertainty over the continuation of pension and other benefits during collective bargaining negotiations was deemed insufficient reason to support their claim they were forced to terminate their employment. *Bartman v. Allis Chalmers Corp.*, 799 F.2d 311 (7th Cir. 1986), *cert. denied*, 479 U.S. 1092 (1984).

C. A voluntary program should be structured in such way as to maximize its desired impact on the targeted surplus group, while at the same time avoiding oversubscription and loss of valuable, key employees.

1. Limiting such benefits to a particular age group does not necessarily render it unlawful under the ADEA. *Cipriano v. Board of Educ.*, 785 F.2d 51, 56 (2d Cir. 1986) (early retirement incentives limited to employees aged 55-60):

> [S]ince the employer's goal in offering early retirement incentives is often to save expenses by reducing the size of the workforce, it is only reasonable for the employer to offer more to those employees who leave at a younger age, saving the

> employer more years of continued full salary, than to those who remain in the workforce and do not confer in the employer the sought-after benefit.

But see Statement of Managers (the Republican and Democratic floor managers' agreed interpretation of the final version of OWBPA), EEOC Compliance Manual (BNA) N:1210:

> Early retirement incentive plans that withhold benefits to older workers above a specific age while continuing to make them available to younger workers may conflict with the purpose of prohibiting arbitrary age discrimination in employment. . . . For example, it would be unlawful under this substitute to exclude older workers from an early retirement incentive plan based on stereotypical assumptions that "older workers would be retiring anyway."

Moreover, legislative history indicates:

> OWBPA was intended to allow the courts to fashion different kinds of *Cipriano*-type challenges. In particular, courts might hold that while employers cannot justify a maximum age cutoff in an early retirement incentive by claiming that incentives are not needed for older workers who are likely to retire soon in any event, employers can justify a cutoff by demonstrating that it provides an incentive for workers in a particular age bracket to retire before they reach the cutoff date and lose the option of choosing extra benefits.

Michael C. Harper, *Age-Based Exit Incentives*, Va. L. Rev. 1271, 1316 (Sept. 1993). *See*, in this connection, *Spink v. Lockheed Corp.*, 60 F.3d 616 (9th Cir. 1995), *rev'd*, 116 S. Ct. 1783, 1792 (1996) (Court of Appeals erred in applying amendments to ADEA and ERISA retroactively).

2 Incentive payment amounts predicated upon a sliding scale to provide greater incentives to those farthest away from normal retirement are lawful in certain circumstances. 29 U.S.C. § 623(l)(1)(B) (pension subsidies and/or Social Security bridge payments lawful). *Lyon v. Ohio Educ. Ass'n & Professional Staff Union*, 53 F.3d 135, 139 (6th Cir. 1995) (no age discrimination though plan provided higher benefits to younger workers with equivalent years of service). *See also Statement of Managers, supra*:

> [E]arly retirement incentives that impute years of service and/or age would satisfy the ADEA. For example, a plan that gives employees who have attained age 55 and who retire during a specified window period credit for 5 additional years of service and/or age would be lawful.

See also pre-OWBPA cases: *Karlen v. City Colleges of Chicago*, 837 F.2d 314 (7th Cir.), *cert. denied*, 486 U.S. 1044 (1988); *Dorsch v. L.B. Foster Co.*, 782 F.2d 1421 (7th Cir. 1986) (lawful plan provided departing employees with equal monthly installments until they reached age 62, even though those closer to age 62 would receive lesser benefits in toto).

3. Other limitations are permissible if objective factors explain the exclusions. *See, e.g., Bodnar v. Synpol, Inc.*, 843 F.2d 190 (5th Cir.), *cert. denied*, 488 U.S. 908 (1988) (limited to employees in nonessential, noncollective bargaining unit); *Trenton v. Scott Paper Co.*, 832 F.2d 806 (3d Cir. 1987), *cert. denied*, 485 U.S. 1022 (1988) (limited to certain facilities).

4. Employer's requirement that pension-eligible employees defer pension benefits as a condition of electing a sweetened incentive program has been found lawful. *Britt v. E.I. duPont de Nemours & Co.*, 768 F.2d 593 (4th Cir. 1985).

5. To guard against oversubscription, employer may wish to consider restricting the total number of "takers"; if so, employer should document, and communicate, the fact that it can only afford so much, or the loss of only so many key personnel in one department/division/unit.

   a. If structured properly in terms of the sequence of offers and acceptances, and made clear in writing, the plan should permit analysis of the number and demographics of the potential acceptances, as well as a determination as to the number to be accepted. Needless to say, however, an employer's refusal to accept an employee's offer to leave cannot be predicated upon reasons of age. Length of service, on the other hand, can govern so as to permit priority for the longest service employees. *See Gray v. York Newspapers, Inc.*, 957 F.2d 1070, 1084-85 (3d Cir. 1992) (case-by-case implementation and secrecy surrounding offers did not support claim of involuntary acceptance).

   b. What is permissible to discourage key employees, whom the employer wishes to stay, from seeking to participate in the voluntary separation program?

   c. What is permissible to minimize the possibility of having to offer voluntary separation benefits to an employee who may have intended to leave anyway?

D. Releases. Under appropriate circumstances, a formal Agreement and Release of Claims should be considered.

1. Advantages.

   a. Likely to spotlight, at the earliest possible time, potential plaintiffs and issues.

b. Minimizes future risks either by deterring individuals from suing or, if they do sue, by possibly foreclosing recovery on such claims. However, releases are always subject to claims of fraud, duress or failure of consideration.

2. Disadvantages. Might precipitate or encourage litigation or, at the very least, arouse employee suspicion or hostility where none previously existed.

3. Legal considerations.

a. Private settlement of employment disputes generally favored by the courts. *See, e.g., United States v. Allegheny-Ludlum Indus., Inc.*, 517 F.2d 826 (5th Cir. 1975), *cert. denied*, 425 U.S. 944 (1976); *Spiridigliozzi v. Bethlehem Mines Corp.*, 558 F. Supp. 734 (W.D Pa. 1980).

b. Prospective claims. Older Workers Benefit Protection Act, 29 U.S.C. §§ 630, 623, 626 ("OWBPA") (no prospective waivers); *Alexander v. Gardner-Denver Co.*, 415 U.S. 36 (1974) (employee cannot be deemed to have waived prospective claims under Title VII); *Adams v. Philip Morris, Inc.*, 67 F.3d 580, 584 (6th Cir. 1995), *reh'g denied*, 1996 U.S. App. LEXIS 548 (6th Cir. 1996) (future claims may not be released except to the extent they stem from past discrimination).

c. Most courts have permitted waivers of claims relating to employment decisions occurring as of the date of the release. *See, e.g., Lazic v. University of Pa.*, 513 F. Supp. 761 (E.D. Pa. 1981).

d. Unasserted claims? Unasserted or unmentioned claims may be held not to have been waived (*see, e.g., EEOC v. U.S. Steel Corp.*, 583 F. Supp. 1357 (W.D. Pa. 1984)) and, accordingly, there should at least be some discussion of a legal claim.

e. Voluntary and knowing. *See generally Adams v. Philip Morris, Inc.*, 67 F.3d at 583 (applying ordinary contract principles); *Pierce v. Atchison, Topeka & Santa Fe Ry.*, 65 F.3d 562, 571 (7th Cir. 1995) (totality of circumstances test); *Cirillo v. ARCO Chemical Co.*, 862 F.2d 448 (3d Cir. 1988) (7-factor test).

i. Representation by counsel. *But see Cox v. Allied Chemical Corp.*, 538 F.2d 1094 (5th Cir. 1976), *reh'g denied*, 551 F.2d 93 (5th Cir. 1977), *cert. denied*, 434 U.S. 1051 (1978) (failure to establish that EEOC conciliation agreement was voluntarily and knowingly signed, where attorney consulted did not explain all terms of the agreement).

ii. Arms-length negotiation of waiver terms; absence of boilerplate language. *See, e.g., EEOC v. U.S. Steel Corp.*, 583 F. Supp. at 1362. *But see Runyan v. NCR Corp.*, 573 F. Supp. 1454 (S.D. Ohio 1983), *rev'd on other grounds*, 759 F.2d 1253 (6th Cir. 1985), *en banc reh'g granted*, 38 Fair Empl. Prac. Cas. (BNA)

5 (6th Cir. 1985), *aff'd*, 787 F.2d 1039 (6th Cir. *en banc*), *cert. denied*, 479 U.S. 850 (1986); *Pilon v. University of Minn.*, 710 F.2d 466 (8th Cir. 1983).

iii. Understandability of the release, including as to the specific statute or nature of the claim in question. *See, e.g., Alphonse v. Northern Telecom., Inc.*, 776 F. Supp. 1075 (E.D.N.C. 1991); *Pilon v. University of Minn.*, 710 F.2d at 468; *Valenti v. International Mill Servs., Inc.*, 610 F. Supp. 36 (E.D. Pa. 1985); *Bernstein v. Consolidated Foods Corp.*, 622 F. Supp. 1096 (N.D. Ill. 1984).

iv. Adequate consideration -- over and above that to which employee would have been entitled under existing policy. *See, e.g., Ponzoni v. Kraft General Foods, Inc.*, 774 F. Supp. 299 (D.N.J. 1991), *aff'd mem.*, 968 F.2d 14 (3d Cir. 1992); *Runyan v. NCR Corp.*, 573 F. Supp. 1454 (S.D. Ohio 1983), *rev'd on other grounds*, 759 F.2d 1253 (6th Cir. 1985), *en banc reh'g granted*, 38 Fair Empl. Prac. Cas. (BNA) 5 (6th Cir. 1985), *aff'd*, 787 F.2d 1039 (6th Cir. *en banc*), *cert. denied*, 479 U.S. 850 (1986).

v. OWBPA requirements. In order for a release to be effective and enforceable as to a claim of age discrimination under the federal ADEA, the OWBPA requires, in addition to i, ii, iii and iv above, employees must have at least 45 days to consider signing (21 days for a release not pursuant to group exit incentives) and at least 7 days to revoke the agreement. Inform employees, in writing, of coverage of program, eligibility and time limits. Release must specifically refer to ADEA.

vi. No specific release, but employee's acknowledgment of voluntariness. *See Ackerman v. Diamond Shamrock Corp.*, 670 F.2d at 69.

vii. Rescission proper where key information withheld. *Cross v. U.S. Postal Serv.*, 34 Fair Empl. Prac. Cas. (BNA) 1442 (E.D. Mo. 1982), *aff'd on other grounds*, 733 F.2d 1327 (8th Cir.), *aff'd en banc*, 35 Fair Empl. Prac. Cas. (BNA) 1520 (8th Cir. 1984), *cert. denied*, 470 U.S. 1051 (1985).

viii. Acceptance "under protest" - *Tribble v. Westinghouse Elec. Corp.*, 669 F.2d at 1196 (employee's decision to request early retirement "under protest" held involuntary); *Anderson v. Montgomery Ward & Co.*, 650 F. Supp. 1480, 1483 (N.D. Ill. 1987), *vacated in part*, 704 F. Supp. 162 (N.D. Ill. 1989) (decision to accept/reject based on company's statements such as "we feel you have a future here; or conversely, 'you should seriously consider the offer'").

f. The "tender-back" doctrine: whether a waiver that fails to meet the requirements of OWBPA is deemed ratified where the plaintiff attempts to rescind the agreement, but refuses to tender back the benefits:

(i) Ratification -- *Blistein v. St. John's College*, 74 F.3d 1459 (4th Cir. 1996); *Blakeney v. Lomas Info. Sys., Inc.*, 65 F.3d 482 (5th Cir. 1995), *cert denied,* 116 S. Ct. 1042 (1996) (*affirming* 879 F. Supp. 645, 648-49 (N.D. Tex.)); *Wamsley v. Champlin Refining & Chemicals, Inc.*, 11 F.3d 534, 540 n.11 (5th Cir. 1993), *cert. denied,* 115 S. Ct. 1403 (1995); *O'Shea v. Commercial Credit Corp.*, 930 F.2d 358 (4th Cir. 1991), *cert. denied,* 112 S. Ct. 177 (1991); *Grillet v. Sears, Roebuck & Co.*, 927 F.2d 217 (5th Cir. 1991); *Hodge v. New York College of Podiatric Medicine*, 940 F. Supp. 579 (S.D.N.Y. 1996).

(ii) No ratification -- *Long v. Sears Roebuck & Co.*, ___ F.3d ___ (3d Cir. 1997) (*see* Feb. 11, 1997 Daily Labor Report (BNA) at E-1); *Raczak v. Ameritech Corp.*, ___ F.3d ___ (7th Cir. 1997) (*see* Jan. 21, 1997 Daily Labor Report (BNA) at A-9); *Fleming v. United States Postal Serv.*, 27 F.3d 259 (7th Cir. 1994), *cert. denied,* 115 S. Ct. 741 (1995); *Oberg v. Allied Van Lines, Inc.*, 11 F.3d 679 (7th Cir. 1993), *cert. denied,* 114 S. Ct. 2104 (1994); *Forbus v. Sears Roebuck & Co.*, 958 F.2d 1036 (11th Cir.), *cert. denied,* 506 U.S. 955, 113 S. Ct. 412 (1992); *EEOC v. Sara Lee Corp.*, 923 F. Supp. 994 (W.D. Mich. 1995); *Elliot v. United Technologies Corp.*, 1995 U.S. Dist. LEXIS 19325 (D. Conn. 1995).

g. A separation package that provides enhanced benefits in exchange for execution of a release has been upheld even where unavailable to employees age 40 or more who decline to execute the release. *DiBiase v. Smithkline Beecham Corp.*, 48 F.3d 719, 727 (3d Cir.) (offered to "all persons willing to sign the release regardless of age"), *cert denied,* 116 S. Ct. 306 (1995).

4. Drafting considerations.

a. Plain language.

b. Include a waiver of tort and contract claims.

c. Encourage the employee to take adequate time to consider whether to sign. Also affirmatively suggest that the employee have the agreement and release reviewed by an attorney. *See Baba v. Warren Management Consultants, Inc.*, 882 F. Supp. 339, 343 (S.D.N.Y.), *aff'd without op.*, 89 F.3d 826 (2d Cir. 1995), *cert. denied*, 117 S. Ct. 119 (1996). Reflect such in the release. NOTE: These and other subjects, as noted in D.3.e.v. above, must be included where a waiver under the ADEA is sought.

E. Regarding the viability of "reverse" age discrimination claims by those ineligible for the voluntary separation incentive plan because of insufficient age or pension ineligibility: *See Hamilton v. Caterpillar, Inc.*, 966 F.2d 1226, 1228 (7th Cir.), *reh'g, en banc, denied*, 1992 U.S. App. LEXIS 30142 (7th Cir. 1992) (restriction to age 50 or older with 10 years of service lawful because "ADEA does not provide a remedy for reverse age discrimination"); *Ludovicy v. Dunkirk Radiator Corp.*, 922 F.2d 109 (2d Cir. 1990) (lawful to restrict plan to employees age 55 and over with at least 15 years of service); *Karlen v. City Colleges of Chicago*, 837 F.2d 314 (7th Cir.), *cert. denied*, 486 U.S. 1044 (1988); *Henn v. National Geographic Soc'y*, 819 F.2d 824, 826 (7th Cir.), *cert. denied*, 484 U.S. 964 (1987); *Dittman v. General Motors Corp.*, 941 F. Supp. 284 (D. Conn. 1996) (plant closing agreement between union and employer that provided for generous early retirement benefits for employees over age 50 upheld; "ADEA does not bar discrimination against the young in favor of the old"); *Wehrly v. American Motors Sales Corp.*, 678 F. Supp. 1366 (N.D. Ind. 1988); *Rock v. Massachusetts Comm'n Against Discrimination*, 424 N.E.2d 244 (Mass. 1981) (no violation of state law as to employees aged 40-55 where employer offered early retirement benefits only to employees over age 55); *Mason v. Lister*, 562 F.2d 343 (5th Cir. 1977) (Federal Employee Early Retirement Act upheld against ADEA challenge by 46-year-old employee with 21 years' service who did not meet the requirements of either 25 years' service or 20 years' service and 50 years of age); 29 U.S.C. § 623(l)(1)(A) (permissible to provide for attainment of a minimum age as a condition of eligibility for early retirement benefits).

F. Exclusion of pension-eligible employees from severance pay benefits held violative of the ADEA. *See* OWBPA; *EEOC v. Borden's, Inc.*, 724 F.2d 1390 (9th Cir. 1984); *EEOC v. Westinghouse Elec. Corp.*, 725 F.2d 211 (3d Cir. 1983), *cert. denied*, 469 U.S. 820 (1984); *McCorstin v. U.S. Steel Corp.*, 621 F.2d 749 (5th Cir.), *reh'g denied*, 627 F.2d 239 (5th Cir. 1980); *Hannan v. Chrysler Motors Corp.*, 443 F. Supp. 802 (E.D. Mich. 1978); *see also EEOC v. City of Altoona*, 723 F.2d 4 (3d Cir. 1983), *cert. denied*, 467 U.S. 1204 (1984); *EEOC v. City of New Castle*, 32 Fair Empl. Prac. Cas. (BNA) 1409 (W.D. Pa. 1983), *aff'd mem.*, 740 F.2d 956 (3d Cir. 1984). *But see Hazen Paper Co. v. Biggins*, 507 U.S. at 604, 113 S. Ct. at 1706:

> When the employer's decision is wholly motivated by factors other than age, the problem of inaccurate and stigmatizing stereotypes disappears. This is true even if the motivating factor is correlated with age, as pension status typically is.

See also Sperling v. Hoffman-La Roche, Inc., 924 F. Supp. 1396, 1406 (D.N.J. 1996) (decision based upon the "ample retirement benefits" to which an individual would be entitled if laid off does not involve "the problem of inaccurate and stigmatizing stereotypes" "that productivity and competence decline with old age"). On the other hand, *see Babich v. Unisys Corp.*, 842 F. Supp. 1343, 1351 (D. Kan. 1994), *recons. denied*, 859 F. Supp. 454 (D. Kan. 1994) (*Hazen Paper Co.* distinguished from situation where employee is about to vest in pension benefits as result of his age, rather than years of service, and employee is terminated to prevent vesting).

V. INVOLUNTARY SEPARATION PLANS

A. ADEA *prima facie* guidelines as applied to reductions in force. *See, e.g., Tuck v. Henkel Corp.*, 973 F.2d 371, 375 (4th Cir. 1992), *cert. denied*, 507 U.S. 918 (1993) (in the protected age group; discharged; meeting employer's legitimate expectations; persons outside class were retained); *King v. General Elec. Co.*, 960 F.2d 617 (7th Cir.), *reh'g, en banc, denied*, 1992 U.S. App. LEXIS 12990 (7th Cir. 1992 (same); *Loeb v. Textron, Inc.*, 600 F.2d 1003 (1st Cir. 1979) (in the protected age group; was satisfying the legitimate business needs of the employer; was nevertheless fired; was replaced by a younger person). Other courts, recognizing there generally may be no replacement in a reduction in force, have omitted this requirement. *See, e.g.*, *Mitchell v. Data General Corp.*, 12 F.3d 1310, 1315 (4th Cir. 1993); *Maresco v. Evans Chemetics*, 964 F.2d 106 (2d Cir. 1992); *Berndt v. Kaiser Aluminum & Chemical Sales, Inc.*, 789 F.2d 253 (3d Cir. 1986); *Stumph v. Thomas & Skinner, Inc.*, 770 F.2d 93 (7th Cir. 1985); *Thornbrough v. Columbus & Greenville R.R. Co.*, 760 F.2d 633 (5th Cir. 1985); *Williams v. General Motors Corp.*, 656 F.2d 120 (5th Cir. 1981), *cert. denied*, 455 U.S. 943 (1982). The Fifth Circuit has required that the plaintiff show s/he was a member of the protected class, was adversely affected and was qualified to assume another position with the employer, and that some direct or circumstantial evidence leads to a conclusion or an inference that the employer intended to discriminate on the basis of age. *Wiliams v. General Motors Corp.*, *id.*; *see also Ridenour v. Lawson Co.*, 791 F.2d 52 (6th Cir. 1986). The Third Circuit has required that plaintiff initially establish "he is a member of the protected class . . . and was laid off from a job for which he was qualified while others not in the protected class were treated more favorably." *Berndt v. Kaiser Aluminum & Chemical Sales, Inc.*, 789 F.2d at 257. However, in *Chiaramonte v. Fashion Bed Group, Inc.*, 932 F. Supp. 1080, 1086-87 (N.D. Ill. 1996), the district court, citing the rationale of the Supreme Court in *O'Connor v. Consolidated Coin Caterers Corp.*, 116 S. Ct. 1307 (1996), rejected the notion that a *prima facie* case of age discrimination cannot be established where the plaintiff has been replaced by a person within the protected age class, but younger).

1. Courts generally have required more of plaintiffs where, in fact, there has been no replacement with a younger worker. *See La Grant v. Gulf & Western Mfg. Co.*, 748 F.2d 1087 (6th Cir. 1984). They reason that in a reduction in force, unsatisfactory performers already have been the first to go before other, generally satisfactory employees, are considered for termination:

   > Unlike the employer who passes over a qualified minority applicant, the employer who fires a qualified older employee as part of a reduction-in-force does nothing inherently suspicious. One expects non-discriminating employers to hire qualified applicants rather than keep looking. To do otherwise raises a fair inference of discrimination. In the reduction in force case, the employer often must discharge qualified employees. The nondiscriminating employer will choose whom to discharge on the basis of their relative contributions to the business. That the one chosen happens to be older by itself raises no fair inference of discrimination -- those who remain may be more productive. The age discrimination plaintiff in this type of case must show more.

   Matthews v. Allis-Chalmers, 614 F. Supp. 11, 14 (N.D. Ill. 1984), *aff'd*, 769 F.2d 1215 (7th Cir. 1985); *see also Simpson v. Midland-Ross Corp.*, 823 F.2d 937 (6th Cir. 1987).

2. One court interpreted the "something more" as requiring a plaintiff to show "some other indirect evidence from which a logical inference of discrimination can be made . . . [such as] statistics showing a pattern or practice of age discrimination or statements indicating that age was a factor in the employment decision." *Bobbitt v. PBA, Inc.*, 31 Fair Empl. Prac. Cas. (BNA) 366, 367 (D. Minn. 1983). *See also Wunderly v. S.C. Johnson & Son, Inc.*, 828 F. Supp. 801 (D. Ore. 1993).

3. In an ADEA case, most courts will permit employers to use the "last refuge" argument to defend a reduction in force action ("Even if the decision appears unwise, wrong or poorly reasoned, it isn't unlawful unless discriminatory").

   a. *Furr v. Seagate Technology*, 82 F.3d 980, 986 (10th Cir. 1996), *cert. denied sub nom., Doan v. Seagate Technology*, 117 S. Ct. 684 (1997) ("[f]inancial evidence suggesting that a decision, in hindsight, may not have been prudent is not evidence of improper motive; the ADEA is not violated by erroneous or even illogical business judgment"); *Hardin v. Hussman Corp.* 45 F.3d 262, 264-65 (8th Cir.), *reh'g, en banc, denied*, 1995 U.S. App. LEXIS 4518 (8th Cir. 1995) (decision based upon "business judgment" does not require evidence of financial distress"); *Bialas v. Greyhound Lines, Inc.*, 59 F.3d 759, 763 (8th Cir. 1995 (decision to terminate older employees because they are more highly paid does not, by itself, support an inference of age discrimination); *Gustovich v. AT&T Communications, Inc.*, 972 F.2d 845, 848, 1062 (7th Cir. 1992) ("The question is not whether the ratings were *right* but whether the employer's description of the reasons is *honest*"; emphasis original); *Dale v. Chicago Tribune Co.*, 797 F.2d 458 (7th Cir. 1986), *cert. denied*, 479 U.S. 1066 (1987) ("The Court does not sit as a super personnel department to reexamine a company's business decisions"); *Williams v. Brooklyn Union Gas Co.*, 819 F. Supp. 214 (E.D.N.Y. 1993); *Arnell v. Pan Am. World Airways, Inc.*, 41 EPD para. 36, 506 (S.D.N.Y. 1986) (ADEA "may not be invoked merely to challenge the wisdom of an employer's decisions"); *Zick v. Verson Allsteel Press Co.*, 644 F. Supp. 906 (N.D. Ill. 1986), *aff'd mem.*, 819 F.2d 1143 (7th Cir. 1987) ("ADEA is about age discrimination and not shabby or numbskull practices").

   b. *But see Cazzola v. Codman & Shurtleff, Inc.*, 751 F.2d 53 (1st Cir. 1984) (company's failure to investigate sudden changes in performance evaluations following change in supervisors was factor in denial of summary judgment).

B. The voluntary separation plan should be implemented in strict accordance with the written design or plan. Failure to follow established policies may be viewed as evidence of discrimination (*Herold v. Hajoca Corp.*, 864 F.2d 317 (4th Cir. 1988), *cert. denied*, 490 U.S. 1107 (1989) failure to follow longstanding policy of first laying off employees with least seniority); *Christie v. Foremost Ins. Co.*, 785 F.2d 584 (7th Cir. 1986)); it also may well give rise to a state law cause of action in jurisdictions that recognize employment contract actions arising from failure to follow personnel policies or personnel manual provisions.

C. Avoid invoking a reduction-in-force plan merely to deal with an individual or a very small group where, in essence, the problem is performance or other like considerations. Such separation "plans" really should apply only to broad groups or employees of a division or subsidiary in which there is a surplus. Courts will likely look suspiciously at any sudden identification of particular individuals as "surplus."

D. Force reduction in an "overall surplus" situation, where the focus is on reducing total numbers of employees -- not on fitting existing employees into a newly redesigned organization scheme.

1. Determine how employees should be terminated to best achieve downsizing while doing the least damage to efficiency and operations. Are there other considerations that militate against seeking to identify the least effective or "least contributing" employees for earliest termination? Is there a reason to consider inverse seniority?

2. Seek to generate relative employee rankings, within well-defined universes, by performance, value to the organization and/or possession of special skills and experience. In generating relative rankings, some subjectivity is permitted. (One employer's supervisors knew only that they were to identify those employees they would "miss the least" and while this was found to be quite subjective, it was not held to be clearly unlawful. *Allison v. Western Union Tel. Co.*, 680 F.2d 1318 (11th Cir. 1982).) *See also Graffam v. Scott Paper Co.*, 870 F. Supp. 389 (D. Me. 1994), *aff'd*, 60 F.3d 809 (1st Cir. 1995) (finding assessment of employees in light of post-RIF job requirements was valid notwithstanding disparate impact on older employees). *But see Weihaupt v. American Medical Ass'n*, 874 F.2d 419 (7th Cir. 1989), *reh'g denied*, 1989 U.S. App. LEXIS 10064 (7th Cir. 1989) (employee's performance in existing job may be irrelevant for determining qualifications for new, restructured position with different responsibilities). The rankings must be followed as closely as possible. *Vaughn v Mobil Oil Corp.*, 708 F. Supp. 595 (S.D.N.Y. 1989).

3. Ensure that <u>all</u> employees are reviewed and that all avenues for obtaining information about employees' performance and essentiality to the business are explored (*i.e.*, do not fail to obtain written appraisals, to talk with the employee's supervisor or obtain from the supervisor a written evaluation of the employee's relative performance level). *See Duffy v. Wheeling Pittsburgh Steel Corp.*, 738 F.2d 1393 (3d Cir.), *cert. denied*, 469 U.S. 1087 (1984). *Cf. Hardin v. Hussmann Corp.*, 45 F.3d 262 (8th Cir.), *reh'g, en banc, denied*, 1995 U.S. App. LEXIS 4518 (8th Cir. 1995) (incomplete review of performance gave rise to pretext argument).

4. Obtain and retain written documentation on employee performance and the justification for employee rankings from employees' supervisors to guard against the possibility they themselves may be terminated in a subsequent force reduction, presenting the problem in litigation of the "disappearing supervisor" or a hostile witness.

5. Rankings can be generated from an existing evaluation system or one specially designed.

a. Factors favoring an existing evaluation system. *See, e.g., Conkwright v. Westinghouse Elec. Corp.*, 933 F.2d 231 (4th Cir. 1991).

   i. It is (or should be) already well-documented and was probably designed by human resource professionals who were not under the time pressure that might apply to the creation of a "new" system.

   ii. Supervisors should already be trained in using it.

   iii. Employees should understand it and, to the extent they have a right or desire to challenge its implementation and administration, will likely already have done so.

   iv. Employees should already be aware of where they stand on the plan, and they may have come to accept those standings, even if they may not know where they rank relative to others.

b. Factors favoring a new evaluation system. *See generally Jones v. Unisys Corp.*, 829 F. Supp. 1281 (D. Utah 1993), *aff'd,* 54 F.3d 624 (10th Cir. 1995) (change from seniority based system to skills based system).

   i. Normal evaluation systems are typically not geared to making hard decisions on termination, but to boosting employee morale or suggesting areas of development for employees to improve their weaknesses.

   ii. Managers may not have a history of "brutal honesty" in writing evaluations under an existing plan, but will have to assume this posture when forced to identify who will be retained and who will be terminated.

   iii. The formal appraisals in the existing system may have been written only after salary planning sessions, as a "bootstrap" to salary results.

   iv. "Rating inflation" may have historically crept in.

   v. An existing system may not provide for relative rankings of employees.

   vi. A special rating system can be designed to include factors relevant to termination, such as whether particular employees possess special skills or abilities needed in the future. The employer may have reason to retain an employee even if that employee is not currently rated at the top for past performance, because the employee has only been on the assignment for a short period, is on a "developmental rotational assignment" into a position that is not within his/her particular expertise, or is newly hired but may still possess skills needed for the future.

Length of service can be a positive factor. *See Coburn v. Pan Am. World Airways*, 711 F.2d at 343.

c. "Special" evaluation systems can bring special legal problems . . . or advantages.

i. Any inconsistency with previous ratings and/or rankings will be very hard to explain. *See Verbraeken v. Westinghouse Elec. Corp.*, 881 F.2d 1041 (11th Cir. 1989), *cert. denied,* 493 U.S. 1064 (1990) (low score on newly-instituted peer review evaluation contrasted with past favorable supervisor evaluations); *EEOC v. Consolidated Edison*, 80 Civ. 1292 (S.D.N.Y. 1982); *Hannan v. Chrysler Corp.*, 443 F. Supp. at 805.

ii. Factors can be added to avoid even the appearance of age bias, and to monitor for adverse age impact. *See Coburn v. Pan Am. World Airways*, 711 F.2d at 343; *Mastie v. Great Lakes Steel Corp.*, 424 F. Supp. 1299 (E.D. Mich. 1976).

7. Review the results of the employee ranking process for statistical imbalance, and, especially where potential issues exist, check whether the documentation available matches the rankings. A "Personnel/Legal Review Audit Committee" offers an opportunity to monitor for results that could be readily challenged by those affected.

E. Force reduction resulting from an "Organization Redesign." Employers are increasingly turning to inside and outside Organization Effectiveness and Design Consultants to suggest new structures to achieve greater efficiency. Terminations in connection with these programs raise slightly different issues than those discussed above.

1. The steps in the "organization redesign" procedure usually involve both identification of the functions that will continue to be performed by the organization, and the creation of a new structure -- theoretically without regard to incumbents' identities or personalities. The existing workforce is then analyzed, level-by-level, from the top down, to determine which employees best fit the newly created organizations and the redesigned jobs. Those left over after the "fitting process" are "surplus" to be placed elsewhere or terminated. *See*, in this connection, *Doan v. Seagate Technology*, 82 F.3d 974, 978 (10th Cir. 1996) ("Congress has recognized potential as a legitimate factor distinct from age"), *cert. denied*, 117 S. Ct. 684 (1997).

2. How broadly to search throughout the workforce for employees whose abilities match available jobs? How broadly to look for open positions in the newly designed organization into which otherwise "surplus" employees might fit? The more established the employer's practice of searching for new positions for employees whose jobs have been eliminated, the easier it will be for a plaintiff to make out a *prima facie* case if the employer does not find, let alone seek, an alternative position for a terminated employee. *See Cronin v. Aetna Life Ins. Co.*, 46 F.3d 196 (2d Cir. 1995) (failure to search for open position for older employee, where employer did so for younger employees, was evidence of discrimination);

Curto v. Sears Roebuck & Co., 38 Fair Empl. Prac. Cas. (BNA) 547, 551 (N.D. Ill. 1984). If employees other than a plaintiff are offered alternatives to termination, the employer's motivation will be suspect. *Fugate v. Allied Corp.*, 582 F. Supp. 780 (N.D. Ill. 1984); *Jacobson v. Pitman-Moore, Inc.*, 582 F. Supp. 169 (D. Minn. 1984).

a. In *Marson v. Jones & Laughlin Steel Corp.*, 523 F. Supp. at 507, the court found no fault when the employer considered the "universe" to be only salesmen in a local center, and did not engage in a company-wide search.

b. In *Weidman v. Western Elec. Co.*, 527 F. Supp. 263 (W.D.N.C. 1981), the employer properly looked at engineers in the same "personnel universe."

c. In *Ruth v. Allis-Chalmers Corp.*, 40 Fair Empl. Prac. Cas. (BNA) 1227 (W.D. Ky. 1986), *aff'd mem.*, 820 F.2d 405 (6th Cir. 1987), the court declined to infer age discrimination from the employer's failure to consider, or train an employee for, another position, nor from its decision not to assume any relocation expense by moving the employee to another location.

3. For all "unassigned surplus," the employer would be well advised to undertake placement efforts (choosing the geographic scope and whether bumping will be considered) commensurate with the overall force situation then existing and the likely availability of open positions. It should not hold out hopes of placement or "go through the motions" of a futile search for other jobs when there simply aren't any available. It should inform employees of a certain date by which they must either be placed or else they will be terminated, and should adhere to its publicized policies and timeframes.

4. It is essential to document decisions on new assignments and alternate placement efforts.

F. Using seniority as a determining (or contributing) factor in involuntary downsizing decisions for management employees may not be desirable; it may even, under some circumstances, raise certain legal questions. *But see Hazen Paper Co. v. Biggins*, 507 U.S. 604 (1993) ("it is incorrect to say that a decision based on years of service is necessarily 'age-based'").

1. It does not take account of the relative potential contributions of employees. *See* E.1. above.

2. Only "bona fide" seniority plans are referenced in Section 703(h) of Title VII as being protected. Terminations of management employees by inverse seniority may not qualify if the seniority "plan" is adopted solely for downsizing and is not used for any other purposes. In this connection, while use of seniority in downsizing is likely to benefit older managerial workers and lessen ADEA concerns (*see* 29 U.S.C. § 623(f)(2)(A): lawful "to observe the terms of a bona fide seniority system"), it could be challenged by recently-hired women and minorities who will be disproportionately affected. *See Pullman-Standard, Div.*

of Pullman, Inc. v. Swint, 456 U.S. 273, 289, 102 S. Ct. 1781, 1790 (1982) (evidence that operation of seniority system had adverse impact on group protected by Title VII may be used in considering totality of circumstances to determine if discriminatory motive present).

3. Consider combining seniority with performance (using broad categories of employee performance levels) and terminating probationary and other less senior employees first within each performance ranking group, starting with the lowest ranking performance band.

G. Selection for involuntary termination should not be based on certain factors that generally have been held to be unlawfully age-related.

1. The higher cost of employing older workers who, by virtue of longer service, have higher salaries, is generally an impermissible factor under EEOC interpretations, 29 C.F.R. Sec. 1625.7(f), unless the dollar argument is tied to productivity per dollar of salary cost, as alluded to in *Loeb v. Textron, Inc.*, 600 F.2d at 1008. *See also DiCola v. Swissre Holding Inc.*, 996 F.2d 30, 32-33 (2d Cir. 1993) ("salary is not a surrogate for age" where "the employer is seeking to adjust costs to match productivity, rather than to eliminate a salary differential based on longevity").

a. *Bialas v. Greyhound Lines*, 59 F.3d 759 (8th Cir. 1995) (even if terminated because of status as higher-paid employees, "this evidence does not in itself support an inference of age discrimination"); *Anderson v. Baxter Healthcare Corp.*, 13 F.3d 1120, 1125-26 (7th Cir. 1994) (applying rationale of *Hazen Paper Co. v. Biggins*, *supra*, to the use of salary considerations, the court held the employee "could not prove age discrimination even if he was fired simply because Baxter desired to reduce its salary costs by discharging him").

b. *Watkinson v. Great Atlantic & Pacific Tea Co.*, 585 F. Supp. 879 (E.D. Pa. 1984) (management statements focusing on "senior force" with higher cost per person hour held admissible to establish plaintiff's case).

c. *Franci v. Avco Corp.*, 538 F. Supp. 250 (D. Conn. 1982) (undue employer focus on reducing salary and fringe benefit costs led to the layoff of older, more highly compensated employees).

d. Where objective measures of employee output per salary dollar cost can be derived, they may be a permissible consideration, even where there is an adverse impact on older workers. *See Donnelly v. Exxon Research & Eng'g Co.*, 12 Fair Empl. Prac. Cas. (BNA) 417 (D.N.J. 1974), *aff'd mem.*, 521 F.2d 1398 (3d Cir. 1975).

2. Eligibility for early retirement benefits cannot be a factor in an involuntary termination decision. *McCorstin v. U.S. Steel Corp.*, 621 F.2d at 754. Nor can it be used to justify terminating employees who are pension-eligible rather than laying them off and giving them recall rights. *But see also* cases cited in IV. F. *supra*.

VI. OTHER SUGGESTED APPROACHES TO MINIMIZE LIABILITY AND/OR RISK OF SUIT

Freeze hiring and/or "backfilling" surplus employees' jobs. The employer will have a hard job of explaining if it is simultaneously hiring new employees while terminating "older" employees -- unless the skills involved are discrete and separate. *See James v. Sears, Roebuck & Co.*, 21 F.3d 989, 994 (10th Cir. 1994); *Tuft v. McDonnell Douglas Corp.*, 581 F.2d 1304 (8th Cir. 1978); *Deutsch v. Carl Zeiss, Inc.*, 529 F. Supp. 215 (S.D.N.Y. 1981).

NOTES

NOTES

13

RESPONDING TO AN EEOC CHARGE OR OSHA INVESTIGATION

Joseph R. Damato

TABLE OF CONTENTS

I.

YOUR EMPLOYEE AS YOUR CO-DEFENDANT: SOME CONSIDERATIONS

I.

YOUR EMPLOYEE AS YOUR CO-DEFENDANT: SOME CONSIDERATIONS

A. INTRODUCTION[1/]

More and more, plaintiffs suing their former employers for wrongful discharge or employment discrimination also sue individuals--their supervisors, co-employees, company officers, or even directors--as well. In these situations employers and their counsel need to carefully consider whether to undertake a joint defense.

Putting forth a joint defense will usually be cost efficient and consistent with the employer's common law obligation to indemnify an employee who lawfully carries out in good faith his duties to the Company. In addition, a joint defense will typically not undermine the employer's position or increase its risk of liability since the codefendant's conduct--presumably as a member of the employer's management--will often be attributed to the employer for liability purposes in any event. Other factors favor joint representation as well. For instance, maintaining the good will and confidence of managerial employees may depend upon putting forth a single defense of the corporation and the manager in question. And, usually, a unified defense is a strong defense.

When, however, the employer and the individual supervisor are jointly sued and the initial investigation discloses that the supervisor might have acted wrongly and outside the scope of his or her employment--as often occurs when sexual harassment or criminal action by the supervisor is alleged--a joint defense may be rejected on the grounds that the interests of the employer and the supervisor are in conflict.

The issues relating to potential conflicts of interest are made even more complex by the factual uncertainties typical of the early phases of litigation. The question of whom the company's counsel will represent in any action must generally be answered at a very early stage, often before the facts have been fully developed. This fact increases the likelihood that

---

[1/] The current status of the law in your own jurisdiction may differ from that reflected here. The law presented here is meant to illustrate the issues you may face in this area, and is not intended to be exhaustive. Also, this discussion relates to issues you may face in civil actions only. A treatment of the issues to be addressed in a criminal law context can be found in the materials prepared by William F. Pendergast.

an actual conflict of interest may emerge after the case is under way and result in the disqualification of counsel from representing any of the parties in the litigation.

B. CHECKLIST OF CLAIMS AND DEFENSES IN ACTIONS NAMING INDIVIDUAL DEFENDANTS

1. Plaintiff's attorneys are suing individual codefendants under a wide range of theories.

a. The particular claim asserted against the individual defendant may have a direct bearing on whether company counsel chooses to defend that employee. The theories asserted against individuals may also prove to be legally untenable and therefore subject to a motion.

b. In most cases when there is a joint defense, it will be desirable to seek dismissal of the claims against the individual defendants if possible, and to remove those individuals from the case.

2. Many wrongful termination complaints include a cause of action for intentional or negligent infliction of emotional distress, and generally focus on alleged employer misconduct stemming from the termination decision and the manner in which that decision is carried out. Many plaintiffs also include a cause of action for defamation, directed against either the company, or a managerial employee, or both. The allegations relating to these theories often describe specific conversations or meetings, such as the exit interview, and are therefore often directed against the managerial participants as individuals.

3. Privilege as a Defense: The defense of privilege often will prevail against these tort claims.

a. If the allegedly defamatory statement was truthful, it is absolutely privileged.

b. Employer responses to inquiries from administrative or other governmental agencies will also be privileged.

c. Statements to other employees, fairly explaining the basis for the discharge, or statements uttered as part of the investigation leading to the discharge, may be protected by a qualified privilege, depending upon the absence of malice.

4. The Managerial Immunity Defense: Individual supervisors and other company officials who may be codefendants in these tort causes of action may assert a defense based on the doctrine of "managerial immunity."

a. If the complaint alleges that the individual defendants were the agents and employees of the defendant employer and acting within the course and scope of their employment in doing the things alleged, the managerial privilege may be available to them. See Scopas v. Armstrong World Indus., 114 L.R.R.M. 2933, 2934 (C.D. Cal. 1983); Becket v. Welton, Becket & Assocs., 39 Cal. App. 3d 815, 114 Cal. Rptr. 531 (1984).

5. Breach of Contract and Related Defenses: Managerial codefendants may not be held accountable for the employer's alleged breach contract or breach of the implied-in-law covenant of good faith and fair dealing, since the individual defendant is not a party to the employment contract forming the basis of the implied covenant. See Cleary v. Am. Airlines, Inc., 111 Cal. App. 3d 443, 168 Cal. Rptr. 722 (1980).

a. Supervisors and managers acting within the scope of their employment on behalf of their employer in carrying out the termination also cannot be held liable for interfering with the contract. See B., Inc., v. Miller Brewing Co., 663 F.2d 545 (5th Cir. 1981); Crossen v. Foremost-McKesson, Inc., 537 F.Supp. 1076, 1077 (N.D. Cal. 1982).

b. On the other hand, third-party employees who, for personal reasons unrelated to the nature and scope of their employment, engage in intentional and malicious acts designed to create employment problems for the plaintiff, may be subject to a claim for intentional interference with contractual relations.

C. ISSUES TO CONSIDER ONCE THE ACTION IS FILED

1. In evaluating whether or not to engage in a joint defense, the corporation should consider a variety of issues, in addition to the potential for conflicts of interest:

a. Will the testimony of the prospective jointly represented codefendant be consistent with testimony of others?

b. Are there defenses or evidentiary matters peculiar to the codefendant that might be better handled outside joint defense?

(1) For example, a sexual harassment claim against a corporation and manager where plaintiff also asserts a common law tort against the manager, to which the manger might respond that his attentions were invited. As a practical matter, would this defense to the tort claim reduce the corporation's defense to the issue of the manager's credibility on the possibly unrelated claim?

c. Would discovery or trial strategies be altered by the joint representation of the corporation and codefendant employee? Are there objections to be made or privileges to be asserted--or waived--on behalf of one party and not the other?

d. Will a joint defense lead to emphasis of one party at the expense of another?

e. Will a joint defense either inhibit the corporation's full investigation of the matter or hamper settlement?

f. What are the cost considerations involved in a separate defense?

(1) Is it appropriate for the company to advance litigation expenses for a codefendant?

(2) If so, how should it be structured and memorialized?

g. Would a company decision not to undertake the joint defense of a managerial codefendant damage the company's rapport among its managerial employees?

h. If a joint defense is undertaken, what representations should be made to the individual codefendant at the outset concerning the conditions of the joint defense?

i. What statements should be made at the investigation stage, so that a company attorney does not inadvertently create an attorney-client relationship through interviewee's expectation or disclosure of confidential information in belief joint defense already undertaken? See Bernstein v. Crazy Eddie, Inc., 702 F. Supp. 962, 988 (S.D.N.Y. 1989).

D. THE OBLIGATION TO INDEMNIFY

1. California Law

Section 2802 of the California Labor Code provides as follows:

> An employer shall indemnify his employee for all the employee necessarily expends or loses in direct consequence of his discharge of his duties as such, or of his obedience to the directions of the employer, even though unlawful, unless the employee, at the time of obeying such direction, believed them to be unlawful. Cal. Lab. Code § 2802.

a. There has been very little case law in California interpreting this provision but it is clear that section 2802 requires an employer to defend or indemnify an employee who is sued by third persons for conduct occurring in the course and scope of his employment.

b. In Douglas v. Los Angeles Herald Examiner, 50 Cal. App. 3d 449, 123 Cal. Rptr. 683 (1975), the question of when this obligation arises was addressed, at least implicitly. According to the appellate court, "when an employer refuses to defend an employee in an action which may or may not be unfounded for conduct which may or may not have been within the course and scope of his employment and it is ultimately established that the action was unfounded and the employee acted within the course and scope of his employment, then the employer has an obligation . . . to indemnify. . . ." Id. at 465 (emphasis added).

c. Does the Douglas decision require an employer to defend immediately upon the employee's tender of defense?

(1) The decision appears to permit an employer who believes that the conduct complained of falls outside of the course and scope of employment to decline the tender at the outset of the litigation. At that point, the employee will be faced with finding his or her own counsel.

(2) If, however, the claim is ultimately found unmeritorious, or if it is later established that the conduct was within the course and scope, the employer may be obligated to pay the cost of defense.

(3) At this juncture, at least, there appears to be no reservation of rights rule analogous to that which is present in the insurance industry.

E. THE PROBLEM OF CONFLICTS OF INTEREST

1. The Company Attorney's Obligations

a. Absent some form of inquiry into the potential for conflict of interests, a company attorney's choice to represent multiple parties may violate the requirements of Fed. R. Civ. P. 11. Unioil, Inc. et al. v. E.F. Hutton & Co. 35 al., 802 F.2d 1080 (9th Cir. 1986).

b. The Code of Professional Responsibility, which governs attorneys, will affect the company lawyer in joint defense situations.

(1) Canon 4 provides "A Lawyer Should Preserve the Confidences and Secrets of a Client."

(2) Canon 5 deals with a lawyer's obligation to exercise independent professional judgment on behalf of a client. DR 5-105(c) allows employment by multiple clients if "it is obvious [the attorney] can adequately represent the interests of each" and "if each consents to representation after full disclosure of the possible effect of such representation. . . ." Model Code of Professional Responsibility DR 5-105(c).

(3) Canon 9 states that a "Lawyer Should Avoid Even the Appearance of Professional Impropriety."

2. No Per Se Rule

Representation of the defendant employer and a codefendant by single counsel does not per se create a conflict of interest or violate the Canons.

a. See, e.g., Katz v. Morgenthau, 709 F.Supp. 1219 (S.D.N.Y. 1989) § 1983 Claims); Smith v. City of New York, 611 F.Supp. 1080 (S.D.N.Y. 1985); Clay v. Doherty, 608 F.Supp. 295 (D.C. Ill. 1985) (§ 1983 Claims); Lee v. Hutson, 600 F.Supp. 957 (N.D. Ga. 1984) (§ 1983 Claims); Manganella v. Keyes, 613 F.Supp. 795 (D.C. Conn. 1985; Feng v. Sandrik, 636 F.Supp. 72 (N.D. Ill. 1986) (sex discrimination); Kerry Coal Co. v. United Mine Workers, 470 F.Supp. 1032 (W.D. Pa 1979), aff'd, 637 F.2d 957 (3d Cir.), cert. denied, 454 U.S. 823 (1981).

b. See also Doe v. A Corp., 709 F.2d 1043 (5th Cir. 1983) (the corporation and the benefit plan for its employees had the right to waive any possible claim of conflict resulting from the attorney's joint representation); International Union v. Allis Chalmers, 447 F.Supp. 766 (E.D. Wis. 1978) (the simultaneous representation of a contributing employer and ERISA fiduciary in the Union's NLRA, ERISA, and securities law lawsuit did not conflict); D.S. Magazines, Inc. v. Warner Publisher Servs., 623 F.Supp. 624 (S.D.N.Y. 1985).

3. Company's Defense May Create Conflict

On the other hand, even when the codefendant employee has consented to joint representation, the employer's defense that the employee was acting outside the course and scope of employment (thereby opening the employee to potential individual tort liability) is a conflict requiring disqualification and even setting aside a judgment after the fact. Dunton v. County of Suffolk, 729 F.2d 903 (2d Cir. 1984), modified, 748 F.2d 69 (2d Cir. 1984); cf. Shadid v. Jackson, 521 F.Supp. 87 (E.D. Tex. 1981); Katz v. Morgenthau, supra, 709 F.Supp. 1219.

a. Thus consent alone will not necessarily cure a conflict when a conflict in the presentation of a defense, or potential for that conflict, is readily apparent. Id. See also Rice v. Baron 456 F.Supp. 1361 (S.D.N.Y. 1978) (dicta).

b. See also O'Reilly v. Executone, 135 A.D.2d 999, 522 N.Y.S.2d 724 (3d Dept. 1987) (permitting attorney's withdrawal from representation of employee, on grounds that employer's defense that the employee's conduct not attributable to employer would be raised at trial.)

4. Is Consent Informed?

Assuming that all defenses will be consistent and consent is asserted, the principal question will be whether the consent is informed.

a. Unified Sewerage Agency, Etc. v. Jelco, Inc., 646 F.2d 1339 (9th Cir. 1981) ("it is not sufficient that both parties be informed of the fact that the lawyer is undertaking to represent both of them, but he must explain to them the nature of the conflict of interest in such detail that they can understand the reasons why it may be desirable for each to have independent counsel"); Smith v. City of New York, 611 F.Supp. 1080 (S.D.N.Y. 1985); City Consumer Servs., Inc. v. Horne, 571 F.Supp. 965 (C.D. Utah 1983); Lee v. Hutson, 600 F.Supp. 957 (allowing attorneys to solicit informed consent even after disqualification is sought); In Re Grand Jury, 446 F.Supp. 1132 (N.D. Tex. 1978) (the court denied a motion for disqualification of attorneys for conflcit of interest in multiple representation, when a hearing was held and the court questioned individuals, and allowed individuals to question the court, concerning the nature of their waivers).

b. Effective May, 1989, California adopted Rules of Professional Conduct relating inter alia to adverse interests, disclosure, and informed, written consent.

5. Difficulties in Managing the Lawsuit

Even with informed consent, counsel must insure that the second element of DR 5-105(c) (whether it is obvious to the attorney that he can adequately represent both defendants) is met.

a. In Oneida of Thames Band v. State of N.Y., 757 F.2d 19 (2d Cir. 1985), the court held that the potential for a conflict does not preclude joint representation under this standard. Rather, the test is whether joint representation "would make the day-to-day conduct of the trial unmanageable or even difficult." Id. at 22.

(1) See also City Consumers Servs. Inc. v. Hovine, 571 F.Supp. 965 (C.D. Utah 1983) (an objective standard should be used--namely, does the lawyer possess substantial doubt that he can adequately represent the interest of each client?).

6. The Problem of "After-Discovered" Conflicts

A real conflict may develop during discovery or at trial requiring the attorney to withdraw from representation of one of the codefendants.

a. The question then presented is whether the codefendant from whose case the attorney has withdrawn may seek disqualification of the attorney under Canon 4 or 9.

(1) For example, assume that on the eve of trial the codefendant employee informs his defense attorney in a discrimination case that he or she was drunk or under the influence of drugs when the incident at issue took place, thus creating an "outside scope" argument.

(2) After withdrawal, may the attorney use this information on behalf of the corporation or does his or her disqualification from the entire case necessarily follow? See Rice v. Barion, 456 F.Supp. 1361 (S.D.N.Y. 1978).

b. The standard law under Canon 4 is that an attorney who has represented a party previously on a matter "substantially related" to the subject matter of the instant lawsuit is subject to disqualification.

(1) The Canon's purpose is to preserve confidences and provide clients with unrestrained representation.

(2) Therefore, many cases hold that the presumption of exchange of confidential information is nonrebuttable. See, e.g., In Re Corrugated Container Antitrust Litig., 659 F.2d 1341 (5th Cir. 1981).

(3) The Second Circuit appears, however, to allow a party to rebut the presumption. See generally United States Football League v. Nat'l Football League, 605 F.Supp. 1448 (S.D.N.Y. 1985).

7. Expectation of Confidentiality

At least one court has held, interpreting Canon 4, that an attorney is not to be disqualified at the behest of a former client if the former client had no expectation of confidentiality. Allegaert v. Perot, 434 F.Supp. 790 (S.D.N.Y. 1977):

> At the time these law firms are claimed to have acquired their information, neither the corporation nor anyone connected with it had any expectation that either of these law firms would keep secret from their primary clients any information acquired in the course of any services individually performed. . . .
> Id. at 800.

a. See also E.F. Hutton & Co. v. Brown, 305 F.Supp. 371 (S.D. Tex. 1969). A client's simple consent to adverse representation, however, is not consent to the use of confidential information. In Re Corruption Container Antitrust Litig., 659 F.2d 1341, 1348 (5th Cir. 1981).

8. Waivers of Conflict

Inaction by a former client in seeking to disqualify may constitute a waiver of conflict. International Sound Technicians v. Int'l Alliance, Etc., 611 F.2d 266 (9th Cir. 1979); cf. In Re Corrugated Container Antitrust Litig., 659 F.2d 1341, 1348 (5th Cir. 1981).

9. Payment of Fee

An attorney whose fee is paid by the corporation for representation of a codefendant employee and who adequately discloses the fee arrangement may not be subject to disqualification. See In Re Special Grand Jury, 480 F.Supp. 174 (E.D. Wis. 1979); In Re Special February 1975 Grand Jury, 406 F.Supp. 194 (N.D. Ill. 1975); Compare N.Y. Bus. Corp. Law § 724(c) (McKinney).

10. Vicarious Liability

In New Jersey it has been held that a corporation may be found vicariously liable for punitive damages in a wrongful discharge case by engaging in a joint defense. See Cappiello v. Ragen Precision Indus., 192 N.J. Super. 523, 471 A.2d 432 (1984).

11. Withdrawal

In New York, at least one court has allowed attorneys to withdraw from representing the individual while continuing to represent the corporation, notwithstanding joint representation through a motion to dismiss. *O'Reilly v. Executone*, 135 A.D.2d 999, 522 N.Y.S.2d 724 (3d Dept. 1987).

II.

INSURANCE COVERAGE OF LABOR RELATED LAWSUITS

II.

INSURANCE COVERAGE OF LABOR RELATED LAWSUITS

A. GENERAL CONSIDERATIONS

1. There are many different types of insurance policies arguably covering different types of alleged employer misconduct. However, even when a particular claim initially appears not to be covered, it still may be, because rules of construction relating to insurance policies are liberally applied in favor of the insured. Uncertainties or ambiguities in a contract be interpreted against the drafter of the language, and it is usually the insurance carrier that drafts the language of the policy.

2. Insurance policies, considered by the courts to be "adhesion contracts," are liberally construed in favor of the insured and strictly construed against the carrier for public policy reasons as well. General policy provisions "are interpreted broadly so as to provide the greatest possible coverage to the insured." State Farm Ins. Co. v. Partridge, 10 Cal. 3d 94, 101 (1973). "[A]ny uncertainty or ambiguity must be resolved against the insurer and, if semantically possible, the policy must be construed so as to achieve its manifest object of indemnifying the insured against the losses to which the policy relates." Pepper Industries, Inc. v. Home Ins. Co., 67 Cal. App. 3d 1012, 1018 (1977).

3. However, if a policy clearly provides that it does not cover a particular kind of lawsuit, like wrongful termination, a court will not impose liability upon the carrier. Giddings v. Industrial Indemnity Co., 112 Cal. App. 3d 213, 218 (1980). In light of this, employers seeking to insure employment litigation should carefully scrutinize their policies when they are written, to make sure such litigation is covered.

4. Insurance companies in recent years, mindful of the strict rules of construction, have clarified their coverage provisions and exclusionary clauses in order to make sure that if employment litigation is not to be covered by the policy, the policy so states.

5. Despite this, it is important that employers sued for wrongful termination or related labor claims do not limit themselves to a cursory review of their insurance policies to determine if there is coverage. Even though a policy's language may at first glance indicate otherwise, there may be at least partial coverage, and so long as there is arguable partial coverage, the carrier has a duty to defend the insured.

B. TYPES OF INSURANCE POLICIES ARGUABLY COVERING DIFFERENT TYPES OF LABOR-RELATED LAWSUITS

The common types of liability insurance that arguably cover employment-related claims are the following:

1. Comprehensive general liability: covers loss by reason of liability to pay damages on account of injury or property damage caused by accident. "Injury" should not necessarily be narrowly construed as "bodily injury." Some policies provide that "injury" includes not only "bodily" injury but also injury from "racial, sex, marital, ancestry, physical and mental handicaps, age, sexual preference, and pregnancy, or religious discrimination, false arrest or imprisonment, malicious prosecution, libel, slander, defamation of character or invasion of privacy." Further, some comprehensive general liability policies cover contractual liability, which arguably could cover any and all contracts, including a collective bargaining agreement or an employment contract.

2. Comprehensive personal liability: similar to comprehensive general liability but applies to damages imposed by law on an individual. Such a policy might include a broad form of extended coverage, which would cover employees acting within the scope of their authority.

3. Errors and omissions liability: covers special risks such as negligence, omissions, mistakes and errors inherent in the practice of a particular profession.

4. Workers' compensation and employer's liability: covers basic workers' compensation litigation and arguably covers California Labor Code Section 132(a) claims.

5. Excess and umbrella liability: generally provides coverage in areas which might not be included in basic coverage and/or liability in excess of the insured's primary insurance coverage.

6. Directors' and officers' liability and general partners' liability: covers the actions of a company's directors, officers, and certain employees who, while acting within the scope of their duties, incur liability to another party.

7. Homeowner's liability: will not cover a business but if an individual supervisor is named as a defendant in a wrongful termination lawsuit, the supervisor should check his or her own homeowner's policy and consider tendering the defense of the lawsuit to the carrier.

C. NONCOVERAGE OF CERTAIN CAUSES OF ACTION OR DAMAGE CLAIMS

1. Punitive Damages

California is one of only eight states in the country that specifically provides for noninsurability of punitive damages. California Insurance Code Section 533. See also, California Civil Code Section 1668, making unlawful any contract (including an insurance contract) which exempts anyone from responsibility for willfully injuring another. City Products Corp. v. Globe Indemnity Co., 88 Cal. App. 3d 31, 35 (1979). Twenty-two states do allow punitive damages to be insurable or allow such in cases of vicarious liability. Other states have either not yet determined the issue or do not allow punitive damages at all, leaving aside the question of whether they are insurable. Therefore, it is important that employers consult counsel to determine which state law governs their insurance policy.

2. Despite the general noninsurability of punitive damages in California, the California Supreme Court has held that merely because an act is "intentional" or "willful" within the meaning of traditional tort principles does not make it "willful" so as to exonerate the insurance carrier from liability under Insurance Code Section 533. An Act would be willful (and thus not insurable) only if done with a "preconceived design to inflict injury." Clemmer v. Hartford Insurance Co., 22 Cal. 3d 865 (1978), as modified January 17, 1979.

3. An insurance company always has the right to state clearly in a policy that it will cover only "accidents" or "unintentional acts," and the courts will not extend these policies to intentional acts. Two cases dealing with wrongful termination illustrate this point.

a. In St. Paul Fire & Marine Ins. Co. v. Superior Court of Yuba County, 161 Cal. App. 3d 1199 (1984), the insured had a policy covering claims for bodily injury resulting from "an accidental event." This term was defined by the policy to mean something the insured "didn't expect or intend to happen." The insured was sued for wrongful termination and the court, in a lawsuit brought by the insurance company for declaratory relief, held that the termination was "not an unintentional, unexpected, chance occurrence," and thus there was no potential liability on the part of the insurance company under the policy. The carrier did not have a duty to defend the insured employer.

b. In Commercial Union Ins. Co. v. Superior Court, 196 Cal. App. 3d 1205 (1987), the court expanded the ruling made in St. Paul. As noted above, the insurance policy in St. Paul defined the accident as something that was unexpected. In Commercial Union, the policy defined the injury as something that was "neither expected nor intended by" the policyholder, who in this case was an employer being sued for wrongful termination. The complaint included an allegation that the plaintiff suffered severe emotional distress as a result of the termination. The employer tendered the defense of the lawsuit to the carrier, contending that he did not expect the employee to experience this type of injury. The carrier rejected the tender of the lawsuit, so the employer sued the insurance company, making the same argument to the court. The court rejected the argument, concluding that the policy did not cover intentional acts, including a termination of employment.

4. On the basis of these two cases, insurance companies today are not having difficulty arguing successfully to the courts that wrongful termination litigation is not covered by a standard liability policy covering "accidents." Thus, in order to make sure that this type of litigation is covered, an employer should insist that the policy so state.

D. DUTY TO DEFEND THE INSURED EMPLOYER

1. Broader Than Duty of Coverage: The duty to provide a defense to a lawsuit is broader than the duty of covering the claims within that lawsuit. The duty of defense attaches when at least one of the claims in the lawsuit falls, or may be construed to fall, within coverage of the policy. Further, the general rule is that an insurance company must provide a defense as to all allegations in the complaint if it has a duty to defend against any of the allegations, even though some of them (or even most) might ultimately result in recovery for damages not covered by the policy. California Union Ins. Co. v. Club Aquarius, 113 Cal. App. 3d 243, 248 (1980).

2. Where there is a potential for liability under the policy, a defense must be provided. State Farm Fir & Casualty Co. v. Drasin, 152 Cal. App. 3d 864, 869 (1984).

3. Even where the allegations of a complaint may not, on their face, give rise to a duty to defend, there still may be facts not expressly referred to in the complaint that give rise to coverage. Previews, Inc. v. Calif. Union Ins. Co., 640 F.2d 1026 (9th Cir. 1981). Gray v. Zurich Ins. Co., 65 Cal. 2d 263 (1966;,

4. A claim or a cause of action may be construed to require coverage even in the face of statutory or express noncoverage. For example, a sex discrimination claim, while worded in terms of intentional misconduct, does not require "intent" as a necessary element. This is true with respect not only to federal law but also a claim brought pursuant to the California Fair Employment and Housing Act. Thus, neither California Insurance Code Section 533 nor an express exclusion

of coverage for intentional acts in an insurance policy will preclude a defense for a sex discrimination claim if it can be otherwise arguably covered.

5. When an employer's carrier denies a duty to defend, the employer should not necessarily accept the denial, believing the carrier knows best when it comes to understanding what the policy requires. Often the duty to defend is present and if the carrier wrongfully denies a tender of the defense, the exposure for the carrier could be substantial.

E. INSURED'S RIGHT TO BE DEFENDED BY COUNSEL OF CHOICE AT EXPENSE OF INSURANCE CARRIER

1. "Cumis" Counsel

"Cumis" counsel is a shorthand way to refer to counsel whose fees are paid at least in part by a insurance carrier to defend claims asserted against an insured, but who was selected to so defend by the insured itself, and not by the insurance carrier.

The rationale for "Cumis" counsel was anticipated by the California Supreme Court in 1964. Because an insurance carrier's duty to defend the policyholder is more important than the carrier's desire to control exclusively the defense of a lawsuit, the carrier's obligation to defend requires it to pay the reasonable value of legal services and costs performed by independent counsel selected by the policyholder where either (1) facts exist which create a legal conflict of interest between the insurance company and the policyholder, or (2) the insurance company lacks an economic motive for vigorous defense of the policyholder. Tomerlin v. Canadian Indemnity Co., 61 Cal. 2d 638 (1964).

Often an insurance carrier will concede that it has a duty to defend the insured, but will then issue a "reservation-of-rights" letter setting forth bases for later asserting noncoverage of ultimate liability. The most common example of this is where the insurance company asserts that it will not be liable for punitive damages based on serious or willful misconduct or intentional acts on the part of the insured.

In 1984, a California court of appeal held that this situation poses, virtually as a matter of law, a conflict of interest between the insurance company and the insured. San Diego Navy Federal Credit Union v. Cumis Ins. Society, Inc., 162 Cal. App. 3d 358 (1984).

Since 1984, however, Cumis has been refined and limited by case law and by statute. For example, in Foremost Insurance Co. v. Wilks, 206 Cal. App. 3d 251 (1988), the court held that a punitive damage claim by itself was insufficient to create a conflict between the insured and the insurer, thus triggering a duty under Cumis to provide the insured with independent counsel. This ruling is consistent with the Tort Reform Act of 1987, more fully discussed below.

If the insurance carrier does not issue a reservation-of-rights letter, a Cumis conflict of interest is not present and unless a separate potential conflict of interest is present, the insured does not have the right to be represented by its counsel of choice at the carrier's expense.

2. California Tort Reform Act of 1987

As could be expected, the Cumis decision caused substantial controversy. Insurance companies found themselves beset by numerous claims of a conflict of interest, with their insureds insisting upon independent counsel of choice. Further, insureds (and their counsel) insisted that independent counsel be paid their normal fees, which were often higher than those of law firms retained by the insurance companies. Thus, the insurance industry persuaded the California legislature to pass the Tort Reform Act of 1987. The Act, codified in Civil Code Section 2860, provides, in pertinent part:

> a. If the provisions of a policy of insurance impose a duty to defend upon an insurer and a conflict of interest arises which creates a duty on the part of the insurer to provide independent counsel to the insured, the insurer shall provide such counsel to represent the insured unless, at the time the insured is informed that a possible conflict may arise or does exist, the insured expressly waives, in writing, the right to such counsel. An insurance contract may contain a provision which sets forth the method of selecting such counsel consistent with this section.
>
> b. For purposes of this section, a conflict of interest does not exist as to allegations or facts in the litigation for which the insurer denies coverage; however, when an insurer reserves its rights on a given issue and the outcome of that coverage issue can be controlled by counsel first retained by the insurer for the defense of the claim, a conflict of interest may exist. No conflict of interest shall be deemed to exist as to allegations of punitive damages or be deemed to exist solely because an insured is sued for an amount in excess of the insurance policy limits.
>
> c. When the insured has selected independent counsel to represent him or her, the insurer may exercise its right to require that the counsel selected by the insured possess certain minimum qualifications which may include that the selected counsel have (1) at least five years of tort litigation practice which includes substantial defense experience in the subject at issue in the litigation, and (2) errors and omissions coverage.

The insurer's obligation to pay fees to such independent counsel selected by the insured is limited to the rates which are actually paid by the insurer to attorneys retained by it in the ordinary course of business in the defense of similar actions in the community where the claim arose or is being defended. This subdivision does not invalidate other different or additional policy provisions pertaining to attorney's fees or providing for methods of settlement of disputes concerning those fees. Any dispute concerning attorney's fees not resolved by these methods shall be resolved by final and binding arbitration by a single neutral arbitrator selected by the parties to the dispute.

d. When independent counsel has been selected by the insured, it shall be the duty of such counsel and the insured to disclose to the insurer all information concerning the action except privileged materials relevant to coverage disputes, and timely to inform and consult with the insurer on all matters relating to the action. Any claim of privilege asserted is subject to in camera review in the appropriate law and motion department of the superior court. Any information disclosed by the insured or by independent counsel is not a waiver of the privilege as to any other party.

e. The insured may waive its right to select independent counsel by signing the following statement: "I have been advised and informed of my right to select independent counsel to represent me in this lawsuit. I have considered this matter fully and freely waive my right to select a defense attorney to represent me in this lawsuit."

f. Where the insured selects independent counsel pursuant to the provisions of this section, both the counsel provided by the insurer and independent counsel selected by the insured shall be allowed to participate in all aspects of the litigation. Counsel shall cooperate fully in the exchange of information that is consistent with each counsel's ethical and legal obligation to the insured. Nothing in this section shall relieve the insured of his or her duty to cooperate with the insurer under the terms of the insurance contract.

Civil Code Section 2860 has been upheld by a California appellate court. _Centennial Ins. Co. v. Murat_, 206 Cal. App. 3d 1199 (1988)

Because Civil Code Section 2860 has now been upheld, insured employers will have to accept its restrictions on independent counsel. This means at the very least that legal fees of such counsel may not be covered competely by the policy, and even the right to have such counsel (whose fees are to be paid by the insurance company) may not be available. Of course, each situation must be separately analyzed, so insured employers should check with counsel about their particular case.

F. TENDERING THE DEFENSE OF THE LAWSUIT TO THE INSURANCE CARRIER

1. It is imperative for an employer who is sued to provide notice immediately of this fact to its insurance carrier and tender the defense of the lawsuit to the carrier.

2. It is important for an employer to clearly identify itself in its tender of defense and include the policy number of its insurance. If, due to an employer's carelessness in notifying its insurance carrier of a lawsuit against the employer, the carrier mistakenly denies its duty to defend, the carrier may be successful in defending itself later in an action by the insured alleging a bad-faith denial of the duty. California Shoppers, Inc. v. Royal Globe Ins. Co., 175 Cal. App. 3d 1 (1985).

III.

HANDLING THE DISCRIMINATION CHARGE AT THE ADMINISTRATIVE LEVEL

III.

HANDLING THE DISCRIMINATION CHARGE AT THE ADMINISTRATIVE LEVEL

A. IMPORTANCE OF EEOC INVESTIGATIVE PROCESS

1. Employers often minimize the importance of handling the discrimination charge while it is before the EEOC or state agency. This can be a serious and costly mistake because the outcome of investigation and conciliation procedures generally have a significant impact on (1) whether or not there will be a subsequent lawsuit based on the charge and, if so, (2) what the outcome of the lawsuit will be. Keep in mind also that the very same principles set forth here apply to charges before other administrative agencies handling employment disputes.

B. INITIAL RESPONSE TO THE CHARGE

1. Upon receiving a charge, first consider whether it is timely. EEOC charges in deferral states (both California and Nevada are deferral states) must be filed within 300 days of the alleged discrimination; in non-deferral states within 180 days. State FEP laws have their own time limits for filing charges.

2. Internal Investigation

a. As soon as the charge is received, the Company should conduct a thorough and intensive investigation.

b. Information that is discovered or generated will be susceptible to discovery if the charge leads to litigation. If a charge is initially determined to be a likely lawsuit, an immediate decision must be made as to whether counsel should be retained to protect the confidentiality of certain information generated during the investigation. To preserve attorney work product and attorney client privilege defenses:

-- whenever possible, counsel should direct the investigation

-- all investigative reports and papers should indicate that they are prepared solely for the use of Company counsel.

c. All witnesses or persons who have knowledge of the facts should be interviewed. It is especially important to talk to persons who may be less willing or unwilling to talk later in an adversarial context.

d. All pertinent records and documentation should be gathered, reviewed and put in a safe place.

e. Members of management involved in the charge should understand that, if their recollection of the facts changes, they should not hesitate to alert personnel or counsel to their fresh recollection of events.

C. THE INVESTIGATION

1. General Considerations

a. Proceed with care and deliberation. An inaccurate or poorly thought out response may result in a charge not being resolved at the administrative stage. If that happens and the case ends up in court, it will be extremely costly and time-consuming.

b. Be courteous, reasonable and as cooperative as possible in dealing with the investigator. There is a sharp distinction between asserting the rights of the employer and being hostile to government agents.

c. Make sure that any requests for information or documents are in writing. Do not respond to oral requests.

2. Responding to Interrogatories

a. If the EEOC sends a set of interrogatories, be very careful about the type and extent of information you submit.

b. Just because the agency asks for certain information does not mean that it is relevant. The Company (with the assistance of counsel if necessary) should determine what information is pertinent to the precise claim of the charging party, and only that information should be supplied.

c. Whenever possible, try not to hand over raw data, such as actual personnel files or payroll records. Such information may be used by the agency to develop other information and might later be used against the employer in a lawsuit. Answers to interrogatories should be carefully and conservatively developed.

3. The Position Statement

a. A position statement usually is the most effective tool for the employer during an investigation. It presents the employer's position as effectively as possible by setting forth both the factual and legal reasons why the charge has no merit.

b. The position statement can be submitted at the beginning or end of an investigation, or with responses to interrogatories. This depends on the particular charge.

c. A position statement can be as detailed as deemed necessary, but it should address all aspects of the charge, be carefully prepared and supported by persuasive data.

d. A thorough and persuasive position statement is worth the time and effort it requires for several reasons:

-- Because they are overworked, inexperienced or because they simply do not understand the facts or the way the law is applied, investigators may omit crucial facts in reports to their superiors who must determine the merits of charges. A position statement helps to assure that the facts and law will be presented to agency decisionmakers in their most persuasive light.

-- Once in the agency file, a position statement which makes it clear that the case has no merit or that there is substantial doubt that the plaintiff can win may convince a charging party or his/her attorney that litigation should not be pursued. If suit is filed, the position statement may help to obtain satisfactory settlement.

-- If the Company has a strong case, an initial investment of time at the investigative stage to prepare a convincing position statement may help to avoid the enormous amounts of time and expense required for litigation.

e. See attached Appendix A (page 29) for an outline of a typical position statement.

6. <u>Subpoenas</u>

If the agency wants more information than employer is willing to submit, it has the power to issue subpoenas, compelling the attendance and testimony of witnesses and the production of records and documents. If the agency issues a subpoena, the Company must decide whether to comply or resist. Courts will refuse to enforce subpoenas which are too broad, seek irrelevant material, or fail to specifically describe the evidence sought.

D. <u>THE FACT-FINDING CONFERENCE</u>

1. The fact-finding conference is a face-to-face meeting between the person who filed the complaint, the charging party, and the company representatives who have first-hand knowledge of the charge.

2. The agency uses the fact-finding conference to try to obtain quick settlements of individual charges. Where settlement is not possible, the facts adduced enable the agency to determine what further investigation is needed, and in some rare cases, to make a cause or no-cause decision.

3. Procedure

a. Depending on the agency involved and the agency's docket, the conference may take place within a few weeks after the charge is filed, or it may be months or even years before a conference is held.

b. Attending the conference are the charging party (and perhaps his/her attorney), the supervisor or manager involved, a personnel officer (and/or Company attorney), the agency's investigator who runs the meeting, and sometimes another agency employee who takes notes of the proceedings.

c. Settlement negotiations are kept confidential and off the record, but all other aspects of the conference are on the record.

d. Under EEOC procedures, at the fact-finding conference "each allegation of the charge will be closely examined and fully discussed; the charging party will be allowed ample time to explain and support each allegation [and] the respondent [will receive ample time] to present and defend its position."

4. The importance of the fact-finding conference cannot be overstated for the following reasons:

a. The fact-finding conference is an opportunity to air your case before the agency, and it gives the agency an opportunity to dismiss a baseless charge.

b. Because the conference is on the record, what is said becomes a part of the agency's file. Many employers have found their cases damaged by an inadvisable remark or information furnished during the conference.

c. The conference is the only face-to-face meeting with the charging party. A thorough and effective presentation may help persuade the charging party toward a reasonable settlement or against filing suit.

5. Guidelines for the Employer in handling the fact-finding conference

a. Be sure that you have conducted a thorough investigation of the charge. Try to anticipate the arguments that the charging party will make and have the facts or testimony available to refute those arguments.

b. Make sure that the supervisors or managers who are involved understand what will happen at the conference and that they are fully prepared.

c. Especially where you have a strong case, try to ensure that the record of the conference is correct and complete. Your presentation should be organized, your representatives should not speak too rapidly, and you should keep your own notes of what is said in the event of any future disagreement.

6. Guidelines for the persons actually involved in the fact-finding conference

a. As much as possible, give objective descriptions of events or actions and avoid vague, subjective comments, such as "she lacked initiative" or "he wasn't management material."

b. Always think before speaking. Avoid spontaneous, off-the-cuff responses.

c. Don't get emotional. Supervisors and managers accused of discrimination may be upset, especially if they think the charging party is lying.

7. Conclusion

The best approach for a fact-finding conference is the same as for other discrimination matters. Be prepared and be factual, and avoid being emotionally subjective.

E. DEALING WITH THE CHARGING PARTY

1. When an employee who has filed a charge is still employed by the company, he or she is very much aware that his or her immediate superior may be angry and will watch for the slightest change in behavior. A thoughtless decision or an angry remark may provoke or be used to support a retaliation charge.

2. Guidelines for supervising an employee who has filed a discrimination charge

a. Don't discuss the complaint. If the employee asks you about it, emphasize that anyone has the right to complain about discrimination and that such complaints do not affect employment status in any way.

b. Avoid taking a "moral" stance. Don't say that filing the charge "hurt the company" or that the employee wasn't "a team player."

c. Don't express disappointment or criticism. Never say to an employee who has filed a charge that you "thought the matter had been straightened out" or that the "charge was a real stab in the back."

3. Supervisors and managers often forget that just because someone sues or files a charge does not mean they are going to win. Representatives of management, especially those who feel victimized by a complaint, must be cautioned that any attempt to get back at the employee can be costly. The weakest discrimination charge can become a strong retaliation case.

F. SETTLEMENT

1. An employer must often decide whether to agree to a monetary settlement, even though the amount to be paid is more than it thinks is warranted, or to run the risk of litigation. This requires some evaluation of how much "principle" is worth. Other considerations in deciding whether to settle a charge are:

a. Whether a settlement would disrupt operations.

b. Whether relations between the company and a union might be adversely affected.

c. What impact a settlement might have on other employees or groups of employees.

d. The uniqueness of the factual situation.

2. Settlement Options

a. No-Fault Settlement: The employer and the agency can negotiate an acceptable settlement agreement which contains a non-admission provision and which disposes of the charge. This is the most common type of settlement. The EEOC encourages these settlements prior to its determination on the merits of a charge. In many cases, it will accept almost any monetary settlement that is acceptable to the parties. There are some terms which the employer should generally seek:

-- withdrawal of the charge;

-- language stating that the employer has no obligation after the settlement agreement expires other than its duty to comply with the particular statute involved.

b. Private Settlement: Sometimes settlement with the agency is not possible or practical, so the second possibility is to negotiate a private voluntary settlement with the charging party. These are often difficult to secure and should be carefully drafted. Any private settlement should contain a non-admission clause and release language. It <u>must</u> require withdrawal of the charge by the charging party.

APPENDIX A

OUTLINE FOR PREPARING A TYPICAL POSITION STATEMENT TO THE EEOC OR STATE AGENCY

A. INTRODUCTION AND FACTS

1. Describe the operation of the department in question and the charging party's work history and job description.

2. Set forth the facts relevant to the charging party's claims in a non-argumentative and straightforward fashion.

3. Conclude with a demonstration of why the facts do not support charging party's claims.

B. REBUTTAL TO CHARGING PARTY'S CLAIMS

1. Either admit or deny each claim and set forth the reasons for your denial, referring to the facts set forth in the first section.

2. If charging party makes erroneous statements or presents irrelevant information, point out the errors and the reasons why the information is irrelevant.

3. Ensure that there are no unanswered questions.

C. RESPONSE TO INTERROGATORIES

1. Answer the relevant interrogatories by providing the requested information in the form requested.

2. If the information requested does not exist, so state.

3. If the request is overly burdensome, state the reason why additional time is requested or why the information is overly burdensome. Attempt to give alternatives, if possible (e.g., request is for 100 personnel files, alternative to files is an index card with job history so that selected individual files may be reviewed).

4. If the request is for irrelevant information, state why respondent believes that information is irrelevant. If possible, offer an alternative which is relevant (e.g., not all hires, but hires for specific jobs; or, not all terminations, but all discharges for particular rule violation).

D. CONCLUSION

1. Reiterate the business reason(s) for the personnel action at issue.

2. Point out any discrepancies within or credibility issues with respect to charging party's claims, and respectfully request that the agency dismiss the charge.

IV.

RESPONDING TO AN INVESTIGATION UNDER THE OCCUPATIONAL SAFETY AND HEALTH ACT (OSHA)

IV.

RESPONDING TO AN INVESTIGATION UNDER THE OCCUPATIONAL SAFETY AND HEALTH ACT (OSHA)

Congress passed the 1970 Occupational Safety and Health Act (OSHA) to provide a means of reducing the ongoing incidence of illnesses and injuries caused by substandard safety and health conditions in the workplace. The original intent of this law was to attack the problem of workplace safety by fostering a cooperative effort among employers, the government and labor (workers and work unions) to identify both causes of illnesses and injuries and feasible corrective means, and to achieve compliance through provision for inspection and penalties. Since the adoption of OSHA, the cooperation envisioned by Congress often has been replaced by litigation over interpretation of standards and penalty assessments. The principles set forth here apply to dealings with the California state OSHA investigations as well. In Nevada, federal OSHA applies.

A. COVERAGE

OSHA covers all non-public employers in the United States, including: workplaces, offices, factories, yards, mills, and construction sites. All employees working for these employers are covered by OSHA, including executives and managers. Workplaces located in states that have assumed administration of OSHA by authorization of the federal OSHA administration are subject to state laws that must parallel OSHA.

B. REQUIREMENTS

Employers are obligated to:

1. adhere to standards and regulations set or adopted by the U.S. Department of Labor Occupational Health and Safety Administration (DOL-OSHA);

2. furnish employment and places of employment free of recognized hazards that are causing or likely to cause death or serious injury, but are not covered by specific standards (the general duty clause);

3. keep records of work-related injuries and illnesses, and report OSHA any workplace deaths or events resulting in hospitalization of five or more employees;

4. allow employees to exercise their rights under the act (e.g., to complain about hazards and participate in OSHA proceedings) without coercion, harassment or discrimination; and

5. comply with abatement orders issued pursuant to OSHA.

NOTE: OSHA personnel are forbidden from giving advance notice of inspections and from disclosing trade secrets learned in the course of inspections.

C. PENALTIES FOR VIOLATION

1. Employer obligations regarding standards, the "general duty," and record-keeping/reporting are enforced by citation/penalty procedures. These provide for penalty assessments up to $1,000 per violation in the case of ordinary violations, up to $1,000 per violation per day in the case of failure to correct previously cited violations, and up to $10,000 per violation in the cases of "willful" or "repeated" violations.

NOTE: Employers also are subject to criminal prosecution under federal law for willful violations of standards that result in death of an employee. In Congress, there is now pending legislation which would increase the criminal OSHA penalties.

2. Amount of Penalty.

Four factors are used to determine the actual amount of penalty, up the maximum:

a. The employer's size.

b. The gravity of the violation, measured by the number of employees exposed to harm, the frequency and duration of exposures, and the potential for serious injury or death created by the violation.

c. The employer's history of prior violations.

d. The employer's "good faith" or overall attitude toward compliance, measured by the quality of overall safety programs, degree of cooperation with OSHA personnel and relative diligence in effecting abatement of potential hazards disclosed through OSHA inspections.

NOTE: OSHA does not provide penalties for employee violations. As courts have interpreted the law, employee compliance is to be secured through lawful disciplinary action by employers who are expected to adopt safety and health rules consistent with OSHA standards and to make compliance with those rules a condition of employment.

The act also provides for criminal penalties--jail terms and fines--for any employer who willfully violates a standard when such violation causes an employee death, and for any person who knowingly misrepresents facts to OSHA, who gives advance notice of an inspection, or who kills an OSHA inspector who is acting in the line of duty. In addition, employers who operate imminently dangerous facilities are subject to a federal court shutdown order upon petition by OSHA. Employers who discriminate against employees for exercising rights provided by OSHA are subject to civil suit for damages upon complaint by OSHA.

D. INSPECTIONS AND INVESTIGATIONS

DOL-OSHA is authorized to conduct on-site inspections and to issue subpoenas for records or testimony to determine whether employers are in compliance with specific OSHA standards, with the "general duty" clause and with various regulations.

An employer may refuse to allow an inspector to conduct on-site inspections. In such cases, OSHA must obtain an administrative search warrant from a court. The standards for obtaining an administrative warrant are somewhat less rigorous than standards required for criminal search warrants. OSHA need only show that:

1. the employer is the subject of a bona fide employee complaint about safety or health hazards; or

2. the employer has been selected for inspection pursuant to a pre-existing and reasonable plan of routine inspections; or

3. the employer is being inspected to ensure that prior violations have been corrected.

Administrative search warrants typically are limited in time--usually thirty days after issuance. Employers who continue to refuse an inspection after issuance of the search warrant face contempt-of-court proceedings.

NOTE: OSHA-issued subpoenas are not enforceable except by court order, but a court-enforced subpoena must be complied with until or unless quashed or modified.

OSHA can only conduct inspections and investigations "during regular working hours, and at other reasonable times, and within reasonable limits, and in a reasonable manner." An employer who believes that an inspection is or has become unreasonable may order the inspectors to leave the workplace or may go to court to seek modification of a warrant or previously enforced subpoena.

E. CITATIONS AND LEGAL PROCEEDINGS TO ENFORCE CITATIONS

Citations for a violation of the act must be issued within six months after OSHA personnel know or reasonably should have known of the violation.

Each citation must describe:

1. the nature of the violation with reference to a standard, regulation, or "general duty" obligation;

2. the degree and circumstances of the violation;

3. the proposed penalty; and

4. a date for correction of the hazard created by the violation.

In the case of "general duty" violations, a citation usually will describe at least one method of correction OSHA believes to be feasible.

A citation must be protested within fifteen working days after receipt, or the citation and penalty will be deemed uncontestable.

> NOTE: Settlements and compromises of issues arising from OSHA citations may occur before protesting--during the fifteen-workday contest period--or at any time before final order. Settlements are encouraged by OSHA, provided the settlement corrects any actual cited hazards and does not have the effect of limiting future enforcement activities.

Employees, or if unionized, their union, may contest citations to the extent they may disagree with the abatement dates proposed. They also may participate as parties in any legal proceedings before the OSHRC or courts. Employees may, but are not required to, file pleadings in order to preserve their party status.

F. EMPLOYER DEFENSES - DEFENSES TO CITATIONS, ABATEMENT DATES, METHODS OF ABATEMENT, AND/OR PENALTIES

1. No Violation or No Hazard: The employer has not in fact violated the standard, "general duty," or regulation listed in the citation, or no hazard resulted from violation, or the employer reasonably had no knowledge of the violation.

2. De Minimis Violation: A violation did not create a hazard, or otherwise did not directly compromise safety or health conditions in the workplace, or was violated only in minor, technical, ways by the employer who provided alternative protections of equal or greater sufficiency as those provided

by the standard. A de minimis violation carries no penalty or abatement requirement.

3. Vague or Ambiguous Standard, or Improperly Communicated Standard Non-Mandatory Standard: A standard may have been violated, but the wording was such that a reasonable person would not know exactly what conduct was prohibited, or the standard was not enforceable by reason of improper issuance, or the standard amounted only to a suggestion, not a directive.

4. Compliance Not Possible or Feasible, Abatement Date or Method Unreasonable: A standard, "general duty"-covered condition or regulation cannot be met by known, available and feasibly useful means, where the employer has applied all known and feasible alternate means of correction and is not lagging behind industry compliance.

NOTE: Defenses based on feasibility are highly controversial. Employers are expected to keep up with the state-of-the-art in compliance programs. Cost of compliance, or relative cost-effectiveness of the standard-prescribed methods, ordinarily is not a successful "feasibility" defense in the face of specifically mandated standards, except in unusual or extreme situations.

5. Employee Misconduct: Non-compliance resulted from reasonably unanticipated employee failure to follow previously established and enforced work rules or an employee has acted in an "idiosyncratic" fashion that was unpredictable.

6. Miscellaneous Defenses: The situation was not timely issued; the citation resulted from an illegal inspection; OSHA's evidence of violation is equivocal or not credible; the wrong employer was cited (the cited employer did not create the hazard, had no power or ability to correct the hazard, or had no employees exposed to the hazard); OSHA has no jurisdiction over the particular condition cited; the violation was not willful, repeated or a failure to be, or was not serious--i.e., likely to cause death or serious injury, the penalty is unreasonable; the date for possible correction is unreasonable.

G. STANDARDS

1. OSHA standards address:

a. walking and working surfaces, ladders, platforms, scaffolds, and means of egress;

b. ventilation, noise, radiation, and hazardous or toxic liquids and air contaminants;

c. personal protective gear use and maintenance;

d. hazardous materials such as acids, corrosives, explosives, flammable and toxic substances;

e. workplace sanitation;

f. medical facilities;

g. materials handling and storage, use, maintenance and construction of cranes and industrial vehicles;

h. welding equipment and procedures;

i. equipment, tool, and machine guarding;

j. electrical apparatus;

k. carinogens;

l. hazard communication; and

m. access to records.

Conditions that are specifically regulated by other federal laws or agencies, such as mines, railroads, aircraft operation, nuclear power generation, etc., are not covered by OSHA. Worker's compensation laws generally are unaffected by OSHA.

OSHA standards have been relied on by some courts as evidence of what would be reasonable conduct, and by other courts as the actual standard by which alleged misconduct or negligence will be judged in civil litigation to recover damages for work-related injuries or illnesses.

> CAUTION: Violation of OSHA standards may give rise to prosecution for battery, aggravated battery, reckless conduct, homicide, or conspiracy to commit such acts, under state criminal laws where prosecutors can show that the employer violated OSHA standards with a reckless or grossly negligent frame of mind or other criminal intent.

2. Variances from Standards: DOL-OSHA may issue variances from standards to employers who can show they have adopted better methods of eliminating hazards than are required by applicable standards or who can demonstrate a need for more time to come into compliance while maintaining adequate temporary protections. DOL-OSHA also may grant modifications of previously ordered hazard abatement requirements.

G. GENERAL DUTY CLAUSE

The "general duty" clause requires an employer to eliminate "recognized" hazards of serious potential for death or injury addressed by a specific or performance standard to the extent there may be feasibly useful means of doing so. Hazard recognition is the key to this obligation. A hazard may be recognized if the existence and means of correction are known in the employer's industry, even if the particular employer is unaware of same.

H. REQUIRED RECORD-KEEPING

OSHA requires each covered employer to keep a log of workplace injuries resulting in death, lost time, restricted work capability, and/or medical treatment, or illness; to prepare a supplemental report of each such illness or injury; and to publish an annual summary of the log. This log must be "conspicuously" posted during the following February. An employer must notify OSHA in cases of an employee fatality or mass hospitalization (five employees or more). The log and supplemental reports are to be available for review by OSHA, NIOSH, and employees.

I. SUMMARY

OSHA Is a complex law that carries severe consequences for non-compliance in terms of penalties, abatement costs, litigation, collateral liability, workplace morale, and public good will. Lack of knowledge of the law or applicable standards no longer is a viable defense, since OSHA has been in effect since 1971 and has received wide publicity.

J. KEYS TO OSHA COMPLIANCE

1. Prepare a written compliance program that addresses all standards applicable to a workplace and periodically review and update the program.

2. Provide for internal enforcement.

3. Closely monitor each OSHA inspection to determine whether the inspection is being conducted in accordance with the OSHA compliance manuals (the so-called Field Operations Manual and Industrial Hygiene Manual). A failure by OSHA to precisely follow its own procedures will be strong evidence that the inspection is unreasonable.

4. Develop contacts with local OSHA supervisors to facilitate prompt resolution of misunderstandings caused by unsophisticated OSHA inspectors' failure to grasp workplace realities. A matter addressed before citation always is less complicated than one addressed after citation.

5. When dealing with OSHA inspectors, remember that the inspector rarely has some ulterior motive to harass or penalize your enterprise; he is only doing a job governed by laws and politics far outside his ability to influence. If there is good cause to believe the inspector is improperly

motivated (e.g., his brother is the union president) call up the OSHA office and ask that another inspect be sent.

REMEMBER:

1. Anything said to OSHA by a supervisor or manager will be recorded and probably will be construed as an admission adversely to the employer's position in the event of a citation proceeding or criminal prosecution.

2. The employer's representatives need not say anything to OSHA about workplace conditions. The representative need only provide logs and other documents required to be kept.

3. Be familiar with the forms used by OSHA to record information gained from inspections so that answers to questions will be recorded on those forms as favorably as possible.

4. Immediately correct any correctable hazards disclosed during the inspection. This will not prejudice the employer's right later to contest a citation, will enhance the employer's ability to obtain credit for good faith, and may lessen chances for issuance of a "willful" citation.

5. After an inspection, give the inspector a name, title, and address to whom any citations should be sent. Otherwise, valuable time will be lost while mail travels within the company.

6. Do not exaggerate the quality of safety/health conditions if describing them to an inspector.

5482a

NOTES

14

CONTROLLING LOST WORK TIME: INTEGRATING ADA AND FMLA INTO WORKERS' COMPENSATION AND STD POLICIES AND PRACTICES

Christopher G. Bell

CONTROLLING LOST WORK TIME

Integrating ADA And FMLA Into Workers' Compensation and STD Policies And Practices

by

Christopher G. Bell[1]

I. Introduction

The Americans with Disabilities Act ("ADA") and the Family and Medical Leave Act ("FMLA") have important implications for responding to workers' compensation claims which are plaguing employers.

The ADA is landmark civil rights legislation, but few in Congress foresaw the breadth and depth of its potential impact on workers' compensation. It is important to understand how the ADA can grant additional rights to injured workers. It does not matter under the ADA whether a person acquires a disability in an occupational accident. An injured worker that has an ADA-covered disability is protected from disability discrimination--and has a right to reasonable accommodation--in addition to some rights and benefits the individual may be entitled to under workers' compensation law. However, the impact of the ADA on workers' compensation is being blunted by developing ADA case law which is restricting the definition of "disability" and who is "qualified" under the law.

How the FMLA interacts with workers' compensation also concerns many employers, but this critical issue was not addressed in the Department of Labor's Interim Final FMLA regulations

---

1 Mr. Bell is a Partner with the national management, labor and employment law firm of Jackson, Lewis, Schnitzler & Krupman in Washington, D.C. Mr. Bell will be opening the firm's 19th office, in Minneapolis, Minnesota, in the Spring of 1997. Mr. Bell is a frequent author and lecturer on the Americans with Disabilities Act. He has co-authored several books including: The Taking Control Process: Beyond Light Duty; and, The Workers' Compensation - ADA Connection: Supervisory Tools for Workers' Compensation Cost Containment That Reduce ADA Liability.

issued June 4, 1993. Only in the final rule issued 18 months later was the workers' compensation interplay with FMLA addressed.[2] Many injured workers will have FMLA rights to leave, job restoration and continuation of health benefits which must be integrated into workers' compensation practices.

This paper discusses the interplay of these three laws and describes some proactive steps an employer may take to reduce unnecessary absence and promote appropriate early return to work in a manner that promotes legal compliance and cuts benefit costs.

II. Understanding the ADA-FMLA-Workers' Compensation Connection: A Hypothetical

The following hypothetical demonstrates how the ADA and FMLA provide the injured worker with additional rights.

A truck driver employed by XYZ Hauling Company ("XYZ") returns his rig to the lot at the end of the day. The driver has been working for XYZ for the past five years. XYZ has 55 employees all at one location. He tells his supervisor that his back really hurt him when he lifted a heavy chain out of the truck. The next day the driver brings in a medical certification form from his doctor. The form indicates that the driver will be unable to perform his driving job for at least three weeks due to degenerative disk disease which will require physical therapy. He presents the form to the supervisor. It is the fourth workers' compensation claim filed by an employee in the last month and the supervisor is mad. He tells the driver not to come back until he is "100 percent." The supervisor says nothing about the driver's rights and obligations under the Family and Medical Leave Act ("FMLA").

The driver sits at home collecting time loss payments. Weeks go by. The weeks turn into two months. The last form from his doctor indicates that the driver now has a permanent lifting restriction; he is not to lift more than 10 pounds. The driver is informed that he will be discharged at the end of 26 weeks of absence unless he is released to return to work by that time. Believing that he might be able to return to work even as a truck driver if XYZ assigns another worker to do the heavy lifting, the driver requests additional unpaid leave until he is released to return to work and asks that another employee be assigned to help him with the lifting. He also asks if there is another job within his medical restrictions to which he might be reassigned. XYZ declines these requests without discussing them with the driver in spite of the fact that there is a vacant dispatcher job for which the driver may be qualified. He is fired after 26 weeks of absence pursuant to XYZ's neutral leave policy.

Finally, there is a $20,000 lump sum settlement of his permanent partial workers' compensation claim. The employee signs a general release and waiver of all claims but the waiver does not expressly mention ADA claims.

---

2 Citations in this paper are to the Department of Labor's Final FMLA regulations, 68 Fed. Reg. 2180 (Jan. 6, 1995).

The unemployed driver soon discovers that $20,000 does not go very far and he asks his lawyer if there is not something else the lawyer can do. The lawyer files a charge with the Equal Employment Opportunity Commission ("EEOC") under the ADA and a complaint with the Department of Labor under the FMLA and later a lawsuit under both laws. The suit seeks double back wages for a willful violation of the FMLA and requests $50,000 in compensatory and punitive damages[3] and a jury trial under the ADA for wrongful discharge and failure to return the worker to work with a reasonable accommodation.

The hauling company got into trouble because management did not realize how the ADA and the FMLA both can provide enhanced rights to ill and injured workers.

A. The FMLA

The injured driver in the example is working for an employer with 50 or more employees. 29 C.F.R. § 825.104. He has been employed by XYZ for more than a year and has worked at least 1,250 hours during the twelve months before he requested leave. And, he works at a worksite with 50 or more employees within a 75 mile radius. Id. at § 825.110. Therefore, the hauling company is covered by the FMLA and the driver is eligible for up to twelve weeks of unpaid leave for any of a variety of family and medical purposes including treatment of his own "serious health condition" that renders him unable to do the essential functions of his job for more than three days. Id. at § 825.114. While the definition of "injury" or "illness" under workers' compensation and "serious health condition" under the FMLA may not be synonymous, from a practical standpoint, many injuries compensable under workers' compensation would qualify as serious health conditions under the FMLA.

In our example, XYZ has failed to meet its obligations under the FMLA in several respects. It failed to notify the driver of his expectations and obligations under the FMLA when he requested leave for an apparent FMLA purpose.[4] In particular, the driver should have been told: his

---

3 Having fewer than 100 employees entitles XYZ to limit its liability for compensatory and punitive damages to $50,000 because of the caps on damages contained in the Civil Rights Act of 1991, 42 U.S.C. § 1981a(b). An employer with 501 or more employees could be liable for $300,000 in compensatory and punitive damages. Id.

4 To designate leave as FMLA leave which draws down an employee's 12 week entitlement, the Employer must comply with three distinct notice requirements. The poster approved by the Department of Labor must be properly displayed. Second, an employer must disseminate written information about the FMLA to all employees. This information must be included in any employee handbook. Third, an employer must promptly issue individual written notice to the employee requesting leave normally within two business days of an employee request for FMLA-qualifying leave. In most instances, notice need only be given once in each six month period on the occasion

(continued...)

leave would be counted against his twelve week annual FMLA entitlement; he would be expected to provide medical certification of his serious health condition (as he did in this case) and the consequences of not doing so; he had a right to substitute paid leave and whether XYZ was going to require such substitution; whether he would be obligated to pay premiums for continuation of health benefits and the arrangements for making such payments; about any requirement for a fitness for duty certificate as a condition of returning to work; about his right to restoration to the same or an equivalent position at the end of the leave; and, about his possible liability for any health insurance premiums paid by XYZ should he not return to work at the expiration of his FMLA leave. Id. at § 825.301(c).

Failure to inform an employee of these rights and obligations may preclude an employer from counting the leave used against the employee's FMLA entitlement thereby increasing the amount of leave to which the employee will be entitled. Id. at § 825.208(b).

Although the FMLA provides only a right to unpaid leave, the driver is receiving workers' compensation benefits pursuant to state law. Presentation of his medical certification form put XYZ on notice that he has suffered an injury requiring him to be absent from work for more than three days under the continuing treatment of his doctor and physical therapist.[5]

(...continued)
of the first employee notice of the need for leave. See, § 825.208(b).

An employee is obligated to put his or her employer on notice that leave is being requested for an FMLA-qualifying reason. If an employee requests leave for a non-FMLA qualifying reason, the absence will not be protected under the FMLA. Johnson v. Primerica, DC SNY, No. 94 Civ. 4869, 1996 (WL 34148 (1/30/96)). The employee must provide the employer with sufficient information, such as the duration of the leave and whether the employee has been hospitalized or is under a regimen of continuing treatment by a health care professional in order for the FMLA to be invoked. Reich v. Midwest Engineering, Inc., Case No. 94-CV-525 (W.D. Mich. (7/22/95)). However, an employee need not refer expressly to the FMLA when requesting leave; the employee need only request leave for a reason that qualifies under the Act. Manuel v. Westlake Polymers Corporation, Case No. 95-30050 (5th Cir. (10/3/95)).

5 Of course, not every medical condition will meet the definition of a serious health condition. One court found that rectal bleeding was not a serious health condition where the employee was not under continuing treatment by a health care provider and was not absent from work for more than three days. Bauer v. Dayton-Walther Corporation, Civil Action No. 94-101, 1996 WL 11071 (E.D. KY 1/5/96)Note, further, however, that an employee may have a "chronic serious health condition manifesting itself in episodic flare-ups which is protected by the FMLA despite the fact that the employee is not absent for more than three days and does not visit a health care provider for treatment of the incident. 29 C.F.R. 825.114(b) (iii).

The Department of Labor's Final Regulations restrict an employer's access to employee medical records for purposes of granting FMLA leave. An employer may not require more documentation than is contained on the Department of Labor's revised health care provider certification form. Id. at § 825.306(a). This is problematic for employers because this form provides an insufficient explanation why an ill or injured worker is currently unable to travel to work, be at work or otherwise do his/her job. However, the Final Rule did provide that an employer's medical advisor can contact an employee's treating physician for clarification of the information contained on the revised form or for confirmation that it was provided by the health care provider, if the employee consents to the contact. § 825.307(a) & 310(b). An employer is also permitted to have direct access to an employee's treating physician if such contact is authorized by workers' compensation law.

An employer with a reasonable basis to question the legitimacy of a medical certificate also may seek, at its expense, a second medical opinion from a physician not regularly within its employ. Id. at § 825.306(a). If there is disagreement between the first and second physician, an employer and employee may jointly agree to a third physician whose determination is binding. Id. at § 825.306(c).

Fortunately, the Department of Labor has also taken the position that an employer may avail itself of the broader access to medical records and the employee's treating physician provided by state workers' compensation laws or employer-provided disability benefit plan. § 825.207(d). Accordingly, had XYZ wished to obtain its driver's medical records and contact his treating physician, it could have done so for workers' compensation purposes. However, an employer would be prohibited from denying FMLA leave on the basis of such medical documentation. An employer's greater access to medical information through the workers' compensation system also applies to return to work physicals. Under the FMLA, an employer is limited to accepting a statement from an employee's treating physician that the employee is released to return to work unless an employee consents to an employer's medical advisor contacting the treating physician for clarification. Id. at § 825.310(a). The FMLA does not permit an employer to contest the return to work release or to require such a release only from an employer's health care provider. Id. at § 825.310(c). In contrast, many workers' compensation laws permit an employer to require submission of a return to work certificate from the employer's physician as a condition of job restoration. The FMLA does not bar an employer from the greater access to medical information or its right to restrict job restoration provided for by workers' compensation law. Id. at § 825.310(b); Opinion Letter from J. Dean Speer, Director, Division of Policy and Analysis, Wage and Hour Division, U.S. Dep't of Labor to David E. Block, Esq., dated February 28, 1994

XYZ did not avail itself of this broader right to medical information and accepted the driver's medical certification form. Since the medical certification form also revealed the driver's need for treatment and his 10 pound lifting restriction, XYZ could conclude that his injury rendered him unable to do his job because of his medical condition. Therefore, the driver was entitled to up to twelve weeks of unpaid leave with a right to be restored to the same or equivalent job if he was released to return to work before the expiration of twelve weeks.

Instead of permitting him to stay out for twelve weeks, the hauling company fired him after 26 weeks. Although a Department of Labor official previously had indicated that such an action would impermissibly count the FMLA leave time against the employee and would constitute unlawful retaliation. See, Id. at § 825.220(c). The present agency view is that a 26 week neutral leave policy would not violate the FMLA. As noted above, specific notice of FMLA rights and obligations and informing the employee of his or her FMLA eligibility must be given to an employee requesting leave before the leave may be counted against his/her FMLA entitlement. Failure to do so within strict regulatory time frames results in an employee retaining his/her FMLA leave entitlement until such time as the employer gives the required notice, according to Department of Labor officials. Because many employers fail to give such notice to their injured workers, this also has the effect of extending the leave entitlement notwithstanding the terms of an employer's neutral leave policy.

The FMLA does not require an employer to return to work an employee who is medically unable to do his job. Nor does it require modification of the job or reassignment to a new position. Unfortunately, the FMLA creates difficulties for an employer attempting to get injured workers back to work and off benefits. Many employers have used "light duty" to bring an injured worker back to work within his/her medical restrictions. Light duty jobs typically are very different from the job an employee was doing at the time of injury. Because the FMLA requires that a worker be restored to the same or equivalent position upon return from leave, an employer may not compel an injured worker to accept light duty work in lieu of exercising his/her FMLA entitlement. Id. at § 825.702(d). Likewise, the Department of Labor has taken the position that an employer may not require an FMLA eligible employee to accept reasonable accommodation instead of FMLA leave. Id. An employer may offer accommodation, or light duty, but may not compel it. On the other hand, if an employee rejects an offer of employment that is within his/her medical restrictions, an employer may contest the employee's entitlement to workers' compensation indemnity benefits. In addition, if an employee voluntarily accepts light duty, an employer may not designate time on light duty as FMLA leave as the employee is working. However, time spent on light duty does not lessen an employee's right to be restored to the same or an equivalent position held at the time leave commenced.

XYZ could incur significant liability for violating the FMLA. The FMLA provides for the recovery of one or more of the following: wages, employment benefits, or other compensation denied or lost to such employee by reason of the violation; or, where no such tangible loss has occurred, such as when FMLA leave was unlawfully denied, any actual monetary loss sustained by the employee as a direct result of the violation, such as the cost of providing care, up to a sum equal to twelve weeks of wages for the employee. §825.400(c). At least one court has held that compensatory and punitive damages are not available.[6] However, several courts have held that a supervisor may be personally liable for violating the FMLA. This is particularly true if the supervisor has acted in bad faith in violating the FMLA.[7]

---

6 See McAnnally v. Wyn South Molded Products, 912 F. Supp. 512 (N.D. Ala. 1996).

7 In what may be the first jury decision holding individual supervisors liable for a violation of the FMLA, a federal jury in the United States District Court for the Northern District of Illinois (continued...)

B. The ADA

Approximately 18% of the 72,687 ADA charges filed with the EEOC through September 30, 1996 came from persons claiming to be disabled because of a "back impairment." Many of these individuals will not have an ADA-covered disability. In order to be protected by the ADA, a person must have an impairment that substantially limits major life activities, have a record of once having an impairment that substantially limited major life activities, or be regarded by an employer as having an impairment that substantially limits major life activities. 29 C.F.R. § 1630.2(g).

Recently, the EEOC issued EEOC Notice 915.002: Workers' Compensation and the ADA (Sept. 3, 1996), which appears to be an effort by the agency to broaden and clarify the ADA's application to injured workers.

However, recent trends in ADA decisions make it increasingly difficult for injured workers to prevail on an ADA claim. First, a growing number of courts are requiring that impairments be permanent in nature in order to state an ADA claim. See, e.g., Oswalt v. Sara Lee Corp., 889 F. Supp. 253, 258 (N.D. Miss. 1995), aff'd, 74 F.3d 91 (5th Cir. 1996)(Missing work for one month because of medication for high blood pressure was not a substantial limitation of a major life activity); Sanders v. Arneson Products, Inc., No. 95-15349, 1996 U.S. App. LEXIS 19500 (9th Cir. 1996)(Psychological impairment lasting only 3 ½ months was not a disability); McDonald v. Commonwealth of Pa., 62 F.3d 92 (3rd Cir. 1995) (less than two month recovery from abdominal surgery insufficient to constitute disability); Evans v. City of Dallas, 861 F.2d 846, 852-53 (5th Cir. 1988) knee impairment requiring surgery was not disability because not permanent). Second, courts under both the ADA and the Rehabilitation Act have held that an individual who seeks and obtains disability benefits claiming to be permanently and totally disabled and unable to work cannot claim simultaneously to be a "qualified individual with a disability and sue an employer for disability discrimination. See, e.g., McNemar v. The Disney Stores, 91 F.3d 610 (3d Cir. 1996); Kennedy v. Applause, Inc., Case No. 95-5501 (9th Cir. 7/31/96); August v. Offices Unlimited, Inc., 981 F.2d 576 (1st Cir. 1992); Beauford v. Father Flanagan's Boys' Home, 831 F.2d 768 (8th Cir. 1987), cert. denied, 485 U.S. 938 (1988).

7(...continued)
awarded $58,000.00 for back pay and benefits to a former hospital nutritionist under the FMLA. Freemon v. Foley, Civil Action No. 96 C 209 (N.D. Ill. Sept. 26, 1996) (Urbom, J. presiding). The jury calculated this amount by adding lost back pay ($53,600) and lost benefits ($9,000) and by subtracting the amount Ms. Freemon failed to earn in an effort to mitigate her damages ($4,600). In this regard, the jury concluded that Ms. Freemon could have earned $12,000 in an effort to mitigate her damages, but only earned $7,400 in the form of unemployment compensation benefits. See also: McKiernan v. Smith-Edwards-Dunlap Co., 1995 WL 311393 at *3 (E.D. Pa. 1995)

Because the driver has a back impairment that permanently restricts his ability to lift more than 10 pounds, he could be viewed by the courts as having a disability because he is substantially limited in performing lifting and also because he may be foreclosed from working in a wide variety of jobs. See e.g., Tuck v. HCA Health Services of Tennessee, 7 F.3d 465 (6th Cir. 1993)(nurse unable to lift patients or heavy objects had disability under the Rehabilitation Act); Thornhill v. Marsh, 866 F.2d 1182 (9th Cir. 1989)(employee perceived to be unable to perform heavy work requiring lifting was regarded as having a disability under the Rehabilitation Act). On the other hand, a great many courts are rejecting that a worker with lifting restrictions is disabled. See, e.g., Ray v. Glidden Co., 85 F.3d 227, 5 AD Cases 991, 992 (5th Cir. 1996)(Inability to perform "heavy lifting" does not constitute a disability); Kiess v. D&H Distributing Co., 5 AD Cases 897 (D. Md. 1996)(Individual whose heart condition restricted heavy lifting not disabled); Vaughan v. Harvard Industries, Inc., 926 F. Supp. 1340 (W.D. Tenn. 1996) (Employee with permanent 20 pound lifting restriction and a 30 minute standing restriction not disabled); Aucutt v. Six Flags Over Mid-America, Inc., 85 F.3d 1311, 5 AD Cases 902, 907 (8th Cir. 1996)(A 25-pound lifting restriction was not a disability); Williams v. Avnet, Inc., 910 F. Supp. 1124 (E.D.N.C. 1995)(Finding that manual punch press operator with twenty-five pound lifting restriction, limited ability to push and pull, and a disability rating in other proceedings of five percent permanent partial disability to the back, not "disabled" under the ADA); O'Dell v. Altec Industries, Inc., 1995 U.S. Dist. LEXIS 15218, 1995 WL 611341 (W.D. Mo. 1995) (Finding that plaintiff with frequent lifting restriction of thirty-five pounds, and occasional lifting restriction of fifty pounds, not "disabled" under the ADA); Otis v. Canadian Valley-Reeves Meat Co., 884 F. Supp. 446 (W.D. Okla. 1994) (Finding that temporary lifting restriction of twenty-five pounds and permanent lifting restriction of seventy pounds did not constitute "disability" under the ADA); and Czopek v. General Electric Co., 1995 U.S. Dist. LEXIS 8607, 1995 W.L. 374036 (N.D. Ill. 1995) (Finding that plaintiff with twenty pound lifting restriction not "disability" under the ADA.)

Even if XYZ could argue that the driver was not disabled, it would be in the company's best interest to investigate further the driver's accommodation requests. Accordingly, XYZ should have considered his request for a reasonable accommodation if he was otherwise qualified, i.e., able to perform the essential functions of his truck driver position with or without reasonable accommodation. The driver requested several possible accommodations that did not receive sufficient consideration by XYZ. As part of its consideration, XYZ had a right to its driver's medical records concerning his back impairment and work restrictions upon the driver's request for reasonable accommodation under the ADA. Id. at § 1630.14(c) App. See, e.g., Grenier v. Cyanamid Plastics, Inc., 5 AD Cases 75 (1st Cir. 1995) (Employer can require applicant to provide medical certification as to his ability to return to work, and as to any reasonable accommodation necessary under the ADA, provided the requirement is relevant to assessment to perform essential job functions); Miller v. National Casualty Co., 61 F.3d 627 (8th Cir. 1995) (Notice by relative that plaintiff had "lost it" and was being hospitalized, without prior knowledge of disability or medical documentation was insufficient to constitute request for reasonable accommodation); Beck v. University of Wisconsin, 75 F.3d 1130 (7th Cir. 1996) (Employee's failure to provide medical records and specify accommodation required justified summary judgment for employer). An employer may need such records to assess the nature and degree of an employee's limitations and to identify possible reasonable accommodations. When used for this purpose, the FMLA does not preclude access to medical records.

The example does not provide enough information to analyze his request for another employee to assist with heavy lifting. We are not told what the essential functions of the driver's position are, whether moving objects weighing more than 10 pounds is an essential function or the number of other employees that may be available to assist the driver when such lifting must be performed. Nor do we have sufficient information to consider the possibility that such an accommodation would pose an undue hardship. Since providing a personal assistant such as a reader or sign language interpreter can be a form of reasonable accommodation in some circumstances, assigning another employee to assist the driver cannot be blithely ignored by XYZ. Id. at § 1630.2(o); But see, Michell v. Lydall, Inc., 1994 U.S. App. LEXIS 2177 (4th Cir. 1994)(Employer not required to hire another person to reduce the workload of a disabled employee); Gilbert v. Frank, 949 F.2d 637, 644 (2d Cir. 1991) (employer not required to assign co-worker to do physically demanding tasks employee no longer able to do); Treadwell v. Alexander, 707 F.2d 473, 478 (11th Cir. 1983) (assigning additional employees to cover plaintiff's physically demanding duties was an undue hardship); Coleman v. Darden, 595 F.2d 533, 540 (10th Cir.), cert. denied, 444 U.S. 927 (1979) (under the Rehabilitation Act, an employer may be required to have someone assist the disabled individual to perform the job, but the employer is not required to have someone perform the job for the disabled individual).

The driver's request for additional unpaid leave raises troublesome issues. Based upon the ADA's legislative history, the EEOC has interpreted the ADA to include additional unpaid leave as a form of reasonable accommodation subject to the undue hardship limitation. Id. at § 1630.2(o) App.; H. Rep. 101-485, Pt. 2, 101st Cong., 1st Sess. 64 (1990). This means that an employer applying a neutral leave policy to terminate a disabled employee may be required to make an exception to that policy as a form of reasonable accommodation. The amount of additional unpaid leave that would have to be provided is not specified in the EEOC's regulations. In its recent Enforcement Guidance on the ADA and workers' compensation, the agency went further, asserting that an employer had a duty to (1) provide additional unpaid lave; (2) hold an employee's job open until s/he returns, and, if this would pose an undue hardship, then (3) transfer an employee to an existing vacancy which may be left open without undue hardship. EEOC Notice 915.002: Workers' Compensation and the ADA (Sept. 3, 1996), pp. 14-15.

However, the courts have made clear that indefinite leave or unanticipated and unpredictable leave is not required. The Courts generally have rejected significant leave or tolerance of unpredictable absence as a form of reasonable accommodation. See, e.g., Hudson v. MCI Telecommunications Corp., 87 F.3d 1167 (10th Cir. 1996)(Request for indefinite leave not an accommodation); Rogers v. International Marine Terminals, Inc., 87 F.3d 755 n.2 (5th Cir. 1996)(indefinite leave not required); Monette v. Electronic Data Systems, 90 F.3d 1173 (6th Cir. 1996)(indefinite leave not required); Myers v. Hose, 50 F.3d 278 (4th Cir. 1995)(indefinite leave not required); Tyndall v. National Education Centers, 31 F.3d 209 (4th Cir. 1994) (presence at the school is an essential function of a teacher position); Jackson v. Veterans Admin., 22 F.3d 277, 280 (11th Cir. 1994) (Rehabilitation Act does not require Federal agency to accommodate periodic, unanticipated absences of probationary employee); Carr v. Reno, 23 F.3d 525, 531 (D.C. Cir. 1994) ("An essential function of any government job is an ability to appear for work (whether in the workplace or, in the unusual case, at home) and to complete assigned tasks within a reasonable period of time.... To require an employer to accept an open-ended "work when able" schedule for a time-sensitive job would stretch 'reasonable accommodation' to absurd proportions and imperil the effectiveness of the employer's public enterprise."); Guice-Mills v. Derwinski, 967 F.2d 794 (2d Cir. 1992) (head nurse with depression was not a qualified individual with a disability because she could not report to work before 10:00 a.m.); Beauford v. Father Flanagan's Boy's Home, 831 F.2d 768, 771 (8th Cir. 1987), cert. denied, 485 U.S. 938 (1988) (Rehabilitation Act does not protect employee who is no longer able to do his or her job due to physical and emotional ailments arising out of pressures of work); Larkins v. Ciba Vision Corp., 3 A.D. Cases 715 (N.D. Ga. 1994) (ADA does not require employer to accommodate employee totally disabled from working); Matzo v. Postmaster General, 685 F. Supp. 260, 263 (D.D.C. 1987), aff'd without opinion, 861 F.2d 1290 (D.C. Cir. 1988) (regular attendance is an essential function); Stevens v. Stubbs, 576 F. Supp. 1409, 1415 (N.D. Ga. 1983) (Rehabilitation Act "does not protect absenteeism or employees who take excessive leave and are unable to perform the prerequisites of their jobs.").

On the other hand, many other courts have recognized that leave may be a reasonable accommodation under some circumstances. See, e.g., Williams v. Widnall, 79 F.3d 1003 (10th Cir. 1996)(Leave for treatment for alcoholism may be required); Schmidt v. Safeway, 864 F. Supp. 991, 996 (D. Ore. 1994)(same); Corbett v. National Products Co., 4 AD Cases 987 (E.D. Pa. 1995)(leave for treatment of disability may be required as an accommodation); Hudson v. MCI Telecommunications Corp., 87 F.3d 1167, 5 AD Cases 1099 (10th Cir. 1996)(in dicta, the court observed that leave for treatment may be an accommodation in some circumstances).

Some courts have held that an employee may use accrued paid or additional unpaid leave. Kimbro v. Atlantic Richfield Co.,889 F.2d 869 (9th Cir. 1989), cert. denied, 498 U.S. 814 (1990) (Failure to make an exception to strict adherence to attendance policy was unlawful failure to accommodate); Fuller v. Frank, 916 F.2d 558 (9th Cir. 1990)(leave for outpatient treatment and a second leave for inpatient treatment required for alcoholic employee as reasonable accommodation); Dutton v. Johnson Cty. Bd. of Cty Commissioners, 3 AD Cases 808 (D. Kan. 1994)(failure to permit employee to use accrued leave violated ADA).

Nor have the courts grappled with the interplay between the ADA and the FMLA. The FMLA's twelve week leave entitlement, including intermittent and reduced leave, may undercut somewhat the employer argument that presence on the job is per se an essential function.

The driver also requested a job transfer. The failure of XYZ to consider the driver for the dispatcher position might violate the ADA depending upon the circumstances. Reassigning an employee who can no longer do a job because of a disability is a form of reasonable accommodation specifically mentioned in the statute as a way of overruling earlier Rehabilitation Act case law. 42 U.S.C. § 12111(9)(B).

The circuits are split regarding whether an employer has a duty to provide reassignment. See, e.g., Schmidt v. Methodist Hospital, 89 F.3d 342 (7th Cir. 1996) (Employer is not required to find another job for an employee not qualified for the job he or she is doing but may not deny alternative employment available under an employer's existing policies); Meyers v. Hose, 50 F.3d 278 (4th Cir.

1995); Jimeno v. Mobil Oil Corp., 66 F.3d 1514 (9th Cir. 1995) (Where collective bargaining agreement permitted termination of unfit employee, employer requirement to find alternative job in company or otherwise reasonable accommodate is not inherent); Daugherty v. City of El Paso, 56 F.3d 695, 700 (5th Cir. 1995) (Only the refusal to reassign for a discriminatory reason is prohibited by the ADA; preferential reassignment is not required.) But see, Pritchard v. Southern Co. Service, 1996 U.S. App. LEXIS 22062 (11th Cir. 1996)(Reassignment is required where employee cannot be accommodated to perform in current position); Benson v. Northwest Airlines, 62 F.3d 1108 (8th Cir. 1995)(Reassignment may be required under the ADA); Monette v. Electronic Data Systems, 90 F.3d 1173 (6th Cir. 1996)("it is true that employers may be required, as a reasonable accommodation, to transfer a disabled employee to a vacant position for which he or she is qualified"); Buckingham v. U.S. Postal Service, 998 F.2d 735 (9th Cir. 1993); Fedro v. Reno, 21 F.3d 1391 (7th Cir. 1994) (Under the Rehabilitation Act, it might be a reasonable accommodation to reassign a postal worker with HIV from Mississippi to California for better medical treatment.)

There is also disagreement regarding the scope of reassignment. See e.g., Buckingham v. U.S. Postal Service, supra, suggests that the an employee might be reassigned across country. On the other hand, two district courts have limited the scope of reassignment to the facility in question based upon the employer's policies and practices. See e.g., Riley v. Weyerhaeuser Paper Co., 898 F. Supp. 324 (W.D.N.C. 1995), aff'd, 77 F.3d 470 (4th Cir. 1996); Emrick v. Libbey-Owens-Ford Co., 875 F. Supp. 393 (E.D. Tex. 1995).

An employer is not required to create a new job or to provide "light duty." See, e.g., Champ v. Baltimore County, Maryland, 884 F. Supp. 991 (D. Md. 1994), aff'd, 91 F.3d 129 (4th Cir. 1996) (Officer who could not perform forcible arrest, shoot with two hands but who could perform temporary desk job was not qualified individual with a disability); Nguyen v. IBP., Inc., 905 F. Supp. 1471, 1486 (D. Kan. 1995)(Light duty is not mandated by ADA and if provided by employer voluntarily, can be temporary); Vaughan v. Harvard Industrics, 926 F. Supp. 1340 (W.D. Tenn. 1996)(Employer who exceeds requirements of ADA by providing light duty is not estopped from arguing that employee is not a qualified individual with a disability); Magel v. Federal Reserve Bank of Phila., 776 F. Supp. 200, 204 (E.D. Pa. 1991) ("[h]owever reasonable accommodation is defined, it does not include creating a new job.").

Note, however, that in its Enforcement Guidance, the EEOC asserts that creating light duty positions is not required, doing so may have a disparate impact under the ADA or other equal employment statutes. In addition, EEOC asserts that light duty positions may not be limited to persons with compensable injuries. EEOC Notice 915.002: Workers' Compensation and the ADA (Sept. 3, 1996), pp. 18-22.

XYZ's failure to discuss these possible accommodations with the driver and make a good faith effort to provide accommodation denied it a defense to his claim for compensatory and punitive damages. Under the Civil Rights Act of 1991, Congress provided employers with a defense to damages for denial of accommodation if an employer makes a good faith effort to provide reasonable accommodation in consultation with the individual requesting it. 42 U.S.C. § 1981a(a)(3).

Moreover, courts are reviewing the totality of circumstances including employer's efforts at providing other accommodations to determine that efforts at accommodation are sufficient. Courts are holding that an employer is not obligated to provide the accommodation an applicant or employee requests so long as accommodation is provided. See, e.g., Riley v. Weyerhauser Paper Co., 898 F. Supp. 324 (W.D.N.C. 1995), aff'd, 77 F.3d 470 (4th Cir. 1996) (No liability for failure to provide reasonable accommodation where employer had discussions with plaintiff, prepared job description and videotape of job to show employee's physician and where employee contacted the Job Accommodation Network); Hankins v. The Gap, Inc., 84 F.3d 797 (6th Cir. 1996)(Employer need not provide accommodation employee requests so long as employee provides effective accommodation); Sharpe v. AT&T, 66 F.3d 1045 (9th Cir. 1995) (Employer sought to accommodate employee with a seizure disorder by placing him on short and long term disability for time to evaluate his condition of employment, re-training for new position, allowed him to apply for another position within company, and offered his old job back. Court held that employer made more than sufficient effort at accommodating employee); Fink v. New York City Dept. of Personnel, 3 AD Cases 1067 (S.D.N.Y. 1994) (Employer which provided readers, tape recorders and audio tape as accommodations for blind employees taking a civil service exam, was found to have provided reasonable accommodation procedures that would ensure that examination would be fair; the fact that the readers were alleged to have been noisy and impaired plaintiffs' concentration amounted to unauthorized and unintentional actions which the Rehab Act was not designed to remedy); Carter v. Bennett, 840 F.2d 63, 67 (D.C. Cir. 1988) (Section 504 of the Rehabilitation Act does not require an employer to provide every accommodation requested.)

Finally, XYZ's workers' compensation attorneys may have failed to gain an adequate waiver of the driver's ADA claims as part of the workers' compensation settlement. While the issue has yet to be authoritatively addressed by the courts, it is likely that an ADA waiver will be held to a "knowing and voluntary" standard. See, Wittorf v. Shell Oil Co., 1994 WL 150810 (E.D. La.) (There is no reason why the "knowing and voluntary" standard should not apply to the ADA.); Callicotte v. Carlucci, 698 F. Supp. 944 (D.D.C. 1988) (Employee with chronic alcoholism and depression did not knowingly and voluntarily waive Rehabilitation Act claim when agreeing to probation and last chance agreement in lieu of termination.) The failure of a workers' compensation release to expressly waive ADA rights may make the release ineffective in barring any later ADA lawsuit. In addition, an employer will have to provide additional monetary consideration for the waiver of the ADA claims to be effective. Accordingly, any settlement of a workers' compensation claim should be accompanied by an express waiver of all claims under the ADA and the waiver should specify the consideration provided for the ADA waiver.

III. The Impact of FMLA and ADA on STD Policies

Suppose our truck driver hurt his back at home, playing touch football. Instead of receiving workers' compensation benefits, the employee is eligible for short term disability (STD) benefits under XYZ's benefit plan. Typical STD policies provide that after the eighth day of absence because of a disability, injury, or illness, the employee will receive anywhere from 50% to

100% of his or her income. In short, the STD policy is an income replacement policy for employees unable to work. In addition, many STD policies authorize leave and grant job restoration rights for a specified period of time.

What constitutes a "disability" under the terms of an STD policy and what constitutes a "serious health condition" under the FMLA are probably co-extensive. A condition that requires an employee to be out at least eight days -- a typical threshold requirement for STD eligibility -- presumptively will be a serious health condition under the FMLA, which merely requires that an employee be out for more than three days. Thus, a condition which entitles an employee to STD will in all likelihood constitute a serious health condition under the FMLA. In our example, therefore, the FMLA outcome would not change whether the employee is covered by workers' compensation or an STD policy.

For purposes of the ADA, however, an employer should consider whether the employee in question has an ADA-covered disability. Because the XYZ driver has an ADA-covered disability, the only change made by the application of the ADA to the STD policy would relate to any right to job restoration and/or additional leave granted by the policy. If an employer creates a right to job restoration or provides additional authorized leave by virtue of eligibility for STD benefits, the employer has created a "floor" from which ADA rights will build. An employer would be hard pressed to argue that it is an undue hardship to provide leave beyond the FMLA-mandated 12 weeks or to hold a job open beyond that time if the employer has already contracted to do so in its benefit plan. Accordingly, an employee entitled to, for example, 26 weeks of STD benefits may assert that s/he is entitled to additional unpaid leave beyond the 26 weeks as a form of reasonable accommodation. Again, this request is subject to the undue hardship limitation which should take into account the hardship created from the date of the employee's initial absence. Nonetheless, if an employer has contracted to provide paid benefits for absence and job restoration for the first 26 weeks, it will be difficult to successfully argue that tacking on another few weeks is unduly burdensome.

IV. Pitfalls to Reducing Absenteeism and Promoting Return to Work

The final FMLA regulations in conjunction with other laws such as the ADA, make it more difficult for an employer to control absences, promote early return to work and cut benefit costs. Here are the elements of the FMLA and ADA you must bear in mind in seeking to control absences and promote return to work.

A. Leave Is An Entitlement

1. Neutral attendance control policies in which an employee is penalized for absences cannot be applied to FMLA leaves.

2. Poor attendance resulting from FMLA qualifying absences cannot be used against an employee when considering eligibility for any term or privilege of employment including bonuses, promotion or reduction in force.

3. An employer cannot require return to work on modified or light duty or with accommodation if the individual's FMLA entitlement is not exhausted.

B. The ADA, Other Laws, Collective Bargaining Agreements or Other Company Policy May Provide Greater, Cumulative Rights

The FMLA final rule makes clear that FMLA is cumulative, providing rights in addition to what is provided by other laws, collective bargaining agreements or more generous company policy. Additional unpaid leave beyond the 12 FMLA weeks, with restoration to the same job is a reasonable accommodation according to the EEOC.

C. Access to Medical Information Is Restricted

The Department of Labor's Final Regulations restrict even further an employer's access to employee medical records for purposes of granting FMLA leave. An employer may not require more documentation than is contained on the now revised Department of Labor's health care provider certification form absent clarification is sought by an employer's medical advisor with the employee's consent.

V. Controlling Absences, Promoting Return to Work and Avoiding Litigation and Liability

There are several steps an employer can take to control unnecessary absences and promote return to work.

A. Establish a Disability Management Committee.

An employee who cannot or should not work because of a medical condition frequently will have overlapping, cumulative rights under several laws and policies. Such an individual may be entitled to benefits and protection under workers' compensation, state disability laws, other state family, pregnancy or nondiscrimination laws as well as the FMLA, ADA or the Pregnancy Discrimination Act. Responding to such an individual's request for leave, work restrictions, light duty or reasonable accommodation requires an employer to understand the interplay of these various laws with company policy. No one department has the time or expertise to provide what is necessary--a coordinated, integrated response. Nor is it realistic that these different, overlapping program responsibilities will be consolidated. Therefore, it is critically important to establish a Disability Management Committee composed of representatives from Risk Management, Human Resources and Legal. Such a committee can be established at a facility or regional level depending upon corporate structure. Representatives who will work together as a team to monitor employees on medically-based leave or work restrictions; to devise for each such employee an appropriate action plan; and to make decisions regarding requests for modified duty and reasonable accommodation.

B. Establish a Strong Disability Management Program Which Applies Appropriate Policies

An employee may be on a FMLA or extended medical leave while recovering from a disabling impairment. Or, an employee may be brought back for on-the-job work hardening in a temporary modified duty position. In addition, the individual may be provided a reasonable accommodation to enable him or her to perform the essential functions of the original position or to enable performance of a different position to which the employee is reassigned. It is critically important that an injured or ill employee with work restrictions understand that after use of applicable leave or modified duty, the employee will be terminated unless she or he can return to the employee's original position or another available position for which the employee is qualified, with or without reasonable accommodation. A good disability management policy has the following elements.

1. Give FMLA notice to FMLA eligible employees on workers' compensation or short term disability benefits. Administrative procedures should be developed to automatically send the required FMLA notice and health care provider certification form after 4 days of absence.

2. Establish, in accordance with the FMLA and ADA a maximum neutral policy after which an employee will be separated from employment. This may be done lawfully under the FMLA if an employee is required first to use the FMLA entitlement and then apply for any discretionary employer-provided leave of absence.

3. Separate leave authorization from pay authorization and tighten eligibility for receipt of paid benefits while on leave.

FMLA only requires an employer to provide unpaid leave. Provision of paid leave, including paid sick leave or short-term disability benefits is governed by employer policy. An employer can establish more stringent eligibility for paid leave than for unpaid leave. For example, an employer could require that receipt of paid leave is contingent upon an employee providing medical records for review by a medical advisor. If an employee wishes merely to submit the health care provider certification form, the employee is entitled to receive unpaid leave but would not be eligible for paid FMLA leave. If the employee submits satisfactory documentation demonstrating inability to work due to a medical condition, the employee receives paid leave. An employer can also tighten eligibility for short-term disability benefits by requiring that receipt of benefits was contingent upon an employee's willingness to accept reasonable accommodation to enable the employee to return to work. Failure to accept reasonable accommodation would result in loss of paid benefits but entitlement to unpaid leave would continue until the FMLA entitlement was exhausted.

4. Treat requests for work restrictions as a reasonable accommodation. Under the ADA, an employer is permitted to obtain sufficient medical information to ascertain whether an individual requesting accommodation is an individual with a disability, whether the accommodation requested is medically necessary and whether the accommodation would enable the employee to perform the essential functions of the position in question. For example, an FMLA-eligible employee who requests to be excused from typing due to wrist pain is requesting reasonable accommodation.

If typing is an essential job function, an employer is not required to so restructure the job but other options such as modification of equipment or reassignment are possibilities. However, the employee is implicitly asserting the basis to be put on FMLA leave by asserting an inability to do an essential job function because of what may be a serious health condition. An employer in this circumstance may put the employee on leave and preliminarily designate the leave as FMLA leave pending receipt of medical certification. The employer then will be able to consider the possibility of reasonable accommodation by requesting a complete set of medical records pertaining to the condition for which the employee is seeking accommodation in order to ascertain the feasibility of an accommodation.

VI. Conclusion

Employers must integrate the ADA and FMLA into their medically-based leave and benefit policies. Gone are the days when these issues could be neatly compartmentalized between Human Resources, Risk Management and Legal departments.

In particular, employers should take the following steps:

1. Integrate the ADA and FMLA into medically-based leave and benefit policies. A neutral leave policy should be revised to ensure that it will not create expensive liabilities under the ADA and FMLA.

2. Employers should adopt a coordinated team approach to medically-based leave and benefits that includes risk management, benefits, human resources, legal and EEO to fashion leave and benefit policies that weave carefully between applicable laws in a way that encourages work rather than the use of benefits.

3. Train managers and supervisors in the interplay between the ADA, FMLA, and workers' compensation. Make sure that managers and supervisors give the required FMLA notice whenever it is learned that an employee is requesting leave for an FMLA purpose such as a work-caused injury resulting in more than three days of absence from work.

JACKSON, LEWIS, SCHNITZLER & KRUPMAN

1625 K STREET, N.W. • SUITE 700 • WASHINGTON, D.C. 20006

(202) 347-5200

(202) 223-8557 FACSIMILE

PRACTICE LIMITED TO REPRESENTING MANAGEMENT IN
LABOR, EMPLOYMENT & BENEFITS LAW AND RELATED LITIGATION

ATLANTA, GA
BOSTON, MA
CHICAGO, IL
DALLAS, TX
GREENVILLE, SC
HARTFORD, CT
LOS ANGELES, CA
MORRISTOWN, NJ

NEW YORK, NY
ORLANDO, FL
PITTSBURGH, PA
SAN FRANCISCO, CA
STAMFORD, CT
WHITE PLAINS, NY
WOODBURY, NY

SAMPLE FAMILY AND MEDICAL LEAVE POLICY[1]

A. Family and Medical Leave

The Leave Policy. You are eligible to take up to 12 weeks of unpaid family/medical leave within any 12 month period and be restored to the same or an equivalent position upon your return from leave provided you: (1) are a regular full-time employee who has worked for the company for at least 6 months; or
(1) are a regular part-time employee who has worked for the Company for at least 12 months and has worked for at least 1040 hours in the last 12 months. A "rolling" 12 month period measured backwards from the date you take leave will be used for computing the period within which the 12 weeks of leave may be taken.

Reasons for Leave. You may take family/medical leave for any of the following reasons: (1) the birth of a son or daughter and in order to care for such son or daughter; (2) the placement of a son or daughter with you for adoption or foster care and in order to care for the newly placed son or daughter; (3) to care for a spouse, son, daughter or parent ("covered relation") with a serious health condition; or (4) because of your own serious health condition which renders you unable to perform an essential function of your position. Leave because of reason of "1" or "2" must be completed within the 12 month period beginning on the date of birth or placement. In addition, spouses employed by the Company who request leave because of reasons "1" or "2" may only take a combined total of 12 weeks leave.

Notice of Leave. You must notify the Company of your need for leave by completing a Request for Family/Medical Leave Form, available from your supervisor or Director. You should give 30 days prior written notice, or as much advanced written notice as possible, to your supervisor.

Medical Certification. If you are requesting leave because of reasons "3" or "4," you and the relevant health care provider must supply appropriate medical certification. You may obtain the Medical

1 The materials contained in this handout were prepared by the law firm of Jackson, Lewis, Schnitzler & Krupman for the attendees' own reference in connection with management education seminars presented by the firm. Since these materials and related discussions are informational and educational in nature and represent the speaker's own views, attendees should consult with counsel before taking any actions and should not consider these materials or discussions thereabout to be legal or other advice. Professional advice should be obtained before attempting to address any legal situation or problem.

Certification Form from your supervisor or Director. Whenever possible, the Medical Certification should be supplied prior to the commencement of leave. Further, the Company, at its expense, may require an examination by a second health care provider designated by the Company. If the second health care provider's opinion conflicts with the original medical certification, the Company, at its expense, may require a third, mutually agreeable, health care provider to conduct an examination and provide a final and binding opinion. The Company may require a subsequent medical recertification. Failure to provide requested certification within 15 days, if such is practicable, may result in delay of further leave until it is provided.

Reporting While On Leave. If you take leave because of your own serious health condition or to care for a covered relation, you must contact your supervisor or appropriate management representative, on the "first and third Tuesday" of each month regarding the status of the condition and your intention to return to work to see how you are progressing and so that we are up to date on any new developments. In addition, you must give notice as soon as practicable (within 2 business days if feasible) if the dates of leave change, are extended or initially were unknown.

Intermittent and Reduced Scheduled Leave. Leave because of a serious health condition may be taken intermittently (in separate blocks of time due to a single health condition) or on a reduced leave schedule (reducing the usual number of hours you work each workday) if medically necessary. If leave is unpaid, the Company will reduce your salary based on the amount of time actually worked. In addition, while you are on an intermittent or reduced schedule leave, the Company may temporarily transfer you to an available alternative position which better accommodates your recurring leave and which has equivalent pay and benefits.

Light Duty. The company will attempt to aid you to return to work as quickly as possible within your medical restrictions. The company may be able to provide you with some temporary light duty work to enable you to return to full duty. If available, light duty may be authorized for up to 60 days. After that point, the Company will attempt to place you in a vacant position for which you are qualified, including your original position if it is available. If you are interested in performing temporary light duty when medically able to do so, please contact your supervisor. If the Company offers light duty within your medical restrictions and you choose to remain on leave, you will lose eligibility for short-term disability benefits. If you accept light duty work, you will receive 100 percent of your current rate of pay and time spent performing light duty will not count against your available medical leave. Your refusal to accept light duty, however, does not affect your FMLA leave entitlement.

Reasonable Accommodations. The Company also will attempt to reasonably accommodate a medical condition to enable you to do your original job. Any accommodation must be medically necessary, effective, and not an undue hardship upon Company operations. If you cannot be accommodated to perform your original position if available, we will attempt to place you in a vacant position for which you are qualified. Such a reassignment may be at your current rate of pay or a lower rate of pay if an equivalent position for which you are qualified is not available. You may meet with your supervisor or Director to discuss possible means of accommodation. Your refusal to accept an accommodation does not affect your FMLA leave entitlement. If the Company offers an effective reasonable accommodation within your medical restrictions and you choose to remain on leave, you will lose eligibility for short-term disability benefits or such refusal may affect your eligibility for workers' compensation benefits under applicable state law.

Leave is Unpaid. Family/medical leave is unpaid leave, although you may be eligible for short or long term disability payments and/or workers' compensation benefits under those insurance plans, which we provide at no cost to you. These plans are generally described elsewhere in the handbook. If you request leave, you must notify the Company if you wish to use any accrued paid time off as part of your family/medical leave including, paid vacation, personal days, and sick leave (sick leave will be applied only when leave is taken for reasons "3" and/or "4"). For more information regarding use of your accrued paid time off, or eligibility for disability and/or workers compensation insurance payments, talk with your Director and/or Regional Benefits Administrator and/or refer to the plan documents (which are controlling).

Medical and Other Benefits. During an approved family/medical leave, the Company will maintain your health benefits, as if you continued to be actively employed. However, if you elect not to return to work at the end of the leave period, you will be required to reimburse the Company for the cost of the health insurance premiums paid by the Company for maintaining coverage during your leave, unless you cannot return to work because of a serious health condition or because of other circumstances beyond your control.

Returning From Leave. When you are able to return to work following a leave because of your own serious health condition, you should attempt to give the Company at least one week's notice by mailing to your supervisor or Director medical certification stating that you are able to resume work. You may obtain Return to Work Medical Certification Forms from your supervisor or Director. This is important so that your return to work is properly scheduled.

Extended Leave for Serious Health Condition. Leave taken because of your own serious health condition may be extended on a month-to-month basis for a maximum of an additional 40 weeks upon: (1) written request to the Company; (2) submission of medical documentation satisfactory to the Company that you have a serious medical condition which precludes you from travel to and from work, being at work or safely and satisfactorily performing an essential function of your position with or without reasonable accommodation; and (3) approval by the Company (which is subject to its business needs). If you do not return to work on the originally scheduled return date nor request in advance an extension of the agreed upon leave with appropriate and sufficient documentation, you will be deemed to have voluntarily terminated your employment with the company. If you request an extension of your leave beyond the initial 12 week period, you must submit medical documentation of your continued serious health condition demonstrating that your medical condition precludes travel to and from work, being at work or safe and satisfactory performance of essential job functions, in advance for each month that the leave is extended. If your serious health condition continues to prevent you from returning to work after an extended leave of absence of 40 weeks, you might be eligible for up to an additional 28 days of leave under limited circumstances: (1) your medical condition must be severe enough to constitute a disability under applicable law; (2) your medical condition must be expected to be sufficiently resolved so that you will be able to return to work at the end of up to 28 days of additional leave; and (3) provision of the additional unpaid leave will not impose undue hardship on the Company.

Please understand that reinstatement from an extended leave of absence (leave beyond the initial 12 weeks of leave) is not guaranteed and will depend upon the availability of a vacancy for which you are qualified.[2]

Also, after a maximum of 40 weeks of extended leave of absence under the circumstances described above (or 44 weeks if eligible for a final 28 day extension), you must be able to return to your original position if it is available or a vacant position for which you are qualified. If you are not able to return to work after all authorized leave has been exhausted, your employment will be terminated.

---

2 Please note that the EEOC takes the position that an employee on leave as a reasonable accommodation has a right to return to his/her same position unless the employer demonstrates undue hardship. However, a majority of courts addressing the issue of extended leave as an accommodation have not adopted the EEOC's position as of this date because such an employee is unable to be in attendance to perform his/her essential job functions. Adoption of a more restrictive job restoration policy has some risk. Please seek the advice of counsel before adopting such a position.

NOTES

NOTES

15

CHECKLIST FOR DETERMINATION OF INDEPENDENT CONTRACTOR STATUS

Laura J. Lokker

CHECKLIST FOR DETERMINATION OF INDEPENDENT CONTRACTOR STATUS

In order to establish an independent contractor relationship, the answers to the majority of the following questions should be yes.

		YES	NO
1.	Have the parties signed an independent agreement?	_____	_____
2.	Does the contract state that the company has no right to control the work performed?	_____	_____
3.	Has the company prepared a letter upon the completion of the work stating that the contractual terms were complied with?	_____	_____
4.	Does the contract state that the independent contractor cannot be fired so long as he meets his contractual obligations?	_____	_____
5.	Does the contract state that the independent contractor has a right to hire and fire assistants?	_____	_____
6.	Does the contract state that the independent contractor will treat assistants as his own employees and will comply with all tax requirements?	_____	_____
7.	Does the contract provide that the independent contractor is solely responsible for providing the labor to achieve the intended result?	_____	_____
8.	Is the independent contractor paid by the job, rather than by the hour?	_____	_____
9.	Is the company ensuring that no type of training is provided by the company for inexperienced workers?	_____	_____

10. Is the independent contractor viewed as a skilled worker? _____ _____

11. Is the independent contractor hired for a specified time period? _____ _____

12. Does the contract set out a completion date or some other termination date of its relationship with the independent contractor? _____ _____

13. Does the independent contractor set his own hours of work? _____ _____

14. Is the independent contractor free to work for any number of persons or firms simultaneously? _____ _____

15. Does the independent contractor advertise and project himself to the public as an independent contractor in business for himself? Does he have business cards? Does he advertise in the yellow pages? _____ _____

16. Does the independent contractor furnish his own tools? _____ _____

17. Does the independent contractor perform his job off company premises? _____ _____

18. Does the independent contractor negotiate the payment for his services with the company? _____ _____

19. Does the contract provide that the customer will pay the independent contractor directly, rather than pay the company who them pays the independent contractor? _____ _____

20. Does the company consistently refer to the worker as an independent contractor in letters, memoranda, invoices, check stubs, and other correspondence between the parties? _____ _____

21. Does the company refrain from instructing the independent contractor as to the sequence in which the work is the be performed? _____ _____

22. Does the company refrain from requiring the independent contractor to submit regular oral or written reports? _____ _____

23. Does the company refrain from sending supervisors or inspectors to the field on a regular basis to check on the work progress? _____ _____

24. Does the company refrain from requesting that the independent contractor do the same type of work as it regular employees? _____ _____

25. Does the company refrain from engaging an independent contractor to do something that is part of the day-to-day operations of the company? _____ _____

26. Is there evidence that the company's competitors are treating similar workers as independent contractors? _____ _____

NOTES

16

CHECKLIST FOR HUMAN RESOURCES DETERMINATION OF CONSULTANT'S STATUS FOR PAYROLL TAX PURPOSES

Laura J. Lokker

CHECKLIST FOR HUMAN RESOURCES DETERMINATION OF CONSULTANT'S STATUS FOR PAYROLL TAX PURPOSES

	Employee	Independent Contractor
1.	Consultant works on premises	Consultant works off premises
2.	Company has control over the means, manner, and terms of work, including order or sequence of work; Consultant must comply with supervision.	S&S has no control over the means, manner, and terms of work; Consultant need not comply with supervision.
3.	Consultant spends full time working for Company, while the agreement lasts.	Consultant spends only part time working for Company and works for other clients during the terms of the agreement.
4.	Consultant performs services only.	Consultant furnishes a final report or some other tangible evidence of his work.
5.	Consultant is paid on a weekly or some other periodic basis.	Consultant is paid for the job.
6.	Consultant is reimbursed for expenses which are accounted for.	Consultant is not paid expenses in addition to payment for the job.
7.	Consultant works set hours, e.g. 9-5.	Consultant can work any hours that he/she elects.
8.	Consultant does not have an independent business.	Consultant does have an independent business.
	a. Consultant is not known in his or her field.	Consultant is known in his or her field.
	b. Consultant works alone.	Consultant hires others to work for him.
	c. Consultant does not furnish any materials. They are all furnished by Company.	Consultant has his own materials to do the job.
	d. Consultant does not hold himself out as being in his own business.	Consultant holds himself out as being in his own business, and has business investments and expenses.

e. Consultant can quit at any time without incurring liability.	Consultant cannot quit without liability for failure to complete the job.
f. Company can terminate Consultant's employment at any time.	Company may be liable in damages for termination unless contract provides otherwise.

NOTES

NOTES

17

TELECOMMUTING: EMPLOYMENT LAW ISSUES

Laura J. Lokker

Reprinted with permission from a presentation, *The Legal Detours of Telecommuting*, Michael A. Blickman, Ice Miller Donadio & Ryan, Indianapolis, IN.

TELECOMMUTING: EMPLOYMENT LAW ISSUES*

Telecommuting, loosely defined as any arrangement whereby employees work at a location other than the main office of their employer, is a growing employment trend. Typically involving employees working from their home, often with the aid of technology links, such as computer modem, ISDN line and fax machine, telecommuting raises a number of potential legal concerns which should be recognized and addressed at the outset.

FAIR LABOR STANDARDS ACT

- Timekeeping and Submission Of Time Records
- Overtime Calculation

WORKER'S COMPENSATION

- Did Injury "Arise Out Of and In The Course Of Employment"?
- Employer's Duty and Opportunity To Assure Workplace Safety
- Opportunity For Employee Fraud

---

*Adapted with permission from presentation, *The Legal Detours of Telecommuting*, Michael A. Blickman, Ice Miller Donadio & Ryan ©1996

INDEPENDENT CONTRACTOR OR EMPLOYEE?

- Degree of Control and Direction By "Employer"
- IRS "20 Factor" Test

ZONING AND OTHER LAND USE RESTRICTIONS

- Zoning Laws Which Prohibit "Operating a Business" Out Of The Home
- Lease Restrictions
- Neighborhood/Condominium Association or Co-op Board Restrictions or Covenants

AMERICANS WITH DISABILITIES ACT

- Qualified Individual With A Disability
- Can Perform the Essential Functions of a Job With or Without Reasonable Accommodation
- Employer's Duty to Provide Work At Home as Reasonable Accommodation
- Is It An Undue Hardship On The Employer?

  -Vande Zande v. Wisconsin Dept of Administration, 44 F. 3d 538 (7th Cir. 1995).

  -Anzalone v. Allstate, 1995 U.S. Dist. LEXIS 1272 (5th Cir. 1995).

WORKPLACE PRIVACY

- Employer's Right To Inspect Workplace
- Retrieval of Employer-Provided Equipment
- Private Home vs. Employer's Right To Oversee Workplace As Safe and Appropriate

CONFIDENTIALITY OF EMPLOYER INFORMATION

- Who Has Access To The Employee's Computer, Documents, Disks, etc.?
- Devise Plan To Protect Confidential Information Before Telecommuting Begins

  e.g. : -Use Passwords

  -Lock Computer System

  -Employee Signs Confidentiality Agreement

EMPLOYEE SELECTION FOR TELECOMMUTING

- Determining Appropriate Criteria For Selecting Employees Eligible.
- Criteria Should Be Business-Based and Nondiscriminatory

  -Avoid Gender-Based Decisions

- Criteria Should Be Applied Uniformly To All Employees

MANAGING PERFORMANCE

- Overcoming Manager's Fear That "Absent" Employees Are Less Productive
- Shift Focus From "Managing Activity" To "Managing Results"

THE TELECOMMUTING CONTRACT

1. Time Records
    - Promise To Record Time and Submit To Employer Regularly
    - Agreement Concerning Employee's Work Hours, Especially If Non-Exempt

2. Access By Employer To Home Workspace To Inspect

3. Confidentiality Of Computer Data and Other Company Records

4. Return of Property Upon Termination (With Penalty For Failure)

5. Responsibility For Equipment Maintenance and Repairs

   (Note: No Paycheck Deduction Without Prior Signed Employee Authorization)

6. Define Whether Independent Contractor or Employee Relationship

7. Insurance Requirements

8. Use Of Equipment: Personal vs. Business Use

9. Access By Others To The Workplace: Limitations, If Any

10. No Guarantee That Telecommuting Will Be Permanent

11. Employment At Will Disclaimer

NOTES

18

EMPLOYEE PRIVACY: AVOIDING LIABILITY IN THE ELECTRONIC AGE

Julienne W. Bramesco

Table of Contents

Introduction

Imagine legal practice without duplicating machines, fax machine, e-mail, or cellular phones. Can you remember life before you had a computer sitting on your desk? These new technologies increase productivity by saving time, labor, and making it possible to monitor in ways we would not have considered twenty years ago. We live in a world with constantly changing technology. Unfortunately, as the new technologies increase productivity, they also create many new sources of liability.

It has, perhaps, never been easier for employers to monitor their employees. Employers can reach employees at remote locations through cellular phones and fax machines. They can access communications from voice mail, pagers and e-mail. Video cameras are smaller and more available than ever. These advances have not, however, been universally applauded. This paper will address some of the legal issues confronting employers created in part by the new technologies.

1

Sources of Privacy Law

Employers do not have unfettered rights in the workplace. Before an employer picks up an extension to see if a call is personal or business, or sets up a surveillance operation, there are a number of laws which should be considered. It is important to note that there is little case guidance for most of these laws, and any surveillance should be undertaken with common sense and consideration of the future implication of the conduct.

Electronic Communications Privacy Act of 1986 (EPCA), 18 U.S.C. §2510 et seq.

In 1986, Congress amended the Federal Wiretap Act to include electronic communications. The ECPA is the basic statute governing electronic communications in interstate commerce. It covers two types of communications: (1) in transit in Title I; and (2) stored in Title II. The prohibitions of the ECPA include the willful interception or use (including attempts to intercept or to procure interception through another person) or disclosure of a wire, oral or electronic communication (18 U.S.C. §2511), and unauthorized access to and disclosure of stored wire and electronic communications (18 U.S.C. §§2701 and 2702).

In order to discuss the EPCA, it is important to understand its definitions.

1. "wire communication" means any aural transfer made in whole or in part through the use of facilities for the transmission of communications by the aid of wire, cable, or other like connection between the point of origin and the point of reception (including the use of such connection in a switching station) furnished or operated by any person engaged in providing or operating such facilities for the transmission of interstate or foreign commerce and such term includes any electronic storage of such communications;

2. "oral communication" means any oral communication uttered by a person exhibiting an expectation that such communication is not subject to interception under circumstances justifying such expectation, but such terms does not include any electronic communication;

3. "intercept" means the aural or other acquisition of the contents of any wire, electronic, or oral communication through the use of any electronic, mechanical, or other device;

4. "electronic, mechanical, or other device" means any device or apparatus which can be used to intercept a wire, oral, or electronic communication other than:

    (1) any telephone or telegraph instrument, equipment or facility, or any component thereof, (i) furnished to the subscriber or user by a provider of wire or electronic communication service in the ordinary course of its business and being used by the subscriber or user in the ordinary course of its business or furnished by such subscriber or user for connection to the facilities of such service and used in the ordinary course of its business; or (ii) being used by a provider of wire or electronic communication service in the ordinary course of its business, or by an investigative or law enforcement officer in the ordinary course of his duties;

    (2) a hearing aid or similar device being used to correct subnormal hearing to not better than normal;

5. "electronic communication" means any transfer of signs, signals, writing, images, sounds, data, or intelligence of any nature transmitted in whole or in part by a wire, radio, electromagnetic, photoelectronic or photo optical system that affects interstate or foreign commerce, but does not include--

    (1) any wire or oral communication;

    (2) any communication made through a tone-only paging device; or

    (3) any communication from a tracking device (as defined in section 3117 of this title);

6. "user" means any person or entity who uses any electronic communication service and is duly authorized by the provider of such service to engage in such use;

7. "electronic storage" means any temporary, intermediate storage of a wire or electronic communication incidental to the electronic transmission thereof; and any storage of such communication by an electronic communication service for purposes of backup protection of such communication.

ECPA applies every time a supervisor listens to the call of his/her employee. Fortunately, however, there are many exceptions to the ECPA's prohibitions. EPCA permits employees of wire or electronic communication providers to intercept, disclosure or use communications under certain circumstances. 18 U.S.C.§2511(2)(a). Employees of the Federal Communications Commission may also intercept communications in the normal course of duty. 18 U.S.C.§2511(2)(b). There are two exceptions to the ECPA which are of most use to private employers. These are consent and the telephone extension exception.

First, the telephone extension exception. Monitoring may be done if the equipment used meets the definition under §2510(5)(a)(1), i.e., is telephone or telegraph equipment furnished to the subscriber or user in the ordinary course of business and which is used in business **and** which is used in the ordinary course of business. There are a number of cases which interpret this exception to ECPA. For example, in Briggs v. American Air Filter Co., Inc., 630 F.2d 414 (5th Cir. 1980), the employer, believing that confidential information was being disclosed to a business competitor, picked up a phone receiver which was "an ordinary extension telephone," listened to and recorded part of a call. The court held that Congress did not intend to prohibit this type of conduct.

The type of equipment used for the interception is important for it can lead to contradictory results. In Epps v. St. Mary's Hospital of Athens, Inc., 802 F.2d 412 (11th Cir. 1986), a supervisor listened to and recorded a conversation disparaging two other supervisors. The court held that the telephone extension exception was met because the equipment met the definition and the employer had a legitimate business interest in contents of the communication, i.e., scurrilous remarks about supervisory employees. In Deal v. Spears, 980 F.2d 1153 (8th Cir. 1992), the Eighth Circuit held that the intercepted calls would not be heard or acquired but for the recording device. The court specifically disagreed with the Eleventh Circuit's finding in Epps that the interception device was exempt equipment. "It seems far more plausible to us that the recording device, and not the extension phone, is the instrument used to intercept the call. We do not believe that the recording device falls within the statutory exemption." See also Pascale v. Carolina Freight Carriers Corp., 898 F. Supp. 276 (D.N.J. 1995).

Even if the equipment meets the test, monitoring must be done in the ordinary course of business for the exception to apply. In Watkins v. L.M. Berry & Co., 704 F.2d 577 (11th Cir. 1983), the court held that the "ordinary course of business" does not mean "anything that interests a company." The fact that the subject of the call was personal meant that it could not have been intercepted in the ordinary course of business, except to guard against unauthorized phone use. Consequently, the length and purpose of the interception are important.

Perhaps more useful and comforting in the employment context is consent. It is not illegal to intercept a communication where one party to the communication has consented to its interception. §2511(2)(d). Consent may be explicit or implied, and is to be construed broadly. For example, in Griggs-Ryan v. Smith, 904 F.2d 112 (1st Cir. 1990), the court found no violation of the statute where Plaintiff was informed that calls were being monitored, and consequently, knowingly agreed to the surveillance; the consent being inferred from the surrounding circumstances. In Griffin v. City of Milwaukee, 74 F.3d 924 (7th Cir. 1996), the court concluded that since police dispatchers were warned that the work station phone calls might be monitored for training, evaluation, and supervision purposes, the plaintiff consented to the recording of her calls. There are limits to implied consent, however, the Griggs-Ryan court specifically referred to Watkins. Even if consented to, the interception is illegal if used for the purpose of committing criminal or tortious acts. §2511(2)(d).

New technology not only has created new ways to communicate, but has also created new ways of storing communications. ECPA distinguishes between the intercepting of communication at the time of transmissions (Title I) and the retrieval of communication after it has been stored (Title II). Title II of ECPA prohibits unauthorized access to and disclosure of stored wire and electronic communications. 18 U.S.C. §§2701 and 2702. This proscription has been held to include stored electronic "e-mail" and pager messages. The requirements for legally intercepting wire communications are more stringent than those for accessing stored electronic communications.

In Steve Jackson Games, Inc. v. U.S. Secret Service, 36 F.3d 457 (5th Cir. 1994), the U.S. Secret Service received a search warrant which authorized seizure of computer data from Steve Jackson Games, (SJG), a company which published books, magazines, role-playing games, and related products. SJG operated an electronic bulletin board which facilitated communication between the company, its customers, and free-lance game writers. When the warrant was executed, the computer which operated the electronic bulletin board was seized. The bulletin board contained 162 items of stored, but unread "e-mail." SJG filed suit claiming violations of the Privacy Protection Act, The Federal Wiretap Act including Title I (interceptions) and Title II (stored communications). The district court held that the Secret Service violated the Privacy Protection Act, and Title II of the ECPA, but it held that there was no "interception" in violation of Title I of the ECPA " because its acquisition of the contents of the electronic communications was not contemporaneous with the transmissions of those communications." The Fifth Circuit affirmed, clearly distinguishing the differences between store wire communications and stored electronic communications and in doing so, established that stored "e-mail" was subject to the less stringent requirements of Title II.

There are exceptions under Title II which are similar to those of Title I. These exceptions distinguish between access and disclosure. The exceptions for access are the provider exemption, §2701(c)(1) and consent by the user, §2701(c)(2). The exceptions for disclosure of the contents of stored communications include:

- consent by the originator, addressee or intended recipient, §2702(b)(3)
- business use, §2702(b)(5)
- disclosure to law enforcement, §2702(b)(6) where a service provider has "inadvertently obtained" stored communications which "appear to pertain to the commission of a crime."

Unlike the provider exception in Title I, many employers are indeed "providers" of electronic communications services. In Bohach v. The City of Reno, et al, 932 F.Supp. 1232 (DN, 1996), the U.S. District Court for Nevada held that the city lawfully accessed and retrieved pager messages from its computer because §2710(c)(1) allows service providers to "do as they wish" when accessing communications in electronic storage."

The courts have also been required to address the recording of stored voice mail messages. In what appears to be the only case on the subject, the U.S. District Court of the District of Montana held that a bank employee did not violate the ECPA because first, there was no "interception since the recording was not contemporaneous with the leaving of the messages, but more importantly, the persons leaving messages **consented** to the recording by having left messages in the first place. Payne v. Norwest Corp., 911 F.Supp. 1299 (1995). But see U.S. v. Reyes, 922 F. Supp. 818 (SDNY, 1996), where the court held that a criminal defendant had an expectation of privacy in his own pager, and that retrieving numbers from the memory of a pager are clearly electronic communications that are in electronic storage.

In these days of runaway litigation, employers are more and more responsible for conditions in the workplace which they have seemingly little control. In order to protect themselves from discrimination lawsuits, particularly sexual harassment, employers have had to monitor what appears to be the private conduct of employees. Can an employer not only access, but take employment action based on inappropriate use of an e-mail system? The answer appears to be affirmative.

In Smyth v. Pillsbury, 914 F.Supp. 97 (E.D. Pa, 1996), the plaintiff, Michael Smyth, was terminated for transmitting inappropriate and unprofessional comments over an e-mail system. The company had repeatedly assured its employees that the e-mail system was confidential and privileged and would not be intercepted. Plaintiff sued claiming violation of public policy, in that employers could not terminate employees in violation of their right to privacy. The court granted Pillsbury's motion to dismiss, finding that the Pennsylvania common law regarding tortious invasion of privacy was not implicated because there was no reasonable expectation of privacy in e-mail communications. Further, the court held, that even if there was a reasonable expectation of privacy, the company's interests in preventing inappropriate and unprofessional comments outweighed such a privacy interest.

State Electronic Communication Laws

The EPCA did not intend to preempt state legislation. People v. Conklin, 522 P.2d 1049 (Cal, 1974). State law, however, cannot be less restrictive than federal law. U.S. v. McKinnon, 721 F.2d 19 (1st Cir, 1983). At last count, 13 jurisdictions require that all parties consent to the interception of phone calls. These include California, Connecticut, Delaware, Florida, Illinois, Maryland, Massachusetts, Michigan, Montana, New Hampshire, Oregon, Pennsylvania and Washington. Additionally, some states have revised their wiretapping statutes to specifically address computer surveillance.

Common Law Torts

If ECPA and the state laws are not enough, employee privacy is also covered by common law torts. Although treatises have been written on these subjects , I will briefly outline the common privacy torts.

Defamation

The elements of a claim of defamation include:

- A false and defamatory statement
- An unprivileged publication to third party
- Fault amounting at least to negligence, and

- Either actionability of the statement irrespective of special harm, or the existence of special harm caused by the publication. Restatement (Second) of Torts §558 (1977).

Defamation claims occur often in the context of job references. Most employers have reacted to this by refusing to give job references. Recent cases, however, are beginning to imply a duty to warn where the employer has relevant knowledge that an employee might be dangerous. Randi W. v. Muroc Joint Unified School District, 929 P.2d 582 (Cal, 1997) holding that the writer of a letter of recommendation owes prospective employers a duty not to misrepresent facts in describing the qualifications of an employee, if making the misrepresentations would present a "substantial and foreseeable risk of physical injury to the prospective employer or third parties."

Intrusion upon seclusion

This claim has been defined as one where a person intentionally intrudes, either physically or otherwise, on the solitude or seclusion of another if the intrusion would be highly offensive to a reasonable person. Restatement (Second) of Torts §652B (1977). For examples, see Busby v. Truswal Systems Corp, 551 So.2d 322, 7 IER Cases 1348 (Ala, 1989), Fayard v. Guardsmark, 5 IER Cases 516 (EDLa, 1989), and Rudas v. Nationwide Mutual Insurance Co., 1997 U.S. Dist. LEXIS 169 (EDPa, 1997).

Publication of private facts

This claim is one where a person gives publicity to a matter concerning the private life of another, if the matter publicized is the kind that would be highly offensive to a reasonable person, and is not of legitimate concern to the public. Restatement (Second) of To rts §652D (1977). An example of this type of claim is Childs v. Williams, 825 S.W. 2d 4, 7 IER Cases 255 (Mo. Ct. App. 1992). Child's psychologist wrote a letter to her supervisor, describing her emotional disorder, and requesting transfer to another position. The court granted judgment for the psychologist, not withstanding the verdict, on the grounds that the employee had waived her right to privacy by providing written releases.

False light

According to the Restatement of Torts, [o]ne who gives publicity to a matter concerning another that places the other before the public in a false light is subject to liability to the other for invasion of his privacy, if

(a) the false light in which the other was placed would be highly offensive to a reasonable person, and

(b) the actor had knowledge of or acted in reckless disregard as to the falsity of the publicized matter and the false light in which the other would be placed. Restatement (Second) of Torts §652E (1977). An example of this tort appears in Ellenwood v. Exxon Shipping Co, 6 IER Cases 1623 (D.C.Maine, 1991), where the court held that merely taking action, i.e. placing an alcoholic employee in another position, does not create a cause of action for false light.

Other potential privacy torts

In addition to those torts clearly identified as "privacy torts", there are several other torts which may implicate employee privacy. False imprisonment is defined as where an actor confines or intends to confine another, and the confine is conscious of the confinement or harmed by it. Restatement (Second) of Torts §35(1977). Assault and Battery, are also torts often claimed by employees claiming invasions of privacy. Restatement (Second) of Torts §§13, and 21 (1977). These torts frequently occur after the use of technology, during the investigation phase.

One of the more egregious cases of this type is Caldor, Inc., v. Bowden, 330 Md. 632 (Md, 1993). Samuel Bowden was a minor employed as a customer service representative in the hardware department of a national retail store, Caldor. One evening, Bowden was asked to report to the upstairs customer service desk. He was escorted to a 10' x 10' windowless office where he was confronted by two loss prevention employees he had never met. Mr. Bowden was interrogated about a theft for approximately two hours. He claimed that he attempted to leave, but that the door was blocked by one of the employees who stated "sit down or we'll help you sit down." He was forbidden from calling his parents, and was told that if his parents called, they would be told their son was not in the store. To make matters worse, the next day, when Bowden returned to the store with his mother to "get to the bottom of things," Bowden and his mother were followed, forced to return to the store, and subjected to racial epithets. Bowden was then handcuffed, escorted to the front door, where he remained in the public view until the police arrived.

The plaintiff, Bowden, sued Caldor alleging false imprisonment, wrongful discharge, malicious prosecution, defamation, and intentional infliction of emotional distress. The jury awarded compensatory and punitive damages on all five counts.

The Privacy For Consumers and Workers Act (PCWA)

In 1993, Senator Paul Simon (D-Illinois) introduced a bill to regulate work place surveillance (S.984, 103rd Congress, (1993)). The bill was not enacted by Congress. The bill defined electronic monitoring broadly to include computer-based information systems. While the law did not entirely prohibit monitoring, it strictly regulated it requiring notices not only to employees but to customers as well.

Title VII of the Civil Rights Act of 1964 as amended 42 U.S.C. §2000(e) et seq.

Title VII prohibits employment discrimination on the basis of race, color, religion, sex or national origin. It protects individuals not only from being treated differently than other employees (disparate treatment) but also from facially neutral practices that have an adverse impact on a protected class. The new technologies have made information more accessible than ever. Even if an employer's search or investigation is legal under specific "privacy" laws, it may still violate the civil rights law. The following types of practices might subject an employer to a claim of adverse impact: (a) drug testing; (b) credit reports; and (3) criminal background investigations including arrests and/or convictions.

Adverse impact can be defended (See 42 U.S.C. §2000(e)-2(k)). The employer must show that the challenged practice is job related for the position and consistent with business necessity.

2

The New Technology & Discovery

Not surprisingly, the new techology: voice mail, e-mail, and computer data bases have created great fodder for discovery. E-mail messages tend to be conversational, brief and "folksy". The same informality that encourages e-mail use, can be damning in employment litigation. Chevron learned this message the hard way, paying a 2.2 million dollar settlement in a sexual harassment case where the evidence included anonymous jokes transmitted over the corporate e-mail system. E-mail messages can also create copyright liability for a company and divulge corporate secrets.

Even more frightening is the prospect that it is very difficult to delete e-mail messages. "Deleted" e-mail messages may be stored indefinitely in computer systems even after the user no longer needs or wants to retain the message. Savvy attorneys now ask for deleted messages and computer hard drives in discovery. Additionally, systems employees are increasingly noticed for deposition.

How is the attorney client privilege affected by these developments? What is the effect of electronic communication on privileged communication between attorneys and their clients? There are no current cases addressing this issue. The ease of use and lasting nature of electronic communications does create new concerns over protection of the privilege. It is likely, however, that communications that are intended to remain confidential, and where the privilege is not waived in some other fashion, remain privileged when transmitted via the internet and other electronic mail systems. Although many warn that the internet is not truly private, computer "hacker" activities are illegal, just as we have seen that wiretapper's activities are illegal. To rule that a privilege was waived, merely, because the communication was electronic seems to be an overly harsh result. Because of the continued development of technology and the lack of clear legal guidance, care is advised in communicating any sensitive matter.

3

How to Balance Employer Rights and Employee Privacy

It appears that for at least today, employers have the greater rights when it comes to monitoring conduct in the workplace. We live in a litigious society, and it is always possible that the wrong facts will hit a judge or member of congress, changing managerial rights once again. It cannot be too strongly stated that common sense should be used in deciding how to use technology for workplace monitoring. Experience shows that the greatest law in your favor is not going to persuade a jury when your facts are objectionable.

The single most important recommendation for balancing employer rights and employee privacy is to have a computer policy. According to the Society for Human Resource Management statistics, while 80 % of companies surveyed use e-mail, only 34 % have written policies.

Be careful not to create zones of privacy. Make sure that lockers, desks, and other working areas are considered employer property or space. In particular, be careful about overstating the private nature of voice mail computer and e-mail systems, as there is an aura of privacy surrounding these systems (use of passwords, etc). Furthermore, do not allow employees to think they have privacy by failing to do surveillance and inspections for which you claim a right.

Secondly, get consent from employees for searches. You can get explicit consent by having a signed policy statement, but consent can also be implied. Many of the telephone cases turn on the fact that the employees had been aware of management's past surveillance.

A company needs to define the proper use of office equipment. There is no way to capture the loss of time and productivity that is attributed to personal use of company materials. Additionally, it is clear that companies will have responsibility for the messages that are transmitted over its systems. At a minimum, a policy should forbid communications that are discriminatory, defamatory, offensive, or otherwise inappropriate and unprofessional. The same care going into written communications needs to go into the drafting of computer messages, which may be maintained in perpetuity.

Be sure to review and revise handbooks and other corporate policies to cover emerging technologies. For example, your policies probably address unauthorized access to a physical area, but do they address unauthorized access to a computer file? In other words, if your company generates office policies, be sure to cover the "virtual office" as well. Make sure that policies are not only generated, but well communicated.

Balance employee privacy issues with legitimate business concerns. Consider, not only is it legal, but is it *fair*. Not only will egregious conduct be more likely to result in a lawsuit, it will be more likely to raise punitive damages. Be wary about creating bad legal precedent, not only for your company, but for management generally.

Finally, be aware of the rapidly changing nature of the law in the area of employee privacy. This is an area ripe for regulation, and we have already seen one attempt on the federal level. Stay current on proposed state and federal legislation, and take political action if necessary.

NOTES

NOTES

19

DISPUTE RESOLUTION AT DARDEN RESTAURANTS

Presented by
Clifford L. Whitehill-Yarza

Dispute Resolution at Darden Restaurants

Be Part of the Solution

Dispute Resolution

A fair, consistent way to resolve differences

At Darden Restaurants, we strive to treat people fairly and with respect, because every job contributes to our continued success. This philosophy extends to the way we handle problems and disputes in the workplace, because we know that even routine differences can get bigger when there are no resources to help solve them.

Our goal is to resolve all workplace disputes in a way that is effective and fair to all parties. In order to do this, we have developed four ways to resolve workplace problems and concerns, while protecting the legal rights of all parties. These options make up our Dispute Resolution Procedure.

Dispute Resolution covers claims for wages and other compensation, tort claims, discrimination claims, denial of benefit claims, claims for violation of state and federal laws or claims under common law. Dispute Resolution does not cover issues such as performance reviews, benefits, pay, layoffs and job elimination. Company work rules cannot be changed by Dispute Resolution. This folder outlines the basics; for more details, refer to your Dispute Resolution Handbook.

Here's How Dispute Resolution Works:

Open Door Policy

The first step in resolving a dispute is to use our Open Door Policy. This means that if you have a workplace concern or dispute, you can feel free to talk about it with one of the managers in your restaurant. If, for any reason, you don't feel you can talk to any of your managers about the problem, you may discuss it with your director of operations or senior vice president. They will listen and try to help you resolve the dispute. At any time in the process you may also call the toll-free Employee Relations number in Orlando.

Our Open Door Policy remains the first — and often the *best* — way to resolve a problem or dispute *before* it becomes a crisis. That's because an open and honest exchange by the people who are closest to the problem provides the best insight and opportunity for resolution. And our Open Door Policy guarantees you can use it *without fear of retaliation.*

Peer Review

If the Open Door Policy does not resolve your concern, you may choose to air your complaint before a Peer Review panel. This panel consists of two employees and a manager (not from your restaurant) chosen from a pool of trained panelists. Let's say you disagree with a management decision and decide to appeal to a Peer Review panel. A neutral facilitator will set up the review and help you prepare. You will present your side of the issue, and the manager would present her or his side. The panel will listen to both sides, consider all evidence, and make a decision. All proceedings are confidential. You'll find more details on Peer Review in the Peer Review brochure.

Mediation

If you (or the company) are not satisfied with the decision of the Peer Review panel, you may submit your claim to mediation. A mediator is a neutral, outside party who is trained in dispute resolution. All costs of mediation are paid by the company. The mediator listens to the dispute and helps you and the company reach an agreement by opening up communications and suggesting options. If both parties do not agree on a solution (or if you or the company decide to bypass mediation), then you or the company may choose to take the dispute to arbitration for a final and binding solution.

Arbitration

Arbitration is the final step in our Dispute Resolution Program. Like mediation, arbitration uses a neutral, outside party to hear the dispute. In arbitration, however, the arbitrator makes a final and binding decision. Both sides present their arguments at a hearing, which is more formal than mediation and less formal than court. The arbitrator then weighs the evidence and makes a decision. If you win, you can be awarded anything you might seek through a court of law. The costs of arbitration are split by you and the company.

Questions and Answers About Dispute Resolution

Q *I'm having a problem with one of my managers, so I don't think talking to anyone in my restaurant will do any good.*

A If you believe you can't talk to anyone in your restaurant about your problem, the Open Door Policy allows you to go to your operations director or SVP. You may also call the toll-free Employee Relations number at Central Office. The important thing is to talk to someone in management as soon as possible.

Q *How do I get Dispute Resolution forms and/or information?*

A Ask your general manager for forms and information, or call Employee Relations in Orlando.

Q *Why would I want to use Dispute Resolution instead of going to court?*

A Unfortunately, our court system is overloaded and slow. In some areas of the country, civil litigation (including workplace disputes) often takes six or seven years to settle. And the cost of litigation puts it out of the reach of most people. Dispute Resolution is much faster and cheaper.

Q *Won't I give up some of my legal rights by using mediation or arbitration?*

A No. Mediation and arbitration protect your rights just like a court of law. In a variety of cases, including discrimination cases, the U.S. Supreme Court has recognized mediation and arbitration as effective ways to resolve disputes.

Q ***Who are the mediators and/or arbitrators used in Dispute Resolution?***

A They are trained, neutral experts who belong to the American Arbitration Association, a public service, non-profit organization that offers a wide range of dispute resolution services to business and government. The organization has established accepted rules and procedures to hear and decide cases, and their decisions are recognized by the court system.

Q ***Why does the company use Dispute Resolution?***

A We have an obligation to both our employees and our investors. Employee disputes that end up in court are costly and time-consuming for all involved, and after lawyers fees are paid, generally neither party gains. Dispute Resolution offers a way to settle these claims more quickly and cheaply, while protecting the legal rights of both parties. In this way, we can devote more of our resources toward improving our business, which benefits employees and investors.

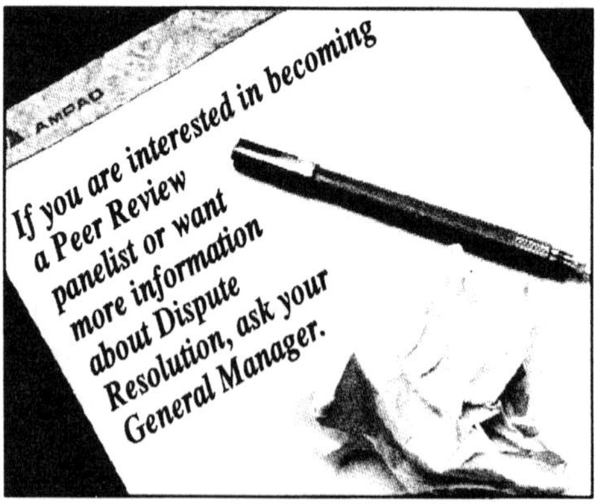

GMRI 0150 (6/96)

NOTES

NOTES

20

DISPUTE RESOLUTION PROCEDURE: DARDEN RESTAURANTS

Presented by
Clifford L. Whitehill-Yarza

Dispute Resolution Procedure

DARDEN
RESTAURANTS

Table of Contents

Introduction

We know that occasional differences may arise between the Company and Employees during or following employment. In most instances, these differences are resolved through our Open Door Policy. However, in disputes where this procedure did not produce a satisfactory result, the only recourse for the Employee or the Company has been litigation, which is costly and time-consuming for all parties. The Company believes there is a better method to resolve these disputes. This method adds three additional dispute resolution steps: peer review, mediation and arbitration, which provide a fair and equitable way to resolve disputes.

Consequently, the Company has adopted a Dispute Resolution Procedure ("DRP"). This Policy will be used to resolve claims or controversies (as defined in the DRP arising out of an Employee's employment or termination), that an Employee may have against the Company or the Company may have against the Employee. These disputes, which have not been resolved through normal personnel channels and the Open Door Policy, shall be resolved through peer review, mediation and, if necessary, exclusive, final and binding arbitration as provided in DRP. Therefore, neither the Company nor the Employee may litigate such claims against each other in a court.

The Dispute Resolution Procedure consists of four options: (1) Open Door; (2) Peer Review; (3) Mediation; and (4) binding Arbitration.

How to Use DRP

Any controversy, claim or dispute subject to the DRP (which has not been resolved through the Open Door Policy) must be submitted in writing on a Peer Review/Mediation/Arbitration Request Form to the restaurant's general manager (if the Employee works in a restaurant), or to the vice president of personnel, within one (1) year from the date the Employee first learns of his/her claim. Any claims not submitted to DRP during this one (1) year period shall be considered resolved and closed and the Employee may not thereafter pursue the claim through the DRP or seek relief from any federal, state or local governmental administrative agency or court, unless otherwise provided by law in which event, the one (1) year period shall be accordingly extended.

Any issue as to this provision or any other time limitation, shall be resolved solely by arbitration as specified in the section on pages 9–14. Nothing in DRP limits an Employee's independent or concurrent use of any state or federal administrative agency. If the matter is returned for resolution directly between the parties (a right to sue letter, for example) it is to be thereafter processed exclusively under DRP, which includes mediation and arbitration to the full extent permitted by law.

What is Covered Under DRP

1. The claims of Employees which may be submitted to DRP are claims for wages or other compensation due (except as herein limited); tort claims; claims of discrimination including but not limited to race, color, sex, religion, national origin, disability, sexual orientation, material status or age; claims for denial of benefits; claims for violation of any federal or state law or regulation or any claim arising under common law. However, the DRP is not available to review performance evaluations, job elimination or layoff decisions, Company work rules, policies or pay rates, or increases and decreases in benefits except to the extent such matters relate to statutory or breach of contract claims.

2. The Employee will be notified within fourteen (14) days after he or she submits a claim to the restaurant manager or to the vice president of personnel whether the claim is eligible for resolution under DRP. If the claim is eligible for resolution under DRP the claim will be handled in accordance with the following procedures.

Peer Review

Procedure

If the Open Door Policy has not resolved your concern under DRP, you will present your complaint to a Peer Review panel made up of two co-workers and one manager. During this process, you will privately present your case to the panel. The manager who made the decision affecting you will also present his or her case. The panel will investigate your complaint and arrive at a final decision.

Peer Review Panel's Decision

Within thirty (30) days after the Employee's claim is presented to the Peer Review Panel, the Panel shall issue a written decision.

Effect of Panel's Decision

If both the Employee and the Company are fully satisfied with the decision, the Employee and Company shall sign a statement agreeing to the Panel's decision within twenty (20) days. The decision of the Panel shall then be final, binding and enforceable against both parties. If either the Employee or the Company is not satisfied with the Peer Review decision, the Employee or the Company shall submit the claim, within thirty (30) days, to mediation as explained in the next section, or proceed with arbitration as explained on pages 9–14.

Mediation

Procedure

Mediation shall be conducted in accordance with the Employment Mediation Rules of the American Arbitration Association ("AAA") in effect at the time the request for mediation is made.

Notice

A written request for mediation by either the Employee or the Company shall be sent to the nearest ("location") office of AAA by certified or registered mail, return receipt requested, with a copy of the request sent in the same manner to the other party. The form for such request may be secured from the AAA office which is listed in the telephone book.

"Location" of the Mediation

The mediation shall take place in or near the city in which the Employee is or was last employed by the Company.

Selection of Mediator

The mediator shall be chosen according to the procedures set forth in the Employment Mediation Rules of the AAA or by the Company.

Costs of Mediation

The costs and fees of mediation and the mediator will be paid by the Company.

Settlement

If the dispute is resolved during mediation, it will be put in writing, signed by the parties, and be binding on both parties and become fully enforceable in a court of competent jurisdiction against either party.

Termination of Mediation Without Settlement

The mediation shall be considered terminated:

1. by a written declaration by the mediator that further attempts at mediation are no longer worthwhile; or
2. by a written statement by either party that they desire to terminate mediation.

Arbitration

Procedure

If mediation has been terminated without a settlement or the Employee or the Company has declined mediation, the claim or dispute shall be submitted to binding arbitration in accordance with the Employment Dispute Resolution Rules of the American Arbitration Association (AAA), except to the extent modified by these DRP or by applicable state or federal law. The arbitration and any decision or award made by the arbitrator will be final and binding on both parties.

Requirements for Arbitration

In accordance with the following Notice Requirement, submission of a timely claim under the DRP is a prerequisite to arbitration. If the Company or the Employee fails to timely submit a claim for arbitration, the claim shall be deemed settled and the Employee or the Company will be barred from arbitrating the claim under the DRP or from seeking relief from any federal or state court unless further time is required by federal or state law.

Notice Requirement

1. The Company or Employee must give written notice of the decision to arbitrate to both the other party and to the nearest ("location") office of the AAA by certified or regis-

tered mail, return receipt requested, within thirty (30) days following the termination of mediation or written notice of the decision not to proceed with mediation (as explained in "Effect of Panel's Decision" on page 5).

However, if these dates occur within one (1) year from the date the Employee first learns of his/her claim, the Employee shall have any additional time remaining in the one (1) year period within which the written notice of the decision to arbitrate must be given. The written notice shall identify and describe the nature of all claims asserted and the facts upon which such claims are based and shall include the relief requested by the Employee or the Company.

"Location" of the Arbitration Hearing

The arbitration shall take place in or near the city in which the Employee is or was last employed by the Company.

Selection of Arbitrator

The arbitration shall be conducted by one arbitrator chosen according to the procedures set forth in the Employment Dispute Resolution Rules of the AAA. The selected arbitrator shall be experienced in law relating to employment disputes.

Date and Duration of the Arbitration Hearing

1. The arbitration hearing will start no later than sixty (60) days following the date of the selection of the arbitrator. However, the selected arbitrator may order the hearing rescheduled if mutually agreed to by the Company and the Employee (in writing) or if good cause is shown.

2. The arbitration hearing shall last no longer than two days. Each party has one day to present his/her position. The arbitrator may, for good cause, extend the hearing and adjust the timing of the presentations.

Representation

Both the Company and the Employee have the right to be represented by counsel of their choice and at their own expense. However, if the Employee notifies the Company that he or she will not be represented by counsel at hearing (at least thirty (30) days before the date of the hearing), the Company also will not be represented by counsel at the hearing.

Subpoenas

Each party has the right to subpoena witnesses and documents for the arbitration hearing by requesting a subpoena from the arbitrator. Any such request shall also be served on the other party. Any objection to the issuance of any subpoena must be submitted to the arbitrator within ten (10) days following receipt of the request.

Designation of Witnesses & Exhibits

At least fifteen (15) days before the start of the arbitration hearing, the Employee and the Company must provide each other and the arbitrator with a list of witnesses, including any expert witnesses, a brief summary of the testimony of each witness and a list of all exhibits intended to be used at the arbitration. Unless so ordered by the arbitrator, witnesses or exhibits which do not appear on these lists will not be allowed to testify or be introduced during the hearing.

Arbitration Transcript

The Company, at its option and expense, may arrange for and pay the cost of a court reporter to provide a stenographic record of proceedings. The Employee may obtain a copy of the record by paying 25% of the reporter's fee or, if not done by the Company, arrange for a court reporter at his/her sole cost.

Post-Hearing Briefs

Either party, upon request at the close of hearing, shall be allowed to file a post-hearing brief. The time for filing briefs and the length will be set by the arbitrator at the hearing.

Arbitrator's Decision

The arbitrator shall issue a written decision within thirty (30) days after the hearing, which shall include a statement of the arbitrator's finding of fact and conclusions of law.

Authority of the Arbitrator to Grant Relief

1. The arbitrator has the authority to grant legal and equitable relief, if requested, including both temporary restraints and preliminary injunctive relief, to the same extent as could a court of competent jurisdiction.

2. Unless the claim or controversy alleges a violation of a specific federal or state statute, the arbitrator has no authority to establish wage rates or wage scales or benefits, to establish performance standards, work rules, food quality and service standards, or similar company policies and procedures.

3. The arbitrator has no authority to hear claims which the Employee did not submit to Peer Review, provided those claims could have been submitted to Peer Review.

4. The arbitrator may give any weight to the decision of the Peer Review panel that the arbitrator deems proper under the circumstances.

Judicial Review

Either party may bring an action in any court of competent jurisdiction to compel arbitration under this Agreement and to enforce an arbitration award.

Arbitration Fees and Costs

1. The arbitrator's fees and expenses, the costs of the hearing facilities, plus any costs owed to the AAA or the arbitrator shall be shared equally by both the Employee and the Company, except that the Employee shall not be required to pay more than the equivalent of two weeks' salary in his/her current position, or the last position held with the Company. Any amount over this limit shall be paid by the Company.

2. Any other expenses incurred by either party during the arbitration process, including attorney's fees, if any, shall be paid by the party incurring the expense. However, if the Employee prevails on a statutory claim which entitles him/her to attorney's fees, the arbitrator may award reasonable attorney fees to the Employee in accordance with such statute.

NOTES

NOTES

21

PEER REVIEW/MEDIATION/ ARBITRATION REQUEST FORM: DARDEN RESTAURANTS, INC.

Clifford L. Whitehill-Yarza

DARDEN RESTAURANTS, INC.
PEER REVIEW/MEDIATION/ARBITRATION REQUEST FORM

We recommend that you read the Dispute Resolution Procedures booklet before completing this form; copies are available from your manager or Employee Relations.

From: Name of employee: ______________________________

Employee number: ______________________________

Address: Work: ______________________________

Phone: ( ) ______________________________

Home: ______________________________

Phone: ( ) ______________________________

Indicate where you would like your notifications sent: ☐ to home ☐ to work ☐ both.

1. Describe the details of your complaint(s) or dispute(s). You may attach a separate statement or relevant supporting documents if you need more space.

____

____

____

____

2. To the best of your ability, indicate the nature of your dispute by checking the applicable category(s) below:

☐ Working conditions
☐ Age
☐ Disability
☐ Marital status
☐ Medical condition
☐ National origin
☐ Race
☐ Religion
☐ Retaliation
☐ Sex
☐ Sexual harassment
☐ Sexual orientation
☐ Other (explain): ____________

____

3. Indicate the type of relief you seek and/or the dollar amount, if any, of your claim(s) (i.e., the amount of damages you seek to recover):

Description of relief sought: ______________________________

____

____

Dollar amount, if any, of claim(s): ______________________________

I hereby authorize the Peer Review panel and the Mediator or Arbitrator to review those portions of my personnel file which may be relevant to the proper investigation of my claim.

Date ____________ Employee's Signature ______________________________

This Peer Review/Mediation/Arbitration Request Form received on this date by ____________________

To be completed by the Dispute Resolution Facilitator and copy sent to employee.

Peer Review conducted on __________ (date) and completed __________ (date). Result ____________________

Mediation conducted on __________ (date) and completed __________ (date). Result ____________________

Arbitration conducted on __________ (date) and completed __________ (date). Result ____________________

White–Employee **Yellow**–GM **Green**–Employee Relations **Gold**–Director **Pink**–Facilitator/Div. Office

NOTES

22

EMPLOYMENT DISPUTES

Carol A. Wittenberg
Susan T. Mackenzie
Margaret L. Shaw

Excerpted from a chapter in *Mediating Legal Disputes: Effective Strategies for Lawyers and Mediators* (Dwight Golann, Ed.), and reprinted with permission of Little, Brown and Company, 1996.

EMPLOYMENT DISPUTES*

By: Carol A. Wittenberg
Susan T. Mackenzie
Margaret L. Shaw[1]

OVERVIEW

Use of mediation to resolve employment disputes is on the rise. Express legislative endorsement is but one indicia of the growing recognition of the viability and acceptability of mediation as an appropriate mechanism for resolving discrimination claims. For example, in enacting both the Americans With Disabilities Act of 1990 and the 1991 Civil Rights Act, Congress specifically included provisions "encouraging" the use of mediation and other alternative means of dispute resolution "where appropriate and to the extent authorized by law."[2] Increasingly, federal district courts throughout the country are referring discrimination cases to mediation under judicially-initiated programs.

Similarly, federal, state and local administrative agencies charged with enforcing anti-discrimination law are experimenting with mediation programs. In New York, the State Human Rights Commission recently trained selected staff to serve as "in house" mediators in designated claims, and it is currently conducting a pilot project of case referrals to outside mediators. The New York City Human Rights Commission has had an in-house mediation program for several years. At the federal level, in 1993 and 1994 the Equal Employment Opportunity Commission initiated a mediation-based pilot project in four field offices. The project was deemed a success and as a follow-up, the EEOC established an ADR task force and announced on April 25, 1995 a wide-ranging effort to encourage ADR in all aspects of the EEOC's activities.[3]

BENEFITS OF MEDIATION

For a number of reasons, mediation is well-suited to resolving employment disputes, whether a case is handled as part of an in-house system or privately by attorneys in lieu of litigation.

(1) Emotionality

Employment disputes usually involve highly emotional issues. It is said that loss of one's job is the third most stressful life event, next only to death and divorce. Whether one's livelihood is at stake, as in a wrongful termination case, or the issue involves a professional relationship that

---

* *Excerpted from a chapter from **Mediating Legal Disputes: Effective Strategies for Lawyers and Mediators** (Dwight Golann, Ed.), Little, Brown and Company, 1996.*

has gone awry, as in a sexual harassment case, the dispute occurs in a highly charged atmosphere. A mediator can help parties vent their anger and frustrations in a nonjudgmental atmosphere that allows them to feel their positions have been heard, and to move on to a more productive, problem-solving stance.

One of us, for example, had the experience of being asked by the plaintiff after several hours of mediation if a one-on-one meeting with the mediator was possible. Her counsel agreed. After telling the mediator that she reminded her of a former boss, an important mentor to her, the plaintiff talked about how upset this case had made her. She also talked about how much the negotiations over dollars were leaving her feeling disassociated from the process and from what she was personally looking to accomplish. The mediator was able to help the plaintiff identify her feelings, think through what she really wanted out of a resolution, and work within the process to accomplish that result. The case settled shortly after this caucus.

(2) Confidentiality

The privacy and confidentiality mediation affords may be particularly important to employees and employers alike in the context of employment disputes. For example, in many of the cases involving sexual harassment claims we mediate, a primary focus of claimants is to have an unpleasant situation stop, stop quickly, and stop permanently. Another goal is to have the individual engaging in inappropriate behavior gain some understanding of the impact of the offending conduct, and to be constrained from repeating this conduct in the future. The impact of a complaint or publication of a complaint on future promotional or other employment opportunities is also a frequently expressed concern. Individual respondents, too, unless they are looking for vindication, may want to get on with their lives and put the incident behind them.[4] Most are concerned about their reputations, and most want their careers to continue uninterrupted.

Employers are almost always interested in confidentiality. This is particularly true in discrimination cases, since publicity regarding allegedly discriminatory practices can affect business generally, and the employer's reputation in the marketplace. Employers are also looking to minimize disruptions to workplace morale and productivity, and recognize that the perception of how any one individual is treated by management may affect the workforce on a more general basis. At the same time, employers are also concerned that, without confidentiality, settlements will create precedent or "benchmarks" for future complainants, or encourage "me too" complaints.

(3) Creativity of Outcome

Mediation is also an informal and flexible process, one that allows for more creative resolutions than either arbitration or litigation. Mediation's creativity is particularly important in employment disputes, where the impact of the controversy can have profound effects on the parties' lives. We also find in many of the litigated disputes we mediate that non-legal and non-monetary issues are as significant a barrier to resolution as the financial and legal aspects.

In certain cases where employee reinstatement is not appropriate, settlements have been reached by retaining a complainant on the payroll in a consultant capacity for a given period of time. For example, in an age discrimination claim we mediated, the settlement called for retention of employment status without pay of a male complainant for a two-year period for the purpose of vesting in certain benefits afforded retirees. In one gender discrimination case we handled, the tailor-made outcome involved keeping the employee on the payroll for a period of time with a new title to assist her in securing alternative employment at a level she felt was commensurate with her skills.

Corporate-wide training on sexual harassment prevention has been a cornerstone of other mediated settlements of individual claims. In a breach of contract case involving a senior executive, part of the settlement involved a guaranteed loan to invest in a new business.

These kinds of solutions often address the parties' real, underlying interests and thus permit a more satisfactory resolution.

(4) Cost Savings

Practical considerations also make mediation of employment disputes a particularly attractive alternative to litigation. The process is likely to be less expensive than litigation, or even arbitration. One attorney who frequently represents plaintiffs in discrimination cases observed that the cost of litigation of a discrimination claim to individual claimants was roughly $25,000 as compared to a $1,000 to $3,000 cost of mediation.[5] A study in the early 1990's estimated the cost to defend a single discrimination claim at $81,000, and put the cost of sexual harassment complaints alone to a typical Fortune 500 company at approximately $6.7 million annually.[6]

We also note that litigation costs per se do not necessarily take into account the indirect, personal and emotional costs to all parties to the litigation. “Soft” costs to employers can include time spent dealing with a case by busy executives. Loss of productivity in the workplace is another frequently mentioned fallout. All workplaces have informal information channels, and we often hear from individual participants in a mediation about the disruptive effects of the case on others in the workplace -- both in terms of time spent on rumor or speculation and concerns about the possible indirect effect of resolution on others not parties to the particular dispute. For instance, at one company we worked with, speculation was rampant about who would be let go or reassigned in the event the case resulted in the reinstatement of a discharged employee.

(5) Speed

Mediation is also likely to be significantly faster than litigation, and this is of particular importance given the dramatic increase in the filing of anti-discrimination claims. The number of sexual harassment claims filed with the EEOC increased from 6,127 in 1990 to 14,420 in 1994. As of 1995 the EEOC had a backlog of over 100,000 cases, with no increase in staff or budget likely. A study by Kleig Associates in the late 1980's and early 1990's indicated that 60% of working women, when asked about legally impermissible conduct, believed they had experienced sexual harassment on the job. Since sexual harassment represents only one form of actionable discrimination, and the already over-burdened courts and administrative dockets render the likelihood of timely relief for valid claims in these forums slim, the need for other prompt and fair resolution mechanisms is apparent.

In our experience, mediation of a routine employment case involving an individual claimant generally can be concluded in one or sometimes two days. While in some cases the parties are unable to reach complete closure in mediation sessions, we have often found that additional follow-up telephone conferences with one or both parties are productive in reaching settlement. These calls can usually be completed expeditiously and within a matter of weeks, at most. This abbreviated time framework is a far cry from that of cases submitted to administrative agencies, the courts or arbitration.

Speed of resolution can be a particularly important factor in employment cases, where the effectiveness of certain remedies, such as reinstatement, is related to the length of time a former employee has been off the job. For some complainants no longer on the payroll, delay can seriously affect financial survival as well. Expeditious resolution can allow employees and employers alike to put the incidents behind them and get on with their lives and businesses.

(6) Success Rate

Finally, mediation enjoys a high success rate. While settlement rates vary, it is not uncommon for mediators to report overall "success" rates of 80% to 90%. An evaluation of the EEOC's pilot mediation program in its Houston, New Orleans, Philadelphia and Washington field offices from April 1993 to March 1994 showed that mediation resolved charges of discrimination less expensively and more quickly, with closure in an average of 67 days as opposed to 294 in the regular charge process. In that pilot program, agreements were reached in 52% of the 267 mediations completed and an astonishing 92% of the participants said they were "satisfied" with the process.[7]

(7) Questions about the Advantages of Mediation

Are there disadvantages to mediation in the context of employment disputes? Of course there are, although we believe that some of the "dangers" we hear expressed are often over-emphasized. Some employers are concerned that the availability of mediation will encourage many more potentially frivolous complaints. Others are concerned that mediation simply adds a layer of time and expense when a case does not settle, an outcome which neither individual claimants nor employers can readily afford.

Even if a case does not settle in mediation, however, other dispute resolution options are not foreclosed. Mediation usually serves to narrow issues and promote more targeted, thoughtful case preparation for all parties. For example, in one case involving separate but related charges of discrimination based on sex and national origin brought against a large, international corporation, the parties were able to resolve the national-origin discrimination claim by developing a new transfer system during the mediation process, thus narrowing the issues for litigation solely to the claim of discrimination based on sex.

There are, of course, some cases that are simply inappropriate for mediation. As one employer's counsel has pointed out to us, it is almost always cheaper to settle a case than to pursue it through any kind of formal dispute resolution process. In addition, there are cases that, upon analysis, are without any apparent merit, and call for the employer to take a firm stance. For example, in one sexual harassment case in which we were asked to factfind, an emotionally unstable employee raised allegations against his manager that could not be substantiated. In another, the employer was not only highly suspicious of the employee's veracity but also concerned that the employee was using the fact of the complaint to test the limits of absenteeism and other personnel policies, feeling protected by the employer's concern over the potential for a retaliation charge.

In other cases there may be real questions about whether a party or its attorney will participate in good faith in a mediation process. We had one experience where after a morning of discussion, including several separate meetings with each side and an exchange of offers and counter-offers, the lawyer representing an employee claiming gender discrimination inexplicably escalated his demands beyond where he had previously indicated his client would be willing to settle. During a private caucus this attorney was unable to offer any rationale other than disappointment that the company was undervaluing his case. Despite the mediator's best efforts to get the discussions back on track, and offers by the company to provide additional benefits to the employee, the case did not settle. We wondered how committed the plaintiff's side had been to the mediation process from the outset.

CHALLENGES TO THE MEDIATOR

There are some special characteristics of employment cases that can challenge the mediator, and may require special approaches and techniques. We discuss a number of these below.

(1) Disparity in Resources

While parties in other kinds of cases may have unequal resources, in employment cases this lack of parity can make it difficult to even get the parties to the table. Claimants and plaintiffs in employment cases often are out of work or face an uncertain employment future, and can only hire attorneys who will serve on a contingency basis. They may balk at the added expense of a mediator, particularly when the outcome of mediation is uncertain. While some employers will agree to pay the entire mediation bill as an inducement to a plaintiff's participation, others are concerned that without some financial investment, a plaintiff will not participate whole-heartedly. There may also be concern that agreement to "foot the bill" will be viewed as signaling a weak case.

In these circumstances, we have found several approaches effective. The first step is to understand thoroughly the parties' concerns. If, for example, the employer is worried about the employee's investment in the process, the mediator can explore not only the nature of that concern, but also what verbal representations by either the claimant or claimant's lawyer might allay those concerns. Perhaps the mediator, after speaking with the claimant, can assess the employee's intentions and communicate them to the employer's satisfaction. At other times an assessment from an outsider familiar with the claimant, such as the employee's counselor or therapist, can be helpful. As an alternative, a mediator can suggest dividing the costs of mediation on a basis other than equal shares, such as payment based on a contribution formula related to the employee's salary level. Another suggestion to explore is having the employer pay mediation costs "up front," with the employee's share deducted from a later settlement or judgment.

(2) Timing

Timing can affect the process and outcome of a mediation of an employment case in several different ways. Where mediation is attempted shortly after an incident of alleged discrimination or harassment has been raised, the claimant may need extra help in getting beyond feelings of anger or outrage over what is perceived as inappropriate or impermissible treatment in the workplace. Conversely, an individual manager or subject of a claim may feel betrayed that a charge was raised, as well as angered over the content of the charge. Often it is important that these kinds of strong emotions are allowed to be expressed, normalized and legitimized before meaningful dialogue about resolving the situation can take place.

At the other extreme, when a case has already been in litigation for an extended period of time, dragging its way through drawn-out depositions and the kind of procedural skirmishing endemic to litigation, positions can become hardened, relationships between attorneys strained, and the parties even more determined to stop at nothing short of what is perceived as "justice." And while mediation can be viewed as particularly advantageous in cost savings, if little or no discovery has occurred, the lack of information about the facts on the part of one or both parties to the employment dispute can hamper productive negotiations.

In one case we handled, for example, an age discrimination claim referred by the court, the plaintiff's attorney had done little investigation prior to the mediation, and thus was unaware of circumstances that called into question the integrity of the plaintiff during his last year of employment. Assisting the attorney to become more realistic about the chances of full recovery at trial became the challenge of this mediation. In another case we mediated involving a sexual harassment claim, outside counsel for the employer, who had recommended mediation, was unaware of some of the conduct of the individual manager who was the subject of the allegations. That case required us to mediate between the employer and the manager as well as between the individual manager and the claimant, and the claimant and the corporate entity.

Mediators handling employment cases need to be especially sensitive to these and other issues of timing. In cases where emotions are running particularly high, the mediator may find it helpful to meet separately with each of the parties before a more structured process begins. In these initial sessions, parties can be assisted in articulating their concerns and thinking through their goals for mediation. Similarly, in cases where relationships between attorneys have soured, for example, as a result of a lengthy pre-trial stage or prior dealings between the two, we have found it helpful to have the attorneys meet with us separately in initial planning sessions in order to vent their personal and professional frustrations and to enlist their input and suggestions in designing measures to manage the problem during the mediation process.

(3) Imbalances of Power

In certain employment disputes, such as those involving sexual harassment claims, a perceived or real imbalance in the power relationship between the parties may itself constitute an impediment to settlement. In several cases we have handled the respondent has been a high-level supervisor or even chief executive and the claimant has been a secretary or other lower-ranking employee. In addition to resources, experience or actual disparity in such factors as status and communication skills, perceived effectiveness and ability to have an impact may be hampering resolution. It is of critical importance that the mediator compensate, not overcompensate, for these disparities, and ensure that the process is fair and non-coercive.

We have found that as a general proposition, particularly in dealing with the individual who feels at a power disadvantage in mediation, movement is better accomplished by pulling rather than by pushing. For example, in one case involving a sexual harassment claim where the facts underlying the claim were perhaps unconscionable but not legally actionable, helping the claimant to recognize the benefits of moving forward with her life was more effective than trying to convince her that she had a weak case.

When an issue of power imbalance is articulated or apparent, it is helpful to take the time to consult with the parties before the "real" mediation begins in order to structure the mediation process to accommodate the particular needs of the parties. We discuss whether the complainant or the attorney wants to make an opening statement and, in some cases, the circumstances under which the complainant will make a statement. We have observed that complainants who prepare a statement for the initial joint session tend to feel a degree of participation that engenders a sense of control over and dignity in the process not otherwise possible. Interestingly, in one sexual harassment case we handled, in which the plaintiff was represented by an attorney not experienced in either mediation or employment law, the plaintiff was encouraged not to take an active role. That plaintiff was never able to overcome her fears of "being taken advantage of" by the other party in order to reach a settlement.

Other process design issues can, similarly, affect balance of power concerns. For example, we often ask if the complainant has considered bringing a "support person" to the mediation session. At times a family member or close friend attending a mediation session with a claimant has been particularly helpful. We attempt to establish whether or not it may be necessary or beneficial to keep the complainant and individual respondent apart at least initially, and to ensure that the space in which the mediation is to be conducted permits separation. We also seek initial guidance from the parties on the timing of joint and caucus sessions.

We routinely schedule pre-mediation conference calls with all involved in the case to work through these kinds of details, and reach verbal consensus on basic procedures. At times, we incorporate these understandings into the written Agreement to Mediate. In sum, we believe mediation offers the opportunity for parties to employment disputes to have complaints handled with a degree of care and thoughtfulness not usually available in other dispute resolution processes.

(4) Desire for Revenge

The strong emotionality that can exist in employment cases often translates into a desire for revenge. Complainants who feel they have been wronged sometimes look for a way to make the employer or the individual charged with harassing or discriminatory behavior "pay." A focus on revenge can present a major obstacle to settlement.

There is no simple way to deal with this in mediation. Sometimes, particularly in cases where the complaint has already prompted the employer to take preventative measures, explaining the full impact of the complaint on workplace policies and procedures or on individual careers of others can help the complainant change to a posture more conducive to resolution. It has been our experience that the full extent of changes already made in the work setting often have not been fully or effectively communicated to the complainant, particularly in the heat of litigation. Other approaches we have found effective in handling the desire for revenge is to have the individual respondent contribute out of his own pocket to a financial settlement proposed by the employer. In some cases, such a contribution has been sufficient to assuage the complainant and to bring about a settlement.

(5) Negotiation by Numbers

A situation that sometimes arises in the mediation of employment cases is where one or both parties get fixed on a settlement figure and refuse to budge. Finding a new framework for analysis, one that appears objectively fair, can help parties stuck on numbers save face and ultimately agree on a different figure to settle the case.

In an age discrimination case we handled, for example, the plaintiff began the negotiations demanding $150,000. After a few rounds of offers and counter-offers, the plaintiff refused to go any lower than $75,000, and the defendants were stuck at $25,000. Because the plaintiff had left the defendants' employ some time before, the opportunity to offer additional benefits or other in-kind elements of resolution was very limited. The defendants simply believed the plaintiff had no case. The plaintiff disagreed, and felt he had already made a huge concession by halving his demand. The plaintiff refused to negotiate further until the employer showed some significant movement. Thus it was incumbent upon the mediator in this situation to reframe the terms of the debate.

In this case the mediator was able to accomplish a recasting of the issues by taking into account the fact that the plaintiff's job had been eliminated within six months after he had been fired. Calculating what he would have earned in after-tax dollars between the time he was terminated until his job was eliminated——less what he had collected in unemployment compensation and including reasonable attorneys' fees——netted an amount that, after consideration, was agreeable to both sides.

(6) Non legal and Personal Issues

At times both parties to an employment discrimination case fail to realize that a non-legal problem is the root cause of the dispute, and addressing that underlying issue in mediation may effectively resolve the entire case. For example, in one case we mediated for an organization involved in multinational and offshore investments, a personality conflict between the head of the accounting department and the head bookkeeper had festered for years. The working relationship between the two had deteriorated to the point that they hurled racial and sexual epithets at one another routinely. Upper management ignored the situation until both employees threatened to file race or sex discrimination charges. At that point, while the organization valued both employees, management could see no alternative to dismissing one or both, given the negative impact the relationship was having on the productivity of the entire accounting department. We were asked to intervene.

With the assistance of the mediator, each party was able to shift focus from placing blame on the other to recognizing their mutual interest in being employed by the organization. Mutually acceptable procedures for personal interaction in the office were identified and reduced to writing. The parties also identified a third employee in the organization whom both trusted, agreeing to have the mediator approach that employee regarding his availability to assist in resolving any future problems. Also during the mediation, the parties recognized that a contributing, if not overriding cause of the deterioration of their personal and professional relationship was an outstanding loan from the department head to the bookkeeper which the department head had intimated was forgiven years ago. The resolution between the parties also included a repayment schedule for that loan.

(7) "Outside" barriers to resolution

In some employment cases the real barrier to resolution may be an individual who is not a direct party to the dispute. In one case we mediated involving a disability claim by an airline manager with over 25 years of service, the claimant was moving toward resolution. However, as the mediation progressed, it became clear that his spouse, who was also present, was so angered by what she perceived as unconscionable treatment by the employer that she considered all offers of settlement by the employer insulting. Egged on by his spouse, the claimant became more obstinant and refused to budge from his initial position.

The mediator dealt with this situation by giving recognition to the wife's feelings, and by helping her understand that her anger was fueled at least in part by resentment over the amount of time her spouse had spent on his job rather than with his family over the years. The spouse was also afforded an opportunity to air her position directly to the corporate representatives who were present. Once she had communicated her feelings, she was able to reorient her focus from the past to the future, and to consider the potential impact of lengthy litigation on her husband's deteriorating health and well-being. Both she and the complainant were then able to focus on what could be accomplished in mediation, and the elements of a mutually acceptable package fell into place.

PREPARING FOR MEDIATION

Once selected, the mediator routinely schedules a conference call with the attorneys. The purpose is to determine the attorneys' familiarity with the process, set ground rules for the mediation, and answer questions or resolve issues that may create barriers to settlement. This step can be particularly useful in employment cases because of the often perceived if not actual imbalance of power of the two parties.

The mediator generally describes the mediation process, including requirements for confidentiality. The mediator may review an Agreement to Mediate over the telephone and advise the parties that they will receive a copy of the Agreement in time to go over and sign it before the mediation session. The parties will be asked whether they wish to make written submissions to the mediator prior to the session to familiarize the mediator with the nature of the dispute and, if so, whether these submissions will be shared with the other side as well as with the mediator.

The mediator will also ask the parties who will be attending the mediation session. Parties want to be assured that there is someone involved in the process on the other side with the ability to respond to issues which may arise in mediation as well as with the authority to settle. Although the ultimate decision-maker may not be able to attend the session, it is important that everyone understand the extent of the mediation participants' authority.

Attorneys or their clients are expected to make a brief statement at the mediation session, setting forth the essential elements of their case. If the attorneys make a statement, we encourage them to present their case in a way that allows the other side to hear the client's concerns without creating an offensive or defensive reaction. In our experience, an adversarial posture at the outset is rarely conducive to fostering productive settlement discussions. The mediator may also discuss whether the claimant will be more fully involved in the process if he or she makes a brief statement.

At the start of mediation, the mediator explains the general process to be followed to everyone present. We often use this opportunity to describe our style of mediation as well. We alert participants that we may utilize joint or separate sessions, or speak to an attorney privately during the day as needs require. Advising participants of procedures at the outset creates clear expectations.

COMBINING MEDIATION WITH OTHER ADR PROCEDURES

In our experience, mediation can be used effectively in combination with other alternative dispute resolution procedures, such as fact-finding or facilitation to address specific needs in particular employment disputes. For example, one of us served as a member of a neutral team under a procedure developed by all parties to resolve a hostile environment/sexual harassment claim. Under the agreed-upon procedure -- embodied in a document which was signed by the parties and the neutral team -- the team first conducted interviews with the claimant and the individual alleged to have created the hostile environment. Any other employee the team deemed relevant was also made available for interview, and interviews could be conducted by one or both of the team members at their discretion. The team also had access to personnel files and any other corporate records.

Under the procedure, the team was to mediate the dispute after conducting interviews, either in joint sessions with both individuals or through separate meetings with each party. If mediation efforts were not successful, the team was to draft a report, with findings of fact on several specific charges. That report was to be shared with the complainant and individual respondent, but not the employer, and was to be followed by a further attempt at mediation. Only if a second mediation attempt proved unsuccessful did the procedure call for submission of a fact-finding report to the employer.

In the actual case, the parties did not negotiate realistically during the first round of mediation. Only after reading the neutral team's findings of fact did each party express an interest in moving from previously expressed "final" positions. The parties were able to reach resolution during the second round of mediation, rendering moot the issuance of the fact-finding report to the employer.

Mediation can be combined with fact finding in other ways as well. In one case we were asked to mediate that involved a sexual harassment claim by a management trainee against two senior vice-presidents of a bank, investigation by the bank's attorneys' had found sexual contact between the complainant and one bank executive, but concluded that the incident was consensual. The bank's attorneys also concluded that the complainant was not being sexually harassed or retaliated against by the second bank executive, who was her boss. Mediation was difficult because the complainant and her attorney had little faith in the investigation conducted by the bank's attorneys, who also represented the bank in mediation. The bank's attorneys were unwilling to engage in serious settlement discussions without independent support for some of the complainant's allegations.

The mediator adopted the role of fact-finder under agreed upon conditions. The names of the other individuals the mediator interviewed would remain confidential, although the substance of their observations would be made available to the bank. The mediator interviewed several of the complainant's coworkers as well as her therapist and shared her preliminary findings with the parties. Mediation then resumed, and the parties were able to resolve the matter.

In another instance involving claims by several employees against one employer, a settlement was reached in mediation which called for the continued intervention of the mediator, but in the role of facilitator. We have also been asked to participate in procedures for evaluating the effectiveness of settlement agreements that address on-going relationships. For example, one of us agreed to participate in a six-month review and "fine-tuning" of settlement terms resolving a dispute between the two chief executives of a membership organization.

CONCLUSION

In all of the examples described throughout this chapter, mediation proved to be an effective process for handling a variety of complaints raised in the employment context. While the degree of emotionality, the overlap of legal and nonlegal claims, and the imbalance of power between the parties to employment disputes may pose unique challenges for a mediator, these factors need not be impediments to the effectiveness of mediation as a method of dispute resolution. Indeed, we would argue that mediation's flexible, consensual approach is particularly well-suited to the employment setting.

We anticipate that the increase in the use of mediation will continue with the encouragement of legislatures, courts and users of the process. As attorneys become more familiar and comfortable with the process, they, too, will view mediation as the preferred method of resolving employment disputes.

---

1. The three authors are principals in the firm of Wittenberg, Mackenzie & Shaw, L.L.C., a New York based firm of neutrals providing ADR services in employment disputes.

2. 42 U.S.C. 12212 and 42 U.S.C. 1981-A.

3. *Alternative Dispute Resolution Alert*, Vol. 1, No. 4 (June, 1995) at 1.

4. One of the concerns that has been expressed about mediation in sexual harassment (or discrimination) cases is that mediation will "cool out" or settle a particular incident or series of incidents, leaving the alleged offender free to continue and the inappropriate behavior free to flourish. While this is a real concern, some precautions can be taken. For example, agreements can specify that in the event of a future charge of harassment against the alleged offender, the complainant will come forward with a formal charge or a sealed letter placed in the offender's personnel file will be opened. Howard Gadlin, "Mediating Sexual Harassment," in Bernice Sandler and Robert Shoop (eds.), *Sexual Harassment on Campus: A Guide for Administrators*, Faculty and Students (forthcoming).

5. Janet Rovin, remarks presented at the Annual Meeting of the American Bar Association, Section on Labor and Employment Law, August 11, 1995.

6. Linda Stamato, "Sexual Harassment in the Workplace: Is Mediation an Appropriate Forum?", *Mediation Quarterly* (Winter, 1992), at 167. Recent jury verdicts in sexual harassment cases and other discrimination suits have also caused employers to consider alternatives to litigation. For example, the jury in the *Weeks v. Baker & McKenzie*, 1994 DLR (BNA) 170 (September 6, 1994), awarded a secretary employed by a law firm $7.1 million in compensatory and punitive damages for conduct by a partner over a 15 day period.

7. Ricky Silberman, "Mediation at the EEOC," *NIDR News* (July/August 1995) at 3.

NOTES

23

ADR FLEXIBILITY IN EMPLOYMENT DISPUTES

Carol A. Wittenberg
Susan T. Mackenzie
Margaret L. Shaw

ADR FLEXIBILITY IN EMPLOYMENT DISPUTES

By Carol A. Wittenberg
Susan T. Mackenzie
Margaret L. Shaw[1]

More and more, disputants, courts, public agencies and legislatures are embracing the use of ADR in employment disputes. Federal, state and local antidiscrimination statutes -- including the Civil Rights Act of 1991 and the Americans With Disabilities Act -- "encourage" the use of alternative means to resolve disputes arising under their acts.

Agencies enforcing these federal statutes and local ordinances have or are developing internal ADR mechanisms. The New York State Human Rights Commission has had a mediation program in effect since 1991, and in it's first year, approximately 50% of approximately 400 cases referred to mediation were resolved.[2] The New York State Human Rights Division has added a mediation pilot project to the menu of ADR options. Similarly, the EEOC, following it's successful pilot project in selected locations, has approved a plan for voluntary ADR programs in all of its regional offices.[3]

Recent statistics demonstrate that individual disputants are also resorting to ADR in increasing numbers to resolve employment

---

[1] The three authors are principals of the firm of Wittenberg, Mackenzie & Shaw L.L.C., a New York based firm of neutrals providing ADR services in employment disputes.

[2] Matthew W. Daus, "mediation Claims of Discrimination," Dispute Resolution Journal, (October-December 1995).

[3] See, for example, "EEOC Approves Plan for Voluntary ADR Programs," World Arbitration and Mediation Report, Volume 6, No. 5 (May 1995) at 97.

disputes. In a recent survey conducted by the White Plains, New York law firm of Jackson, Lewis, Snitzler & Krupperman, over 50% of the 850 human resource specialists and in-house counsel surveyed stated that they used or planned to use a formal ADR process to resolve workplace disputes. This represents a 10% increase from 1983. The survey also indicated that 92% of respondents had received a sexual harassment complaint, an increase of approximately 30% from the previous year.[4] Similarly, a recent Illinois Human Rights Commission study indicates that employers and employees are equally interested in selecting ADR to resolve their disputes, particularly when such a procedure is available early in the process.[5]

These statistics are consistent with our own experience. However, while increased use of ADR can be documented, there is no data to suggest which ADR process is best suited to particular employee disputes. The issue is complicated by the fact that at the core of many issues framed as legal disputes are other workplace issues that have given rise or contributed to the complaint which must be addressed before the dispute can be resolved. In other cases, the parties' version of events is so different that certain factual matters must be resolved before the

---

[4] See report of survey in Employment Law Strategist (March 1996 at page 6.

[5] See Lamont E. Stallworth and Linda K. Stroh, "Who is Seeking to Use ADR? Why Do They Choose To Do So?," Dispute Resolution Journal (January-March 1996), page 30.

issues in dispute can be addressed. In dealing with these types of cases, we have found it most helpful to adopt a flexible approach to fit the particular circumstances of each individual case. This often means combining ADR processes.

We hope that a few examples and case studies will serve to demonstrate the effectiveness of "mixing procedures" in appropriate cases.

Combining fact-finding investigations with mediation

In one case we handled, a junior female faculty member lodged with the Dean of Students a verbal complaint of sexual harassment by her Department Chair. She was concerned that her failure to grant her Department Chair sexual favors would affect her ability to be granted tenure in the next three years. She was also concerned about potential notoriety were she to file a formal complaint, and said she wanted to resolve the matter before putting her complaint in writing.

The Dean of Students contacted the University's counsel, who, after a "discussion" with the Department Chair, called us in to mediate. Before a formal session, we talked with the female faculty member, the Department Chair, and counsel for the academic institution. We found that the Department Chair had little or no recognition that his overtures to the junior faculty member were unwanted. At the same time, the junior professor's position was that the only acceptable solution was to terminate the Department Chair.

After these initial discussions, we recommended a variation on the "classic" mediation process the parties had initially envisioned, to add an initial fact-finding component. We proposed conducting preliminary interviews with the junior professor and the Department Chair, as well as a few others identified by them, and suggested preparing a report to be shared with the two principals. Only in the event that subsequent mediation did not resolve the issues between the two would the University be privy to the fact-finding report. Both the professor and the Department Chair, represented by counsel, agreed to the procedure.

Through the "combined" fact-finding/mediation process, each party was able to articulate his/her individual version of the incidents and gain some understanding of the other's perspective. The settlement terms the parties eventually agreed upon were reviewed by the University counsel, who was also made a party to the final settlement agreement. In sum, the Department Chair agreed to "step down" as Chairman of the department for the next three-year period, the time during which the junior professor would be applying for tenure. The junior professor was given a financial "parachute" that she could claim within three years, together with the guarantee of placement assistance in the event that she decided to leave the institution during that time period. In addition, she was given direct access to the University Provost should she experience any further incidents she deemed to constitute inappropriate behavior or sexual harassment. The Department Chair was subject to a three-year "follow-up" plan, which included counseling and an acknowledgment that any further proven incidents of harassment could result in his separation from the University.

This kind of resolution, which met the underlying interests of both parties, would probably not have been possible through a traditional adjudicatory process or classic mediation.

Combining fact-finding with facilitation

In a different setting, we were retained by a health care facility to investigate a series of employee complaints of "harassment" and other potentially legally impermissible conduct by department management. All employees who worked continuous shifts were invited to speak with us, and we interviewed more than 30 employees over a three day period.

We found no egregious or potentially actionable conduct on behalf of any staff member, and concluded that almost every specific, individual complaint -- standing alone -- would likely be viewed as easily remedial or even "petty". Nevertheless, in the aggregate, the complaints revealed a unit where overall staff relationships and interactions were characterized by mistrust and miscommunication.

Changes in the nursing profession, as well as financial pressure and downsizing at the institution, had altered the work environment in the unit. Staff with long years of service operating under one set of procedures were called upon to adapt to substantially new operations and procedures. Our observation was that unit department management had offered little support for these changes, and the resulting atmosphere of mistrust was seriously impairing the ability of the overall unit to operate effectively. We were persuaded that serious problems in personnel practices and maintenance of professional standards on the unit needed to be addressed as expeditiously as possible.

We drafted a report that detailed specific complaints articulated by staff members, and included our findings concerning these complaints and recommendations for addressing the major problems identified. We also recommended facilitation to help the staff develop a strategic plan to address the new work environment in the unit.

As facilitators, we subsequently worked with a committee to establish overall unit goals. All further discussions of professional and policy matters were related to and tested against the goals of the unit. During the course of the facilitation, we also assisted the group in developing plans to help them meet the new demands of the Hospital while responding to the staff's professional needs. In addition, we explored issues that separated individuals and worked on ways to improve communications and relationships on the unit. The group developed a comprehensive plan that was approved by higher management after being reviewed by the staff.

Combining mediation with advisory settlement

In another setting, mediation was combined with an advisory settlement opinion to close a gap the parties could not otherwise surmount. The case involved a sexual harassment charge brought by a 23-year old female assistant hired by a musical company. The assistant had responded to a posting at her college for a position in the Company's's Boston office, advertised as "requiring significant travel". At the end of the job interview, the musical agent summed up the job as "marriage without sex". The assistant accepted the job, although she later claimed that she had concerns about working closely with the agent. However, she felt that contact with celebrities was too exciting to pass up.

Early on, the assistant traveled with the agent to Los Angeles, San Francisco, Seattle and Miami. The agent told the assistant he was traveling to Bermuda in March for vacation and work and that, if she was "good", she could accompany him on the trip. However, she would have to use her vacation time, since only part of the Bermuda trip was for business. The assistant agreed.

Upon arrival in Bermuda, the assistant learned that their "suite" had only one large room containing a king sized bed. She stayed in the suite with the agent for three nights, sleeping fully clothed in one corner of the bed. On the morning of the fourth day, she became upset and left the room. She befriended a group of polo players who assisted her in returning to the states.

Upon her return to Boston, the assistant noticed that her job duties appeared to be changing. She no longer had contact with celebrities and she no longer traveled. She appealed to the Vice President of Operations for a transfer, and when her request was denied, she left her job and filed a charge of sexual harassment against the Company and the agent. She was re-employed within four months by another company at a job paying a comparable salary.

During the session, the mediator explored the differing perceptions and perspectives of the Company and assistant. Misconstrued comments such as "I need an older man to take care of me" were articulated and clarified. Rumors about each were also articulated and verified or refuted.

The mediator also addressed the potential effect of the assistant's behavior in Bermuda on her case were she to pursue litigation, and the extent of her actual damages, since she had found an equivalent job and had not sought psychological assistance after leaving the Company.

The assistant insisted she would not leave the mediation with less than $75,000, a demand strongly supported by her father. When the mediator proposed that the agent personally contribute to the settlement, however, the assistant and her father indicated a willingness to be flexible.

The mediator then talked with the two attorneys for the defendants, one for the Company and one for the agent, exploring ways in which to package a proposal. The Company was determined not to exceed a settlement package of $50,000, especially because the woman had worked for the Company for less than six months. Although the agent's counsel indicated that his client would be willing personally to help bridge the gap to resolve the case, the mediator was unable to move either side closer to the other's proposed settlement amount.

Finally, the mediator suggested a "mediator's proposal." Our procedure for using a mediator's proposal is as follows: The mediator presents the settlement proposal to both sides, giving them a set period of time in which to respond. Confidentiality of the process is protected, unless both sides agree to accept the settlement proposal. This means that if one party accepts the mediator's proposal and the other side refuses, the refusing party is not told whether the settlement was acceptable to the other side. Both sides agreed to this procedure.

The mediator fashioned two proposals. The first was for $65,000, payable in two installments: $35,000 payable 20 days after execution of the settlement agreement, and $30,000 payable nine months later. The second proposal was for $60,000, payable in full 20 days after execution of the agreement.

The Agency accepted both settlement proposals. The assistant agreed to accept the second proposal, $60,000 payable 20 days after execution of the agreement. Interestingly, neither the assistant nor her father asked whether the agent was contributing to the final settlement. Use of a mediator's proposal made resolution of this dispute possible. The parties were able to focus on the financial amount proposed by the mediator instead of rejecting the other side's proposals for settlement.

Conclusion

Use of ADR to resolve employment disputes is on the rise. Parties need to be flexible in considering approaches for resolving these disputes. Mediation can be used alone or in combination with other dispute resolution procedures such as fact-finding, facilitation or advisory settlement to promote resolution. In certain circumstances, a neutral fact-finder's report prior to mediation may be sufficient to promote settlement. In other cases, it may be necessary to engage in mediation after fact-finding to bring about a final resolution of the dispute. Where intervention of a neutral still fails to bring the parties to resolution, use of a mediator's proposal for settlement may be the only way to bridge the gap between he parties.

In sum, it is helpful for attorneys to look at ADR as a flexible system for employment disputes, and work with the neutral to fashion a process or combination of procedures best suited to the particular circumstances of each case.

NOTES

NOTES

Program Schedule and Faculty

PROGRAM SCHEDULE

Registration will be thirty minutes before the program start. A continental breakfast will be available at that time.

FIRST DAY: 9:00 A.M. - 5:00 P.M.

9:00 INTRODUCTION

The Lessons of Texaco, Avis, Mitsubishi and Astra

Martin F. Payson

9:15 WHAT A PLAINTIFF'S LAWYER LOOKS FOR WHEN EVALUATING A POTENTIAL LAWSUIT

- How plaintiff's counsel goes about assessing the merits of a potential claim
- How plaintiff's counsel assesses the merits of a potential client
- What consideration is given to the amount of a potential jury verdict in deciding whether or not to accept a case
- To what extent are cases accepted because of their perceived quick settlement value
- What consideration is given to the existence and use of a corporate internal dispute resolution mechanism

Kyle M. Francis & Wayne Outten

10:15 Break

10:30 HOW DEFENSE COUNSEL AND HUMAN RESOURCE EXECUTIVES CAN WORK TOGETHER MORE EFFECTIVELY TO AVOID WORKPLACE LITIGATION

- How counsel and human resource executives can define their respective roles in litigation avoidance
- What programs should the legal and human resource functions initiate and monitor to minimize potential claims?
- When should human resources and in-house counsel start to consult about an asserted claim in order to avoid litigation?
- When should outside counsel be brought in to avoid exposing inside counsel being called as a fact witness?

Jackie Gordon, S.P.H.R. & Lynne E. DiStasio

11:30 HOW TO RESPOND EFFECTIVELY TO CHARGES OF SEXUAL HARASSMENT

- What the human resources function can do to deal with sexual harassment complaints to respect the rights of both the charging party and the accused
- How the in-house legal counsel can monitor the investigation without becoming embroiled in the case
- When outside counsel should be consulted in order to be most effective in avoiding litigation

Meryl R. Kaynard & Pamela S. Poff

12:30 p.m. - 1:30 p.m. BUFFET LUNCH

1:30 A FEDERAL PERSPECTIVE: INSIDE THE EEOC

Paul Steven Miller, Commissioner, Equal Employment Opportunities Commission

2:15 QUESTIONS AND ANSWERS

2:30 BREAKOUT SESSIONS-ROUND I

Attendees may choose two of the three sessions in the following topics:

I - WHEN YOU WRITE, YOU MAY BE WRONG

An examination of good and bad employment documents and how they help win or lose a case

II - AVOIDING LITIGATION WHEN RE-ENGINEERING THE CORPORATION

How to restructure your organization to avoid claims of age, sex and race discrimination

III - HOW TO HANDLE GOVERNMENT AGENCY INVESTIGATIONS: WHEN THE EEOC, DOL OR OSHA COME CALLING

- Cooperation versus contention
- When to agree and when to resist — there is a right way

Breakout Discussion Leaders:
Michael I. Bernstein, Joseph R. Damato & Alan M. Koral

3:30 Break

3:45 BREAKOUT SESSIONS-ROUND II
(Choose from above Breakout Sessions)

4:45 QUESTIONS AND ANSWERS

5:00 COCKTAIL RECEPTION

SECOND DAY: 9:00 A.M. - 5:30 P.M.

9:00 WHEN WORKERS CAN'T OR WON'T WORK

- How counsel and human resources can work together more effectively to minimize liability under the "Bermuda Triangle" of workplace leaves of absence: the Americans with Disabilities Act, workers' compensation laws and the Family and Medical Leave Act

Christopher G. Bell

10:15 Break

10:30 MANAGING THE REINVENTED WORKPLACE: HOW TO ANTICIPATE AND MINIMIZE LIABILITY ARISING FROM ALTERNATIVE WORK ARRANGEMENTS

- Temporary and contingent workers
- Employee leasing
- Independent contractors
- Joint employers

Christina D. Harris & Laura J. Lokker

11:30 CORPORATE COMMUNICATIONS AND PRIVACY ISSUES: HOW TO RECOGNIZE AND EFFECTIVELY DEAL WITH THE HIDDEN LIABILITY IN THE NEW ELECTRONIC WORKPLACE - LEGAL AND ETHICAL CONSIDERATIONS

- Electronic monitoring
- Workplace surveillance
- Computer use and abuse
- E-mail and voicemail eavesdropping

Julienne W. Bramesco & Mark E. Faber

12:30 p.m. - 1:00 p.m. BUFFET LUNCH

1:00 IT'S TIME TO CALL THE QUESTION ON EMPLOYERS, THE NLRA AND THE LABOR MOVEMENT

Richard Bensinger, Director of Organizing, AFL-CIO

1:30 QUESTIONS AND ANSWERS

2:00 ALTERNATE DISPUTE RESOLUTION: A CASE STUDY IN HOW TO DEVELOP AND IMPLEMENT AN ADR PROGRAM THAT ELIMINATES WORKPLACE LITIGATION AND EXCESS JURY AWARDS

- Mandatory arbitration
- Binding peer review programs
- Jury trial waivers

Clifford L. Whitehill-Yarza & Martin F. Payson

3:00 Break

3:15 THE ART AND SCIENCE OF MEDIATION IN EMPLOYMENT DISPUTES: A DEMONSTRATION OF HOW MEDIATION IS ACTUALLY CONDUCTED

Margaret L. Shaw

5:15 QUESTIONS AND ANSWERS

OPTIONAL POST-CONFERENCE WORKSHOP: 9:00 A.M. - 5:15 P.M.

STAYING UNION FREE: THE RENEWED CHALLENGE FOR LAWYERS AND HUMAN RESOURCE PROFESSIONALS

Post-Conference Workshop Presenters:
Martin F. Payson & Mark L. Sussman

Morning Session: 9:00 a.m. - 12:15 p.m.

9:00 **How Changes at the NLRB and the AFL-CIO Have Significantly Increased Your Company's Chances of Being Unionized**

- Knowing who the players are
- How NLRB decisions and rulemaking have tilted the playing fields strongly in favor of unions
- How the second Clinton Administration will assist unions in their nationwide organizing efforts

10:00 Break

10:15 **How to Assess the Existence of Workplace Issues That Contribute to Union Organization Success**

- Job security
- Changing demographics
- Corporate restructuring
- An emphasis on the service industries
- The lack of preparedness among first-line supervisors and middle managers

11:15 **How to Recognize the Early Warning Signs of Covert Union Activity and How to Lawfully and Effectively Respond**

- "Salting" of the workplace with union plants
- Union access to parking lots
- Union use of e-mail and voicemail
- Union use of the Internet
- What management can do to control the workplace

12:15 p.m. - 1:15 p.m. Lunch

Afternoon Session: 1:15 p.m. - 5:15 p.m.

1:15 **How to Develop a Step-by-Step Strategy to Preserve Your Company's Union Free Status**

- Defining your company's position on unions
- Developing an issue-free philosophy
- Exercising your rights to communicate under the law
- Convincing employees not to sign union cards

3:30 Break

3:45 **A Step-by-Step Guide to Maintaining A Union-Free Workplace**

- 18 critical steps you can take to minimize your company's chances of being organized
- How to use emerging ADR techniques for both union and litigation avoidance
- How to take advantage of NLRB rules regarding employee participation programs to minimize the need for third-party intervention

5:00 **Questions and Answers**

FACULTY

Chairman
Martin F. Payson
Jackson, Lewis, Schnitzler
& Krupman
White Plains, New York

Christopher G. Bell
Jackson, Lewis, Schnitzler
& Krupman
Washington, D.C.

Richard Bensinger
Director of Organizing
AFL-CIO
Washington, D.C.

Michael I. Bernstein
Benetar Bernstein Schair & Stein
New York City

Julienne W. Bramesco
Senior Attorney
Marriott International, Inc.
Washington, D.C.

Joseph R. Damato
Seyfarth, Shaw, Fairweather
& Geraldson
Washington, D.C.

Lynne E. DiStasio
Associate General Counsel
Metropolitan Life Insurance Company
New York City

Mark E. Faber
General Attorney - Human Resources
GTE Service Corporation
Stamford, Connecticut

Kyle M. Francis
Smith Mullin, P.C.
West Orange, New Jersey

Jackie Gordon, S.P.H.R.
Divisional Vice President -
Human Resources
Builder's Square
San Antonio, Texas

Christina D. Harris
National Vice President
Marketing / Alternative Staffing
AIG Risk Management, Inc.
San Francisco

Meryl R. Kaynard
Vice President and
Assistant General Counsel
The Chase Manhattan Bank, N.A.
New York City

Alan M. Koral
Vedder, Price, Kaufman, Kammholz
& Day
New York City

Laura J. Lokker
Vice President & Senior Counsel
Simon & Schuster, Inc.
Upper Saddle River, New Jersey

Paul Steven Miller
Commissioner
Equal Employment Opportunities
Commission
Washington, D.C.

Wayne Outten
Lankenau Kovner Kurtz
& Outten, LLP
New York City

Pamela S. Poff
Senior Vice President -
Deputy General Counsel
PaineWebber, Inc.
Weehawken, New Jersey

Margaret L. Shaw
Mediator
Wittenberg, Mackenzie & Shaw, LLC
New York City

Mark L. Sussman
Jackson, Lewis, Schnitzler
& Krupman
Woodbury, New York

Clifford L. Whitehill-Yarza
General Counsel and
Senior Vice President
Darden Restaurants, Inc.
Orlando, Florida

Program Attorney: Barry D. Denkensohn

NOTES